By the Renewing of Your Minds

24 August 2001

To David,
    For the renewing of minds,

All best,
Ellen

By the Renewing of Your Minds

THE PASTORAL FUNCTION *of* CHRISTIAN DOCTRINE

ELLEN T. CHARRY

New York   Oxford

OXFORD UNIVERSITY PRESS

Oxford University Press

Oxford   New York

Athens   Auckland   Bangkok   Bogota   Bombay   Buenos Aires
Calcutta   Cape Town   Dar es Salaam   Delhi   Florence   Hong Kong
Istanbul   Karachi   Kuala Lumpur   Madras   Madrid   Melbourne
Mexico City   Nairobi   Paris   Singapore   Taipei   Tokyo   Toronto   Warsaw

and associated companies in
Berlin   Ibadan

First published in 1997 by Oxford University Press, Inc.
198 Madison Avenue, New York, New York 10016

First issued as an Oxford University Press paperback, 1999

Oxford is a registered trademark of Oxford University Press

Library of Congress Cataloging-in-Publication Data

Charry, Ellen T.
    By the renewing of your minds : the pastoral function of Christian
doctrine / Ellen T. Charry.
        p.   cm.
    Includes bibliographical references and index.
    ISBN 0-19-509710-6 (cloth); ISBN 0-19-513486-9 (pbk.)
    1. Theology, Doctrinal—History.   2. Pastoral theology.
3. Spiritual formation.   I. Title.
BT22.C45   1997
230'.09—dc20   96-28092

9 8 7 6 5 4 3

Printed in the United States of America
on acid-free paper

While still in its formative stages, this project took shape as a study in character formation from the following incident. A good friend, Annette, who had dedicated her life to feeding, clothing, and housing the urban poor, was murdered by her sixteen-year-old foster son, whom she and her husband had tried to rescue from the ravages of inner-city crime and poverty beginning when he was six. By the time I met Donald five years later, he was thoroughly conversant with scripture. As his adolescent years hit hard, my husband and I, and the whole church community of which we were all a part, tried to help wean him away from the lure of drugs and violence and back into school. But our efforts ended in disaster when he broke into his foster parents' house to retrieve money he had stored there from a drug deal. When he and Annette got into a fight over the money, he flew into a rage and bludgeoned her into unconsciousness. He put a pillow over her head to finish the job, put her body in the trunk of her car, and went back into the house to clean up the mess. Then he drove the car to an empty parking lot and abandoned it there. Two hours later he was buying jewelry for his girlfriend using Annette's credit card. Three days later his grandmother took him to the police. Donald is now serving a life sentence for second-degree murder. He calls me weekly, trying to figure out what happened and who he is. This book is dedicated to him.

Preface

This book arose from reading classical texts of Christian theology slowly. I first started noticing purpose clauses while reading Thomas Aquinas's treatise on the passion of Christ: Christ was lifted up on the cross to purify the air; he stretched his arms out to bring all nations to himself. I started rooting around for similar comments that indicated why God did such and such, working out details of the biblical narrative. I worked back from Aquinas to Anselm, to Augustine, and finally to Athanasius, and found similar comments: God did all things gently and by persuasion in order to gain our trust; Christ became human so that we might become divine. I saw that the explanations of the divine rationale were to a practical purpose, and that it had to do with the reader: the writers were addressing the readers. I didn't quite know what to do with this thought, so I just kept reading.

It slowly dawned on me that what I was seeing made sense to me from my years of experience as a mother, and that this perspective had been left out of account by modern theology. These older writers thought of God on the model of a good parent. Taking the doctrines of the Christian faith seriously was assumed to change how we think and act—to remake us. The theologians who shaped the tradition believed that God was working with us to teach us something, to get our attention through the Christian story, including those elements of the story that make the least sense to us. They were interested in forming us as excellent persons. Christian doctrines aim to be good for us by forming or reforming our character; they aim to be salutary. They seek to form excellent persons with God as the model, and this in a quite literal sense, not as metaphors pointing to universal truths of human experience that lie beyond the events themselves. In other words, I came to see that the great theologians of the past were also moralists in the best sense of the term. They were striving not only to articulate the meaning of the doctrines but also their pastoral value or salutarity—how they are good for us.

I also noticed that they understood human happiness to be tied to virtuous character, which in turn comes from knowing God. Becoming an excellent person is predicated on enjoying God. For these theologians, beauty, truth, and goodness—the foundation of human happiness—come from knowing and loving God and nowhere else. I realized then why this no longer make sense to us. All of these have become disjoined in the modern world, and especially the postmodern world, with the unsettling consequence that from the point of view of the classical tradition, we are moral and intellectual barbarians.

Although I started this project as an exercise in historical theology, a constructive thesis emerged: when Christian doctrines assert the truth about God, the world, and ourselves, it is a truth that seeks to influence us. As I worked through the texts, the divisions of the modern theological curriculum began making less and less sense to me. I could no longer distinguish apologetics from catechesis, or spirituality from ethics or pastoral theology. And I no longer understood systematic or dogmatic theology apart from all of these. In the older texts, evangelism, catechesis, moral exhortation, dogmatic exegesis, pastoral care, and apologetics were all happening at the same time because the authors were speaking to a whole person. Our neat divisions simply didn't work. Eventually the distinctions between historical and systematic theology and between theology and biblical studies began to weaken, too. I realized that I was uncovering a norm of theological integrity that had become unintelligible to the modern disciplines.

As I worked on the texts I came to think of myself as an Irish monk in a scriptorium, carefully preserving the tradition. Classic theological texts are becoming more scorned than read. I have sought to read the tradition sympathetically because a community that rejects its past is doomed. The shapers of the Christian tradition were trying to do something. When they did it well and when poorly, and when they succeeded and when they failed, are questions that require thoughtful discernment. Yet we cannot make those judgments if we fail to sympathize with these ancient writers. *By the Renewing of Your Minds* cautions against obliterating the past. The goal is to let the dead speak to us.

The selection process for this project was difficult. The theologians and texts included here—Paul, Matthew, Athanasius, Basil the Great, Augustine, Anselm, Aquinas, Julian of Norwich, and Calvin—are certainly not the only theologians who belong in a volume like this. Undoubtedly many readers will find their favorite authors missing or will be puzzled by those who are included. I had two selection criteria. Since the purpose of the exercise is to allow the classical theological tradition to speak, I first limited myself to pre-seventeenth-century theologians, who wrote before the modern disjoining of truth, beauty, and goodness took hold.

The other criterion was my desire to plow frozen ground—to examine precisely the most distrusted of Christian theologians, those who have held sway in Christian theology and who are now widely regarded as useless or harmful. Thus, I have forwarded unlikely texts for demonstrating the salutarity of doctrine: Augustine's *De Trinitate* and Anselm's *Cur Deus Homo* rather than Nyssa's *Life of Moses* or John Wesley's sermons. Nor do contemporary voices of liberation appear, as some might hope. By selecting only the hardest cases from the premodern centuries, I hope to prepare and prompt others to mine Christian theology for the diamonds that I suspect lie embedded there. These readings are not meant to be either definitive or exclusive. They are an invitation to consider how theology intends to shape readers for the good life.

I have assembled the readings in chronological order, and they do converse with one another on occasion. But the order should not mislead the reader into considering this work a history of the major theme being developed or believing that the norm of salutarity is the primary norm guiding all theology. Nothing could be further from my intention. This is not a history in the sense that an idea has unfolded and developed. Rather, it is more like an irrepressible urge that surfaces regularly in the minds of keen thinkers—the urge to render theology of genuine use to believers, even as they are clarifying, organizing, and reinterpreting Christian claims about God, the world, the church, and ourselves.

Many institutions and individuals have had a helping hand in birthing this book. The foundation and institutional support I enjoyed include a post doctoral fellowship at Yale Divinity School, 1989–91, from the Henry Luce Foundation, where the idea was conceived; a year's support from the Louisville Institute for Protestantism and American Culture, while I was in residence at the Center of Theological Inquiry, Princeton, N.J., 1991–92, where it gestated; a Faculty Outreach Grant from the Perkins School of Theology, summer 1993, and a grant from the dean for graduate student assistance in manuscript preparation. These have been a shower of constant grace and support.

Additionally, numerous colleagues have spent many hours in conversation and comment on individual chapters, including William J. Abraham, William S. Babcock, Stephen E. Fowl, Victor P. Furnish, James Gollnick, Rowan A. Greer, Richard B. Hays, L. Gregory Jones, George Lawless, Bruce D. Marshall, Richard A. Muller, William G. Rusch, Donald Senior, David C. Steinmetz, Charles M. Wood, and the Dogmatics Colloquium of the Center for Catholic and Evangelical Theology, which discussed a preliminary draft of the chapter on Basil the Great. I am deeply grateful to each of them for suggestions, corrections, and encouragement.

Special thanks is due to Rebecca Charry and Patrick G. Henry for copy editing, to Donna Yarri for proofreading, and to Lucy Cobbe for manuscript preparation. Above all, I must thank my theological mentor and teacher, Paul M. van Buren, who led me to fine theologians. Finally, this book could not have survived the years of its birthing without the tender encouragement and profound understanding of my husband, Dana, who shared with me every moment of its gestation.

Scripture citations are from the New Revised Standard Version (RSV), unless noted as from the New International Version (NIV). Where a scriptural citation appears in a citation from a theological text, I have reproduced it as it appears there.

Contents

Foreword

Doctrine is pastoral, theology and spirituality belong together, and the purpose of what seems to be practically irrelevant formulas such as God is One and Three is to promote love of God and nourish a godly life. These are the convictions that motivate this book.

They animate it as well. Ellen Charry seeks to infuse the doctrines she discusses with their love-promoting and life-nuturing force. There are not many like her. Most theologians abandoned responsibility for practice to preachers centuries ago, and now that preachers have turned elsewhere, doctrinally informed spirituality and pastoral care are left without a home. Even the cognitive aspect of doctrines, their status as truth claims and their intellectual justifiability or lack thereof, is less and less studied. Seminary courses in systematic and historical theology that once centered on the historic creeds of the churches now seek grist for their mill from other sources. Nor is this surprising. When doctrines are stripped of their practical entailments, as they have been in modern times, they become irrelevant. Reclothing them in flesh and blood so that minds may be renewed is what this book is all about.

It would not have been possible to write it even a few years ago. The binary oppositions of Enlightenment epistemology between reason and faith, theology and spirituality, academy and church were still too strong. Now, however, with the development of new ways of displaying the inseparability of the cognitive, affective, and behavioral dimensions of all beliefs, not least religious ones, it is becoming increasingly possible to be scholarly without bracketing pastoral concerns, and to be pastoral without ignoring scholarship. Ellen Charry is one of the first in a new generation of theologians to begin to utilize these opportunities. Despite our age-induced nostalgia for the past, we historical and systematic theologians who have spent our lives studying the creeds of the churches are tempted to think that we were born too soon. A new springtime seems to be stirring in our moribund disciplines in such works as that of Ellen Charry.

Not that she has written for us, but primarily, if I may risk a guess, for the growing multitudes of confused and confusing seekers after spirituality who receive not a hint from their churches, religion departments, and theological schools of the rich guidance to be found in the traditions from which, without ever knowing them, they have for the most part been alienated. What they will find in a doctrinally normed biblical approach such as Charry's is not, to be sure, what they think they are look-ing for. There is here none of the warm fuzziness and feel-good abstractness of much contemporary Christian as well as non-Christian piety. Instead there is the dis-turbingly anthropomorphic concreteness of a religion centered on an unmistakably Jewish male, wholly God yet completely human, dying bloodily on a Roman gibbet for wicked sinners such as you and me. This ghastly climax of human history is, to be sure, good for us, the fountain of all true happiness and flourishing, but it is so because it cuts as deeply and painfully as a surgeon's healing knife into our hearts and incomparably deeper into the heart of God. This is not a welcome message for some seekers after the spiritual, but for others it is life after death.

I have just tried to summarize what seems to me one of the messages implicit in this book, but the words and the sermonic tone are mine, not those of the author. Moreover, it is a misleading message if it is not used as a guide (or better, a gadfly) rather than replacement for the reading of scripture. The gross distortions of Chris-tian truth with which the church's history is replete have often resulted from the mis-use of good doctrines and not only from what we label false doctrine. Much wisdom on these matters is available to thoses who go on and read this volume in its entirety. They will discover many other different messages derived from both the same and other doctrines and will learn how they can be used to God's glory and not to his shame. It is by attending to the tradition as Ellen Charry has done that Christians can by God's grace relearn the grammar of the faith to the renewing of their minds.

George Lindbeck
Professor Emeritus of Historical Theology
Yale University

PART I

Introduction

1

The Art of Christian Excellence*

GOD FOR HUMAN FLOURISHING

The first Christian theologian prepared Christians for the world's inability to comprehend their vision of human dignity and happiness. First Cor. 1.18–31 begins, "For the message of the cross is foolishness to those who are perishing, but to us who are being saved it is the power of God." The passage then points out that those who have come to understand Christ as the source and strength of their life will be undisturbed by the vicissitudes and temptations of life. Paul's message remains a stumbling block to Jews and foolishness to pagans. But those who know themselves bound up in the life of God are free from the power of the world, for they flourish by knowing and loving God.

Flourishing born of enjoying God also has consequences for our relationships with one another. For Christians "have been taught by God to love each other" (1 Thess. 4.9 NIV). Paul assumed that God not only made us his own, thereby freeing us from the world's power, but went beyond this to teach noble conduct on the horizontal plane.[1] That is, God is not only good to us but good for us: "For God did not call us to be impure but to live a holy life" (1 Thess. 4.7 NIV). God teaches us to love one another for our benefit. This contrasts with ancient pagan morality, which was self-taught, as Epicurus put it, or, from a later Christian perspective, mistaught by pagan religion.[2]

Unless we center in God, Christians claim, we are lost. We do not really know who we are, from whence our life takes its orientation, or where we ought to direct our energies. Without God we are liable to float aimlessly at the mercy of volatile emotions and hormones or be seduced by less worthy companions than the maker of heaven and earth. Or we may turn to ourselves in a misguided search for fame, wealth, or power.[3] Paul put the issue rather starkly when, in admonishing the Christians at Rome to choose formation by God over formation by the world, he wrote, "Do not conform any longer to the pattern of this world, but be transformed by the renewing of your mind. Then you will be able to test and approve what God's will is—his good, pleasing and perfect will" (Rom. 12.2 NIV).

*A segment of this chapter will appear in *Discipling Hermeneutics: Interpretation in Christian Perspective*, Roger Lundin (Ed.), Grand Rapids: Eerdmans, 1997.

For Paul, the mental transformation required for excellent living derives from the Greek observation that knowing goodness precedes being good. Plato taught that virtue requires insight, not simply rule-following. There is a standard of absolute goodness against which we distinguish what is good from what is not in conversation with other seekers. Aristotle realized that becoming good requires practice; the virtuous life is a skilled life. Christians valued both insight and practice by insisting both that moral transformation comes from knowing God and that virtue is acquired by practice. Augustine would nuance this insight, arguing that knowing God was necessary but not sufficient for conformation to God; loving God was also necessary. Augustine thus steered Western Christianity to the view that by knowing God we come to love him, and by loving him we come to know him. And seeing in himself that he could not muster the strength to love God sufficiently to be transformed by God, Augustine insisted on the necessity of prevenient grace. Thomas Aquinas subsequently brought Aristotle's emphasis on practice into central focus to complement the Platonic thrust of the tradition.

This work assumes that thinking of insight-oriented and practice-oriented options regarding the formation of virtue as a forced choice is a false dichotomy. Human beings are too complex and malleable for us to think rigidly about character formation. Current schools of psychology focusing exclusively on insight-oriented versus behavior therapy perpetuate this perceived opposition. A self-examined life is certainly desirable. Yet unless honed by experience, knowledge lacks nuance, since decision-making requires constant shifts in judgment in assessing information and circumstances. Consequently, the approach taken here will highlight both knowing and doing.

The patristic age emphasized sapience as the foundation of human excellence. Sapience includes correct information about God but emphasizes attachment to that knowledge. Sapience is engaged knowledge that emotionally connects the knower to the known. In the West, knowledge of God's grandeur and wrath inculcated a strong sense of sinfulness in the individual who contrasted him or herself with God. In this view, growth in the Christian life turned on the ability to trust God as a father rather than fear him as a master. In the East, the emphasis was on likeness to God, by means of which we turn to him from less worthy pursuits. Both traditions, however, insisted that God is the origin and destiny of human happiness, that knowing and loving God are the foundation of human self-knowledge and direction, and that life's goal is conformation to God.

Beginning with Saint Benedict, in the sixth century, anxiety about one's ability to be sufficiently humble and obedient came to the fore. This eventually led Luther to reassert the mercy of God through the principle of justification by grace through faith, a principle that assured believers that God's love was freely given and not dependent on their success or failure at pleasing him. Although knowing God dominates Calvin's theology, he nevertheless turned Protestantism away from the vision of God as the goal of life and instead stressed the centrality of trust in God's love, even while insisting that God indeed may not elect all to salvation. With the seventeenth century, abetted by the epistemology of John Locke, theology began to dismantle the notion of sapience altogether.

Sapiential theology waned with modernity. Theology came to be thought of as the intellectual justification of the faith, apart from the practice of the Christian life. The wisdom of God has ceased to function in the church as the foundation of the good life. Theology is no longer expected to be a practical discipline, burdened as it is in the modern period with the awkwardness of speaking of God at all. Theology became preoccupied with considerations of the conditions of knowledge. And even this enterprise is now questioned by postmodern descendants of Nietzsche, who dispute the notion of knowledge altogether, asserting that knowledge is simply a front for power. In order to reclaim the sapiential function of theology it will first be necessary to suggest how theological claims may be understood to refer to God.[4] Once it is clear that we may speak about knowing God, it will be necessary to ask how we come to love God.

THE ART OF THEOLOGICAL PRACTICE

This study examines primary Christian doctrines and teachings from the Apostolic era through the Reformation in order to argue that a central theological task is to assist people to come to God. This itself is a contested idea for modern theology, which has moved away from primary Christian beliefs and focused on theological method instead (Wood 1994).[5] This critical reflection engages the principles on which the Christian tradition is interpreted, the epistemic conditions under which theological utterances are justified, the norms according to which authentic Christian beliefs and practices function. William Christian refers to the second-order thought of a religious community as its governing doctrines—criteria for maintaining the identity, clarity of vision, and intellectual health of the community (Christian 1987). These include rules and principles that distinguish what is authentic to a community from what is not, how to maintain consistency among its teachings, how to relate its authentic self-understanding to competing or alien claims (thereby ascertaining the scope of comprehensiveness of its authority), and how to organize rules for deriving and arguing for its teachings.

Second-order thought is helpful in maintaining community identity and coherence, but Christian is clear that issues of method do not exhaust the theological task. Religious communities also have primary doctrines that teach members to form a coherent pattern of life by modeling themselves on exemplary individuals through practices that shape their lives, and by habits of thought and behavior (5). Christian designates primary doctrines as first-order assertions that identify the setting for a religious life and teach about God (in the Christian case) in relation to human life. They also propose right courses of action, virtues, and dispositions to be adopted by members (8). In short, primary doctrines are the practically oriented content of the faith. They enable a religious community to "propose a pattern of life to its members and nurture them in it as best it can" (44).

Second-order reflection should support the primary doctrines of a community and so is indirectly of practical import. For much of Christian history, theology focused on primary doctrines. Only when knowledge itself became problematic was special attention given to second-order thought. One example of a theologian who engaged in both is Thomas Aquinas. He set forth the bulk of his great compendium of Christian theology with a second-order discussion of the conditions of knowledge under which he was operating prior to explaining the faith for believers.

This work follows a similar procedure. The body of this book is concerned with primary Christian doctrines—specifically, their character-forming intentions. This first chapter is a most modest attempt to suggest epistemic conditions under which such a first-order project might again be undertaken. The point is not to jump over modernity and reimpose classical theology but to see if there are not terms on which the classical conversation might be a bit less alien to us so that we might be stirred to take up the task they were engaged in: helping people flourish through knowing and loving God.

Primary Christian doctrines have been under fierce pressure since the Enlightenment. Modernity pressed theology to account for any claim to theological knowledge. As the conditions for knowledge narrowed, religious claims began to be read symbolically. On the symbolic interpretation, religious assertions about humanity, God, and the world, even if they are historically grounded, are significant only as expressions of the collective experience of the community or inner states of consciousness. In either case, they provide a meaningful framework within which one may interpret one's own identity, strivings, successes, and disappointments. The truth of these assertions does not depend on their relationship to transcendent realities. As the scientific understanding of truth came to dominate modernity, theologians came to assign religious claims to the realm of myth and meaning.[6]

The loss of theological realism and the retreat of sapiential theology, while not mutually entailed, happened at about the same time. The modern notions of truth, reason, and knowledge, developed by empiricist and rationalist philosophy and the natural sciences, squeezed out both revelation and sapience as genuine truth and knowledge. However, as just noted, a small place was carved out for theological claims as symbolic terms that render life meaningful. I will argue that theology has been overly diffident in this regard and that the conditions of modern knowledge themselves are broad enough to include—or at least not to exclude—the possibility that religious claims actually refer to God.

I will do this by noting three pivotal moments in the loss of theological realism: John Locke's and David Hume's empiricism as the standard for rationality, and Immanuel Kant's destruction of natural theology and his agnosticism about transcendent knowledge altogether. While the writings of these men may today be seen to admit more ambiguity regarding theological matters than has previously been noted, the cumulative effect of their work has been to channel theology into thinking in the symbolic terms that now dominate the field.

John Locke, building on Cartesian rationalism, opened a gap between faith and reason, a gap heretofore unknown to theology. Locke is generally considered an empiricist because he insisted that the proper source of ideas and knowledge is sense experience. But his *Essay Concerning Human Understanding* also helped birth modern second-order thinking by stressing the role of the reasoning process itself in the formation of knowledge. Locke offered a powerful view of reason as the ability to perceive the coherence or incoherence among ideas by arranging them in an orderly fashion, so that connections among them are clearly perceived and the right conclusions drawn from them (1964, 415–6; bk. IV, chap. 17). The right conclusions drawn in this manner are the truth.

In the following chapter he went on to distinguish the truth of reason—understood as the ability to arrange ideas correctly—from faith, which attaches to revelation rather than to ideas. Faith is believed to come from God and relies "upon the credit of the proposer" or tradition (424). Locke acknowledged that revelation may be above and beyond reason, as in the case of knowing the number of the fallen angels and the reality of resurrection. But in cases where reason is applicable, it should be employed to determine the genuineness of revelation. In his later essay *The Reasonableness of Christianity,* whether intentionally or not, Locke set up the scaffolding by means of which later writers would carry him beyond where he himself went, to discredit all support for revelation that is beyond the compass of reason (1983). In short, Locke forged a notion of knowledge based on sense experience and reason devoid of trust in anything beyond sense data and its own power to ascertain coherence among ideas. He thereby disjoined reason from both faith and sapience, eliminating both from the category of knowledge.

So pervasive has Locke's construal of reason been that the loss of sapiential knowledge has not been noticed. Theology largely accepted Locke's *tour de force* and abandoned sapience as genuine knowledge. But upon further reflection, while Locke's argument may have some merit, one must finally ask whether all knowledge is exhausted by the objective disengaged terms Locke set down. As I will argue here, classical theology did not claim to know God on Locke's disengaged terms in the first place, in which case it may be inappropriate to discredit it on his terms. Indeed, it is anachronistic to think of theology on the model of detached scientific knowledge because sapience did not claim to be objective.

The norm of sapience claims that the truth to be known is for the well-being of the knower. While modern knowledge builds on a healthy dose of skepticism, sapience has trust built in from the very outset. In this sense, theological knowledge is more like trust in a mother's love that guides a daughter in finding her way in the world, or the reason employed by a driver who obeys road signs because those who set them are responsible for public safety. In the former case it is certainly rational that the daughter acknowledge the mother's ability to discern what is truly in her best interests. In the latter case it is surely rational that the driver on a mountainous road trust that the traffic signs are reliable and authoritative whether or not he or she knows anything at all about the person who mapped the terrain. In both cases reason is employed, knowledge is assumed, and trust is essential. This knowledge is what Locke relegated to the realm of faith, accepted on the credibility of the proposer.

The knowledge Locke's reason aims for, by contrast, is correctness. It is knowledge that is assumed to arise from the process of ratiocination alone, disengaged from the source of the knowledge. Sapience, on the other hand, enriches the knower in a sense at once more personal and intimate than ratiocination alone can give. Sapience establishes a bond of common purpose, even care and concern, between the knower and the known that is foreign to ratiocination, which looks instead for agreement and disagreement among propositions. Indeed, there seems to be little common ground between the impersonal reason of Locke (and Descartes) and the engaged pursuit of wisdom characteristic of premodern theology. My question to the moderns is whether reason devoid of trust is really possible—that is, whether the disjunction between reason and faith actually functions. More on this below, after we have sketched the demise of theological knowledge as truth.

Another pivotal moment in the attack on theological realism came through David Hume's two-pronged attack on theology.[7] He challenged both natural theology, with his demolition of the teleological argument, and divine revelation, with his attack on miracle, leaving theology apparently without foundation or warrant for its claim to know God. In part V of his *Dialogues Concerning Natural Religion,* the skeptic protagonist, Philo, attacked inferential support for theism, on which the argument from design was based (Hume 1970). The world as we know it from experience, Hume argued, does not imply an orderer analogous to the human mind, only perfect and infinite. On the basis of what we might today call clinical judgment, observation, and experience of the world, God might just as well be a team of gods, a vegetable, or a spider as an omniscient, omnipotent, incorporeal deity.

This argument disqualifies precisely the engaged reason employed by our trusting daughter and experienced driver noted above. The daughter relies on past experience of a wise and loving mother, rather than fear of punishment, while the driver relies on long years' experience on the road rather than simply a desire to avoid a citation. Yet it will be objected that these examples do not hit at the heart of Hume's attack on inferential knowledge because the daughter knows her mother and the driver knows that the Department of Motor Vehicles is responsible for traffic safety. But the believer will respond that the testimony of scripture, the collective experience of the religious community, and the effects of divine care in her own life are as effective as the knowledge possessed by the daughter and the driver of our examples, both of whom ground decisions in past experience. They base their judgments on accumulated reliable cases.

In section X, "On Miracles," of his *Enquiry Concerning Human Understanding,*

Hume assumed that a miracle is a violation of a law of nature (1988). He used the principles being developed by experimental science to destroy trust in the received testimony of religious authorities. While both rely on observation, that of experimental science is far more reliable because it is observer-independent, uniform, and repeatable. It can rule out inaccuracies, preferences, and erroneous judgments by the observer, as well as variations in circumstance of the event itself. Religious testimony for miracles, on the other hand, forces one to rely on interested observers many times removed from the recipients of their testimony, which cannot be subjected to subsequent corroboration. The relation such observers posit between cause and effect may be in error or falsely imagined. With this argument Hume replaced the authority of interpretive judgments, made by participants in events, with the reliability of scientific repeatability, performed by those disengaged from the events. Discerning judgment gave way to scientific observation as the standard for truth.

Hume's arguments, however, would be incomprehensible to the theologians to be examined here, for they assumed both that God is trustworthy, even if imperfectly known, and that discerning judgment is relevant to truth. The legitimacy of *a posteriori* reasoning is taken for granted by Athanasius, Basil, and Calvin, who all rely on inference. Athanasius, for example, argued for the truth of Christianity (and by implication the deity of Christ) over paganism from its moral fruits, not its rationality. Basil argued for the dignity and equality of the Holy Spirit with the other two trinitarian persons from its agency as sanctifier. Calvin argued for the goodness of God from creation. None of them would be as bothered by the unrepeatability of events attributed to God and the ultimate unknowability of God, as are the modern scientifically minded. Unrepeatability does not damage credibility because God works in certain ways at certain times, and for certain reasons. That we should doubt that God is behind events that we cannot duplicate would be an odd argument to them.

The attack on transcendent knowledge by Immanuel Kant is a third pivotal moment in the parochialization of modern truth and knowledge.[8] In response to Hume's attack on scientific reasoning, Kant's *Critique of Pure Reason* shifted attention from what we can know of objects to how we know anything at all (1965). His interest in the structure of the knowing mind and the conditions under which knowledge is possible, led him to conclude that the mind, while itself active in the creation of knowledge, is nevertheless restricted in its powers to knowledge of phenomenal data. The noumenal dimension of reality transcends its grasp. As he put it, we have no knowledge of the thing-in-itself. The paralogisms and the antinomies of the Transcendental Dialectic, with its destruction of the traditional theistic proofs and critique of the use of reason that developed them, put an end to the hope that reason could produce knowledge of God as well as to the discipline of metaphysics as it had traditionally been undertaken. So, while Locke had stymied reason's recourse to revelation, first Hume and then Kant turned around and tamed reason ostensibly beyond its usefulness for theology.

It is not immediately clear, however, that Kant's criticism of noumenal knowledge is quite as devastating to theology as has often been assumed. Theology itself has repeatedly taken offense at metaphysical speculation. Scripture does not engage in it. And the Fathers, although they spoke in the Neoplatonic idiom of their day, rarely if ever speculated on the existence of God. Gregory of Nyssa, for example, warned against it at the outset of *An Answer to Ablabius* and urged "that His nature cannot be named and is ineffable. We say that every name, whether invented by human custom or handed down by the Scriptures, is indicative of our conceptions of the divine nature, but does not signify what that nature is in itself" (1954, 259). Language about God directs believers' thinking properly but does not explain the nature of God. Similarly, the *via negativa* and the *analogia entis,* of Byzantine and medieval Catholic theology, were offered as weak alternatives to direct knowledge of God because of the recognized limits to human reason.

This apophatic bent is not to suggest, however, that the Fathers denied all knowledge of noumena as Kant did. But the positive knowledge that they claimed for theology, while reliable, was not intended to be the hard knowledge Kant criticized. The use of reason in theology had started out as assistance to revelation by theologians like Anselm and Thomas. But in spite of their insistence that faith should seek understanding, reason as a tool of absolute knowledge took on a life of its own that bent in the direction of denying the intelligibility of Christian claims unless knowledge of God was empirically or rationally demonstrable. Knowledge of God that takes the apophatic warning seriously, on the other hand, is open to refinement. This is similar to clinical knowledge that balances experimental and inferential knowledge with clinical judgment and objective knowledge.

Kant's critique of the classical proofs for the existence of God may be more of an asset to theology than has often been recognized. For it permits theology to turn its attention from strong rational proofs, on the model of basic science, to a softer rationality that views transcendent knowledge as reliable though mutable. This broader view of reason may help theology reclaim its distinctive vision of knowledge of God that aims to form and transform believers whose trust in divine judgment and mercy is nurtured through scripture, creed, and worship. The fragility of that trust reminds Christians of the need for prayer to prepare properly for knowing God.

I have suggested that the modern concepts of truth and knowledge developed in stages. Locke separated faith from knowledge, denying the importance of trust as an element in truth. Hume insisted on the repeatability of events as a sign of their truth and disallowed inferential reasoning, tentativeness, and discerning judgment. Kant pointed out that the conditions for knowing lie within the mind itself and that human knowing cannot transcend the limits of time and space within which the mind operates.

In what follows I argue that the modern understanding of reason and truth constructed by Locke, Hume, and Kant is too narrow to be adequate for theological claims. It may even be that some fields within science itself are not up to the rigorous standards they proposed, although I leave that for scientists to argue. Instead I will turn to one subfield of modern knowledge, clinical medicine, that relies precisely on aspects of knowledge that Locke, Hume, and Kant excluded. Trust and discerning judgment based on accumulated cases, including moral judgment, inference, and tentativeness, are all as requisite for adequate medical knowledge as is hard scientific fact.

Although the analogy to medicine is not paramount throughout the specific treatises to be examined here, the theme of Christianity as therapy runs throughout Christian theology. Indeed, theology as spiritual medicine can be traced back to Plato.[9] The patristic age, heavily influenced by Neoplatonism, maintained the therapeutic model for knowledge of God. Augustine frequently referred to knowledge of God as healing the eyes of the soul. Later, Calvin thought of knowing God like a pair of corrective lenses so can enable one to see rightly. The word "cure" itself has both medical and ecclesiastical meanings. And perhaps nothing catches the image so well as a well-known spiritual: "There is a balm in Gilead to make the wounded whole; there is a balm in Gilead to heal the sin-sick soul." Christianity is medicine for the soul.

I use the medical model here as an epistemic tool to suggest grounds upon which contemporary readers might be able at least to sympathize with the claims made by our premodern theologians that God effects spiritual transformation. I believe that the practice of medicine is sufficiently akin to the practice of classical theology that it provides a basis for moderns to regain minimal respect for the possibility that it is as sensible to be grateful that the Holy Spirit sanctifies us as it is to thank the researcher who discovered lithium to control manic-depressive illness, for example. Specifically, I will argue that theology and medicine both require three elements working harmoniously, only one of which is hard science. Both rely on experimental knowledge which is open to revision; both use inferential knowledge based on accumulated cases; and both employ clinical judgment.

The goal is to present a case for what Janet Soskice calls a cautious critical theological realism, the position that theological terms are not "logical ciphers but as terms which putatively refer to possibly real entities, relations, and states of affairs" (1985, 120–4). While the parallels do not mesh in every detail, I think the similarities are close enough to suggest that grounds for trust in the power of God to effect spiritual transformation need be no more stringent than grounds for trust in modern medicine. In this way I shall cautiously try to chart grounds for claiming that from a Christian perspective, knowing God is really—not merely symbolically—the basis of human excellence.

There are varied and pointed similarities between the efficacy of medicine in curing physical ailments and the power of God as the agent of human transformation. As I have already noted, both are clinical arts that require knowledge, careful judgment of a total situation (including inference and interpretation of data), and cooperative trust among the parties involved. Both arts must be applied with caution in every circumstance.[10]

First, medicine, like theology, requires information. It relies on knowledge of the human body and of the processes of health and disease (to the extent that these are known), of diagnostic procedures, and of medications—their side effects and interactions with other drugs and conditions. Theology requires scriptures, creeds, and a tradition for interpreting them to effect spiritual healing, the equivalent of basic science. It requires a grasp of human psychology generally, of the personality dynamics of specific individuals, and of the practices of the faith. Theologians interpret the doctrines of the faith and apply them to their knowledge of human psychology in given social settings.

It might be objected that we have better knowledge of the workings of health and disease than we do of God's work of sanctification. I do not consider this objection a strong one, however, as there are many diseases scientists do not understand and others they cannot treat. In fact, there might be support for the view that spiritual deformity in the form of sin is better understood than some diseases and that therapy for it is more readily available. The fact that various Christian traditions understand the process of spiritual healing differently (Catholics rely more on the sacraments, while Protestants rely more on the Word of God) should not deter support for this view. Medicine also has a variety of treatment modalities at its disposal, and judging among them requires careful discernment and attention to their application in any given environment. Mention of the role of judgment in theological practice brings us to another similarity between medicine and theology.

A second component of success in both medicine and theology is highly skilled judgment—the ability to interpret clinical data based on the knowledge at hand. Competent medical practice requires careful initial evaluation and continuous reassessment on the part of medical practitioners. Health care workers must ask the right questions of the patient—who must supply the right answers—in order to render a correct diagnosis and construct a treatment plan appropriate to the patient's situation and resources. Clinical judgment has guided medical practice for centuries. In this day of high-tech medicine, judgment is less visible, not because it is less reliable now that we have more precise diagnostic tools but because economic pressure and the litigious mood of the society require physicians to protect themselves. Indeed, clinical judgment may, in some cases, be superior to empirical diagnostic tests, which may prove false or misleading. Physicians may need to reassess the treatment they recommend and be ready to adjust or change a course of therapy and determine when it is incomplete or ineffective.

Theological practice also relies on careful assessment of available knowledge. While there is a standard set of core Christian beliefs that unite Christian traditions, their interpretation is very broad. Employing these doctrines in the cause of spiritual and moral healing requires the same degree of judgment by the skilled practitioner, the theologian or pastor, within the known body of theological knowledge.

Recently, there has been renewed attention to the use of cumulative case arguments in philosophy of religion.[11] Rather than a formal chain of deductive reasoning to demonstrate the existence of God *a priori,* reliance on personal judgment is again being recognized as a legitimate form of reasoning in building a case for theistic belief. Cumulative case arguments evaluate a series of considerations based on available evidence to arrive at a reasoned conviction. While this may be jarring to those schooled on deductive reasoning, it should come as no surprise to those who accept inductive reasoning and interpretation of evidence in the practice of medicine.

An important example of inferential reasoning that illuminates the parallel between theology and medicine comes from clinical pharmacology. Many conditions are controlled not with medication but with proper diet, exercise, surgery, or simply palliation in cases in which no treatment is available, including the common cold. Nevertheless, medication is essential in many cases. What the general public rarely realizes is that the action of many medications is poorly understood or unknown.[12] New medications are mostly discovered by tedious processes of trial and error, and often by accident. Placebos are effective on occasion, explained more by trust in the physician than by pharmacological action. That is, there is a degree of mystery in the pharmacology of many medications; their authorization for use by the Federal Drug Administration is based on success in clinical trials regardless of the objective demonstration of their action in the research laboratory. Conversely, drugs that can be shown to work in the laboratory may fail in clinical trials on human subjects. Drugs are trusted and prescribed based on their demonstrated effects, not their theoretical cogency.

The situation in medicine goes directly to the heart of David Hume's criticism of inference in theology. Hume argued that what we take to be the effects of God's work—for our present purpose we will focus not on creation, as he did, but on sanctification—do not yield sure knowledge of God, or indeed any knowledge at all. But he may have made a hasty judgment here. The fact that Christian faith and practice do transform believers' lives parallels the medical evidence that a medication may be effective against an illness whether the mechanism of the disease or the medication is well or poorly understood. Theoretical models of science are intentionally constructed and subsequently modified with further research and understanding, especially in the face of clinical trials.

Theological language is not very different. It too has a theoretical component; standardized language to describe the Person of Christ and the Trinity are theoretical constructs. But the experience of faith or sanctification provides crucial evidence for their adequacy or need for adjustment. Just as poorly understood medications are prescribed based on clinical evidence, the power of God to effect spiritual transformation is trusted by Christians even though human language for expressing the reality of God, like the action of the drug, remains elusive and may later call for modification.[13] In this sense, clinical medicine and theology both employ a soft rationalism whose findings are useful even if they later need to be adjusted in light of subsequent cases or information.[14]

The third and final analogy between medical and theological arts is the need for trust and obedience. Although a patient will rarely have as much medical knowledge as the physician, the patient bears a degree of responsibility for her own treatment, beginning with knowing when to seek medical help. To be successfully treated, patients must trust the caregivers and obey the course of therapy. Abuse of medication, diet, or exercise, or failure to persevere with a course of treatment, will thwart the finest medical efforts. At the same time, trust in the physician may be more important than the biochemical effects of medication itself. Cardiac patients have been known to languish when their physician became ill. Often there are several courses of treatment that could be tried, and the decision may not always rest with the physician, or even with the patient, but with the patient's family (or a clerk in a managed care company). On the other hand, too much knowledge is not always helpful either. Physicians do not treat themselves, nor should they treat their own family members. Fine physicians respect their own limits and fallibility.

Theology, too, is based on more than knowledge and sound judgment. While, as in medicine, there may be spontaneous spiritual transformations parallel to spontaneous remissions that point to the objective power of God to heal without our cooperation, most reform takes place in a broader context. Usually the believer must trust God, be acquainted with the teachings of the church, participate in rites and practices of the church, and be nourished by a supportive community. In short, trust and obedience are central to the successful practice of both medicine and theology.[15]

Now, of course, theology, like medicine, contains elements of risk and uncertainty that can never be overcome. As we saw previously, even the hardest scientific cores of medicine, medications themselves and diagnostic tests, contain elements of uncertainty. Some patients will get better without intervention, while others will succumb to their illnesses regardless of care. Some diagnostic screening tools, like the common Pap smear, return 20% false negatives. On the theological side, some persons will succeed in resisting the grace of God, while others will never mature spiritually; God's grace will transform others to their surprise, or in spite of their efforts to avoid God.

Additionally, in both medicine and theology there is malpractice as well as good practice. Medical practices like bleeding and poultices proved to be harmful and were abandoned. Similarly in theology, ascetical practices like starvation and social isolation, once thought to bring people to God, are now seen as detrimental to human flourishing and therefore at odds with obedience to God. Knowledge in theology and medicine is revisable within limits set by their respective traditions. One strives constantly for excellent medical and theological practice, knowing that there will always be instances of malpractice in the hands of incompetent or sinful practitioners, and improvements in the disciplines through continued learning over time. Evidence of malpractice or financial greed in medicine, though troubling, are not generally taken as good reasons to turn to shamanist practices instead. Theological malpractice should likewise encourage the highest integrity among theology's practitioners. It is not a reason to dismantle or abandon the tradition.

The point of this extended comparison is that knowledge in both theology and medicine is malleable, involves unknowns and risks, and calls for caring and trust. The doctrine of the Trinity has always been held to be a mystery opaque to human understanding, just as the actions of aspirin and lithium elude pharmacologists. At this point the analogy with medicine requires caution, because while there are some medications whose mechanisms are unknown or poorly understood, many others are well understood and experimentally documented. There may be considerably greater uncertainty regarding the reality of God than in clinical pharmacology, although beliefs about God, like our understanding of health and disease, are refined through clinical practice. This is to acknowledge that while both medicine and theology contain elements of mystery, these areas may be greater in theology (although the degree of trust necessary to garner the fruits of these arts may not be).

Still, there are broad parallels. Successful practice in either field requires knowledge as well as skilled judgment of the available facts, some of which, like the actions of aspirin and lithium and drugs undergoing development and testing, is gathered inductively—just as knowledge of the power of God may legitimately be derived, with qualification, from the experiences of transformed believers.[16] In short, belief in the power of the Holy Spirit, prayer, the sacraments, and the doctrine of the atonement may strain credulity no more than faith in aspirin—which may fail to cure a simple headache.

The subjective side of medical and theological arts stands more revealed. While God's grace may be effective even in the most unsuspecting individual, it probably flourishes best, like medicine, under proper conditions of receptivity to God, trust in the rites of the church, and support from a worshiping community. Of course, God, like medical science, sometimes works miracles, and may be rebuffed.[17] And like all medications, in inexpert hands the power of God for good may be distorted. Indeed, the church has caused much harm at times. The proper practice of Christianity, like the proper practice of medicine, requires compassion and care and a watchful eye. In neither case can good treatment be limited to mechanical application of rules or practices.

In conclusion, moderns can best appreciate and learn from the texts and thinkers studied here if they can sympathize with the theological assumptions under which they worked: God's being, work, and teaching, as well as the practices of the church, are genuine knowledge that may effect salutary human transformation when applied prudently and caringly in the proper setting and under optimum circumstances. I have tried to show that for classical theologians, as for modern medicine, effective practice requires integrity, knowledge, skilled judgment, and care, yet neither discipline is ever free of mystery and risk. Theology should be as trusted and criticized as medicine, and medicine should be as criticized and trusted as theology.

On this view, moderns may be comfortable enough with theological language to understand and engage the arguments being made by these doctors of the church for the formative power of the knowledge of God even if there are points on which one may disagree with them. A cautious critical realism, on the model of medicine, is not a naive realism that uncritically accepts all theological claims at face value. Rather, the idea is that although it may be necessary to adjust theological language and even doctrines, although there are examples of failure in theology, and although conditions for effective theological treatment are not always optimum, Christian claims are not incredible; all of these circumstances are present in modern medicine, to which people flock ever more devotedly.

ARETEGENIC INTERPRETATION OF CHRISTIAN TEXTS

The Enlightenment challenged the epistemic status of Christian claims. Concomitantly, historical criticism also obscured the pastoral aspirations of theological texts. Scholarly attention to the debates and circumstances surrounding the formation of Christian doctrines crowds out implications of texts for Christian living. This work, too, is primarily historical rather than constructive. But it undertakes doctrinal exegesis neither by reconstructing the historical circumstances surrounding the writing of a treatise—although these may provide helpful supporting evidence—nor by explicating the meaning of the religious claims being made there, but by attending to how the text influences the psychological disposition of the anticipated reader. In addition to asking about the author's intent, these studies raise the normative question of how helpful these classics are in furthering effective Christian practice.

In joining the normative question to the historical, these interpretations follow in the footsteps of Hans-Georg Gadamer, whose work in philosophical hermeneutics challenged the assumption of historical criticism that scientific objectivity in the humanities mandates an unbridgeable distance between original author and contemporary interpreter (1988). Gadamer pointed out that classic texts are those that reveal truth that transcends their moment in history. The texts constitute a tradition that subsequent interpreters must engage within the horizon of their own historical location in order not only to further understanding of that tradition but also to understand themselves as members of that tradition (253–8).

Gadamer folded the normative moment of application, which had been introduced by Pietism but was lost with the emergence of historical consciousness, back into the art of interpretation, early considered to be composed of understanding *(intelligendi)* and interpretation *(explicandi)* (274–6). Gadamer insisted that interpretation includes the element of proclamation, in which the text exercises its saving effect precisely as a religious text (275) without losing its historical integrity. Contrary to historical criticism, he argued that the cognitive and edifying dimensions of theological texts constitute one, not two, interpretive processes. In short, he reintroduced the interpreter into the interpretive process in what he described as the principle of effective-history, the interpretation of a historical text by someone addressed by the text, someone whose own historicity is taken up in the interpretive act (267).

By admitting the subjectivity of the interpreter into the interpretive process, Gadamer opened a space for the reclamation of sapiential knowledge, as theology understood itself in the premodern period. He recognized the relationship between the knower and the known, and, by implication, the responsibility of the interpreter to assist the reader in participating in that relationship. He spoke of this relationship as a rehabilitation of the notion of prejudice—the predispositions, expectations, or "fore-meanings" the interpreter brings to the text (236). These structure the reading and therefore may be responsible for misreading, but are themselves in turn challenged by the author when unanticipated ideas confront the interpreter "[who] is prepared for [the text] to tell him something" (238). In his recognition of interpretive involvement, Gadamer may be merely bringing into the open what in fact has been the case all along but which the Enlightenment's hope of objectivity failed to admit: the modern notion of truth and knowledge, which excludes the knower from the knowledge, is unrealistic and too narrow to be genuinely useful.

The approach taken here, that classic theological treatises provide guidance for the reclamation of the pastoral function of doctrine, already reveals methodological prejudices. On one level, the decision to turn to the tradition for guidance simply respects the standard view that Christian theology itself is a historically recognizable tradition within which continuous reinterpretation seeks to be Christianly faithful. At another level, however, the decision to grant a measure of authority to that tradition is now based on the judgment that secular culture seems to have spent its moral and intellectual capital and therefore now provides only diminished assistance to theology. Indeed, while there may still be areas in which theology may learn from secular philosophies and ideologies, it may also be possible that theology has something to contribute to secular modes of thought. On a third level, Gadamer's argument for effective historical consciousness points out how painfully limited one's own historical vantage point is and how much in need it is of conversation with those who have trod this path before. But perhaps more significantly, the turn back to the tradition suggests that we moderns need the older authors' understandings of human psychology, of how knowing and loving God function in people's lives. We also need their views of their pastoral responsibility, as well as their insights into God's strategies for human flourishing. Needing to listen to them is not to be confused with agreeing with them. But unless we listen to them, we have no check on the prejudices and limitations of our own time and place.

I have been arguing, following William Christian, that one of the tasks of primary religious doctrines is to guide believers. In this regard there is no reason not to consider our theological forebears at least as intelligent and insightful as we are, despite our disagreements with them. Thus, I have chosen to clear a path for constructing a genuinely pastoral Christian theology by returning to the theological tradition itself. I am persuaded that over the course of centuries of action and reaction to the ups and downs of theological practice, theology has lost its ability to address questions of happiness and perhaps even goodness. Alasdair MacIntyre has pointed this out for moral philosophy, and Charles Taylor has chronicled the career of this loss since the Enlightenment (MacIntyre 1984; Taylor 1989). Their narratives can be paralleled in theology.

With this prologue to the interpretive task, I come to the constructive thesis of this work, the theme that binds the various essays together: the classic theologians based their understanding of human excellence on knowing and loving God, the imitation of or assimilation to whom brings proper human dignity and flourishing. Seeking the various divine pedagogies articulated by classic theologians should provide grounds for reclaiming a genuine pastoral Christian psychology that grounds human excellence in knowing and loving God. As I argue below, for Paul the cross and sealing by the Holy Spirit change a person's status before God, dignifying those who had been aliens or sinners. For Athanasius, the resurrection destroyed the fear of death, empowering people to take God, rather than reifications of human sin masquerading as pagan gods, as the model for human striving. For Augustine, knowing the triune God should promote human dignity and uplifted behavior based on the principle of the *imago Dei*. In various ways all the thinkers to be examined here held that knowing and loving God is the mechanism of choice for forming excellent character and promoting genuine happiness.

Each theologian examined here embraced both objective and subjective dimensions of the work of God as well as a holistic notion of the person to whom God's grace is directed. This integrated vision is not the only way the formative task has been construed, however. At times one or another human faculty, such as reason or experience, has been appealed to so strongly that other faculties, notably the emotions, have been neglected. In this regard, one important impetus behind this work is the feminist insight, similar to the concern of Pietism, that some theological traditions have at times been so driven by cognitive concerns as to deny the role of affect and experience in religious knowledge. Other thinkers have been so sensitive to the reality of human sinfulness that they have taken suffering to be redemptive in its own right, a view that is not supported by the biblical materials or the tradition's strongest theologians. By seeking a holistic view of the formative task of theology, this work responds to both these feminist concerns.

Christian doctrines function pastorally when a theologian unearths the divine pedagogy in order to engage the reader or listener in considering that life with the triune God facilitates dignity and excellence. I call this the "salutarity principle." What is good for us does not always mean comfort or immediate gratification, although surely there are times when what is good for one is immediately gratifying. It takes until age eight or ten for a child to *want* to brush her teeth twice daily, for example. But in the long run, the discipline gives way to the realization that one is securing one's dental health, in which one comes to take pleasure. It is similar with spiritual health. Reflecting on the quality of one's life before God is a taste to be cultivated.

Because the salutarity of doctrinal interpretation is not generally foremost in the study of theological texts, I suggest a neologism to try to capture the moral shaping function of Christian doctrines in the hands of the theologians to be examined here. The word I have settled on, the adjective "aretegenic" (and its noun "aretology"), meaning "conducive to virtue," derives from the standard ancient Greek word *areté*, known from Aristotle as the word denoting moral excellence, frequently translated as "virtue," and from *gennao*, "to beget."[18] "Aretegenic" will serve to indicate the virtue-shaping function of the divine pedagogy of theological treatises.[19]

I have pointed out that beginning with Paul, Christian theologians, although at times ambivalent about it, have generally believed that the being, work, or teaching of God can promote excellence. What constitutes excellence from a Christian point of view, however, is harder to pin down. At times Christian excellence has centered on a specific virtue, like love, humility, self-denial, or self-sacrifice. At other times clusters of virtues, such as the three theological virtues—faith, hope, and love—have been highlighted. The cluster approach does not exclude non-Christian construals of virtue, either. The New Testament includes standard pagan virtue and vice lists, primarily among the epistles.[20] And Aquinas interpolated the four cardinal virtues into Christian construals of human goodness as the core of the *Summa Theologiæ*.

This work does not identify a specific Christian norm of human excellence against which subsequent construals of goodness are judged. It focuses not on character traits but on various mechanisms of character formation. It does acknowledge that character traits expounded in the New Testament, e.g., in the Sermon on the Mount and the epistolary literature, will recur in various Christian construals of human excellence; but its examination will center on the recurrence of imitation and modeling themes, beginning with Paul.

COLONIZING THE MIND

Saint Paul's insight that character reform requires a renewing of the mind (Rom. 12.2, echoed in Eph. 4.23) is implied by literary critic Wayne Booth's discussion of the character-shaping force of nontheological texts in *The Company We Keep* (1988, 139, 298). Reading, Booth argued, attempts to colonize the mind. Indeed—to stop a bit short of an outright mental takeover—careful development or leading of the mind should lead to improved character. Or, to state the point more modestly, development of character will not happen without knowledge. This parallels the premise of insight-oriented psychotherapy: that the mind must be reorganized before behavioral change can take place. But once thinking is targeted as the locus of character formation, other critics—beginning with Aristotle and continuing with his current students Alasdair MacIntyre and Martha Nussbaum—will remind us that moral formation engages the whole person, not just the mind, so the emotions and behavior must not be left out of account.[21]

Recognizing the psychological effects of reading suggests that theological texts have rhetorical intentions of their own. This is where aretegenic analysis or criticism differs not only from modern philosophy but also from much modern theology, for it focuses both on what the author meant the text to do for, to, or with the susceptible reader and on the ideas the author conveyed. This is not to suggest that the meaning of the text recedes from view; rather, the author intends the ideas to enhance the reader's quality of life. The proposal for aretegenic reading, then, is that attending to the psychological dynamics and rhetorical art of a text may disclose its moral shaping potential.

Reading discursive texts aretegenically is new not only for theology but also for philosophy and literature.[22] Black and feminist literary critics pointed out that certain texts—for example, Mark Twain's *Huckleberry Finn,* and Rabelais's *Gargantua* and *Pantagruel*—may teach demeaning views of blacks and women. This stimulated Wayne Booth to examine the ethical potential of reading. But once awakened to the possibilities of harmful narratives, Booth was perplexed by the heavy stress of modern literature and philosophy on the decontextualized, isolated individual who is on her own in the task of moral construction. He pointed to the role of fictional characters in providing a community of friends who may stimulate the moral imagination.

Martha Nussbaum, perhaps stimulated by feminist objections to the exclusion of the emotions from the intellectual life, turned to ancient Greek dramatists and modern novelists to argue that truths of human life can be better grasped through emotional engagement stimulated by literature than by abstract philosophical treatises that appeal only to cognition (1990). She also turned to Aristotle to support the role of insight and intuition, the priority of particularity over generality, and the role of the emotions in moral formation (54–105). Another philosopher, Richard Eldridge, turned to both poetry and fiction because the rule-driven theories of modern moral philosophy, particularly Kantianism and Utilitarianism, ignore the role of concrete cases through which abstract rules may be instantiated and in which the individual may discern those rules' most helpful application (1989). Both scholars contribute to reclaiming sapience.

Nussbaum and Eldridge share common ground with my argument for the analogy of theology with medical practice by reserving room for induction in preferring a case method and looking to experience to supplement rule-driven theories of ethics. And both recognize the importance of discernment and judgment. All three critics add the importance of friendship in the shaping of the mind, a dimension that is probably more central to theology than to medicine, although it is also evidenced by the importance of trust in the physician for healing and comfort when cure is unavailable. Additionally, all three point to the cumulative effects of reading and the influence of characters as models for moral formation.

As a group, then, these three secular scholars point to certain limitations in modern literary criticism and philosophy, which treat the self as an isolated mind seeking to live by moral rules, bereft or fearful of emotions, unguided by friends, unaided by those who have struggled to live the good life before them, and detached from the world. Perhaps Descartes, thinking away in his locked heated room and eschewing the world, epitomizes this caricature. The social and affective dimensions of human formation, as well as the ease with which we learn from specific situations and from other persons, have all been left out of the standard account. As a group, these scholars begin to respond to powerful Enlightenment trends that have become the air of individual autonomy in which moderns live and move and have their being. None of these writers has considered that theology might be a source of help in addressing this rather bleak and, one might opine, unrealistic portrayal of the modern individual. I will leave a discussion of whether theology might not in fact offer assistance to late modernism for another venue.

Here I will simply point out how those who read secular literature as an instrument of moral guidance in part reinforce and in part diverge from the proposal of an aretegenic reading of theological texts. To the extent that theological texts work on the subjective side like any secular text, discussions of how texts engage and influence readers will be of interest to theology. But in the process of thinking through this parallel it should be kept in mind that Christian theologians recommend the company not of fictional characters, which readers pick and choose from at will, but of the Lord of the universe. Additionally, they assume that prayerful writing and reading of theological texts, like prayer and works of charity, are spiritual disciplines undertaken by those open to the inspiration and guidance of the Holy Spirit. Finally, Nussbaum and Eldridge turn from discursive argument to drama, fiction, and poetry because philosophy does not have texts that can carry the weight of aretegenic questions. These writers must straddle two sets of literature, whereas theology has many texts that unite the cognitive and affective tasks in one document.

Booth cuts a wide swath for the influence of texts, including everything from Yeats's poems to television commercial jingles. But he fails to distinguish the ability to make judgments about the salutarity of the text from the types of judgment that a person influenced by that text would make in real life. All he offers the reader is that texts seek to shape readers in their own image and to realize certain aims by inviting readers to dwell within them. They thus invite ethical judgment on whether it is good or bad for us to accept the invitation (92, 97). The discerning reader, along with the ethical critic, is responsible for the final judgment as to which narratives will receive a serious hearing. Criteria for making that judgment, however, are not easy to come by. Booth does not provide an epistemology of discernment or offer criteria of goodness whereby texts may be judged.

The closest Booth comes to identifying the process of discernment whereby the reader learns to make judgments (on the text, and presumably from there to real life) is what he calls "coduction": a narrative-appraising method that compares experiences which we have had in the past and upon which we rely for making judgments in the present (71ff). Text and experience merge in either confirming or modifying previous attitudes and judgments. In this way, we absorb the new notions of the world that we find in the text, then we decide whether to carry them over, or sometimes unconsciously practice them in our real lives (151).

Moral discernment is clearly far more complicated than Booth's suggestion of coduction lets on. It is not possible here to develop a full epistemology of discernment linked to moral formation, although that would be helpful in applying the insights of the texts at hand to contemporary Christian formation.[23] Even without articulating a precise process of moral discernment, though, we can sketch a few common themes that appear to tie together the literary and theological interest in moral formation. First, the text must arouse awareness of a lack and create desire. The successful author will make the reader want to have more of something that she comes to see she lacks after experiencing the text. In the case of the theological texts we will examine, that awareness may be of feeling distant from God, and the resulting goal may be to want closeness to God or a more intentionally God- or Christ-guided life. There must also be an ability for self-transcendence—seeing oneself from another vantage point, with the possibility of change. Stories—in our case, the stories of God enfolded in the doctrines—pattern and direct desires, each implying that it is the best, or at least the most desirable. Booth points out that the discerning reader will be on the lookout for helpful authors, those who have something to teach, friends who invite us to "a richer and fuller life than [one] could manage on [one's] own" (223). Even an innocent reader, who begins by reading for pleasure, may end up being morally stimulated in spite of herself (229). While some readers may intentionally decide to assimilate new moral behaviors, education by influence is often more subtle. It creeps into one's thinking subliminally if sufficiently reinforced. There is then no such thing as resistance to influence; there is at most a choice among influences.

Wayne Booth boldly appropriates this counter-modern view in his adaptation of Harold Bloom's *The Anxiety of Influence* (1973).[24] Booth recognized the modern insistence on self-formation and the consequent anxiety of being influenced by others as patently spurious. In reading, one is occupied by a foreign world that may become one's own (139–40). He even promotes what he calls "hypocrisy upward" or faking it: practice in emulating the virtues and skills of others until they become internalized or habitual (253–4).

That people are influenced by the images and models that surround them, of course, may work for woe as well as for weal, as Hollywood and Madison Avenue make painfully clear. From a Christian point of view, God is the primary moral influence on the believer. Spurring the reader to attend to God becomes an important task of aretegenically interested doctrinal exegesis. Of course, many of the theologians we will encounter believe that the reader, especially if a Christian, is already befriended by God, either through faith and baptism, simply by virtue of being created in the image of God, or by divine election. Still, they write because those so befriended need further assistance in attending to that accompaniment. Thus, theological attending for them is itself an act of obedience.

Writing as a literary critic, Booth rejects God as the source of moral guidance. Yet the need for external guidance cannot be stilled. Fictional characters have taken the place of God as the model for moral formation. But given writers' hesitations to take up the challenge of moral responsibility for readers, or society at large, or even truth itself, one wonders whether some authors might not squirm uncomfortably at having moral responsibility thrust upon them. Richard Eldridge fills the gap between the authority of God and the isolated individual with the modern values of respect for persons and the pursuit of justice that he finds in the work of Joseph Conrad, William Wordsworth, and Jane Austen.

Martha Nussbaum points to an author's contribution to the reader's well-being. Through the text the author imaginatively portrays or suggests thoughts, feelings, wishes, and movements that set a standard of correctness, a norm of the ethical life that carries authority to the reader (9). Again, one sees vestiges of the need for guidance, the tacit admission of the inability of the reader to achieve moral stature alone, behind the insistence on authorial prerogative. The novelist reigns where God once guided.

Moral achievement, Nussbaum argues, is visible in the love between a father and daughter portrayed by the characters in Henry James's novel *The Golden Bowl*. Each sacrifices for the sake of the other, renounces personal gain, preserves the dignity or promotes the well-being of the beloved, or creates new or richer bonds between persons (153). Nussbaum's interpersonal ethic requires a balance between individuation and bondedness. The reader sharpens these skills when confronted with specific situations by which standing values and attitudes may be revised in the quiet of one's reading chair. In effect, the models and vicarious experiences offered by reading provide a protected and more efficient means of self-reflection than the emotional bumps and bruises one is likely to receive by trial and error. Drama and novels help do the work of moral discernment and skill development without the embarrassment of making mistakes in public; the fictional characters make our mistakes for us while the wily reader painlessly, or at least less painfully, reaps the benefits of the fictional character's exploits.

Nussbaum's ethic is quintessentially interpersonal and late-modern. Ethical behavior is the expression of love and care between individuals in loving relationships. The self is formed in relationship, from being loved and by successfully returning love. From a Christian point of view, the interpersonal ethic is naive, as it lacks a doctrine of sin. Grounding one's sense of self in the ability to give and receive love is an invitation to frustration and failure. In the Christian view, even those who love or try to love are sinners who inevitably turn in on themselves rather than turn outward in selfless love. Christians—backed up by the love lyrics of popular music as well as the plots of many operas and contemporary films—believe that humans are incapable of selfless love without the aid of divine forgiveness and the empowerment of the Holy Spirit. Indeed, the high rate of divorce, child neglect, domestic violence, and the violence children now commit against other children all suggest the romantic naiveté of considering interpersonal relations an adequate foundation for ethics. The interpersonal model fails because it offers no transcendent ideal and presents no bar of judgment against which one's conduct may be evaluated.

Be that as it may, Booth and Nussbaum agree on a point that is of interest to theology: particular fictional characters influence the formation of moral standards, prior to formulating general rules and principles, by offering images of how things might be in real life. Nussbaum especially encourages the reader to see the novel as a paradigm of one's own life, by suggesting that in similar circumstances the reader should act likewise. And finally, reading socializes readers by creating a cultural construction that binds the reader to others (1990, 166). In short, fiction accompanies readers and offers them alternative visions of how they should live.

Here again, fiction stands in for religion. For fiction can claim to bind the reader together with others; but although the reader may be lifted momentarily into the company of great and exemplary characters, unless the reader makes a serious commitment to them or lives in a community that reinforces the values and behaviors they lift up, the new friends vanish the moment the book is closed. The social context provided by reading, designed to lift the reader out of isolation, is of limited scope. The company we keep must carry over into life. Unless we induce our real-life friends to read this novel, or see this film, and then discuss it with them, or become college teachers so that we can talk about our favorite books with our students, we are still on our own in interpreting and making the final judgment on whether the world offered by the author merits our redesigning ourselves.

While Nussbaum employs drama and fiction instead of ethical theories to guide character formation, Richard Eldridge, as noted above, is interested in literature to supplement and guide moral philosophical principles of respect for persons and the pursuit of justice. The principles by themselves are devoid of context and emotion, while real people are embedded in social matrices that demonstrate how such principles may variously be applied. Like Nussbaum, Eldridge realizes the difficulty of having an abstract principle shape a person's life but wants to hold to the importance of moral principle more tightly than does Nussbaum. He is not especially interested in the emotional appeal of narratives either, although he recognizes their strength. Rather, he is interested in the examples that literature supplies because they enflesh *a priori* principles of right.

Like Booth and Nussbaum, Eldridge turns to narratives and poetry in order to contextualize and balance deliberation and action, because they "reflect to us the most serious demands on and possibilities for our moral lives as persons" (33). They shape action and self-understanding by providing instances of respect for persons so that the individual can test and practice acting on the principle through a corps of stable embodied cases. Thus exemplars are essential to Eldridge too, who argues that "we can attain moral consciousness only as we see our personhood and its demands reflected in the lives of others that are recounted to us in narrative art." (60).

Literature nudges the moral imagination in small spurts. General principles must be either supplemented with (Eldridge) or prior to (Booth) models of moral selfhood. Yet there is no specific model for emulation. There are only momentary options and imperfect examples. Moral formation is occasional and dynamic. Eldridge would agree with Booth that moral personhood happens in the process of critically considering the lives of fictional characters set against still earlier understandings put before us in worlds through which others have moved (4). Yet it seems that for Eldridge there is no forward movement, no noble end. There is only taking up salient concerns one by one, to examine a principle and perhaps use it temporarily until another presents itself. Examples gained from fiction or poetry do not encourage or upbuild. On the contrary, they prepare us for realistic acceptance of the failures that pervade real lives. What is needed, he says, is "the criticism of nonsovereign reminder, a criticism that leads us to see our own dimensions of possible partial success and failure in expressing and sustaining our personhood in the world with others against the background of the partial successes and failures of the protagonists of the narratives we read" (17). Moral personhood is finally a bleak and meandering nonaccomplishment, so to speak. Fictional characters accompany and soothe us with the sense of their failure, cushioning our own.

Perhaps Eldridge, a secularist working on the far side of Enlightenment optimism, wants the formation of moral personhood to quell exuberant self-assurance about one's moral potential. "All we can do . . . is engage in, take our bearings as agents and evaluators from, *insistence, criticism, redescription,* or *reading,* directed at cases in the service of the elaboration of a *perspicuous representation* of who we are, of what our nature as persons is and demands of us" (emphasis in original) (20). His secular project, although promising companionship from fictional characters, looks joyless and uninviting, even banal. There is no flourishing, no happiness here. There is only trying on characters who will probably fail to reach any moral height of respect for persons and justice, eventually to be replaced by others who walk through the pages of another novel.

Despite differences in nuance, in strikingly similar ways these critics have turned to literature to clarify and turn attention to the possibilities and prospects for structuring the mind morally, by stimulating the emotions and providing models for practice prior to or concomitant with rational principles. Where Booth sees forward movement in the process, Eldridge would perhaps be disinclined to see progress. Where Nussbaum envisions narratives that promote an ethic of love, care, and responsibility, which Carol Gilligan has articulated as a distinctively feminine ethic, Eldridge sees individual cases as instantiating general rules of justice, a typically masculine ethic (Gilligan 1982). Yet together they are trying to find a middle way that avoids God as the source of moral value on one hand, yet recognizes the need for external help in moral formation on the other. All recognize the need for outside influence in structuring character, tacitly rejecting the sovereign self of modernity. But God for them is not an option, so fictional characters must suffice.

The modern critics share a basic insight with pre-Reformation Christianity, an insight derived from Aristotle: by and large we become what we know and are what we do. Surely what we come to know butts up against our genetic endowment. But the influence of the environment cannot be gainsaid. Some may eventually try to cast off who they have become or what they know to become someone else. Others will be negatively influenced by what they know. Still others will fail to resist what they know to be bad for them. But by and large, whether intentionally or inadvertently, willingly or unwillingly, reflectively or innocently, we become what we know. Excellent character doesn't just happen—it is formed, crafted among other things by literary or visual examples that companion, expand one's world, stimulate the imagination, engage the emotions, sharpen discernment, and promote practice vicariously. In conclusion, the three secular critics examined support the view of character formation practiced by classical theology: that moral formation requires emotional engagement with concrete models for emulation and a social context within which to practice them.

For theological purposes the degree of success secularists achieve in charting a path for secular moral formation is less important than the support they lend to the subjective dimension of character formation: the power of particular models to provide a suitable moral environment for shaping character.[25] Such an environment must supply a social context for practicing skills, provide concrete models for emulation, create opportunities for self-reflection, and enlist the emotions in the pursuit of excellence. One additional element on the subjective side that theology can provide, but literature cannot, is numerous and live conversation partners for the journey in the form of a living community within which to practice moral discernment.

Still, secular critics can offer no support from God, nor do they seem to garner much support from the secular tradition of moral philosophy, although Eldridge leans gently on the Enlightenment, and Nussbaum on a psychology of interpersonal relations. Christian thinkers and critics, I have argued, are not working alone. They rely on God to authorize their positions and the guidance of the Holy Spirit to set their hands properly to the task of leadership in the community. And I have suggested that there may be reason not to dismiss their trust.

What, then, do these secular scholars offer theology in its quest to discern the dynamics of Christian moral formation? My argument is that these literary and philosophical critics encourage theology to reclaim its distinctive voice. The turn to fiction for transforming truth, truth to live by, should, above all, encourage Christian theologians to reclaim the sapiential authority of their own beliefs.

A second support for theology from the turn to literature for wisdom encourages theology to reclaim the emotions.[26] In theology's case this will mean attending to how God understands and renders us vulnerable for cultivation by engaging our hopes and aspirations as well as expanding our minds. That is, theology assumes that God is psychologically sophisticated. An aretegenic reading of doctrinal interpretations offers a notion of rationality that embraces the emotions as integral to the process of discernment and moral deliberation. Although few theologians appeal directly to the emotions, many do seek to engage the reader's vanity, pride, or emotional insecurity in order to call forth the reader's best self and pull it yet higher, or to inculcate certain attitudes and behaviors. Paul, for example, variously shamed and praised his readers, rousing them to live up to their best selves. Athanasius appealed to the reader's fear of death in order to heighten the joy at having it overcome by Christ. Anselm appealed to the fear of punishment for wrongdoing in order to deepen trust in the power of the cross. Calvin alternately induced trust and fear of God, to stimulate the virtues of awe and gratitude.

Recognizing the need for concrete examples as teaching models that intrude on the reader's world and invite reflection is another area in which these critics encourage theology to return to itself. In theology's case, of course, the examples will be provided by the identity and work of God in the form of primary Christian doctrines.

Finally, as I have just argued, the literary turn may free theology from exclusive dependence on a narrow rationalism that excludes knowledge gained from inference, experience, prayer, and worship. In the case of literature's interaction with the individual reader, this happens in isolation. But in the case of theology, the process occurs in community—the community of the received texts of the tradition as well as of the living reading community. The community's accumulated wisdom structures internalization of models within the context of a tradition, as Alasdair MacIntyre has artfully pointed out. But the reading community also provides a context for the sociality lately reclaimed as central to moral development.[27] Again, this goes back to Aristotle's *Ethics*, which stressed the importance of friendship and formation in virtue as the formation of skills. Communal practices such as participation in prayer, liturgy, sacraments, works of charity, and study all strengthen Christian identity. That is one reason why Christian communities have been fussy about ordering these communal tasks.

In conclusion, the turn to literature by moral philosophy and the turn to virtue by literary criticism bring to literature and philosophy a debate raging in psychology and education between cognitivists, who follow Plato, and behaviorists, who follow Aristotle, as noted at the outset of this chapter. The former believe that behavioral change and learning begin with knowledge, while the latter hold that behavioral change and experience create fresh patterns of thought. Among our critics, Nussbaum sides with Aristotle, while Eldridge tries to strike a balance between them. Booth does not address the issue directly but seems to follow Aristotle in his emphasis on practice, models, and formation of self as a craft.

The current state of the question in literature and philosophy, as suggested by the critics examined here, does not offer theology a clear path to follow. And the debate itself may be overly polarized. All the discussion does is offer a discipline hampered in modernity by the desire to justify itself scientifically the invitation to return to its own resources—indeed, to be itself.

Still, it will be helpful for theology to reengage the cognitive-behaviorist debate. It is probably the general impression that theology has preferred the Platonic over the Aristotelian approach. That is, theologians have by and large assumed that knowing God creates the proper conditions for loving God rather than the reverse. But concomitant with dedication to knowing God, the church has stressed participation in Christian community and practices as a way not only of reinforcing the knowledge of God but also of shaping the mind so that knowledge of the love of God fits into a life prepared to interpret it properly.

Adequate discussion of this debate is not possible or even necessary here, as it will be explored further as we proceed. What is important is to note that the premodern theologians I will treat did not believe that a choice had to be made. While some emphasized knowledge and others practice, they might be puzzled at the idea that they do not reinforce one another. Modern cognitivist theory recognizes that different persons learn differently, some primarily by thought and reflection, others primarily by experience. Age may also be a factor in how people learn.

For our purposes there is no reason to believe that a choice must be made. In some cases, knowing God through study and preaching will be assumed to lead to loving obedience and behavioral change. In other cases the experience of being loved by God or the formative power of prayer or care for the poor will create their own knowledge of God. Perhaps for most theologians and the believers for whom they care, both approaches are mutually reinforcing, although temperaments vary. Again, the analogy to clinical medical practice comes to mind.

SALUTARITY IN DOGMATICS

Finally, a word should be added about salutarity as a task of Christian theology. One recent theologian concerned with the salutarity of Christian doctrine is Karl Barth, who criticized both Augustine and Calvin on what may be identified as the grounds of salutarity. Barth rejected the Augustinian doctrine of original sin as "an extremely unfortunate and mistaken one" (1956, 500). The notion that sin is sexually transmitted is offensive because it encourages moral irresponsibility. How can one take one's own sinfulness seriously if the fault lies with parental hormones? What Barth takes to be the pastoral point of the doctrine of original sin is lost if "I cannot acknowledge or regard myself as responsible" (500). The doctrine of original sin ought to point to "the voluntary and responsible life of every[one]" (501). In other words, Augustine's teaching on the hereditariness of sin obscures the fact that the purpose of the Christian teaching on sin is not to condemn us but to point to our responsibility for sin, our helplessness in averting it, and thereby turn us Godward. While this end in itself is salutary, that moral responsibility is in itself an important element in moral formation is apparently not lost on Barth either. Yet his interest was not in pointing out that the Christian doctrine of sin reinforces a secular notion of moral responsibility but in stressing the morally uplifting consequences of turning to God. And if previous theologians have failed to address this issue adequately, they must be corrected.

Barth also criticized Calvin's teaching on the Christian life, developed under the rubrics of mortification and vivification. Barth's concern is not that the categories are inadequate but that Calvin "obviously suffers . . . from a curious over-emphasising of *mortificatio* as the expense of *vivificatio*" (1958, 575), which is contrary to the New Testament's teaching on conversion. "What we have called the divine call to advance is in Calvin so overshadowed by the divine summons to halt that it can hardly be heard at all." The result is that Calvin's "presentation is not merely stern, as is inevitable, but sombre and forbidding" (575). And his preference for mortification over vivification obscures what we are to learn—that "it is in view of the Yes pronounced to [us] in the omnipotence of the divine mercy that there arises this falling-out with ourselves and we hear the inexorable No to our being in the flesh" (576). The pastoral point of the doctrine is to lift us from death to the new life for which we are elected by God, and this, Barth argued, Calvin failed to do. The aretegenic presupposition behind Barth's recommendation to emphasize vivification is that underlining what he characteristically calls God's Yes to us builds us up into the dignity to which God calls us. Calvin's lugubriousness, on the other hand, supports a punitive and guilt-ridden identity that Barth considers incompatible with God's grace. Barth is not motivated by the modern psychological insight that a guilt-ridden personality is unhealthy (although he was probably not unsympathetic to that view) and that Christian theology should be adjusted. Rather, as a theologian he believed that God calls us not to be bent over in shame but to stand tall in light of divine grace. And because God is good for us, God's call to new life must be good for us also.

Barth apparently grasped the importance and delicacy of the pastoral power of the doctrine of sin. He argued that Augustine and Calvin distorted the doctrine so that it could not set us on a wholesome and morally responsible path of life in response to election by God. As a theologian his task was to point out and correct the earlier errors and thereby restore the doctrine to its proper aretegenic purpose. We will see other theologians who take a similarly critical approach to their task. Augustine, for example, was correcting Christian Platonism, just as Plato corrected Homer. Anselm corrected Augustine for failing to stress divine mercy. Julian chastised medieval Christianity for overemphasizing divine wrath. Correction of the tradition has always been a central dogmatic task, one traditionally pursued without fanfare in order to avoid disparaging one's teachers and the tradition as a whole.

Before leaving the question of critical judgment on the salutarity of any given aretegenic formulation, a note must be added on the criteria for judging salutarity. While making normative judgments on the salutarity of aretegenic proposals evaluated here is not the main purpose of the work (simply articulating them is the goal), there will be times when normative judgments will be called for. Barth may have concurred with secular psychological insights about what is emotionally healthy and what is not, but his theological judgments were primarily guided by the revelation of God in Jesus Christ. Still, at least from the two texts examined above, Barth was not opposed to secular psychological insights into modern understandings of emotional health. His point about criteria for theological judgment was that psychological insights should be tested against the standard set for knowledge of God in Jesus Christ.

As I argued earlier, judgments on the fittingness of any particular aretegenic proposal, when called for, will be made in conversation with the witness of Christian scripture and tradition, recognizing the appropriateness of conversation with non-Christian understandings of excellence and flourishing. There may be central points at which the Christian and the modern secular notions of human excellence substantially agree. But to the extent that modern psychology, like theology and philosophy, has severed happiness from goodness, modern psychology may be ill-equipped to judge Christian aretologies.

Notes

1. In writing this work I have struggled with the question of gender with regard to pronouns for God. Since this work focuses solely on figures who wrote in the premodern period, when there was no question regarding the use of masculine pronouns, I have decided to respect their thought world because to do otherwise would be artificial and jarring. This should not be interpreted as excluding other possibilities for current theology but simply as respecting those from whom I seek to learn. The English translations used in writing this work were all done before the question of inclusive language was raised. We cannot, for example, tell whether the word "man" in a text translates the more general *homo* or the more specific *vir* in Latin, or the more general *anthropos* or the more specific *aner* in Greek. It has not been feasible to make original translations of all the texts used. The result is an unduly masculinized text that, while it accurately reflects standard scholarship, may well misrepresent the intentions of the original authors, or at least what they might have written had the questions of inclusive language been put to them.

2. Abraham J. Malherbe suggested that Paul may have intentionally contrasted a Christian understanding of moral formation to Epicurus's view (1986, 104–5). The notion that paganism morally miseducated, and that God does a better job of moral education, is a common theme in Pauline and deutero-Pauline theology (e.g., Rom. 1.1ff; 2 Cor. 6.14–7.1; Eph. 2.1–7) and subsequent Alexandrian thought, notably Clement, and Athanasius of Alexandria.

3. Augustine lamented this in his *Confessions*, X:36–8 (Augustine 1991a).

4. Scholarly attention to the practical character-forming effects of Christian doctrine first began in the mid-nineteenth century. In an essay criticizing this approach, John Henry Newman argued that men like Thomas Erskine and Jacob Abbott reduced Christian doctrine to a moral instrumentality and denied the mystery of God by rationalizing the doings of God in humanly useful terms. He did not deny the importance of the moral shaping function of doctrine but insisted that salutarity not be used as a norm for judging the adequacy of Chris-

tian doctrine. He was also concerned that a focus on instrumentality would undermine the realistic claims made by Christian doctrines. I will argue for both the realistic referential and the instrumental dimensions of Christian doctrine in holding to both the objective and subjective sides of the doctrines examined herein (Newman 1910).

5. The situation has been succinctly stated by David Dawson in a discussion of literary theory and theology: "Academic theology turned into theological method at about the same time that practical literary criticism turned into literary theory, and perhaps for much the same reason—as an apologetic or protectionist strategy by humanists who found themselves increasingly marginalized by the rising prestige of science and technology in the university" (1995).

6. The religious existentialism of Paul Tillich, Rudolf Bultmann, and John Macquarrie all reinterpret theological claims in this direction.

7. This section on Hume was enriched by the work of Terence Penelhum and J. C. A. Gaskin (Penelhum 1993; Gaskin 1993).

8. My thinking on Kant was refreshed by the work of Karl Ameriks and Allen W. Wood (Ameriks 1992; Wood 1992).

9. For the moral dimensions of Plato's philosophy, see Cushman (1958).

10. For a thoughtful treatment of the economic and bureacratic pressures on physicians that endanger fine medical practice along the lines described here, see Adson (1995).

11. Mitchell 1973; Abraham 1987.

12. For example, the actions of Wellbutrin and Ludiomil, used to treat depression, are unknown. The actions of Blenoxane and Megace, palliatives to treat carcinoma, are poorly known, as is the case with Ritalin, used to treat children with attention deficit disorders, and Esidrix, used to fight hypertension.

13. In medicine, theoretical models are often modified by experimental trials. In theology, practice has often guided theory, following the ancient rule *lex orandi lex credendi.*

14. Another example would be the desire to enrich language for God beyond monarchical and feudal language, which once seemed definitive but now is seen by many as inadequate to fully capture the grace and mercy of God.

15. The importance of trust and obedience in both medicine and theology do not, of course, deny that both arts may be improperly used and need to be critically examined or censured at times. But this model is developed not for corrupt but for healthy and proper instances of medical and theological practice.

16. Argument along these lines is more fully developed in the work of Patrick Sherry (1984), Grace Jantzen (1987), and William P. Alston (1993).

17. See Alston's discussion for the conditions under which sanctity is achieved (1993).

18. The single appearance of *areté* in the New Testament is Phil. 4.8, at the end of a list of virtues that Christians learned by imitating Paul and in which they are to persevere to remain in the peace of God.

19. I will sometimes interchange "aretegenic" with "pastoral" and "practical." Although they are roughly similar, "aretegenic" conveys more precisely the moral shaping function, whereas "pastoral" and "practical" have of late been construed more broadly.

20. Rom. 1.29–31; 1 Cor. 6.9–11; Gal. 5.19–23; Col. 3.5–17; 1 Tim. 1.8–10; 3.2–7, 8–13; 6.3–5; 2 Tim. 3.2–5; Tit. 1.7–9; James 3.13–8; 2 Pet. 1.5–7.

21. An interesting treatment of the role of rhetoric in reshaping theology is David Cunningham's recent work (1991).

22. Wayne Booth, one of the first to examine the role of literature in moral formation,

understands why this is the case in literature, where the notion of moral responsibility of the author to persons fictionalized in a text, to readers, or to society at large, or truth itself is largely deemed a subliterary consideration, while aesthetics and form are the primary considerations (125–34). But he is surprised that the ethical dimensions of theological texts are similarly disregarded. In an off-hand comment he observes, "Even advertisements in religious journals seldom even hint that reading a touted book might not only teach some important doctrine—that kind of claim is found everywhere—but actually change the reader's character for the better" (236).

23. The original Christian epistemology of discernment is, of course, Augustine's, presented through his famous analysis of "the palaces of memory" in Book X of his *Confessions*, which I shall attend to more fully in time. Recent theological treatments of the epistemology of moral judgment are by James M. Gustafson (1986) and L. Gregory Jones (1990).

24. Bloom invented the phrase to describe the ways poets deal with the influence of earlier poets on their own work.

25. I have written elsewhere of the use of literature as a replacement for scripture by marginalized groups (Charry 1991).

26. If, as I am arguing here, Christian theologians must take their moral responsibilities to their readers quite seriously, the field of literature has another word of advice to offer. It is probably not hyperbole to say that theologians are notoriously poor writers. Many theological texts are simply uninviting. Martha Nussbaum's discussion of the importance of style's matching content is especially germane here (3–53). In short, the conversation with these secular scholars suggests that theology should attend more carefully to how it communicates with readers.

27. Emphasis on sociality in recent philosophical and ethical discussion is often linked with narrative in theology. The work of Stanley Hauerwas is of particular importance in this discussion (1975; 1981).

PART II

New Testament Foundations

Christianity arose as a volcanic eruption within a first-century Judaism in crisis, and in turn precipitated a crisis within the crisis of an occupied nation under religious, political, and economic pressure from the greatest power on earth. The New Testament represents the igneous rock of this eruption, an acrimonious struggle within Judaism over the identity of God and God's people, over the definition of civility and social order, over the meaning of scripture and of hope itself. In some ways, the remaining rock has never cooled.

Underlying all these dimensions of the struggle lay a single and far-reaching question that great empires had often failed to resolve effectively: whether the local tribe or culture is the final arbiter of truth and thus demands loyalty or whether larger harmonious units that sublate diversity within a broader unity can bind diverse groups together by creating a new identity with its own standards of moral conduct. It is the old problem of unity and diversity. Christians argued that Judaism's doctrine of election rendered its claims about God's universality incoherent. Jews saw Christians as interlopers and apostates who denied the truth of God and the heritage of the tradition. In the end, no coherent conversation was possible across this divide.

The Jewish response to the crisis, catalyzed by Roman occupation and concomitant disrespect, was to circle the wagons in order to protect Jewish purity and piety in a barbaric time. The Christian response, on the other hand, was to reach expansively into the world to transform it under a new moral and theological vision. Two of the many trenchant voices to address these questions were Paul and the author of the Gospel of Matthew. Paul argued that with the cross of Christ, God had inaugurated a new way of reconciling enemies and establishing his universal reign of grace and glory, a reign that would encompass all people. Matthew argued that with Jesus, God had issued a new moral law that demanded rigorous standards of self-scrutiny and other-directedness. The differences between them are pronounced, but they agreed that from the very crucible of Judaism's struggle with Rome, a new day had dawned; that God was its architect; and that their task was to make this known and to persuade Jews and gentiles to risk being redefined by the cross and the teachings of Jesus.

2

Co-optation into the Work of God

Paul and His School

Paul and his followers were concerned with Christian formation. From their letters we can piece together how they understood God's work in forming Christians. The letters sought to persuade former social and theological adversaries, gentiles and Jews, that God had joined them together as his people and that their behavior was to reflect this change. Paul labored with and invited Jews, but especially pagans, to grasp, try on, and settle into the new identity and life with God accomplished through the cross.

An aretegenic analysis of the letters suggests that Paul and his followers viewed Christian identity as an ontological status given by God in the cross of Christ. Pagans are co-opted by God in the cross. They are then individually consecrated to Christ in baptism and empowered for new life by the Spirit. This identity comes to fruition in community through proper teaching, example, and worship.

The context for this discussion on Christian formation has been set by the tradition of Pauline scholarship, a tradition that once spoke of Paul's Christ mysticism but now speaks of Paul's insistence on the believer's participation in Christ. Briefly, this school developed as follows. Albert Schweitzer interpreted Paul's talk of being in Christ as mysticism that found its origin in Palestinian Judaism (1931). Subsequently, W. D. Davies softened the distinction between Hellenistic mysticism and Pharisaic Palestinian Judaism and eschatological and rabbinic modes of thought that had polarized Pauline scholarship in the first half of the twentieth century. Davies argued that Paul was a rabbinic Jew thoroughly fluent in Hellenistic thought. He stressed the rabbinic components of Paul's soteriology: communality, vicarious righteousness, obedience, sacrifice with repentance and moral improvement, and expiation of sin through death (1955).

E. P. Sanders, relying on and correcting Davies on several points, examined transfer terminology in Paul's soteriology (1977). The crux of Paul's soteriology is not expiation of sin, but participation in Christ through dying and rising with him. This participation is not union with Christ in a cosmic sense, as Schweitzer thought, but a transfer of lordship in which, by belonging to or participating in Christ, one receives forgiveness for past offenses, is liberated from the power of sin, and receives the Spirit. A consequence, but not the goal, of this participation is righteous living. In opposition to Rudolf Bultmann, Sanders holds that juristic language is subordinated, not preliminary to, participation language, which is the core of salvation. New life in Christ is a transfer of eons, but Sanders does not especially associate this transfer with the adoption language so prevalent in Paul.

After arguing steadily for Paul's soteriology as participationism, Sanders strikingly concludes that apart from the new self-understanding, stressed previously by Bultmann, he has no category within which to understand the reality of being in Christ on which Paul stands. Sanders, in the end, finds himself alienated from Paul. "To an appreciable degree, what Paul concretely thought cannot be directly appropriated by Christians today" (523).

This brief examination of formation motifs in Paul takes up precisely the point at which Sanders concludes. Although he might find Paul's soteriology of new being in Christ useless for contemporary Christians, it is quite important for understanding what salvation does in the lives of believers, precisely the point of this inquiry.

This discussion of the dynamics of Christian formation also attends to rhetorical strategies Paul used. To become a Christian is to be taken up into the drama of God's plan for creation. To impress this upon his readers, Paul encourages, ennobles, and exhorts readers in one sentence and embarrasses, humbles, and chastises them in the next. This keeps the readers or hearers of his letters slightly off-balance, and ever more attentive. Their lives and destinies are no longer their own, and the excitement Paul exudes is palpable.

GOD'S CO-OPTATION OF PAGANS

Paul knew from experience that becoming a Christian was a dangerous and risky undertaking: dangerous because Christians were persecuted, risky because it demanded personal transformation. Christian formation required being both humbled and exalted by a theological identity based on a powerful and fresh understanding of the work of God. Psychologically, Jews and pagans being reoriented as Christians followed different courses. Jews distinguished themselves as children of God, based on Deut. 14.1: "You are the children of the Lord your God." Gentiles were in the divine image based on Gen. 9.6b, "for in his own image God made humankind," but were not members of God's people.[1] Christian claims about Jesus challenged at least two central tenets of Jewish identity. One was that membership in Israel was by birth, for the Christians claimed that membership was by faith in Christ. The corollary was that through the death of Christ, God had made pagans children of God, too. Thus, Jewish followers of Jesus had to rethink both their relationship to God (now through Christ rather than through the law) and their relationship to pagans, who, in the Pauline view, received a true theological identity and were now also children of God.

Gentile Christians faced a different set of challenges. They first had to learn about the God of Israel and then reconceive themselves as his own. Paul understood both sides of this transformation process, although, since his apostolate was largely to gentiles, he is clearer regarding their situation than that of his Jewish sisters and brothers.

One arresting aspect of Paul's theology was his firm belief in God's commitment to pagans. Pharisees, who scrupulously sought to protect themselves from any hint of idolatry, strictly regulated their contact with pagans in order to avoid impurity.[2] Paul shared with other Jews the dim view that paganism was crude, violent, and licentious.[3] He exhorts his converts to turn from the unchastity carried over from their prior pagan lives (1 Thess. 4.3–5; Rom. 6.17–21). Second Cor. 6.14–7.1 transposes the standard Jewish injunction against associating with gentiles to the new converts from paganism.[4] Eph. 4.17–9; and 5.3–11 and Col. 3.5–7 sustain this view.

Yet despite his resonance with the standard Jewish view of pagans, Paul took an unusual approach to them. Rather than shunning pagans, Paul taught that through Christ, God had co-opted them into the covenant and created a new community of all the children of the promise to Abraham. Paul went out of his way to remind his churches (often at the outset of his letters) that God's plan to save them was from eternity, even though hidden until the coming of Christ (Rom. 1.2; 1 Cor. 2.7; Gal. 3.8–9, 14ff; cf. Eph. 1.3–5, 8–14; 3.5–6, 8–9). Of these, Gal. 3.8 and 14, as well as Gal. 4.8–9, specify that this intention includes both a summons for idolaters to turn from their lostness in sin and idolatry and a promise that they will be (or perhaps have already become) children of Abraham and will worship God (cf. Eph. 3.5–6, 8–9).

Paul grounds his argument for God's embrace of pagans in scripture (Rom. 1.2; Gal. 3.8–9; 4), although the divine plan remained hidden (1 Cor. 2.7, cf. Eph. 3.9), or misunderstood until Paul's own reading. Perhaps Paul's attempts to explain the delay represented either a gesture toward Jewish critics who read scripture differently or simply an effort to account for the occurrence of paganism. But the call and promise of God's relationship with pagans preceded scripture. It is prior to the creation of the world (1 Cor. 2.7; cf. Eph. 1.4; 3.9), a mystery realized only in God's own good time, but promised in Gen. 12.3 (Gal. 3.8–9).

The rhetorical effect of this eternal promise is to uplift pagan self-esteem. Paul's insistence on the eternal divine intention illustrates his sophisticated understanding of what constitutes a theological as opposed to a natural identity and what its aretegenic implications are. Pagans knew that Jewish election stretched back at least to Abraham. Paul points out that pagans have an analogous election. They too have a history that extends at least back to Abraham. The parallel history and identity that Paul provides for his readers ennobles them and sets the stage for their ability to boast in the Lord. Later, Paul would cash in on this theology of co-optation by stressing the moral demands that flow from it: though they, like Jews, could now boast in the Lord, they could boast nowhere else.

While on one hand they could now boast of God's interest in them, on the other, Paul is careful not to allow them to boast too much. Not only scripture but the very creation calls out to pagans to acknowledge God (Rom. 1.20) and recognize "that they were without excuse" when they "worshiped and served the creature rather than the Creator" (v.25). Paul's rhetoric points in two directions here. On one hand, pagans should be ashamed of themselves even before Christ. But at the same time, according to Gal. 4.2 and 4, paganism was a stopgap for the immature "until the date set by the father" (v.2), until "the fullness of time had come, [and] God sent his Son" (v.4). This two-pronged rhetorical approach, shaming with one hand while encouraging with the other, is typical of Paul's rhetoric. He kept gentiles in mind of their inappropriate behavior, while stressing their new identity at the same time.

Another element of Paul's strategy is to assure his baby Christians that they are fully in God's hands. They are not on their own. Paul imbues them with God's concern for them before creation, again with Abraham, at present, and for the future. Thus, they would become accustomed to thinking of themselves as eternally, if incipiently, part of God's elect, awaiting co-optation and destined to share in God's grace and glory without the law. This history gives the auditors of the gospel a new dignity: God is preoccupied with *them,* and their turning to him in gratitude for his action in Christ constitutes a central component of a cosmic drama. A further feature of Paul's pastoral strategy is to uplift the new Christians' dignity. God had been worrying about them even before they worried about themselves.

Paul not only shed abroad news that God had long been harboring plans for pagans but also taught that, unbeknownst to them, God had already effected that plan. Through Christ, crucified pagans have been co-opted by God, and Jews, already co-opted by God, are to accept this long-awaited work of God (Gal. 2.15–6). Now everyone has to figure out how to live together in light of this new situation. Numerous passages in the authentic and deutero-Pauline corpus focus on different aretegenic aspects of co-optation. I will examine four pericopæ that highlight the moral implications of the new community of faith.

Galatians 3.26–4.20 exhibits the bidirectional rhetorical style noted above. Galatians 3.26–4.7 reminds new Christians of what God has done for them, and then 4.8–20 embarrasses them for idolatrous recidivism. In 4.3–7 Paul uses his readers' knowledge of slavery in the political realm to depict the spiritual state of all pagans, even those who are wealthy landowners. They were theologically enslaved to false gods but have been manumitted, redeemed from this condition and adopted as children or heirs of the God of Israel through his Son. This spiritual liberation—the pagan's analog to the Exodus, perhaps—ennobles them further by distancing them from their old identity.

True theological identity is given when one is clothed with Christ in baptism (3.27). Unity in Christ marginalizes other dimensions of identity. True identity is the theological identity that comes from being Abraham's child (3.28–9). Subordination of biological and cultural identity to God's work in Christ redirects attention from self to God.

Paul embarrasses the new Christians into repenting of their past behavior by reminding them of their life before they knew God (4.8)—a life enslaved to elemental spirits—in contrast to their life now that they understand that they belong to God (v.9). Paul also recalls their recent upstanding behavior toward him when he visited them (v.14). Their current behavior is shameful on three counts: in comparison with their new status as children of the Father (v.7), in contrast to the fine welcome they gave Paul in the past (v.14), and with regard to the gratitude that their release from paganism demands (v.9). Paul is exasperated yet patiently pastoral: "My little children, for whom I am again in the pain of childbirth until Christ is formed in you, I wish I were present with you now"(v.19). In short, their mentor embarrasses them into returning to the current task of being formed in Christ.

In addition to telling his readers that God is obsessed with them and has elevated them to a noble identity, Paul presses his readers to marvel at the import of the divine action. Being elected by God is not to be taken lightly; simply confessing Christ and joining the Christian community are insufficient. The new theological identity carries moral responsibility, as is evident both in the Galatians passage examined above and in Romans.

Romans 1–3 exhibits a rhetorical strategy related to that of Gal. 3.26–4.20. Romans begins with a review of who the readers are (1.1–7) and a prayer of thanksgiving for them (1.8–15). Then Paul sets his readers up with false flattery by enumerating pagan sins, leading the readers to think that they, who have renounced paganism, would be among the recipients of God's power for salvation (1.18–32). Then, employing rabbinic rhetoric, Paul turns on his readers: if pagans have no excuse, "therefore you [who already claim to cling to God] have no excuse" (2.1). The potentially flattering contrast with their former life is a lead-in to excoriating them for their "hard and impenitent hearts" (vv.5ff). And in the Galatians 4 passage examined above, Paul chastises their celebration of Jewish festivals (v.10). Romans 2 "reads the riot act" to the new Christians, an understandable response from a frustrated mentor. Their lives are to reflect the ennoblement that God has achieved for them. Here again is the two-pronged strategy: First he flatters his converts with their importance in the eyes of God, then he uses the foothold that that self-image gives him to embarrass them for not living up to their new dignity.

In Rom. 2. 17–24 Paul turns to the Jews, chastening those who sin despite the law. He accuses them of claiming to teach (gentiles? other Jews?) the law as the embodiment of knowledge and truth, while failing to live according to the precepts of the Decalogue. Paul, himself a preacher among the gentiles, is outraged because this blasphemes rather than promotes faith in God abroad. Obedience to the moral aspects of the law is, for Paul, a more genuine expression of honoring God than simply being a member of the covenanted people by virtue of circumcision (Rom. 2.25–9). In other words, faithful Jews, for Paul, are those who live morally and do not claim their circumcision merely as a badge. The "inwardly" of verse 29 is not an emotional state of mind; it refers to practicing what one preaches, enumerated in verses 19–23. For some Jews perhaps, in Paul's view, circumcision had become a cover for disobedience to the law; it was no longer working as an instrument of righteousness. Paul concludes that Jews with the law and gentiles without the law are all sinners equally (Rom. 3.9ff). Paul is even-handed in his criticism. God has been equally gracious to Jews and gentiles, so all are without excuse.

God's promised action in Christ, which co-opts gentiles into life with God, provides Jews with a fresh means of atonement, since they disobeyed the first, anticipating the destruction of the Temple. Now (3.21), Christ's death on the cross demonstrates God's righteousness and love, which reconcile those who have faith in the power of his death, which "passed over the sins previously committed" (3.25). It is not self-evident how the reconciliation wrought by Christ's death leads Jews away from the moral laxness of which Paul accuses them and into a morally upright life, however. For on the face of it, the reconciliation accomplished through Christ's death might be construed as providing the same excuse previously provided by circumcision. What the cross of Christ plainly does do, however, is confront Jews with God's love for pagans and press Jews to enter into a reconciled community with them. Perhaps the message of the cross for Jews is its condemnation of the sin of xenophobia.

The explanation of how the cross reconciles in chapter 3 is interrupted by a passage demonstrating that co-optation is authorized by Abraham's faith. When Paul resumes in chapters 5 and 6, his argument seems to run something like the following: Christ's death reconciles all of us to God and saves us from God's wrath; Christ's dying for us is a free gift; it displays God's righteousness for many, leading to eternal life (5.21). Paul never denies that the law had also displayed God's righteousness; rather, perhaps because it went unheeded by disobedient Jews, God has revamped the whole system. In the cross of Christ, God has brought Jews and gentiles together. They must transform their lives accordingly. "God proves his love for us in that while we still were sinners Christ died for us" (5.8). Knowing that God's righteousness and love have been freely given is the point at which Jews link up with former pagans. All who believe that Christ's death reconciles them to God and who consecrate themselves to Christ as an expression of that faith die to sin and rise with him to new life (6.4).

Ephesians 2.11–22 spells out the implications of Paul's theology for life together in the new community. It begins with the Pauline style of reminding the audience of its former and new identity in a sparklingly clear summary of pagan co-optation as developed in Galatians:

> remember that you were . . . without Christ, being aliens from the commonwealth of Israel . . . having no hope and without God in the world. But now in Christ Jesus you who once were far off have been brought near by the blood of Christ. . . . So then you are no longer strangers and aliens, but you are citizens with the saints and also members of the household of God. (vv.12, 13, 19)

The new citizenship and identity that ground their hope and dignity are truer than any they could have acquired on their own.

The author repeats himself in the next chapter: the mystery of Christ is that "the gentiles have become fellow heirs, members of the same body, and sharers in the promise in Christ Jesus through the gospel" (3.6). The point is that even if they do not know or understand it, "nobodies" have been made "somebodies" by the cross of Christ (cf. 1.1.26–31). And they had better "wake up and smell the coffee," for they are no longer the people they once were. Now they are claimed by God, and the structure of Israel has been redesigned to accommodate them.

In both texts the recollection to which the readers are called is strikingly noble. The point is that they are not to be commended for abandoning paganism and its sinful lifestyle. These passages do not even focus on the forgiveness of sin, which would inculcate gratitude (along with sheepishness). The accent (at least in 1 Thessalonians and Galatians) is on the unsolicited new dignity they have been granted as the people of God, even if later they backslide. Recalling who they once were, or thought they were, and who they really are burns the gift into their psyches as they are socialized into the new community of Jews and former idolaters. Impressing upon them the reformation of the law and the reconfiguration of Israel for their sake certainly conveys how serious God is about their salvation and how gracious and powerful to effect it.[5]

Pointing to the power and graciousness of God sets the readers up for attending to their role in the divine plan. They must look to the horizontal consequences of the co-optation of the gentiles; one harmonious global community results from God's destruction of the wall that had guarded Jewish purity. Eph. 2.11–22 invokes a shocking metaphor. It is startling enough that the author believes that God has transformed the law for the sake of pagans and adopted them in the hope that on these terms they will abandon idolatrous practices. But he goes on to remind them that *they* are the community built upon the foundation of the apostles and prophets, the community whose cornerstone is Christ Jesus. The church of Jews and gentiles is now the household of God and is called to behave in accordance with that identity.

Neither the authentic nor the deutero-Pauline letters uses the threat of expulsion from the household of God as a weapon to get the new Christians back on track. While there is a sense of frustration at the enormity of the task of overcoming life-long attitudes and practices that are now dysfunctional and therefore corrupt the community, there is no hint of a punitive attitude on the part of the pastoral guides. The sole source of exhortation and encouragement in the Christian life is the power and grace of God. Christianization required gentiles to abandon both pagan sacrifices and Jewish rites and practices and establish a relationship with the sovereign God of history, revealed in the cross. This may have been more or less emotionally accessible to them depending on their familiarity with some of the popular mystery cults.

Jewish Christians, on the other hand, had to abandon their ancestral traditions in order to embrace God's action in Jesus Christ. They had to reconceptualize God's love and righteousness as universal, now disclosed through Christ's sacrifice, and share their identity as God's beloved with those whom they had heretofore considered religiously defiling. So, while Paul's theology ennobled gentiles, it humbled Jewish believers in Jesus, who had to acknowledge the genuine universality of God and accept gentiles as full members of the covenant through the cross. They had to adapt to the reconstruction of the people of God. Psychologically, the dynamics are quite different for the two groups.

The final passage to be examined in this section on new identity in Christ is 1 Cor. 1.18–31. It points to the aretegenic consequences of the message of the cross, for Christians living in a non-Christian culture, by exegeting the psychological implications of the new identity in Christ. The passage assumes the theology spelled out in Romans and Galatians discussed above and perhaps, though not explicitly, the ability of Jews and gentiles to settle into community together. Here the emphasis is on the spiritual implications of the mechanism God has used to effect this radical reconstruction of the household of God.

What appeared to be a simple political execution disclosed a new perspective on God. What is so remarkable about this common death? The scandal of the cross here may be viewed from two directions. Theologically understood, the cross is more powerful than the wisdom of Greece, the power of Rome, or the authority of Jerusalem. This unsightly event creates a new dignity for idolaters and reconciles adversaries in a way that the greatest political empires and the oldest religious tradition they knew could not achieve. It provides a theological perspective on worldly and ecclesiastical power structures that highlights their inability to effect either spiritual dignity or social harmony.

In addition to correcting the erroneous self-understanding of those who cling to the powers of Rome and Jerusalem, there is a personal perspective from which to interpret this passage. For Paul and those who accept his gospel, one's theological identity becomes one's primary identity. Belonging to Christ renders negligible every other source of security—wealth, education, noble birth, or political or ecclesiastical power. One stands tall in the world because one is God's own. Righteous and sinners, wealthy and poor, privileged and marginal are all of equal value to God, not because of who they are but because of who God is.

Now the point of 1 Cor. 1.18–31 is that those who grasp the wisdom of the cross are truly wise. They seek nobility, status, power, and dignity in the proper place: the cross. From this vantage point they see that the standards of the world are vacuous and that one's proper dignity and identity are to be found in knowing oneself to be a child of God by the power of the cross of Christ. If Jesus' death is the means of making one a child of God, all proper power and authority derive from this relationship and from no other source. Worldly power is irrelevant to who we really are. Whoever finds her true identity in the cross understands that worldly power, while it may be necessary and should be stewarded properly, is no source of self-esteem. The only power worth having is the power of knowing that one is beloved of God (cf. Phil. 3.8). Thus, the seductive power of the world has been broken for those who understand and trust in the power of the cross; others remain perplexed and angry.

So God used what is weak and seemingly powerless, a Jewish peasant from a "hick" town, to show those lured by the world's standards of self-esteem that God is the source of personal security, strength, and spiritual power. The world's vision of self-esteem no longer seduces those who are freed from dependence on worldly notions of power and prestige by trusting in the accomplishment of the cross. The power of the world's standards has paled. The point is not that one should renounce worldly power, for authority and responsibility have their proper place, as Paul suggests later in the letter (12.14–31). It is rather that Christians are to understand that power and honor, while perhaps politically important, are subordinate to true and proper dignity, which comes only from "life in Christ Jesus, who became for us wisdom from God, and righteousness and sanctification and redemption" (1 Cor. 1.30).

From the materials examined thus far, we see that Paul endorsed an aretology of co-optation, the view that Christian excellence comes from a status given by God. There is none of the shame and guilt that would mark later Western theology. Excellence comes from learning what God has done on a grand public scale that sets one's life in a fresh context and gives it new direction and meaning. Christian identity is first acknowledged and then chosen, so to speak. One acknowledges God's work, then decides to live by it.

On Paul's view, one's dignity derives from this identity and not from any natural identity of birth. This makes becoming a Christian a confusing undertaking, for one must sort out one's old self from one's new, God-given status. For pagans, the transition requires letting go of the gods of Rome or Egypt and recognizing the God of Israel. For Jews the transition requires letting go of the law and relinquishing exclusive claim to God's electing grace. For both groups, God has challenged the sources of status and power by which they gauged themselves, whether Rome or Jerusalem, and established wisdom, power, and nobility in what appears to be an expression of weakness and failure: the cross of Christ.

CONSECRATION OF BELIEVERS

We have seen that Paul viewed Christian identity as a theological status given by God that co-opts pagans and draws believing Jews into a new community that requires a new self-understanding. The first step in Christian formation involved recognizing what God has done. The second step involved being consecrated both outwardly and inwardly to this work of God that has taken place in the cross of Christ.

Paul appreciated that the renewing of the mind, which was necessary for Christian formation, required decisive action, symbolic rites and practices in which believers can profess their new identity, and commitments. Baptism is the act in which believers are consecrated to Christ and absorb his power. Paul employs a multitude of images to capture the drama of the event: newness of life, new creation, or a new self (Rom. 6.4; 2 Cor. 5.17; Gal. 6.14–5; cf. Col. 3.9–10); becoming or being formed, conformed, created, or indwelt by Christ or the Holy Spirit, or transformed into the image of Christ (Rom. 8.9–11, 29–30; 1 Cor. 6.19–20; 2 Cor. 3.18; 6.16b–7; Gal. 2.20; 4.19; Phil. 3.21; cf. Eph. 2.10; 3.17); belonging to Christ (Gal. 5.24); putting on or being clothed with Christ (Rom. 13.12b, 14; Gal. 3.27, 29).

This pervasive theme of "enchristing" or participation in Christ suggests how radical a shift becoming a Christian is. Christians not only had to divorce themselves from their former ways of thought and life; they also had to deal with each other on a fraternal basis that ran against the grain of both Jewish and pagan society, a radicalness summed up by Galatians 3.28. Given the mutual mistrust of Jews and pagans in the ancient world, this was not an incidental matter. Lifelong identities, beliefs, values, personal relationships, habits, and categories of thought had to be erased and replaced. Stripping off the old and taking on a new self, becoming a new creation, was not literary hyperbole; it was literally true and personally threatening.[6] New life in Christ required a decisive act of separation from the past and participation in the new present reality.

Paul chose violent and fearsome metaphors to describe the formation process. Death and slavery are perhaps the most odious possibilities one can face. Yet these are the images Paul repeatedly uses in speaking of the participation of new Christians in the identity of Christ. Believers replace their personalities by rehearsing Christ's death, beginning with the consecratory washing of baptism. To look closely at how consecration effects this enchristing, I will examine 2 Cor. 5.14–21, Romans 6, and subsequent elaboration of this teaching on formation in Colossians 2 and 3.

Theological identity made known through preaching the cross is followed by the remodeling of the personality in an experience of spiritual death and rebirth by participating in the cross through baptism. Second Cor. 5.14 reinforces the objective nature of Christian incorporation by recalling that the death of Christ was an event meant for everyone, even those who do not yet know of it or confess it. Yet baptism is also a subjective event in which one experiences Christ's resurrection in oneself. Baptism is spiritual resurrection realized, even though bodily resurrection awaits another day.

In 2 Cor. 5.14–21 God's reconciliation of the world to himself in Christ (v.19) marks a change in history that calls for the replacement of improper with proper obedience. Those who once were enemies of God or under obedience to the law but who now boast "in Christ" now live "for him who died . . . for them" (v.15). They are now instruments of this reconciliation, under orders to take up the reconciling work of God in Christ.

The work of Christ, reconciling the world to God, passes through Christ into those who are bound to God and one another through him. Believers are enchristed, made into extensions of Christ's reconciliation and righteousness. The reconciliation of Jews and pagans into one harmonious body, illustrating the righteousness of God, points to the social dimension of God's reconciliation.[7] Paul's seemingly odd plea to those who know they have been reconciled to God (v.18) to *be* reconciled to God (v.20), the pervasive indicative-imperative dynamic in Paul, reflects the transition the believer needs to make—from simply recognizing the new status conferred by God's gift and call, to internalizing it so that one's actions and personality proclaim Christ's work as an act of obedience to God.

While the 2 Corinthians passage focuses on the call for believers to embody Christ's work in their lives and ministry, Romans 6 describes the symbolic incorporation of the individual believer into the death of Christ. The emphasis here is on what happens to believers ("we who died," "all of us who have been baptized," "we have been buried with him," "so that we too might walk . . . ," "we have been united with him," "we have died with Christ, we also will live with him" [vv.2–8]). Through consecration to Christ the believer experiences the reconciling action directly. Dying and rising with Christ overwhelms the power structures of the world—state, religion, gender, race, and class. Baptism inaugurates a consecrated life in which believers are to "present yourselves to God as those who have been brought from death to life, and present your members to God as instruments of righteousness" (v.13).[8] They are to become those whom they have been made.

There is no doubt about the close connection between the consecratory rite and the moral transformation to follow. Those united with Christ in his death "must consider yourselves dead to sin and alive to God in Christ Jesus" (v.11). Paul urges Christians to relinquish attachments to the wrong source of strength: "We know that our old self was crucified with him *so that* the body of sin might be destroyed, and we might no longer be enslaved to sin" (v.6). Forgiveness for past offenses is the first step toward this goal. Obedience to God, proper teaching (v.17), and the practice of proper behavior are goals of the transformation. There is nothing automatic or purely confessional about it; it is hard work. Christian excellence involves an exchange of orientation, loyalty, and focus in life that Paul calls enslavement: putting oneself at the disposal of, and being directed by, God. Baptism requires one to accept the teaching that God has claimed believers for himself. Consequently they bind themselves to God and take on the new life of righteous living in Christ. For he died for Jews and pagans so that they, knowing him, might now live toward him who has reconciled them with himself and one another.

There seem to be two aspects or even sequential stages to the new life of which Paul speaks in Romans 6. One is the spiritual renewal that predominates in the passage. But the theme of eternal life is also prominent (vv. 5, 22, 23). Enslavement to God means sanctification now and eternal life later (22–3). Thus, the co-optation of gentiles looks backward, the release of Jews from the law focuses on transformation in the present, and all look expectantly ahead to eternal life.

The final passage to be discussed under the theme of enchristing is its deutero-Pauline expression in Colossians 2 and 3. This section encourages Christians to persevere in the Christian life and not return to the Law or paganism, and in this regard it is similar to the Galatians 4 passage discussed earlier. But Col. 2.12–3 also recalls the dying and rising metaphor of Romans 6. Its parenetic rhetorical pattern is by now familiar. It begins with a rehearsal of what has happened to the readers.

Then it reminds the readers of their obligations. Living in Christ requires identifying with him. The fullness of God that dwells in Christ now dwells in them and should direct them; spiritual resurrection into the power of God who raised Christ from the dead means that believers are "alive together with him" (v.13). The emphasis of the Colossians passage is on the triumph of God in the cross (vv.14–5), a triumph believers are to both celebrate and absorb. After recalling them to their divinely accorded status, as one might expect, the writer embarrasses them (2.20–3) with their failures to remain at the ennobled level to which God has brought them: new life in Christ.

The indicative-imperative dynamic recurs in 2.20 and 3.1–4: since you have died with Christ, why do you still seem to be oriented toward the world instead of toward God? Christians are to live the resurrected life to which they have been consecrated. The psychology implied by Paul's theology is a substitution model. After the old personality is stripped off, the new self is to be molded and crafted, shaped according to the image of God (3.10). Christ is the prototype for the compassion, kindness, humility, meekness, patience, forgiveness, and peace that are to rule the new self (v.12). The new life and moral determination combine the new theological dignity gentile Christians have as children of God with the empowerment that comes from being united to him through the death and resurrection of Christ. Not only have they become "God's chosen people" (v.12), but Christ has overtaken them.

Analysis of these passages suggests that the doctrine of the cross functions aretegenically when the believer is consecrated to Christ through participation in his death. Christ's experience becomes the model for the believer's spiritual transformation. Similarly, the substitution that takes place in consecration is the assimilation of Christ's personality and character to one's own. Only by setting one's own experience and personality within Christ's can reconciled living become a reality.

The dramatic rhetoric of death of self and enslavement to God are designed to impress upon readers the seriousness of Christian consecration. Christians are putting their souls and bodies on the line, starting life over, and setting off on an uncharted journey behind an executed Jew.

Empowered by the Spirit

The third moment in Christian formation, the empowerment of the believer by the Holy Spirit, carries the theme of being overtaken by God yet further. Paul recognized the need for ongoing divine guidance. The Holy Spirit bestows the power to redraft one's character (Gal. 5.16–26), channel one's talents and energies outward for the common good of the church (1 Cor. 12.1–11), and direct the mind toward living a godly life in anticipation of the eschaton (Rom. 8 and 1 Cor. 2.6–15).

The gift of the Spirit marks the calm after the storm of initial Christianization. In the Gospels and Acts, the Spirit is a gift of God's presence that fills believers. God pours it out upon or into them at baptism (Matt. 3.11; 28.19; Mark 1.8; Luke 3.16; John

1.33; Acts 1.5) and other significant moments (Luke 1.35; Acts 1.8; 2.4, 17; 4.31 etc.). As with the Johannine vision of the Paraclete, for Paul, the Spirit empowers and guides the believer in obedience to God on an extended basis. Spirit language is gentler than the dying and rising imagery or the stripping off of the old self examined previously, suggesting an ongoing process of formation that follows upon the radical break with one's past required by Christianization.

Paul more frequently refers to the Spirit than to the Holy Spirit and identifies it with both the Spirit of God (1 Cor. 2.10; 2 Cor. 1.22; 3.3; cf. Eph. 2.22) and the Spirit of the Lord (2 Cor. 3.17). Its presence in the believer is frequently a pledge or deposit of future resurrection or eternal life (2 Cor. 5.5; Gal. 6.8; cf. Eph. 1.14). In Rom. 5.3–5 the sorites on character-building ends in hope enabled by the possession of the Holy Spirit, suggesting an eschatological perspective.[9] Paul calls on believers to allow this pledge of future redemption to direct and sanctify their lives while they wait. The gift of the Spirit allows for centering and recognizes the need for continuous divine accompaniment and guidance.

Galatians 5.16–26 follows the format of Greek moral exhortation, found also in Col. 3.5–17.[10] In both passages, behaviors practiced and attitudes admitted under paganism are listed first, followed by a list of the behaviors and attitudes to rule the Christian. The listing of sinful behaviors follows a similar pattern: sexual immorality, idolatry, improper speech, and sinful emotions. The lists of virtues in the two passages overlap somewhat, but the Galatians list is the longer.

What differentiates the two passages is the theological context within which they are set. The Colossians passage intertwines the imperative and the indicative, exhorting the readers, "Put to death, therefore, whatever in you is earthly" (v.5), while observing that they have already "stripped off the old self . . . and clothed [themselves] with the new self . . . which is being renewed in knowledge according to the image of its creator" (vv.9–10). The description of being renewed by virtue of the knowledge they possess then passes back into the injunction to "clothe yourselves with love" (v.14) and to allow the "peace of Christ" (v.15) and the "word of Christ" (v.16) to take over. In short, the Colossians 3 passage was discussed under the motif of enchristing because the imagery is all christological indwelling, beginning with a rehearsal of dying and rising imagery in verses 1–4.

Galatians 5.16–26, by contrast, uses pneumatological language to describe the transformation of the believer as a gift of the Spirit. Paul urges his readers to see life led by the Spirit as contrasting sharply with their former life. The choice seems to be between obedience to immediate self-gratification and long-term gain: short-term pleasure versus inheriting the kingdom of God (v.21). The Spirit is not identified in this passage, but the reference to "the Spirit of his Son" in 4.6 suggests that Paul is most probably thinking of the Spirit of Christ, for he recalls the dying and rising imagery of Romans 6 in Gal. 5.24–5. In other words, baptism sets the believer into Christ; receiving the Spirit propels the believer forward, internalizing the new identity.

The christological imagery in the Colossians passage and the pneumatological imagery in the Galatians passage have similar effects on the believer. The language of dying and rising with Christ in baptism and living by the Spirit provide the strength needed to break with the past and cultivate Christian virtues (vv.22–3). Life in the Spirit acts out the nobility of God. The community is not given a new identity and then left on its own, but is continuously led by God. The impetus for moral transformation comes from embracing God's actions. The virtues and the strength to inculcate them are likewise provided by God. Excellence comes through conformation to the image of his Son (Rom. 8.29) and by submitting to the guidance of the Spirit (Gal. 5.25).

While Gal. 5.25 suggests that the Spirit guides believers after baptism, 1 Cor. 12 presents the Spirit as the basis of community order. The Spirit is at once the source of individual gifts (vv.8–11), the plumb line for using them in the service of the church (v.7), and the standard of unity in the body of Christ (vv.12–31). Paul assumes that all are gifted with skills that upbuild the church and that those who live in the Spirit use them to that end. Telling believers that their gifts are from God and are needed by the church reinforces the believers' theological identity and motivates them to contribute energetically to the body without getting caught up in their own ego needs. Self-confidence is strengthened by knowing that they have been called to serve. They assess their skills and abilities in order to discern and develop them for the good of the body. It is not the distinctiveness of one's gifts but their origin in the Spirit that binds the members of the community together.

Paul's teaching on spiritual gifts encourages a balanced sense of self-worth, yet gently warns of the abuses of power and the proneness to competitive jealousies and rivalries to which people are vulnerable if they mistake the sociological structures of the community for its theological basis. Church members do not construct community by bringing their talents and treasure; God has constructed community by giving Christ. Responding gratefully to God's gift, however, requires all to contribute their gifts and make sure that all gifts are appreciated. Expecting believers to contribute to and reflect upon the commonweal encourages and exercises the patience, humility, gentleness, and kindness that are described as the fruit of the Spirit in Galatians 5 and the new self of Colossians 3, suggesting that the Spirit plays a particularly aretegenic role in Paul's pastoral strategy.

The final passages for examination in this discussion of the Holy Spirit are 1 Cor. 2.6–16 and Rom. 8.1–17, where being led by or walking in the Spirit suggests having the mind of Christ. First Cor. 2.6–16 argues for a theological understanding of church leadership based on the immediately preceding discussion of the power of the cross as the proper locus for understanding personal power. Paul, who grasped the secret wisdom of God in the cross, "understand[s] the gifts bestowed upon us by God" (v.12). Indeed, he has no less than "the mind of Christ" (v.16b), which enables him to interpret spiritual things properly and authorizes his leadership.

His ability to discern God's wisdom in the cross is a gift of the Spirit. Only the spiritually gifted should exercise Christian leadership. The ungifted do not receive leadership authority because they would misunderstand the cross and hence misuse their power. Paul's authority to guide and direct the Corinthians in their Christian babyhood is from the Spirit of God. The teachings of his competitors are not from God at all and mislead these "infants in Christ" (3.1) away from the wisdom of God, which uses what is lowly to bring powerless uneducated plebeians (1 Cor. 1.26) into communion with God.

Paul's own co-optation by the Spirit authorizes his leadership of the Corinthians. By exercising the virtues and desisting from the behaviors that carry them away from their dignity in the cross, the community as a whole grows into its proper theological identity. As they come to see themselves as God's field and God's building (1 Cor. 3.9), their judgments will increasingly reflect the power of the wisdom of the cross that Paul teaches them in place of human wisdom, which relies on nobility of birth, secular wisdom, and political power.

Romans 8.1–17 seems to extend Paul's claim in 1 Cor. 2.16 about the theological foundation of church leadership to church members. Those who walk according to the Spirit of Christ set their minds on the things of the Spirit—life and peace in the conviction of having been adopted by God. Formation by the Spirit turns believers away from sin, enables them to persevere through adversity, and targets the eschatological future of being finally conformed to Christ (vv.24–5).

Setting the mind on the things of the Spirit orders life for the baptized, once they grasp that they have received the Spirit of God (8.9). Life in the Spirit is a process of growing into the new self that has been given. It is not alien but now belongs to the believer, who has made a break with the world in accepting baptism and the new life it bestows. Cultivating the Spirit means thinking of oneself as never unaccompanied by the Spirit, who empowers one for a godly life of peace and freedom from sin (vv.10–1). While from an external point of view life in the Spirit may seem burdensome, from a Christian perspective it is the expression of true freedom.

It is clear that the work of the Spirit continues the work of the cross as the agent of Christian excellence. Whereas the cross co-opts and consecrates believers to God, the Holy Spirit accompanies and guides believers in their life in community. The Spirit, like the cross of Christ, is an agent of humility. Just as the death of Christ shames other understandings of wisdom and definitions of status, the Holy Spirit's gifts, distributed among leaders and members of the community for the common good, lend to the believer's life a dignity that is genuine but not self-generated. On the contrary, it promotes gratitude and thanksgiving.

Like the aretegenic power of the cross, the aretology of the Spirit is both public and social. The Christian who knows herself to be accompanied, perhaps even propelled, by the dignity of the Spirit for a life of holiness is responsible to God in public, as it were. She is no longer acting on her own. Similarly, the gifts of the Spirit are of social value; they help other Christians live up to their new identity and to dedicate their gifts to the common good.

THE DISCIPLED COMMUNITY

Ephesians was written to worshiping communities composed of Christians whose heads were perhaps turned back toward the pagan lifestyle they once enjoyed, or who flirted with syncretism, in order to call them back to their Christian identity (Lincoln 1990, lxxxiv–v). The letter was probably read aloud, perhaps even in a worship service as an instrument of both ecclesial and individual formation. The public orientation of all the New Testament letters highlights their function of setting public norms of character and behavior on both the personal and community levels. Additionally, the focus on prayer and public worship brings to the fore the power of religious practices to reinforce experientially theological identity.

Ephesians follows the Pauline pattern. It establishes a theological foundation to clarify and reinforce the identities of the readers and then offers moral guidance on that basis. The ecclesial setting sustains the authority of divine guidance for communities as well as individuals that we saw in the 1 Corinthians passages examined earlier.

Ephesians grounds human excellence in theological realities, much the way secular proposals ground human excellence in fictional narratives by which readers may judge themselves, only with far greater authority and emotional vigor. It links theology, in this case christology, to parenesis (an exhortation of what kind of persons Christians are to be). Indeed, God's mercy and power, working in tandem, fund Christian virtues and behavior more broadly, according to Ephesians and Pauline theology. For Ephesians, two astonishing accomplishments of divine power and mercy drive this home in chapter 2. The rescue of believers by the cross and resurrection of Christ attests divine power, while the destruction of the seemingly intractable enmity between Jews and pagans attests divine mercy.

The author highlights the moral implications of God's mercy in bringing sinners into life with Christ (2.4–5). The blood of Christ lavishes God's grace on those who discover themselves in the midst of the mystery of the divine plan for creation (1.7–10). The death of Christ, expressing the love of God for his earthly children, leads us into loving one another (5.1–2). The resurrection of Christ brings a new way of life (2.4–10) to foreigners. Obedience to the passions of the flesh passes away when one is "made alive together with Christ" (2.5). And the author concludes the section on the transformation from death to life (2.1–10) by reminding his readers that "we are what he has made us, created in Christ Jesus for good works, which God prepared beforehand to be our way of life" (2.10). The dignity of Christians may not be their own doing, but utilizing it properly is now their responsibility. Once one grasps the extent of God's power, one is assured that throwing one's lot behind God will not be in vain. Christians are accompanied by God and try out their new lives in one another's presence; the anxiety of being alone is quelled so that Christians may rejoice with as well as correct one another, learning all the while how power is to be used and mercy expressed.

The second startling accomplishment of divine mercy and power discussed in chapter 2 is Christ's power as an instrument of interethnic peace, now viewed in its social dimension. The destruction of the wall dividing Jews from pagans (2.14–22) not only expresses divine power, and so inspires awe, but causes everyone to rethink fundamental categories of their identity. The new identities enable the creation of a new ecclesial reality. Here the impurity of past animosities, jealousies, and resentments gives way to "a holy temple in the Lord; in whom you also are built together spiritually into a dwelling place for God" (2.21–2), echoing 1 Cor. 3.16–7 and 2 Cor. 6.16. The author's point is not that since God has torn down the fence that protected Jews from pagan impurities, all ought to live gratefully, although that is surely implied. Rather, he goes further theologically. God has so reconciled former enemies that former instruments of interethnic contempt and scorn are now a holy temple (2.21), a dwelling place for God (2.22), the body of Christ (4.12), the church. God no longer dwells with only one group, but in the new community that cannot be whole unless both Jews and gentiles are present. This theology inspires hope; God can bring purity from what from this distance can be seen to have been impurity, although at the time it appeared normal. In short, participation in Christ through the ordered life of the Christian community is the ground of hope for social as well as personal transformation. Ephesians is explicitly aretegenic; it argues that God confers dignity and encouragement upon believers who now see themselves differently because they are different people and must comport themselves accordingly.

The author, following Graeco-Roman moral tradition (Malherbe 1986, 135–8) and Jewish Neoplatonism (Wild 1985, 128–33; Kurz 1985), urges believers to allow the work of God to restructure their identity. They do not work out or discover their identity but, rather, encounter it by having been redeemed by God. The exhortation to submit to Christ appears in a cascade of images throughout the letter, as the author crafts phrases designed to energize the letter's recipients for Christian living. They are the church that is created, joined together "in him" (2.21); it is his body (4.12). By growing into Christ, believers achieve Christian maturity (4.13–6). They are encouraged to experience themselves as having been raised with Christ to new life (2.6), to be indwelt by Christ (3.17), and to be filled with the fullness of God by knowing the love of Christ (3.19). The power to put away the old self and the energy to put on a new self come from learning Christ who renews the mind (4.20–3). The mind is renewed and behavior changed when one realizes that human life attains greatness because people have been taken into the plan of God—indeed, into the life of God—for the redemption of the world.

Christians' growth into a new self is variously phrased as being clothed in the likeness of God (4.24), or, using a military metaphor, in the armor of God (6.11–7). Just as their ability to live a new life comes from knowing themselves as raised with Christ, their ability to love former enemies requires that they learn from the model of Christ's sacrifice for them (5.1–2).

While Paul and Ephesians insist that renewing the mind is central to the task of moral reform, Ephesians also recognizes the role of specific practices in shaping the mind. On one hand, the self is emptied of prior identity, which is replaced by the dignity bestowed by God, as we saw in Romans 6 and 2 Cor. 5.16–21. On the other hand, cultivating the Christian mind requires following regular patterns of study and apprenticeship as the new self grows into the divine plan in which believers have been set. Christian excellence comes with learning of Christ, having one's mind renewed, following Christ's example, and identifying with the events of his death and resurrection. The Christian is no longer on her own in crafting an identity or finding a meaning for the personal experiences of her life or the cultural mores of her community of origin. The importance and dignity of life come from being a player in a cosmic drama. Ephesians embeds the formation of Christian excellence in the redemptive work of God.

Ephesians does not simply restate the theological foundation for Christian identity and behavior, however. It recognizes the formative power of socialization and moral discernment, illustrating Alasdair MacIntyre's emphasis on the importance of induction into a moral tradition through social practices (1984, chap. 15). The author of Ephesians understands that following baptism, prayer, thanksgiving, and corporate worship are the means of experiencing the theological doctrines that provide a new identity. The letter begins with praise of God and recounts the works of divine redemption of which the readers are themselves beneficiaries (1.3–14). It continues with prayer for the addressees (1.15–23), reminding them of who they now are, theologically speaking, and how they are to live in the knowledge of God revealed to them through the preaching of the gospel (3.6). The writer understands public worship as a rhetorical instrument of Christian formation (Lincoln 1990, lxxxvi). Individuals think outward from the broader social context in which they live. Christian dignity, while a gift of God, is reinforced publicly through socialization in community. The virtues, standards, and moral character of the persons who transmit that social reality are models for the self that is forming. Ephesians grasps the pastoral importance of preaching and worship for what we have seen as Wayne Booth's coduction: the assimilation of a broad range of ideas for moral reflection.

The writer realizes that formation in Christian excellence is the responsibility of the Christian community and its leaders, and it often flies in the face of tempting competitors. Public prayer and thanksgiving in the company of wholesome friends catches believers up in God's call "to be holy and blameless before [Christ] in love" (1.4). Without public expectations they may become caught up in fractiousness, slander, and gossip. Interestingly, the section on the church and its responsibilities and gifts (4.1–16) precedes the section on renewal of righteous living. Chapter 4 verses 11–3 points out that the social structure of the church itself contributes mightily to individual moral formation and must therefore be carefully tended. On this model, a primary ecclesial responsibility is to train Christians by helping them see more and see more pointedly. Community norms, practices, and structures stimulate moral maturity.

For Ephesians, formation in Christian excellence is undertaken intentionally, based on the knowledge of believers' new identity. Like the undisputed Pauline letters, it contrasts new Christians' former shame to their present dignity (Lincoln 1990, 118, 125, 326–7). The author regularly recalls his readers' shameful past and present honor (e.g., 2.1–6, 11–3) in order to strengthen them to shun the past, put off the old life, and take on the new life with Christ—a life of love and forgiveness, holiness (4.1–3, 17–24), truth, peace, and inner strength (6.11–7) (Lincoln 1990, 118–21). Looking back and forth from the past to the present and toward what awaits them in the future reinforces the possibility of healing and of change enabled by the power of God. When Paul tells them, "I pray that you may have the power to comprehend, with all the saints, what is the breadth and length and height and depth, and to know the love of Christ that surpasses knowledge, so that you may be filled with all the fullness of God" (3.18–9), he suggests that Christian sanctity requires intellectual comprehension as well as experiential engagement with the love of Christ. The implication is that these riches constitute genuine happiness.

Christian excellence is spiritual maturation effected by both a rehabilitation of mind and practiced behaviors that renew the self in the likeness of God (4.17, 23–4). The imperatives of verses 17–24, urging readers not to return to the darkness of pagan futility, suggest that Christian behavior cannot be coerced. Although the author realizes the important role sociality and communal leadership play in Christian formation (4.11–3), the decision to luxuriate under the lordship of Christ and be guided by the Christian community, rather than wallow in impurity, must be undertaken intentionally. Humans are socially influenced but not socially determined.[11] Theologically speaking, Christian formation is the work of the grace of God. Practically speaking it requires the intentional care of pastoral leadership and the willingness of the believer to allow God's grace to be transforming. The constant exhortation throughout the Pauline and deutero-Pauline corpus attests to the challenge Christian formation poses to other lifestyles. Christian excellence requires concentration of mind and heart.

Finally, the author enlists enthusiasm for the formation of human excellence. He recognizes the necessity of eliciting uplifting emotions that shape goodness. In this regard, Ephesians specifies but exceeds secular proposals like Richard Eldridge's, which see emotional engagement with specific cases as plodding at best. The first half of Ephesians is rhetorically and psychologically sophisticated. The author's blessings and prayers remind readers of their privileged role in God's plan for all creation and sets prayer as a norm of communal formation (Lincoln 1990, xxxvi). Christians' lives are not their own; God's call to them came "before the foundation of the world to be holy and blameless before him in love" (1.4), as part of "a plan for the fullness of time, to gather up all things in him, things in heaven and things on earth" (1.10). Their participation in impurity and unrighteousness would be selfish and demeaning, for it would obstruct God's plan to redeem the cosmos. Christian living is not a private and personal but a public and corporate responsibility to God.

At the outset of the letter the writer immediately honors the readers by telling them that they are important. But their importance lies not in what they have done or might do but in their place in the cosmic work of God. He makes what in modern parlance might be called a therapeutic alliance with the audience. Although in the course of the letter he will warn them against untoward behavior, he first soothes them, addressing them as faithful saints (1.1, 15). He reminds them of their proper dignity and, at the same time, calls forth their best selves.

He recalls the power of God, which raised Jesus from the dead and is now working for and in them so that they will look forward to reaping the benefits of "the riches of his glorious inheritance among the saints" (1.18). He reminds them of the privilege and responsibility of having been chosen by God for life with Christ. The words "riches," "gifts," "blessings," "grace," "chosen," and "inheritance" appear repeatedly throughout chapters 1–3 to assure the readers of the honor bestowed upon them and to heighten their sense of their new and proper dignity. This exalted stature identifies the demands laid upon them by membership in the household of God as honorable responsibilities befitting the dignity to which God has called them. The obedient life is a gracious and dignified life, and the author encourages them to submerge themselves in life with Christ as the way to a more fulfilling, exuberant, and wholesome life (3.14–9). In short, the carefully crafted rhetoric of Ephesians grants Christians dignity and responsibility. And chapter 4, which begins an explicit moral exhortation, appeals for Christian excellence on the grounds of Christians' new dignity: their calling to conformation to the likeness of God, which is righteous and holy (4.24).

A psychological insight of the author of Ephesians is that critical self-reflection is more likely from those with a strong sense of their own dignity. He does not flatter his readers but makes them proud—not because of their own accomplishment, for they have done nothing to deserve the gifts from which they derive their new identity. They experience confidence in being laborers in God's vineyard, and on that basis alone, he expects their best.

In sum, Ephesians is a work in pastoral theology for the church because it explicates the morally formative power of the work of God. It recognizes that while Christian excellence is theologically grounded, it is socially constructed and liturgically reinforced and is therefore a pastoral responsibility. At the same time, without denying the sovereignty of grace, it recognizes the challenge that Christian living presents to those living in a society that espouses other values. It is rhetorically and psychologically sophisticated, creating Christian excellence through the call and work of God in Jesus Christ.

These formal features of the letter identify its aretegenic project. But the material content of Christian excellence advanced in the last third of the letter is not secondary to the practices that craft it. The purity, righteousness, and holiness advocated in general terms throughout the letter become concrete admonitions starting at 4.25 and continuing through the household codes of chapter 6.

As I noted earlier, the author of this letter, following Pauline precedent, appreciates the power of public norms and sanctions in shaping personal behavior. Admonitions to moral behavior are proclaimed publicly, so that the communal ethos enforces the standard of human goodness required by gospel fidelity. Shaping Christian character occurs primarily in the community, through worship and events like the reading of this letter.

The primary behavioral locus of Christian excellence, according to Ephesians, is the mouth. Although work, sexual behavior, and family responsibilities are treated seriously, the point of origin of Christian character for this text seems to be speech. Sins of the tongue are elaborated at length: lying (4.25), evil talk (29), "bitterness and wrath and anger and wrangling and slander, together with all malice" (31) are all to be put off.[12] Obscene, silly, and vulgar talk educe licentious behavior and therefore have no place among believers (5.4); "only what is useful for building up, as there is need, so that your words may give grace to those who hear" (v.4.29) is to be put on. The point is that sinful speech and emotions belie the believer's dignity as one "marked with a seal for the day of redemption" (4.30). They are sinful not only as shameful acts but also because they betray God. Beloved children of God live the life of love taught by the cross of Christ himself (5.2). Falsehood, violence, sexual impurity, and dissension damage the trust and integrity of the body of Christ established by the Holy Spirit of God. Christian sanctity is not a private affair; it builds up and knits the community together for the glory of God. "Locker room talk," gossip, sexual acting out, anger and quarreling, and drunkenness are to be avoided because they are harmful; they rend the body and obstruct the work of God (Lincoln 1990, 297, 306).

Contrariwise, control of these vices is not left to the private anguish of the spurned or ashamed individual. The wholesome company Christians keep and their participation in salutary communal practices aid in minimizing these vices. Christian maturation happens by practicing holy living in a worshiping community: "psalms and hymns and spiritual songs among yourselves, singing and making melody to the Lord in your hearts, giving thanks to God" (5.19–20). Again, the sociality of formation by liturgical participation comes to the fore.

The household codes (5.21–6.9) follow the exhortation to reject paganism and adopt a Christian life in keeping with standard Graeco-Roman forms of parenesis. In the ancient world, the extended household was the basic unit of society. A well-ordered state required well-ordered households. Household codes spelled out lines of authority and responsibility for familial relations in three hierarchically structured tiers: husbands and wives, parents and children, and masters and slaves. The householder was a ruling-class adult male who had responsibility for the physical and spiritual welfare of his wife, children, and slaves. Proper household management was the building-block of society at least from Aristotle through Augustine.[13] Marriage, childrearing, and work order personal life and thereby support an ordered society.

A general principle of mutual submission out of reverence for Christ (5.21), enunciated in relation to the identity of the church (4.2–6) and in regard to individual behavior (4.25–32), prefaces the codes. Christ rules in the church, over individual behavior, and in the family. That Christ orders marriage, childrearing, and work relationships is then made explicit in the discussion of each realm. Wives are to be submissive to their husbands as they are to the Lord (5.22–4). Similarly, husbands are to love their wives like their own bodies and to nurture them as Christ nourishes the church (5.25–30). Children are to obey their parents, and parents are not to anger their children "but bring them up in the discipline and instruction of the Lord" (6.4). This exhortation is in keeping with the rest of the letter, which teaches care and respect for one another. Such a requirement presumably implies love and respect for children as well. Slaves, like wives, are to obey their masters as energetically as they obey Christ (6.5–8). And masters are not to threaten them, for they too serve the same Master (6.9). The theme running throughout the codes is that the *ecclesia,* not the *civitas,* is the foundation of marriage, family, and work relationships. In short, Ephesians teaches that the lordship of Christ rather than secular authority grounds the social structure.

There is little doubt that these household codes no longer support the social structure, at least in North America. Tolerance of slavery has been undone, at least in the West. The subordination of women is increasingly challenged around the world. And parental authority has also been undermined over the last quarter century, at least in the United States and within its sphere of influence. Indeed, marriage and family as the primary source of socialization are being radically challenged around the globe. But distaste for the lack of a modern norm of equality in the codes should not prevent the student of scripture from appreciating the theological foundation of household responsibilities, which transcends the particular ordering of roles in the letter to the Ephesians: submission to Christ as the foundation of all human relationships.

Christians did not challenge the patriarchal social structure that dominated both the Graeco-Roman and Jewish worlds, although there are indications that Gal. 3.28 gave rise to instances of social unrest (Balch 1981, 9–10, 106–7, 119). But they did challenge the civic foundation of household management by replacing loyalty to the state with submission to Christ. Grounding relationships in Christ may have appeared to civic-minded pagans as unpatriotic.

The author of Ephesians (like the author of Colossians) was caught between two norms for social organization—one from the Graeco-Roman world, the other arising from the Christian confession of Christ as Lord. The Graeco-Roman (and Jewish) norms of household and civic responsibility were based on relationships of dominance and submission. The Greek experience with democracy had been disheartening, and the Romans preferred the order that comes from clear lines of responsibility in a hierarchically ordered society with few rights for any but Roman citizens. With the coming of Christ, God, rather than the householder, became the head of the household and the polis. But these biblical writers were not able to see that the lordship of Christ undermines the hierarchical structures they knew. They, and the Christians who followed them, were unable to visualize a social structure that both honored the lordship of Christ and distributed responsibilities and skills necessary for preserving family and society evenly.

The notion of equality did not exist in the ancient world. Perhaps the ancients feared that equality would lead to anarchy. In any case, the church not only did not introduce the notion of equality, or mutuality, but resisted these notions strenuously when others finally did. There can be little doubt that over the centuries the church itself, instead of submitting to the lordship of Christ in exercising its responsibilities, as counseled by 1 Cor. 1.18–31, often adopted precisely the structures of domination of the world. The visible church is as fallen an institution as Christians could ever hope to see.

Still, despite this flaw, if we squint it may be possible to imagine what it would be like for the church to be governed by the lordship of Christ and the Spirit along the lines set forth by Paul. Even Ephesians 5 and 6 offer principles of incipient mutuality based on acceptance of Christ's lordship. Perhaps the full possibilities of and tensions among all these Pauline and deutero-Pauline texts have yet to be understood.

In conclusion, Ephesians exemplifies aretegenic theology—theology conducive to salutary formation of believers whose dignity lies not in their own power but in their obedience to Christ. It sets reflection on the work of God in Christ in a cosmic context that has direct bearing on the life of local churches. The purpose of theology, on this model, is to strengthen the Christian identity of church members by helping them grasp the dignity accomplished for them by Christ, which separates them from non-Christians. The lordship of Christ pervades one's life—in the family, at work, in the church, and among friends. Although Ephesians does not address the question of interaction with strangers, one can extrapolate from the exhortation of 1 Cor. 10 23–11.1 that Christian norms apply there as well. They are to invade one's personality, emotions as well as ideas. The responsibility of Christian leaders is to help believers drink of the majestic power and mercy of God so that God defines believers' dignity and directs their responsibilities to one another, now that they are the dwelling place of God.

Assessment

This concludes our survey of the elements in Pauline and deutero-Pauline aretology. It appears that they form a comprehensive picture of Christian formation in Christianity's earliest days. It is a picture that in some ways was not carried forward by subsequent Western theology, which became focused on issues of guilt and shame in the medieval period and on faith as the means of overcoming fear of divine rejection with the Protestant Reformation. While these themes may be found in Pauline theology, they are not dominant. Despite the anxious tone of Romans 7, Paul is, on the whole, more interested in how the work of God transforms believers than in their inner state. Three aspects of this dynamic suggest a distinctively Pauline aretology.

First, Christian excellence is based in divine actions. The cross of Christ makes Jews and Greeks co-participants in the drama of redemption. This action of God does away with boasting in one's personal identity. People who recognize what has happened in Christ become different people because they are now related to God in a new way as a result of God's action on their behalf. When grasped and internalized, being related to God in this way becomes the foundation of human dignity and nobility. Living in an eschatological reality gives even the quotidian details of daily life a fresh vivacity.

Baptism is another action of God that grounds Christian identity and shapes character. Baptism publicly and formally transfers the echatological reality to each believer. It grafts individuals into the body of Christ, so that they acquire a history and a calling in God. In this they give up a degree of autonomy and submit to being guided by the Holy Spirit. Under the authority of the Holy Spirit they practice righteous living. All that one can do is acknowledge these events and live in loyalty to God.

Second, Christian excellence comes from adjusting to ontological realities. Christian self-esteem, then, is not from any feature of our own identity or natural endowment that we are to actualize, reclaim, or live into. It comes, rather, from who God is: the one who makes peace where there was division, the one who brings hope of eternal life, the one who brings life out of death. Christians are endowed by this God, conformed to Christ, and indwelt by the Holy Spirit. Therefore, they see wisdom where others see humiliation, and dignity where others experience pain. Life has been set in parameters established by God.

The third feature of Pauline aretology is that it is public and social. The actions of God that make Christians are public events that place the Christian community in the public eye. These actions create public standards that Christians apply in family life, in business, and in public life. Believers' actions and relationships are now filtered through the God-given dignity that one has. The gifts of the Spirit are given not to enhance personal power or status but to upbuild the community. One's body is no longer one's own, for example; it is the temple of the Holy Spirit. One's freedom must be curtailed if it spiritually endangers others. One's speech must be guarded so that Christ's peace prevails in the community. In short, one's conduct and relationships transpire in the presence of God and with the help of the armor of God, through the gifts of the Holy Spirit.

Christians who accept the Christian life are never alone, or left to fend for themselves. They are always accompanied by the cross of Christ, their baptism, and the Holy Spirit, and resocialized by public practices and a strong community ethos that reinforces their identity. They are surrounded by God's grace, which they did nothing to merit. Indeed, they have become instruments of divine grace, ambassadors for Christ, messengers of reconciliation, as Paul put it. Christians are now responsible to God for the reconciliation and righteousness they enjoy. Paul urges them to make the most of it.

Notes

1. *Mishnah* (hereafter *M*), *Abot* 3.14, edited near the close of the third century, likely reflects long-standing theological beliefs to this effect. The *Mishnah* reads: "Precious is the human being, who was created in the image [of God]," and cites Gen. 9.6. "Precious are Israelites, who are called children to the Omnipresent," citing Deut. 14.1. (Neusner 1988, 680).

2. Biblical laws prohibit practices associated with idolatry (Lev. 19.26, 28, 29, 31; 20.1–6) and association with idolaters (Exod. 23.13, 24, 32–3; 34.12–6; Deut. 7.1–5, 25–6). In Paul's day these regulations were being adapted to accommodate the commercial ties that existed between Jews and gentiles. A full tractate of the *Mishnah, Abodah Zarah* (*Ab. Zar.*), is devoted to this theme.

3. Neusner 1988, 662; *M. Ab. Zar.* 2:1.

4. Paul makes a similar transposition in 2 Cor. 6:16–8. He collocates scripture texts that refer to Israel as if they were directed to gentiles! Although a clear distortion of the texts, it illustrates the intensity of his insistence on a genuine theological identity for gentiles.

5. It is perhaps worth noting that Paul does not liken the co-optation of the gentiles to a legal verdict, as medieval theology later would. The divine action is more like an edict than a verdict. It is as if, during the Cold War, the U.S. president had declared all Soviet citizens to be henceforth U.S. citizens, entitled to all rights and privileges of that status.

6. A helpful discussion of the trauma of conversion in general in the ancient world is Malherbe (1987, 36–51).

7. The social dimension of reconciliation following upon the triumph of the cross is taken up in the Greek Fathers, especially evident in Athanasius of Alexandria's work examined below.

8. Rom. 6.12–23 uses the word "righteousness" four times. The point of the passage is to persuade the reader to submit to righteousness as its slave. There is no suggestion of imputed righteousness. Rather, righteousness is an independent norm that the believer can know and internalize as one's own.

9. This passage is strikingly similar to two variant rabbinic sorites that appear in *M. Sotah* 9.15 (Neusner 1988, 466) and *Baraita* Ab. Zar.* 20b (Montefiore and Loewe 1974, 476). In both cases the gradual building of a pious character depends on the Holy Spirit, who is the proximate instrument of resurrection.

*Baraita: legal material contemporaneous with but not included in the codified *Mishna* (ca. 200 C.E.).

10. Abraham Malherbe identified formal features of classical parenesis as follows: it appeals to information already known by the recipients as a reminder; it is generally applicable to new situations; the writer compliments the readers for what they are already doing and encourages them to continue; it offers specific examples for imitation; it may contain brief or extended admonitions (1986, 124–5).

11. For an interesting discussion of the role of reference groups in shaping Christian identity, see Meeks (1990).

12. Andrew Lincoln points out that in the case of lying, stealing, and evil talk there is a clear parenetic pattern. First, the vice is identified negatively: for example, "Let no evil talk come out of your mouths." Then its virtuous counterpart is invoked instead: "but only what

is useful for building up" (293–15). These motivational contrasts are then taken out of the private realm and placed in the context of the community. A rationale is offered that links the desirable behavior to the well-being of the community: "so that your words may give grace to those who hear."

13. For Aristotle, management skills, and particularly political statesmanship, are similar to but not identical with the art of being a householder, which is training for public leadership (1963, 382–5, *Politics*, book I, chaps. 1–2). For Augustine, an ordered society requires ordered harmony and peace that stem from love of neighbor. And this begins with the responsibility for the members of one's own household, one's wife, children, and servants, "not with pride in taking precedence over others, but with compassion in taking care of others" (1984, 874; *City of God,* XIX:14). See also Stambaugh and Balch (1986, 123–4).

3

Authoritative Teaching

The Sermon on the Mount

THE SETTING FOR MATTHEAN PURITY

Matthew's gospel captures the emergence of a besieged community of followers of Jesus who promulgated a radical Jewish soteriology and ecclesiology that was at odds with those whom Matthew experienced as powerful opponents (i.e., scribes and Pharisees). Hostility toward the author's adversaries pervades the text. The impression is that the piety advocated here, at least in the aggregate, was a subversive teaching forged in conflict with other candidates for the form Judaism would take in light of Jesus and the destruction of the Temple.

To appreciate Matthean Judaism we must briefly identify the religious climate within which it developed, as well as the parties and issues to the dispute. While no point in these matters is uncontested, some general observations are possible. Although then, as now, most people were not passionately involved in religious issues, those who were engaged in debate and controversy (Overman 1990, 6–34). The less observant were probably content to let the religious tone of the day be set by those who were, and respected their dedication to debate and live out their religious convictions vigorously. There were parties that disputed respectfully, like the Houses of Hillel and Shammai and Pharisees and Saducees, as well as sects that were soteriologically exclusive, believing only themselves to be the truly faithful remnant of God's people, like the Essenes and the communities that produced 4 Esdras, Baruch, and the Psalms of Solomon.[1]

Matthew's community seems to fit into the latter category of a sect, given the angry feelings of marginalization and persecution at being denied power, and the soteriological denunciations of Jews who disagreed (Matt. 7.19; 21.43–4). There was also some degree of self-righteousness among the more passionate sects at the apparent impiety of others, especially since there was no centralized authority that sought to impose uniformity of belief and practice. A group of Essenes, for example, withdrew to the desert in protest over the corruption of the Jerusalem priesthood, perhaps hoping to administer the cult one day themselves.[2] While these disputes of style and legal debate divided the sects from one another, they were all concerned with purity and piety as spelled out in scripture and adapted to the times.

As E. P. Sanders has reminded us, the various strands of Judaism of the day, Palestinian as well as diaspora, all sought to interpret the Law of Moses in order to achieve purity, which was the responsibility of faithful Jews (1990, 245–6). Purity may well have been associated with righteousness, too. While some things were pure or impure by biblical decree (like fish as opposed to pork and shellfish), scripture, like any constitution, called for interpretation. And various parties went about this task with different interests.

Sanders argues that Pharisees distinguished themselves from Sadducees by self-consciously developing nonscriptural customs and standards of observance. Sadducees stayed closer to the text (1990, 108). At least for the Pharisees, categories of pure and impure were determined by what appears to be a germ theory of contamination by touch or proximity. The various groups debated over what Sanders refers to as "tidying-up" biblical rules of purity. The Pharisees focused on food, utensils, furniture, clothing, and the human body, all of which could become impure by contact with a corpse, semen, a menstruant or other person with bodily emissions, certain insects, and things and persons associated with idolatry. Re-establishing purity by extending biblical precepts was accomplished not only through cultic sacrifice but also through washing one's clothing and by immersion. The Pharisees extended purity by adding regular handwashing as a precautionary measure.

Another important element involved in Pharisaic piety had to do with tithing. Untithed agricultural products or prepared foods were also considered unfit for use, perhaps based on the Pharisees' desire to carry priestly requirements into lay life. This had implications for commerce between Pharisees and other laity as well as between Pharisees and pagans, who could not be trusted to ensure the standards of purity to which the Pharisees adhered and who were impure because of idolatry in any case. It could be that purity and tithing were related. If something pure were touched by something impure, the whole was rendered impure; for something pure to be made fit to eat, a piece had to be taken off, originally for the priests, rendering the whole usable. Touching and taking parts to and from the whole rendered it fit or unfit.

While it is difficult to draw firm conclusions about the role Pharisees played in the Tannaitic Judaism of the *Mishnah*,[3] it may not be unfair to suggest that there is considerable similarity of concern and orientation to piety and purity, even if later teachers modified or rejected specific Pharisaic points.[4] Pharisaic and Tannaitic purity worked from the outside in. Piety is expressed behavior rather than faith or values. That is not to say that internal criteria were not important, but they did not dominate the legal literature produced by the heirs of first-century Judaism.

Tannaitic Judaism's preference for external over internal piety is evident in a parable attributed to R. Eleazar ben Azariah, who flourished 80–110 C.E.

Anyone whose wisdom is greater than his deed—to what is he to be likened? To a tree with abundant foliage, but few roots. When the winds come, they will uproot it and blow it down, as it is said, "He shall be like a tamarisk in the desert and shall not see when good comes but shall inhabit the parched places in the wilderness" (Jer. 17.6). But anyone whose deeds are greater than his wisdom—to what is he to be likened? To a tree with little foliage but abundant roots. For even if all the winds in the world were to come and blast at it, they will not move it from its place, as it is said, "He shall be as a tree planted by the waters, and that spreads out its roots by the river, and shall not fear when heat comes, and his leaf shall be green, and shall not be careful in the year of drought, neither shall cease from yielding fruit" (Jer. 17.8). (Neusner 1988, 681; *M. Abot* 3:17)

Tannaitic piety, of which the Pharisees represented one expression, irked Matthew. Jesus, the Son of God, had let loose a new understanding of purity that worked from the inside out, not from the outside in. The new purity was cultivated not by separation from others, or by reifying the memory of the Temple cult and priesthood, but by the creation of a new eschatological community of Jews and gentiles committed to building one another up in the new righteousness.

The destruction of the Temple must have sobered everyone. Even in a corrupt state, the sacrificial cult was not only a known way of life; it was obedience to God's law, and it was now unavailable as a means of purification. In a society where, despite their differences, all the groups agreed that Judaism pivoted around purity assured by the sacrificial system or its equivalent, the crisis was of major proportions. Leadership was needed. The Essenes, having rejected "civilization" for the purer life of desert asceticism, had taken themselves out of the running. The priests (and the Sadducees, by virtue of their close alliance with the priests) were rather helpless—indeed, unemployed. That left the Pharisees; the Tannaim, who might have had Pharisees among them (Matthew's scribes?); and perhaps the various groups of Jesus-followers.

The Pharisees had been in existence for about two hundred years by Matthew's time. While their fortunes had waxed and waned, they were not averse to political power, although we have no indication that they sought it after the Temple burned. But from the vantage point of a demoralized and perhaps confused and oppressed populace, they offered clarity, stability and, perhaps most significantly, a plan for securing the ritual purity that had been available in Jerusalem at a moment when God's house had been desecrated by pagans. It is conceivable that the uneducated classes would seek the equivalent of sacrificial purity on the model honed by the Pharisees over two centuries.

In approaching the debate between the Pharisees and the Matthean community, it is important to keep in mind two further points made by Sanders. While the Pharisees may have worked out more stringent standards of purity than those observed by the general public, they did not seek to impose these on their neighbors (1990, 249). They did, however, separate themselves at table and in commerce from those who might defile them. While this may have been experienced by other communities as elitist and exclusive, it may not have been intended as such. Indeed, the popularity and trust the Pharisees came to enjoy among the general population attests to the fact that they were viewed by many as a source of comfort rather than oppression, as the fledgling Christians experienced them.

Sanders's other point is that whatever the degree of stringency or separateness from defilement Pharisees or Essenes or others may have observed, this form of purity is not to be mistaken for soteriological exclusivism and thereby legalism, meaning obedience to behavior that wins divine favor (1990, 242). Purity and defilement were unavoidable constants that recurred throughout life and in death. One could not attain a state of purity and remain in it. One was, rather, repeatedly defiled and purified. Jewish ecclesiology held that membership in the household of God (the closest we have to rabbinic soteriology) was by birth or conversion, not by observance of purity laws. The idea found in the letter to the Hebrews, that Christ's sacrifice atoned for sin once for all, had no counterpart in Judaism and probably met with perplexity. For these Jewish groups there was no sailing above becoming soiled by the world, but only repenting and repeatedly being washed and cleansed.

Matthean purity was of another sort and to a different end. Whether the Matthean redactor was himself a Jew or gentile, and whether he wrote in Israel or in Syria, are less important for my purpose here than the tasks he set himself. The Matthean community must have viewed the destruction of the Temple as an opportunity to spread its faith and piety, to offer itself as a contender for leadership in redefining Judaism at this decisive moment. Judging from the anger and frustration that pour forth from the Gospel, Matthew's community was rebuffed. But whether they came from Jewish or gentile families, they considered themselves the rightful heirs of Judaism on biblical grounds, so I designate them as Matthean Jews, who opposed Pharisaic Jews. The crisis gave renewed energy and eschatological meaning to the person and teachings of Jesus. Matthew and the other evangelists, following Paul, came to see the two events together as God's charting a new path for Jews and gentiles to tread together. Their offering for the future of Judaism differed in at least three fundamental ways from the forming rabbinic option. Matthean Judaism (1) held to a radically different understanding of authority (based on Jesus), one that rejected traditional and contemporary Jewish authority, (2) centered on a new view of purity that was both internal and soteriologically exclusive, and (3) radically transformed Jewish ecclesiology into a community of Jews and gentiles as the people of God.

All told, the Matthean option presented a vision of Judaism that most Jews could neither recognize as their own nor accept as legitimate. Thus, I suggest, the Matthean charge of hypocrisy against Jewish leaders was an unfortunate choice—in essence, a misnomer.[5] Matthean Jews hoped that the non-christian Jews would rethink their devotion to purity, tradition, and Israel in light of Jesus and could not graciously accept their negative decision. The pair of metaphors about the difficulty of adapting old garments and utensils to new circumstances in Matt. 9.16–7 testifies to the mismatch. Matthean and Tannaitic Jews judged one another to be misguided. By the time of this written form of the argument in the Gospel, the two communities were talking past one another.

Of the three issues identified as decisive breaks with Tannaitic Judaism, the issue of authority is perhaps most evident. While various schools, individual pairs of scholars, and parties rigorously debated with one another in the process of interpretation, they did share common ground, just as Paul and the Gospel writers did. The Tannaim developed and commented on authorized materials received in the tradition that they claimed stretched from Moses to their own day in order to adapt selected biblical laws to contemporary circumstance. Disagreements between Hillel and Shammai, Pharisees and Saducees, and so forth occurred over how this adaptation should be undertaken. The tradition they forged, however—one relying on traditional chains of authorities, like the genealogy that opens *Abot* (Neusner 1988, 672)—controlled interpretation of scripture by means of their famous "fence around the Torah."

In contrast to this careful development of legal opinion, Matthean Jews claimed Jesus as the source of divine authority and the Sermon on the Mount as his alternative fence around the law that based purity on internal rather than external criteria. Matthean piety saw in Jesus' interpretation of scripture the authorization of a new purity and rejected the traditional lines of legal authority. Matthean Jews cast aside the chain of tradition that authorized contemporary teachers. Matt. 1.1–17 sounds the alarm by opening the Gospel with an alternative chain of authority beginning not with Moses but with Abraham, and even reaching back to Christ, effectively locating the authority of interpretation in Jesus rather than in contemporary scholars, scribes, or teachers developing Mosaic Law. Matt. 15.1–20 clearly states the opposition between the two forms of authority and piety. This move is reinforced by the transfiguration story, which does locate Jesus in relation to Moses as well as Elijah (17.1–13).

The second central issue in the Matthean revolt against first-century Judaism was the understanding of purity. I have suggested that purity was defined from the outside in and was considered to be nonsoteriological by the dominant groups. The Matthean community, by contrast, understood salvation to be centered in a purity that proceeded from the inside out and was soteriologically decisive.

Following Hans Dieter Betz's suggestion that the Sermon takes the form of an epitome, a synopsis of a larger work created for pedagogical purposes, we can look to the Sermon as the epicenter of Matthean purity, a summary of Jesus' teaching elaborated throughout the Gospel and containing within itself a further terse summation in the Beatitudes (1985). Like the *Mishnah*, the Sermon adapts and extends scriptural precepts. Like the Pharisees, the Sermon selects issues from everyday life, seeking to regulate sexual behavior, commerce, ritual practices, and social relations. The difference between the commended separateness of the Pharisees and the commanded ethical standard of the Sermon as a whole and in its parts is that the latter is based on a norm of radical other-centeredness and rigorous self-criticism, a standard that even this Gospel itself had difficulty adhering to. Pharisaic piety understood purity to depend on separation from that which defiles—an understandable choice, given repeated pagan desecration of the Temple and land stretching back to the Babylonians. Matthean piety, by contrast, understood purity to result from involvement with others that expressed purity of heart, first evidenced not by Jews at all but by gentiles, in the story of the wise men who converted to the new king of the Jews despite political danger (Matt. 2.1–12). The chasm between the two views made civil conversation and debate in the frame of reference that Jews were accustomed to impossible. There was only nonconversation between Pharisaic and Matthean piety.

In comparison with the precision with which Pharisaic precepts monitor minute details of daily life, the Sermon gives focused yet general guidelines for conduct and virtues. It applies these guidelines to specific circumstances (bereavement and persecution), with other examples presumably to be filled in by the disciple. Yet the Sermon presents these principles as the teaching of Jesus, whose authority stems from Abraham himself. Matthew's standards of comportment are studded with threats that whoever disobeys will be thrown into hell. He was militantly uncompromising.

The *Mishnah* presented the ideal disciple of Abraham as generous, modest, and humble, and excluded the grudging, the arrogant, and the proud from the designation (Neusner, 1988, 688–9; *Abot* 5:19) but attached no soteriological decisiveness to these traits. The Beatitudes, by contrast, define the privileged or, as *makarios* is usually translated, the "blessed of God" by these virtues. In short, Matthean purity stresses virtues—even in adverse circumstances—in a way that was unknown in Pharisaic piety.

Defining the privileged of God by the new purity of meekness, irenicism, and ingenuousness leads to the last point of Matthean dissension from developing Tannaitic Judaism. The standard Jewish groups debating in the first century all understood membership in the covenant to be achieved by birth in Israel.[6] Purity was important but not soteriologically or eschatologically decisive. Matthew makes the startling claim that purity as defined by virtues taught by Jesus in the Sermon on the Mount, not by birth membership in Israel, is the crux of membership in the covenant.[7] That is, Matthew not only decried the apparent elitism of Pharisee and Essene and the presupposition that distanced the pious from the less observant and pagans in order to protect personal purity; he also insisted that the new standard of other-centered purity in relation to both the less observant and pagans is soteriologically loaded. This rendered Matthean piety truly sectarian in a way that Pharisaic piety was not. The immanent reign of God, around which Matthew's gospel pivoted, would include those from all nations who qualify as disciples of Jesus on

Matthew's new terms (Matt. 8.11–2; 19.28–30; 20.1–16; 25.31–46). This goes beyond simply countenancing a gentile mission. It attacks the very core of Jewish identity, the distinctiveness of which was a central Pharisaic concern. And at a time when the Jewish parties were struggling to find a way to settle in for the long term without the Temple, Matthew's eschatological fervor must have been even more disconcerting.[8]

Given the comprehensive attack on the presuppositions of first-century Judaism that is evident in Matthew's Gospel, it is not surprising that the writer warns his followers of impending persecution, although Pharisees and scribes were not known for harshness. But it is understandable that this group of claimants to Judaism, perhaps both Jewish and gentile Christians, would arouse deep anger; they challenged the foundation on which post-70 C.E. Judaism was being constructed. They rejected received authority, the very notion of ritual purity, and the definition of the covenant and Israel's belonging to God. Perhaps in this light the deceptively simple claim that John and then Jesus went about the countryside proclaiming "Repent, for the kingdom of God is at hand" assumes a more threatening reality, at least for Jews invited to decide for an eschatological community. For repentance, according to the virtues outlined in the Beatitudes, rather than purification by washing or sacrifice, was to be the decisive factor in determining who was among the privileged of God!

Before we examine the text itself, I will make two further introductory points. The absence of a strong doctrinal dimension in the Sermon has often been discussed by commentators, and some are uncomfortable with its unabashedly ethical focus.[9] The ethics of the Sermon delivered by Jesus are dependent on his authority but are not, on the face of it, christological, as, for example, Pauline ethics are, or riveted on faith in Jesus, as John's Gospel is.[10] But I have suggested that the doctrinal basis of Matthean piety is soteriological and ecclesiological. That is, Matthean Judaism was at loggerheads with emerging Tannaitic Judaism in arguing that interior purity is soteriologically significant, that religious authority has been radically redefined by God through Jesus' teaching and example, and that the people of God has been radically reshaped. Matthew laid down a gauntlet to the authorities and was clearly the underdog in the struggle for control of emerging Judaism.

The discussion of Matthean Judaism as an alternative to other offerings of the day should not, however, leave the reader with the impression that the main point of this Gospel is polemical. While Matthew cannot help but speak to his opponents, he is also speaking to potential converts, and those who have already thrown their weight behind the new option, in order to comfort and encourage them, to build them into a new community based on the teachings of Jesus by instructing them in the faith, and to prepare them to suffer for the truth and purity they now profess. His point is that in Jesus there is a new revelation of God that indicates that purity does not require separating oneself from others, as Pharisaic doctrine taught, but involves how we live together, even under trying circumstances. The teaching of Jesus makes disciples into new persons who bond together in a community to try out the teaching in safety. The Sermon looks beyond the persecution they experience or anticipate to craft a community of the faithful that is willing to live under the stringent standards required by Jews and gentiles who choose to follow Jesus. In essence, as the numerous references to the international scope of the teaching attest, it is a radical experiment in multicultural community based on a personal moral code that construes itself as the nucleus of the reign of God.

THE STRUCTURE OF THE SERMON ON THE MOUNT

The following reading of the Sermon, beginning with the Beatitudes, divides it into four major sections:[11]

1. Invitation to discipleship (5.3–16). The Sermon begins with an impersonal list of character traits or circumstances that carry with them divine privilege (5.3–10). Verses 11–2 challenge Jesus' hearers to join this privileged company. Verses 13–6 are a pair of encouraging metaphors.

2. Jesus' teaching in opposition to other interpretations of the law (5.17–48). Verse 17 adopts a negative rhetorical style. Verses 17–20 introduce the theme of the section: Pharisaic requirements of the Law are too lax. Jesus will present an alternative righteousness. The remainder of the chapter (21–48) takes the form of six antitheses. Jesus teaches behavioral patterns that stem from underlying virtuous character traits. This is the Matthean "fence around the Torah."

3. Prohibitions of negative role models (6.1–7.6). This section presents behavior to be avoided. The models are offered in three groups: one using religious customs to elicit a pious demeanor (6.1–18), a second using attitudes toward possessions as the means of developing God-centeredness (6.19–34), and a third to urge self-scrutiny (7.1–6). Again, character traits, both those to be cultivated and those to be avoided, are implied.

4. Parenetic encouragement and concluding warnings and threats (7.7–27). This section is divided among positive encouragement in implementing Jesus' program (7.7–14), warnings about the difficulties and traps that lie in wait along the way (7.15–20), and the threat of fearful consequences that await those who disregard Jesus' teaching (7.21–7).

The structure I have just outlined is as follows:

   I. Invitation to discipleship 5.3–16
        Beatitudes 5.3–10
        Address to auditors 5.11–2
        Exhortation to auditors 5.13–6
  II. Jesus and the Law 5.17–48
        Intensifying Law and prophets 5.17–20
        Antitheses 5.21–48 (positive models of discipleship)
 III. Negative models of discipleship 6.1–7.6

> Quiet piety 6.1–18
> God-centeredness 6.19–34
> Self-scrutiny 7.1–6
> IV. Concluding exhortation 7.7–27
> Encouragement 7.7–14
> Warnings 7.15–20
> Threats of punishment 7.21–7

An Aretegenic Reading of the Sermon on the Mount

The Invitation to Discipleship

The character portraits drawn by the Beatitudes describe ideal disciples in terms of both character traits (humility, modesty, righteousness, mercy, ingenuousness, and irenicism) and misfortune (mourners, the persecuted). The phrases echo scripture and Mishnaic material and are in turn, as one would expect from an epitome, elaborated upon in other sections of the Sermon and in the larger context of the Gospel as a whole.

The Beatitudes are short, stylized pronouncements following a standard form. Each begins with the adjective *makarios,* mentions the trait or condition for which a special status is granted by God, and concludes by enumerating various synonyms for the reward granted (in effect an explanation of the adjective). Those who meet apparently any of these standards will be rewarded. Note that there is no suggestion that the list is cumulative. Both virtuous character traits and misfortune qualify one for God's special concern. *Makarios* translates *ashrey* in the Septuagint, the first word of the Psalter (see note 10). It implies the joy that comes from the privilege of divine favor and hints at reward. It served Matthew's purposes well. The first eight Beatitudes are written in the third-person plural, presupposing a distance between the privileged of God and the gathered crowd. This is to say that Jesus begins by admonishing the crowd to examine themselves to see if they think they might be among the privileged of God—an unnerving prospect, no doubt. It is a rather circuitous invitation.

From that point on, however, Jesus addresses his audience directly. His concern is not only to offer a new picture of purity but also to support those who adopt it to endure the persecution they will face as his disciples. He challenges them to join the ranks of the privileged of God, which entails suffering in his name: "Blessed are you when people revile you and persecute you and utter all kinds of evil against you falsely on my account" (Matt. 5.11). Thus, the Beatitudes challenge hearers to undertake the new piety and to risk personal misfortune as a follower of Jesus.

While at first glance the Beatitudes appear as an idealistic moral challenge, they also offer assurance and celebratory congratulation, as Robert Guelich has pointed out (109–11). That does not, however, deny the ethical demands that accompany the privileged status.[12] A distinction between reward for righteousness and encouragement to endure persecution is not possible for Matthew. The traits and circumstances enumerated in the Sermon are not alien to first-century readers and auditors. Many of the phrases and ideas are familiar from scripture, an indication that Matthew was arguing against Pharisee-influenced piety on scriptural grounds. Although it is not the only text behind the Beatitudes (the opening Beatitude echoes Prov. 16.19–20 and 29.23), Ps. 37 has particular prominence here and at several other points in the Sermon. It is a psalm of consolation and encouragement for those who persist in righteousness yet are greeted with contempt by the wicked, who surround them and seem to flourish. Six times the psalmist assures the beleaguered righteous ones that they will inherit the earth. God will vindicate them and punish their persecutors. This is the situation in which the evangelist finds the Jesus-followers in relation to the emerging Tannaitic Judaism. The following are loose parallels between the Sermon on the Mount and Ps. 37:

Matthew	Psalm 37
5.5 Blessed are the meek, for they will inherit the earth.	37.11 But the meek shall inherit the land, and delight themselves in abundant prosperity.
5.6 Blessed are those who hunger and thirst for righteousness, for they will be filled.	37.28–9 The righteous shall be kept safe forever, but the children of the wicked shall be cut off. The righteous shall inherit the land and live in it forever.
5.8 Blessed are the pure in heart, for they will see God.	37.18 The Lord knows the days of the blameless, and their heritage will abide forever.
5.9 Blessed are the peacemakers, for they will be called children of God.	37.37 Mark the blameless, and behold the upright, for there is posterity for the peaceable.
5.10 Blessed are those who are persecuted for righteousness' sake, for theirs is the kingdom of heaven.	37.39–40 The salvation of the righteous is from the Lord; he is their refuge in the time of trouble. The Lord helps them and rescues them; he rescues them from the wicked, and saves them, because they take refuge in him.

MATTHEW	PSALM 37
5.16 In the same way, let your light shine before others, so that they may see your good works and give glory to your Father in heaven.	37.6 He will make your vindication shine like the light, and the justice of your cause like the noonday.
5.22 But I say to you that if you are angry with a brother or sister, you will be liable to judgment.	37.8a Refrain from anger, and forsake wrath.
5.42 Give to everyone who begs from you, and do not refuse anyone who wants to borrow from you.	37.21–2 The wicked borrow, and do not pay back, but the righteous are generous and keep giving.
	37.26 [The righteous] are ever giving liberally and lending, and their children become a blessing.
6.25 . . . do not worry about your life, what you will eat or what you will drink, or about your body, what you will wear. . . .	37.8b Do not fret—it only leads to evil.
	37.25 I have been young, and now am old, yet I have not seen the righteous forsaken or their children begging for bread.

Full treatment of the relationship between the Sermon and Psalm 37 must await another format. Here I only identify common themes running between the two texts. Righteousness brings long-term rewards and blessings from God. Generosity without regard to the future reflects trust in God's providential care. Although the wicked lie in wait to trap the righteous, the latter trust that God will rescue them from being wrongly accused, or perhaps from succumbing to the temptation to evil. Perseverance in goodness is necessary, and hardships are to be expected. God vindicates those who turn from evil and trust in him and live humbly, generously, peaceably, and without anger in the face of opposition and persecution.

The parameters of the new piety not only replace external purity with internal; they also carry with them a new sense of dignity that comes with intense self-discipline and restraint. Performance of pious practice takes on a whole new life here.

The point is not really faith versus practice. Both forms of piety are concerned primarily with practice, with right living. One way of putting the difference might be to say that dignity in the legal sense comes when those who know themselves to be God's beloved meet their obligations to God in this regard as precisely as possible. It is an ethics of duty and propriety. Matthean ethics is based on the dignity that comes of refining one's character as worked out in relation to others and of holding to a strenuous moral standard when misunderstood and marginalized. There is no question but that both are vulnerable to virtuosity and self-satisfaction.

Matthew nestled the Beatitudes in the biblical heritage. God authorized Jesus to reclaim this biblical heritage of promise and exhortation. Matthew saw the Jesus movement as a biblically based objection to Pharisaic nonscriptural innovation. As new as they are, Matthew implies that the Beatitudes are not really new teaching at all. Rather, Jesus, perhaps following the Pharisaic model, extends or expands the themes of Psalm 37, most notably with the teaching of love for one's enemies. Psalm 37.8 counsels against anger toward evildoers but does not urge love for them, for example. Despite emendations to the biblical injunctions, they are the biblical promise of salvation. Those who long to rebuild the Temple distort the biblical conviction of Hosea that is so important to Matthew: "For I desire mercy, not sacrifice, and acknowledgment of God rather than burnt offerings" (Hos. 6.6, cited in Matt. 9.13 and 12.7). Jesus concludes the list of the Beatitudes with the reminder to his hearers that they are in good company: "Rejoice and be glad, for your reward is great in heaven, for in the same way they persecuted the prophets who were before you" (5.12).

Far from being an unrealistic list of demands, the Beatitudes, read in the context of Psalm 37, offer encouragement to the beleaguered band of Jesus-followers and uplift them in the face of rejection. Privilege, promise, invitation, and exhortation go hand in hand. The note of celebration tempered by the tone of girding for battle in the face of age-old obstacles continues with a rabbinic-style pair of metaphors that liken those who choose biblical faithfulness to salt of the earth and light of the world (5.13–6). Salt is needed to make food palatable; light, too, is needed by all. The metaphors suggest that those who accept the invitation realize that the world needs them; they are commissioned. "Let your light shine before others, so that they may see your good works and give glory to your Father in heaven" (5.16). Righteousness here is not, as for the Pharisees, a sign of obedience, but a tool of evangelism. Aware of the awesome risks his hearers faced in becoming his disciples, Jesus invites them to think of themselves as God's vanguard and to be open about their good works, which is the evangelical responsibility of disciples. They are to preach the gospel with their lives.[13] It is an exhilarating and awesome challenge.

This first section of the Sermon should have the effect of galvanizing the crowd once they conceive of themselves as the privileged of God, as opposed to those who think their privilege is assured by birth. It sets standards, warns of trials to come, and undergirds the mission with a sense of ultimacy. It molds hearers into a group bonded together by God's mission in a hostile environment. The second section urges the crowd to choose sides in Jesus' dispute with the powers that be.

Jesus' Opposition to Pharisaic Judaism

In 5.17–6.48 Jesus specifies his opposition to traditionally authorized teachers by countering their fence around the Torah, built of jurisprudence, with his own fence, built of strength of character, a standard more demanding than that of the scribes and Pharisees. Verses 17–20 respond to the unspoken question in the air following Jesus' implicit attack on Tannaitic scripture interpretation: is he counseling suspension of the Law? No, he says. Jesus, like the Pharisees, is extending the Law, only in a different direction. While on one level Jesus attacks the Jewish leadership, on another he confronts each hearer with a new way of judging her own conduct and attitudes.

The first antithesis concerns anger (5.21–6), although it takes its cue from the Decalogue's injunction against murder. Jesus does not talk about how to try capital cases or distinguish premeditated murder from voluntary and involuntary manslaughter, as would the *Mishnah* (Neusner 1988, 612–6; *Makkot* 1:9–2:8). Nor does he dwell on punishment as a deterrent. This does not mean that he shrugged off the system of jurisprudence that developed under Tannaitic tutelage. It does mean that in this summary of the essential elements of his teaching, his interest lay elsewhere, but in a direction not wholly incompatible with later Mishnaic developments. The scholars of Matthew's day and beyond were intentionally constructing a law code to stand in for the Temple. Jesus' direct address to his audience suggests that he believes himself to be addressing people who want to practice righteous living, and he draws them into his conversation on those grounds. For this purpose Jesus focuses on the inner state of mind of an individual and some of the interactions between individuals that can eventuate in violence, exhorting his listeners to nip it in the bud or resolve the dispute peaceably. Cutting off violence at its source is Jesus' aretagenic fence around the Law.

He enumerates four cases or application scenarios for his hearers to consider: anger (v.22a), verbal insult (v.22b), past injury where restitution has not been made (vv.23–4), and litigation (v.25). What I am calling an application scenario is used in the first and fifth antitheses on anger and retaliation.[14] It is a set of hypothetical cases or incidents each beginning with "if," that invite the hearers to apply Jesus' teaching to a broad range of situations, suggesting that Jesus does not offer an alternative set of rules but instead digs for principles to guide behavior.

In the antithesis on anger, the scenarios seem to be listed in order of publicness—from anger, the most private, to litigation, the most public. Jesus counsels self-examination and action on the part of the responsible party so that no disciplinary action need be taken. The righteous disciple, whose character we already understand from the Beatitudes, is to take the initiative both within her own heart, in the case of anger, or own mouth, in the case of verbal insult, and to extirpate the emotion or resolve the situation. Although this antithesis begins with murder, it functions as an umbrella for a broad range of interpersonal problems and legal cases. They are united by the perpetrator's responsibility for initiating rectification of the situation, even when, as in the case of anger, the victim may be unaware that she has been injured. The character trait being advocated is not named. It combines self-scrutiny with self-discipline for correcting wrongs one has committed without the intervention of any outside authority, most especially the injured party. The point seems to be that the injured party should not need to seek restitution because the perpetrator seeks to rectify the situation spontaneously. It creates a broad fence around the law against murder, not only to prevent violence but to transform the disciple from one who might murder into one who runs to rectify even minor wrongs she has committed. It puts teeth into the command to irenicism of Ps. 37.37 and Matt. 5.9.

The second antithesis focuses on lust (5.27–30). Again Jesus warns his hearers to take a giant step back from the circumstance that ends in trouble. His fence around the law prohibiting adultery is mind control: "don't even think about it," assuming such a posture is possible.[15] It could be an amplification of Ps. 37.18 and Matt. 5.8.

The next antithesis deals with divorce (5.31–2), which is mentioned again in 19.3–12, in the form of a taunt at Jesus from some Pharisees. While perhaps from a modern standpoint Jesus' opposition to divorce for any reason other than unchastity may appear harsh, it needs to be appreciated in the context of Mishnaic divorce law. A subsequent Matthean text sheds some light on this, so even though the full text of the Mishnaic tractate on divorce, *Gittin*, was not yet in its final form, we know from Matt. 19.7 that written divorce certificates were a requirement and from Matt. 19.3 that grounds for divorce were debated (this accurately reflects *Gittin* 9:10). The phrasing of the question in 19.3—"Is it legal for a man to divorce his wife for any cause?"—inadvertently discloses a further important point of Mishnaic law: initiation of divorce was restricted to men, although in rare cases a woman could sue for divorce through the court.

Proper observance of legal divorce proceedings was extremely important. Divorce itself was an institution designed to protect women from abandonment. A bill of divorce entitled the woman to financial compensation, without which women were financially at risk and prohibited from remarrying.

The debate about the grounds for divorce raised in Matt. 19 points to the vulnerability of women to the whims of men. The two verses in chapter 5 summarize Jesus' teaching on divorce as consonant with that attributed to Shammai, recorded in *Gittin* 9:10 (Neusner 1988, 487). The Mishnah records Hillel as granting divorce for virtually any reason at all, while Shammai protected women against frivolous divorce. Matt. 19.7–8 tells us why Jesus followed Shammai. "[The Pharisees] said to [Jesus], 'Why then did Moses command us to give a certificate of dismissal and to divorce her?' [Jesus] said to them, 'It was because you were so hard-hearted that Moses allowed you to divorce your wives, but from the beginning it was not so.'" The stricter procedure acts as a check on male hardheartedness and flippancy. Jesus' teaching urges compassion for women. If these scenarios are exemplary and meant to stimulate thinking along a broad front, this teaching could suggest compassion for anyone in a dependent position—an application of 5.7, the beatitude on mercy.

The antithesis concerning oaths (5.33–7) is a rather straightforward standard of integrity. Oaths imply a dual standard of truth that Jesus ruled out for those who follow him. Verse 33 assumes that vows to God are taken under oath to assure that they will be acted upon. Forbidding oath-taking suggests that Jesus' concern is not for vows taken under oath but for horizontal dealings among people. "Let your word be 'Yes, Yes' or 'No, No'" raises personal integrity in all dealings to the level of vows to God. It may exegete the standard of righteousness of Matt. 5.6.

The teaching on retaliation (5.38–42) comes from Deut. 19.18–21, concerning the number and integrity of witnesses in capital cases and border disputes. Jesus first gives the general principle, "Do not resist evildoers," then follows it with five application scenarios, recalling the form of the first antithesis on murder, which had four. The first scenario counsels nonresistance to physical assault. The second has to do with litigation. The third focuses on generosity of spirit and time. The last two scenarios in this set exhort charity in giving and lending money. The group of application scenarios spans the gamut from not resisting physical violence to being generous with possessions, and it is not immediately evident that nonresistance to evildoers is the theme that unites them. The Deuteronomy text is a pretext for probing for an unnamed character trait that finds expression in this broad group of attitudes and behaviors. The trait sought implies detachment from one's own body and possessions, regardless of the justice of the case.

Whereas serving the cause of justice and deterrence are the recurrent themes of the Deuteronomy passage, faithfully followed by *Makkot*, where phrases from Deut. 19.19 and 21 are cited, Jesus shows no interest in justice. And Matthew has no compunctions about completely inverting the meaning of the earlier text. His concern is with building a fence around the disciple's character so that she becomes selfless.

The final antithesis (5.43–8) carries the teaching to its pinnacle in the exhortation to the disciples that they can stretch to the perfection of God, whose love extends beyond the just and the righteous to the unjust and the unrighteous.[16] It is one thing for God to send rain on the unjust along with the just. It is another for plain folks to love those who have wronged them. Here Matthew's own community is put to the test. Jesus' teaching goes well beyond the hope and consolation modeled for the righteous by Psalm 37. There (and in the Beatitudes) the disciple is encouraged to try on the demands based on the promise of reward or special privilege in the eyes of God. The antitheses, by contrast, mention only threats of punishment for disobedience (5.20, 22, 26, 29–30).

With Jesus, then, Matthew suggests, there is no characterologically neutral ground. Whereas the hearers of the Sermon perhaps had confidently considered themselves persons of good character, Jesus presents everyday interpersonal interactions and feelings as issues of paramount importance, liable to divine judgment. Hearers of the Sermon are beset with new standards of self-assessment. Who has not experienced anger, lust, hardness of heart? One's every feeling is suddenly under God's scrutiny. The rhetoric aims at making the hearers uncomfortable.

The final injunction, "Be perfect, therefore, as your heavenly Father is perfect" (Matt. 5.48), concludes and perhaps sums up the antitheses. They are not so much rules as models for emulation. What I have called application scenarios are hypothetical situations by means of which the disciple can begin to think through what an alternative attitude or behavior would be for any given situation. Jesus is offering an alternative interior purity consisting of a dense concentration of demanding character traits: aggressive self-scrutiny, self-control, compassion, integrity, selflessness and, finally, love of enemies, traits that are essentially limitless in application. Except for the teaching on lust, the antitheses all deal with situations in which the individual is possibly imposed upon, experiences hurt, inconvenience, or some sort of discomfort, and would naturally respond in a self-protective manner or to reestablish a prior satisfactory state that has been disturbed by some intrusion. Jesus' teaching in each case elaborates a basic theme. Disciples are called to rise above self-gratification even when wronged; and in the teaching on lust, they are to rise above self-gratification when it is not to rectify an injustice or dissatisfaction but to gratify desire.

The application scenarios stimulate thinking along a broad range of issues so that the disciples will not only pledge their loyalty to Jesus but will also begin to engage in the self-examination necessary for pursuit of the ideals of discipleship on their own. The foundation of Jesus' ethic is imitation of the perfection of their heavenly Father; the basis of its method is self-criticism.

Negative Models of Discipleship

The second section of the Sermon seeks to woo disciples away from Tannaitic righteousness in matters of interpersonal conduct and to build an alternative structure that could be internalized and applied independently of legal authorities. The third section (6.1–7.6) employs a different rhetorical format. Instead of antitheses to specific Tannaitic or biblical laws, Jesus offers his own admonitions and warnings, which touch on issues of etiquette, detailing the styles of meekness and modesty that were enumerated in the Beatitudes and that extend character ethics beyond the reach of biblical Law. The rhetoric first identifies negative role models to be shunned and is followed by positive models for emulation.

The negative models are presented in three groups of injunctions, each beginning "be careful not to" or simply "do not." The first group deals with visible acts of piety (6.1–18), the second with concern for one's life and possessions (6.19–34), and the third with self-scrutiny (7.1–6). Whereas most of the issues raised by the second section of the Sermon had to do with responding to a sense of personal injury, the third section deals with self-presentation and the nonverbal communication that accompanies routine activities, both religious and secular. Other versions of Judaism made no distinction between sacred and secular either.

The first three scenarios urge modesty in piety, encouraging what might be called a low religiosity profile. He begins with almsgiving. The fifth antithesis (5.42) touched on almsgiving from the perspective of generosity as a norm. Here (6.1–4) Jesus seems to assume the generosity of the pious and turns to how it is to be undertaken. He warns that it must be done unobtrusively, and he does not hesitate to point a critical finger (despite his own teaching on the subject in 7.1–4) at those who seem to be deaf to this teaching. The point of almsgiving is not, as Aristotle taught, to seek honor among one's peers so as to gain stature in the community, but to be rewarded by God. And to this end, philanthropy must be quiet.

The theme of quiet piety continues in the second scenario (6.5–15), on prayer and forgiveness. *M. Berachot*, which deals with liturgical etiquette and obligation, does not stress quiet piety. On the contrary, if one recited the *Sh'ma* (a standard first-century practice) too softly, there was a question as to whether one had fulfilled the biblical command (Deut. 6.7) to recite it (*Berachot* 2.3). Again, at least from a Tannaitic perspective, the Matthean charge of hypocrisy is probably not one that most pious Jews would recognize in themselves. They are merely observing the Law to the best of their ability. Jesus is presenting a different approach to piety, one that shifts attention from the act itself to the tone or style that accompanies it. Here again, we run into different interpretations of obedience. Halachic (Law-observant) Jews of the period took biblical precepts to require literal compliance. The *Sh'ma* (Deut. 6.4–9; 11.13–21; Num. 15.37–41) led to concrete practices like phyllacteries, *mezuzzah*, fringes, and recitation of the text itself, each of which required public display in order to be faithfully fulfilled. One can imagine, then, the confusion aroused in those who found themselves the targets of advocates of quiet piety.

As with the teaching on almsgiving, here a positive model follows the negative so that there is no ambiguity as to what constitutes proper behavior. The Lord's Prayer, with its parallels to both the *Amidah* (perhaps related to the shortened form of "the prayer" discussed in *M. Berachot*) and the *Kaddish*, perhaps models piety by its brevity. The teaching on love of enemies comes in for a reprise (6.14–5), perhaps a tacit recognition of the strenuousness of the demands made upon Jesus' disciples.

Fasting practices exemplify the final scenario on modest piety. Fasting during the period of the second Temple and after was quite common. It took two forms, one public and one private. Public communal fasting (following the practices described in Leviticus and Jonah) was practiced in times of need and in preparation for apocalyptic revelations. It was a highly visible, publicly supported community undertaking to pray for rain in the autumn and to seek rescue in times of public stress. Personal and private fasting atoned for sin. Individual fasting followed or accompanied personal trauma, or was a private expression of public concerns, and probably increased after the destruction of the Temple.[17] Perhaps after the fall of the Temple, fasting became the province of an elite class of ascetics. Excessive fasting came in for rabbinic censure (Montefiore, 1938, 445, 528). Matthean recommendations on fasting seem to stand in this tradition. At a time when fasting as a sign of mourning for the Temple may also have been a patriotic expression of defiance of Roman power, Matthean teaching may have smacked of betrayal of national purpose in the eyes of Jewish nationalists.

The second set of negative models (6.19–34) returns to "secular" subject matter: acquisition of worldly goods. The unifying theme of the section, disdain for possessions, echoes a similar idea found in Ps. 37 regarding sufficiency of food in the face of danger from adversaries, as noted above. Just as in the previous section, where Jesus promoted selflessness even in the face of injustice, here he casts aside concern for worldly goods. In light of the eschatological context within which Matthew wrote, the reasons behind this contempt for possessions are surprisingly uneschatological. His argument is not that the reign of God is at hand and treasures will be useless. The first reason given for not storing up treasures is that even under normal conditions they do not last; theft and decay take their toll. It is not worth putting effort into acquiring things that do not endure. But the more important reason for avoiding materialism is that accumulating goods distracts one from God, "for where your treasure is, there your heart will be also" (6.21). Self-absorption is a waste of precious time in God's beautiful world, and important problems have a way of finding us anyway. We do not need to add to our problems by worrying about trivialities like our clothes, our bodies [our weight], or storing things away in barns [our pension]. Against these enduring temptations, the evangelist, echoing the psalmist before him (Ps. 37.4), encourages hearers to "strive first for the kingdom of God and his righteousness" (Matt. 6.33).

In the previous section on the Sermon we concluded that the underlying orientation toward which the scenarios point is detachment from taking personal offense, or, stated inversely, cultivation of a weak sense of self-importance. We see the same theme recurring here through detachment from self-important postures and positions in society and possessions.

The final negative model is the shortest of this group (7.1–5). It is not a blanket prohibition against judging others. Certainly Matthew does not hesitate to judge others liberally throughout his gospel. Rather, it is an exhortation to self-criticism, a position in line with the above interpretation of the theme unifying the antitheses. Chapter 7 verses 1–5 confronts the hearer with the norm of self-honesty. Under these conditions the foibles of others appear in a different light. This theme returns in the Golden Rule of verse 12.

Verse 6 is enigmatic and not obviously connected to its context. Rhetorically it fits with the prohibitions of chapter 6, beginning with the "do not" that characterizes the teachings of the chapter. Its content, however, is not a prohibition but a warning, similar to the maxims that characterize 7.7–20. On the reading of the opposition of Matthean to Tannaitic piety developed here, the metaphors of dogs and swine could be a play on the frequent rabbinic references to gentiles, with the Tannaim themselves now cast in the role of those beyond the pale of God's people. Matthew's denunciation of Jews who failed to respond positively to his new piety was unnuanced, as is evident in 3.10, 12; 10.15, 16–8; 11.20–24; 12.42, and so forth. On this reading, then, 7.6 brings out the force of the self-critical stance of 7.1–5.[18] Rhetorically this verse presses the disciples to huddle ever closer together, to conceive of themselves, perhaps understandably, as the persecuted righteous; it drives a moral wedge between them and their opponents. Despite his embrace of the gentile mission, which flies in the face of Pharisaic separatism, Matthew ends up reinscribing it in a new guise.

The teaching of the Sermon ends here. The remainder (7.7–27) is parenesis. It consists of encouragement (7.7–11) reminiscent of that following the Beatitudes (5.13–6), maxims reminiscent of *Abot* (vv.12–4), and warnings and threats of punishment (vv.15–27).

ASSESSMENT

The aretegenic force of the Sermon on the Mount can be characterized as follows. In the first part, the evangelist presents Jesus' hearers with a notion of the privileged people of God that challenges the Jewish doctrine of election by appealing to scripture. He invites his hearers to consider themselves among the privileged by becoming his followers, and he prepares them for the suffering they will endure. He reassures them that they and their mission are of paramount importance, that they are capable of accomplishing it, and that through their lives God will be glorified. In this process Jesus offers his followers a sense of importance and dignity that comes from cultivating the sort of inner purity that requires great restraint (nonretaliation, love of enemies, peacemaking, modest piety) under stress.

Echoing the promises of Psalm 37, Matthew creates a determined *esprit de corps* among the beleaguered disciples to encourage them to hold to the new piety, which would triumph as the way for Jews and gentiles to live as God's privileged. They are bound together by the rightness of their cause against the perverseness of their opponents. One can readily envision a crowd caught up in the verve of this vision.

As the details of what is entailed by this blessedness unfold, group pressure holds followers together as Jesus takes them deeper into the standards of character and behavior he requires. One can imagine members of the audience flinching as issues of anger, lust, compassion, and possessions hit home. There is something for everyone here, and the whole, while causing discomfort, also offers an opportunity to break with the past and be bound together in the new community. Group pressure perhaps keeps some weaker members from quietly slipping away.

Matthean righteousness accumulated: in some cases it transformed character traits found in scripture and Tannaitic and pre-Tannaitic texts or added some not found there, and it proffered the whole as an alternative to contemporary purity. Matthean righteousness focused on the manner and style with which religious and legal obligations and all interpersonal dealings are to be carried out. It viewed personal deportment, interpersonal interactions, and even legal transactions (e.g., divorce) in ethical terms. Understatedness, self-control, irenicism, humility, personal integrity, compassion, unstinting generosity, self-scrutiny, assertiveness in rectifying misdeeds, and detachment from possessions and all forms of self-aggrandizement constitute the new purity for those who would be perfect after the model of God. To counter the sense of being overwhelmed by these demands of righteousness, the evangelist interspersed the teaching with words of reassurance and encouragement (5.13–6; 7.7–12) as well as threats and warnings against failure or desertion of the cause (5.20; 7.24–7).

Matthew presents the new righteousness as an accessible teaching, although not a facile one. It is propounded with numerous examples and instances so that hearers may begin to apply the new standards of conduct to themselves and extrapolate from those given to others. Although the piety it opposed was based on a system of legal obligations, the righteousness espoused in the Sermon does not assume that legalism *per se* is problematic. The core of Matthean piety is proactive, not reactive. It entices readers with an understanding of righteousness grounded in other-centeredness—an orientation to the needs of others that sets their welfare above one's own. Matthew's fence around the Law confronts hearers with this stringent standard for self-examination. Other-centeredness is to be cultivated in every aspect of life; it destroys any division between civil and religious obligation. God demands other-centeredness in everything.

Some will object that Matthean virtue is interiorized and individualized. While it is true that Matthew challenges his audience to internalize Jesus' teachings, one must appreciate that Matthew was taking a system that stressed formal obligations and pointing to the deeper understanding of self that behaviors actually express. The question of obedience to God goes far beyond what one is to do—it crafts what kind of person one is to be. Matthew turned attention from correct performance to the agent's self-concept, from behavior to character.

Notes

1. E. P. Sanders distinguishes full sectarianism, which carried with it soteriological exclusivism, from the stance of parties or groups that were more interested in group solidarity and distinctiveness, concluding that the Pharisees were a party but not a sect (1990, 236–42).

2. Tractate *Yoma* in the *Mishnah* may shed light on the Essenes' concerns. Although the *Mishnah* had reached its final form at the end of the second Christian century, there can be little doubt that *Yoma* meant to capture events from the late second Temple period, at least for posterity, if not in hopes of restoration (Neusner 1988, 265–79). And given the negative view of the events recorded there, there is little reason not to trust the report, at least in its general outline. *Yoma* recalls the scene within the precincts of the Temple in prepara-

tion for the Day of Atonement. It vividly attests to the illiteracy and ill-preparedness of some of the high priests, who had to be carefully instructed, exhorted, and guarded to remain sexually pure for their duties (1:3–6). It also attests to confusion and disorganization concerning proper execution of the rites, to the point of someone breaking his foot in a rush to see who would clear the ashes from the altar (2:1–2). And it reports petty competition and turf battles among individuals who would not share their skills and knowledge concerning the rites (3:11).

3. "Tannaim" is the term used to refer to teachers whose opinions are recorded in the *Mishnah,* who lived between 10 and 200 C.E. They are usually identified in pairs within five generations. Pharisees were doubtless included among their number, and beliefs and opinions probably overlapped among various teachers.

4. See Meier for a review of recent opinion (1976, 7–9, 14–21). I tend to concur with Ulrich Luz that the redactor was probably a Jewish Christian working within a Jewish Christian community committed to the gentile mission (1989, 84–7).

5. One can only be a hypocrite if one betrays one's own principles; one is not a hypocrite if one betrays another's standards of faith and life.

6. E. P. Sanders has pointed out that membership in the people of God was based on birth or full conversion. While moral conduct was certainly presupposed by covenant membership, it was never the means of entry into that status, which was a gracious gift (1977, 147–82).

7. A liturgical construction of psalmic hymnody from a later period illustrates the issue. The Babylonian Talmud *(Berachot* 4b) recommends that Ps. 84.4–5, and 114.15 prefaced to Ps. 145, be recited as a complete liturgical unit three times daily. The Talmud is regulating its recitation, not constructing the unit, which may have already been in use. It is rare in Jewish liturgy to find intentionally constructed units of this type, although the *Sh'ma* itself, in use in the first century, is a similar construction. This is the only Psalm text that comes in for such frequent recitation. Each of the three prefaced verses is a beatitude beginning with *ashrey/makarios.* They proclaim the privileged of God as the nation that dwells in God's house and belongs to God, and they form an introduction that clearly establishes their redactor's "Israelology": Israel is the people of God. Matthew also spells out his ecclesiology in the Beatitudes: the humble, suffering, and meek are the privileged of God. Since it is unlikely that Jewish liturgy included the Psalm texts at this time, it would be incorrect to suggest that there is a direct confrontation going on through these texts. But it is clear that first-century Jews defined the people of God as birthright Israel and legally constituted converts and that Matthew is proposing a different doctrine of election. Perhaps the community to which Matthew's text gave rise directly or indirectly spurred the Jewish response.

8. Benjamin Helfgott argued that the Tannaim recognized the threat to the Jewish doctrine of election posed by Christianity and responded in some cases with stony silence or by reasserting the Jewish doctrine (1954, 135).

9. For a history of the argument about the dogmatic dimensions of the Sermon from Carl Stange and Gerhard Kittel through Hans Windisch and others, see Warren Kissinger (1975, Part I).

10. Robert Guelich argues that the Beatitudes are christological in focus (1982). The blessings bestowed are evidence of the inauguration of the reign of God in the ministry of Jesus. But this ignores the aura of expectation of the Kingdom that pervades the gospel and most of the parables. Even granting that Jesus' ministry inaugurates the Kingdom, the suffering endured by his followers turned them to the future for their ultimate vindication.

11. The structural analysis followed here is closest to that suggested by Dale C. Allison Jr. (1987). It deviates from Allison's analysis on the following points. Allison distinguishes 6.1–18 (the triad on almsgiving, prayer, and fasting) from 6.19–7.12 (on storing treasure), taking the first as the Christian cult, the second as social teaching. I take 6.1–7.6 as a unit based on the rhetorical style of prohibitions, dividing the whole into three groups: 6.1–18, 19–34, and 7.1–6, as will be explained below. I attach 7.7–11 to the conclusion of the Sermon.

12. Guelich has argued that the Beatitudes have been reshaped by Matthew to bring them in line with Isa. 61.1, 2. The argument turns on Matthew's focus on the poor, the broken-hearted, and mourners—a strategy that stresses people's conditions rather than their ethical accomplishments. Guelich's interest is in de-emphasizing the ethical tone often associated with the Beatitudes and to stress instead the soteriological dimension of Jesus' ministry. Rather than seeing the traits of humility, modesty, and righteousness as entrance requirements for the reign of God, Guelich sees the Beatitudes as the fulfillment of the biblical promise of salvation for those who are impoverished and helpless (110). This distinction between ethics and promise is, however, a peculiarly Protestant invention, alien to Matthean piety and perhaps influenced by recent developments in liberation theology. Matthew is interested in underscoring the promise of salvation to those who are pursuing the new righteousness yet receive only contempt from their friends, neighbors, and family. But he is also interested in expounding the new righteousness, which he believes to be the only righteousness worth pursuing. Ironically, the emphasis on ethics in the Beatitudes that Guelich seeks to soften is precisely the point that irritated Matthew's Jewish opponents.

13. The exuberance expressed in this passage seems to be in tension with the quiet piety espoused in 6.1–18. But it is a paradox, or perhaps an irony. Precisely the understatedness that Jesus preaches renders his teaching worthy of proclaiming abroad.

14. Robert C. Tannehill has identified the antithesis on retaliation (Matt. 5.39b–42) as illustrated by a series of "focal instances," which are stated forcefully and concisely yet are open-ended, with no clear limit, and leave room for complex situations. They forcefully call attention to one aspect of a situation to stimulate the hearer's thinking in a specific direction, to stimulate the moral imagination by shocking the hearer into examining the situation from a new perspective (1970).

15. A passage in *Abot* may provide some parallel to this fence around adultery, although the sin is not named. The text is in *Abot* 1:5, cited in the name of Yose ben Yohanan of Jerusalem, a pre-Tannaitic teacher:

> Let your house be wide open. And seat the poor at your table. And don't talk too much with the woman. (He meant his wife, all the more so is the rule to be applied to the wife of one's fellows.) In this regard did sages say, "So long as a man talks too much with a woman, (1) he brings trouble on himself, (2) wastes time better spent on studying Torah, and (3) ends up an heir of Gehenna." (Neusner 1988, 673)

The text is terse and has been through layers of redacting. Yose's intention is not clear to us. Neither is the relationship between hospitality to the poor and the dangers of too much conversation with women. Nor is it clear who is meant by "his wife." Is it one's own wife under all circumstances? the woman of the house while entertaining? What is clear, however, is that too much conversation with women, especially married women, can lead to trouble. Torah study protects against what could lead to adultery. In a culture that considered one's own wife taboo essentially half her life, controlling sexual desire was a central concern. As misogynist as the text sounds on first reading, it may have hoped to protect women, especially given the harshness of the biblical punishment for adultery.

16. Careful readers will note that Matthew did not cite scripture precisely. The thesis statements of the antitheses beginning "You have heard that it was said" are usually citations of scripture. In the case of the last antithesis, however, Matthew cites "love your neighbor" from Lev. 19.18 and adds to it "and hate your enemy" as if it were part of the scripture verse, which it is not. Guelich suggests that this interpolation was mandated by the following verse (5.44a, "love your enemies") in order to make the starkness of the antithesis work rhetorically (227).

17. According to the *Mishnah,* during the Second Temple period fasting was observed by the community on special holy days, for rain, and by individuals on Mondays and Thursdays (cf. Luke 18.12). It involved abstinence not only from food and drink during the day (for minor fasts) but also from work, bathing, anointing, wearing shoes, and sexual activity (Neusner 1988, 308; *Ta'anit,* 1:6) and included anointing with ashes (308–9; *Ta'anit,* 2:1). Haircutting and washing of clothing is also prohibited in certain instances (310; *Ta'anit,* 2:7). The fasting practices, with the exception of abstention from food and drink, also applied to mourners. Prayers for rain, accompanied by fasts, were the responsibility of the whole community, led by the priests. If after a specified period of time the prayers were not answered, the restrictions were intensified and extended.

18. Given Matthew's own judgmental attitude toward those who disagreed with him, he would condemn himself were he examined for hypocrisy!

PART III

Patristic Voices

*O*nce past the explosive events of the first century, Christians set about transforming the various environments in which they found themselves. Christianity spread in both Greek- and Latin-speaking lands. Neoplatonism replaced Judaism as the dominant intellectual mindset within and against which Christianity had to find its voice. Paganism became its main rival.

By the fourth century, Christianity had spread so widely that men showing leadership ability were being pressed into episcopal service from metropolis to hamlet. These bishops were the primary theologians, pastors and administrators of the church. Their thought was shaped partly by theological controversies but equally by the experience of being local pastors responsible for assisting former pagans, rather than former Jews, become Christians. In this regard, the patristic age takes its inspiration more from Paul than from Matthew.

Bishops from western Asia and northern Africa were particularly vibrant at this time. This section examines three of them: Athanasius of Alexandria and Basil of Caesarea, both of whom wrote in Greek, and Augustine of Hippo, who wrote in Latin. These bishops of learning and broad vision were able to think the Christian faith through carefully, with one eye trained on the spiritual needs of their parishioners and the other on the church's interaction with the dominant culture, for they flourished as the church inherited the mantle of empire. That is, they believed that God's work in Jesus Christ provided a firm foundation for a moral society. Indeed, they understood the unpacking of Christian doctrines as *paideia*, much as Plato's philosophy had understood itself after Athens's military debacle at the hands of Sparta in the Peloponnesian War which revealed the cracks in the moral and religious foundation of that society. Theologians had not only to explain Christian claims but also to create a morally coherent culture that would educate and form persons for the change of ages happening in their own day.

Although differences that would eventually separate East from West begin to appear early, one feature central to their age marks them all: they agree that God respects us. This respect is evident in our being in the image of God, in our creation by the Word of God, and in our intelligence, all of which teach us of God himself. Further, they insist that this identity is the key to our turn to God, the basis of our salvation. Turning to the beauty, truth, and goodness of God is an expression of our proper strength, dignity, and power.

4

Defeating the Fear of Death

Athanasius of Alexandria

THE BISHOP AS CATECHIST

In a slender volume on light as a basic image in patristic thought, Jaroslav Pelikan noted the morally transforming power of salvation for Athanasius (1962, 95–111). "'In thy light do we see light' (Ps. 36.9b) meant to Athanasius that the light of God, which had shone forth in Jesus Christ, had penetrated the darkness of the world and had transformed men by bringing them salvation" (95). As long as we note that the transformation wrought by salvation is not automatic or forensic but concrete, really taking place through formation of a new self-concept grounded in knowing the Father of Jesus Christ, we will understand Athanasius well. Charles Kannengiesser also noted Athanasius's pastoral concern as he catechized the educated among his flock through *De Incarnatione Verbi* (1988).

The evangelical urgency that Kannengiesser notes in Athanasius applied especially to Alexandrians. In the fourth century Christianity still enjoyed the bloom of youth, energizing and refreshing converts from paganism. Athanasius expected spreading reports of God's venture to transform the minds and lives of individuals by quite literally lifting them out of paganism one by one.

To ferret out Athanasian aretology, I shall rely principally on Athanasius's duplex treatise *Contra Gentes* (*CG*) and *De Incarnatione Verbi* (*DI*) (1971). This work is especially helpful, since it was written before the bishop became embroiled in rancorous controversies. Here we hear Athanasius speaking pastorally, expounding a basic theme of patristic thought: Christianity returns us to the beauty, truth, and goodness of God, and to our proper immortal and incorruptible identity. I will also use his *Third Discourse Against the Arians* (*Ar. III*) as it explains this vision (1986).[1]

THE PERSISTENT LURE OF PAGANISM

The paired treatises narrate the story of the ruin and rescue of the human race from its pristine creation, to its incremental dissolution, through its transformation, gradual ascent from evil, and repair under divine tutelage. The flow of the story forms an inverted bell curve. The *CG* is reminiscent of the lock-step deterioration of the human estate in Jean-Jacques Rousseau's eighteenth-century *Discourse on the Origins of Human Inequality*. For Rousseau, sadly, the rescue operation had yet to commence, while Athanasius was sure that God's plan to save us from ourselves was already operational in Christ.

The *CG* divides into three sections. Chapters 1–29, the bulk of the piece, is a moral argument against pagan claims. Chapters 30–4 lay out the psychology that can be enlisted to fight the problem. Finally, chapters 35–47 point to the ordered aesthetic of creation, which invites us to another way of thinking and living. It becomes the basis of the christology developed in the *Ar. III*.

Athanasius analyzes the human problem as a loss of dignity and self-respect caused by wandering away from God. Dignity, which is required to direct human life rightly, was buried, lost, and forgotten through generations of fumbling around in the dark. The good life—that is, the virtuous life—was trashed beneath indignities that misused body, mind, and spirit. In this we disrespected ourselves. The problem began when we forgot who God is. This led to losing touch with who *we* really are: creatures destined for eternity in light of who created us. This loss led to idolatry, which in turn destroyed human dignity and turned human intercourse into a jungle of violence, corruption, and deceit. In short, civilization was on the verge of collapse. And God saw that it was not good at all.

The tragedy commences with people forgetting or turning away from God; it culminates in murder, adultery, and war. The psychology at work in Athanasius's etiologic tale of how things frayed so badly is telling. God created us in great dignity, Athanasius tells the reader, able to know both how things really are and, therefore, how best to live, yet free to live imprudently. Our best self is blessed and graced by God so that one can

> rejoice and converse with God, living an idyllic and truly blessed and immortal life. For having no obstacle to the knowledge of the divine, he continuously contemplates by his purity the image of the Father, God the Word, in whose image he was made, and is filled with admiration when he grasps [God's] providence towards the universe. He is superior to sensual things and all bodily impressions, and by the power of his mind clings to the divine and intelligible realities in heaven. (7; chap. 2)

Distracted by things closer to hand, however, we become confused, lose the power we received from God to live a properly ordered life, and clutch at evanescent pleasures. Eventually the threat of death, through which we will lose these bodily pleasures, takes hold of us, and fear begins to control our thinking (11; 3). Instead of focusing on God, we begin to reify our fears, giving them a life of their own. This created the basis for polytheism, the creation of images to catch the imagination of wandering minds. Paganism encouraged the imitation of false, immoral gods. Self-degradation emerged from the deification of human, animal, and imagined creatures and animate and inanimate objects, both living and dead forms. These evil imaginings set a bad example, for they were associated with contumacious conduct. They spread rape, incest, bodily mutilation, adultery, drunkenness, and physical violence (33; 11). Idolatry, Athanasius suggests, is stimulated by fears of death and the loss of physical pleasure but ends up engendering moral turpitude:

> For those who hate the adulterer who assaults their own wives are not ashamed to deify the exponents of adultery; and though they do not have intercourse with their sisters, they worship those who do. Although they admit that pederasty is evil, they venerate those who are accused of it; and they do not blush to attribute to those they call gods things in which the laws do not permit men to indulge. (35–7; 12)

In short, paganism is born of despair that reproduces itself.

Athanasius's favorite form of argument is *a posteriori*. He infers truth from its practical results. It is plain to him that gods who promote debauchery by example must be false, while the one who promotes peace and harmony cries out to be confessed as true and good: "For acts must correspond to natures, so that the actor is known from his effect, and the action can be known from its nature" (45; 16). That we become what we know is at the heart of his concern to point out the socially destructive consequences of turning to the creature rather than the creator. Instigated by forgetting or turning from God—in whose image we are made and who stands as moral exemplar to us—the debauched exploits of the gods degrade us:

> all without exception polluted and were polluted. They were polluted by committing these murders, and they polluted their own temples by the smoke of such sacrifices. From these practices evil has spread in abundance among men. For seeing their demons rejoicing in what they did, they straightway imitated their gods by committing such crimes, thinking they were doing the right thing by imitating what they supposed to be superior beings. Hence men gave way to murder and infanticide and all kinds of licentiousness. (69; 25)

The *CG* confronts readers with the debauchery and immorality characteristic of paganism in order to squelch any lingering desires readers might have for it. The details make the reader cringe and distance herself from the temptations that could never be far off in Alexandria.

Having boldly set forth the problem, the second section of the *CG* explains the psychology by which the mind may be healed from this chronic debilitating affliction, for our wandering from God must be reversible. As Athanasius tells his reader from the outset and repeats regularly, the Christian faith is therapeutic because it leads followers back to the Father of Christ.[2] And since it produces goodness, it must be true.

Athanasian psychology, like patristic thought generally, demarcates humans from brute animals by our ability to think and to make sound judgments (85; 31).[3] Intelligence draws a direct line from God to us. This homologeneity between God and us is the basis of one's proper dignity and self-respect. We can operate as thoughtfully as God, and our destiny is to abide with God. Properly ordered thinking should wean people from devotion to debasing fantasies of the imagination that impugn their intelligence, thereby demeaning God's gifts. Paganism is an act of disrespect for both ourselves and God.

Here we have the basic psychology of the patristic age: human dignity comes from our relatedness to God, as given by God in creation. Unlike in the modern view, our dignity is grounded not in that which individuates us from others or demonstrates our self-sufficiency but in that which links us to God by virtue of his grace. Human dignity is seen in our connectedness to God, not in our autonomy. What is required is that one understand the objective state of things correctly: who God is and who we are as a consequence of his love, power, and respect for us.

Intelligence, itself an expression of our dignity and connection to God, guides the senses through its powers of memory. That we can remember the past and carefully think things through enables us to look beyond the vicissitudes of this life. Dreams, in which the mind acts apart from the body, also suggest that the self is more than a body; the uplifted part of the self speaks of its immortality (89–93; 32–3). Intelligence governs the body's natural inclinations, which run in opposite directions and can be destructive, much as the creator symmetrizes and orders the natural opposing forces of nature harmoniously. The power to order one's life functions like the divine principle of order (*Logos*) that suffuses creation.[4]

Athanasius builds the reader's strength of character, indeed nobility, by linking human *logismoi* with the divine *Logos*. He concludes that "the soul has an idea of the contemplation of God, and is its own path, taking the knowledge and understanding of God the Word not from outside but from itself" (93; 33). Augustine would make this idea—that knowledge of God comes from recognizing the self as the image of God—central to his thought. Like Augustine, Athanasius believed that whoever strays from this self-understanding abandons her best and strongest self, becoming vulnerable to self-destructive forces run amok (93; 34).

Athanasius blamed social and moral deterioration on our forgetting our deep linkage with God and consequently developing disordered thought patterns. To set up the cure, he points out that we are equipped to know God properly through our intelligence. In the last section of the *CG*, he carefully explains the divine orderliness evident in creation, with which we are out of tune and to which we must be returned.

The beauty of creation (*Logos*) overcomes the obstacles divine transcendence and invisibility pose to knowing God. Divine wisdom and power can be inferred from the orderliness and harmony of nature (97; 35). By describing antagonistic forces of nature harmoniously balanced against one another, Athanasius points to the divine aesthetic, which contrasts sharply with the anarchic picture of reality given earlier. He points to God's ability to reorder destructive forces to a constructive end. Each created thing occupies its rightful place within the whole; each aspect of the creation contributes its gift—heat, light, nourishment, rest, and so on—for the proper maintenance of all. The classical aesthetic of balance, order, and respect among potentially destructive forces like water, fire, and darkness speaks of "a superior being and master, who joined them together and to whom the elements themselves yield and obey as slaves their lord" (101; 37).

The beauty and intelligence of God set the tone against which pagan debauchery and violence protrude ever more shamefully and needlessly, given that we were created to live in the ordered beauty of God. Through the long description, the reader is gently cradled by the confidence of knowing that God's intelligent beauty and order rule creation. Yet at the same time, the reader is nudged to use her own intellect accordingly. The rhetorical dynamic shows disobedience or flaunting of the divinely established norm of reconciliation, peace, and harmony to be a source of collective human embarrassment.

The middle section of the *CG* offers a completely positive picture of benevolent leadership of the natural world by the Word of God. This invites the reader to live intelligently, in harmony with the created order, and to extend its peace and tranquillity into the social sphere, where human freedom holds sway. Indeed, Athanasius sees God's concern for the human situation as the heart of the matter: "the . . . Father of Christ . . . through . . . his own Word . . . guides and orders the universe for our salvation" (111; 40).

Athanasius's rhetorical strategy aims to encourage. After bringing his reader to blush at paganism's disrespect for God's creation in the beginning of the work, he informs the reader that God is not angry, disappointed, or vengeful, but simply eager to return us to ourselves—for he ordered the whole universe for our benefit (113–5; 41). By reordering our minds in harmony with the intelligent beauty of God's creation, we can return to our true selves. Rhetorically, the dynamic of the treatise appeals only to our self-respect. We shall discuss the alternative way of life under the leadership of God's Word when we turn to Athanasian christology as developed fully in the *Ar. III*.

CURING A DISORDERED MIND

Having descended to the depths of human dissipation, and presented the norm to which we should be conformed through God's Word, in the second treatise Athanasius turns to God's strategy for solving the problem. Against imaginary and dissolute gods, God again marshals his Word, whom the reader now recognizes as the true source of her identity. God's intelligence, instantiated in the incarnate Logos, now reveals immediate knowledge of God and true knowledge of ourselves, leading us in a radically different direction through actions that model the truth: love, compassion, personal integrity, and genuine care.

God saves us from ourselves by renewing us in his image, reforming our minds, and shaping our actions to their proper end (*DI* 137; 1). Athanasius pictures God as wrapped up in love for us. So much did God care for us that he gave us special grace at creation to enable us to share in his beauty and live eternally (141; 3). When we scuttled the gift and became disordered of mind, we naturally began to suffer the consequences of the loss of divine grace: corruption of the body at death and the loss of the possibility of resurrection in the future (143–7: 4–5). Athanasius never presents the two-pronged result of corruption and permanent death as punishment meted out by an angry God. God's respect for us never wavers.

Now, rather than be roused to anger, God responds with a profusion of love and compassion. Rather than teach us obedience through a display of authority and power, God acts like a parent wishing to model excellent behavior for children (149; 6). God is so moved by our unhappiness at the consequences of our rejection of grace that he takes it upon himself to undo the suffering and restore us. Since the source of our distress came through perverting our God-given intelligence, it is requisite that the capacity for an ordered life be returned to us. And here the caring dimension of God's strategy on our behalf is not separated from the ordering capacity: "our own transgression called forth the mercy of the Word, so that the Lord came even to us and appeared among men. For we were the cause of his incarnation, and for our salvation he had compassion to the extent of being born and revealed in a body" (143; 4). Athanasius painstakingly points out how important displaying goodness, compassion, and mercy were to God in taking this matter in hand (147; 6). The reader cannot help but contrast God's course of action with the very different concerns of the pagan gods described in the *CG*.

The circumstances called for dramatic action to straighten us out and reorient us to God. To this end, according to Athanasius, the *Logos* took a body, a pure body, and surrendered it to death. By raising Christ back to life the Father shows us that bodily corruption has been overcome. Thus, the fear of death and corruption that fueled paganism was extirpated from human hearts. Christ's death and resurrection show us the hope of our own future, thereby destroying the fear we had acquired from clinging to physical pleasures.

Athanasius, of course, does not distinguish among the Incarnation, the cross, and Christ's resurrection as scholastic theology later would. Having the one who himself need not die take a mortal body, undergo death, rise again, and ascend to heaven shows us in a concrete historical event that God has restored incorruptibility and immortality to us: "God became human that we might become divine" (269; 54). Yet this restoration is not the whole story. Rather, immortality and incorruption are the point of entry in a display of God's love that so concentrates the mind that it succeeds in weaning us from one way of life to another: "when the race of men . . . had descended to corruption, God the Word of the all-good Father did not neglect them, but effaced the death which had fallen upon them by the offering of his own body, and corrected their negligence by his teaching, and reformed all men's estate by his own power" (157; 10). God's respect for us shines clearly through his actions.

The Incarnation, cross, and resurrection teach us to know the Father so that we realize that without knowing God our existence is pointless; we sink to the most animal level of our being (163; 12). Although creation itself bespeaks divine providence, we neglected to take proper note of this and, degrading ourselves, sank into sin. So God gave the law and sent us prophets and saints, "holy instruction [not just for the Jews but] for the whole world about the knowledge of God and the conduct of one's soul" (163; 12). But this strategy failed. Despite human resistance to the knowledge of God, God persevered, finally saving us from self-destruction through the hope offered by Christ.

For Athanasius, Christ's story is not simply the gift of hope. It is an effective means of severing us from the idols, demons, animal sacrifices, magic, and astrology that we think make us happy, "in order that, understanding through such grace the image, I mean the Word of the Father, and recognizing the Maker, [men] might live a happy and truly blessed life" (161; 11).

Christ as the gateway to knowledge of the Father is a major theme of this dual treatise.[5] The point of the Incarnation is "in order that through it men might be able once more to know him" (165; 13). The Father's goal is to reclaim us by renewing our misshapen minds, which cling to immediate gratification. The reclamation effort is not simply to regain our loyalty; it is also to reorient us to who we really are: "the Word of God came in his own person, in order that as he is the image of his Father, he might be able to restore man who is in the image" (167; 13). The incarnate Logos shows us that we prodigally squandered the Father's gift of intelligence, in which we are like him. Like a good teacher, who "condescends to teach by simpler means those who cannot profit by more advanced things" (169; 15), the Incarnation brought God down to eye-level: "the Word of God took to himself a body and lived as a man among men, and took the senses of all men, in order that those who supposed that God was in corporeal things might understand the truth from the works which the Lord did through the actions of his body, and through him might take cognizance of the Father" (171; 15). And again, "For this reason he was born and appeared as a man and died and rose again, weakening and overshadowing by his own works those of all men who ever existed, in order that from wherever men were attracted he might lift them up and teach them his true Father" (171–3; 15).

Christ's life and ministry are equally salutary. Forgiveness of sin is another tactic—a way of finding the lost and teaching the world about the Father (167; 14). Likewise, the miracles surrounding Jesus' birth and his healings of the congenitally ill reveal his earnestness in wanting to help us, "in order that those who were unwilling to know him by his providence and government of the universe, yet by the works done through the body might know the Word of God . . . and through him the Father" (169; 14).

Still, Athanasius holds the center of the Christian faith to be Christ's death and resurrection (181; 19). He reviews the argument that the incarnation recreates the image of God in us and regains our immortality. But the goodness of God is most fully dramatized after Christ's death. His resurrection stands as a promise of our future incorruption, just as his ordered world stands as the symbol of our lives ordered by the beauty of God (*CG* 3).

The realization that death is only temporary is the turning point in the destruction of idolatry. By restoring incorruption through the resurrection, God finally succeeds where the prior strategies of prophets and Christ's ministry and teaching failed to calm people's anxiety sufficiently for them to look to him. Now the knowledge of God has people abandoning pagan idols and dedicating themselves to the worship of God alone. Athanasius is exuberant at the spread of Christianity. When we cling to Christ, the debauchery, crime, and impieties of paganism are reversed. Idolatry is ousted, and the worship of God is spreading rapidly. It is finally the goodness, mercy, and compassion of God that pull people out of paganism and give them an alternative model for their thought and behavior.

The results of the spread of Christianity are striking. It transforms not only religious life but social and political life as well. Tribal gods are replaced by worship of the one God, reducing internecine wars and ethnic violence. People desist from sexual immorality and violence of all sorts. Peace and harmony break out in the wake of Christian faith. All of these occurrences prove that Christ is truly the Son of God, the savior of the world.

> Thus, those brought up in Christ do not wage war against themselves, but are drawn up to oppose the demons with their virtuous lives and deeds, and putting them to flight they mock their prince the devil. So in their youth they are temperate, in temptations they are constant, in troubles they endure; insults they bear and deprivations they disregard. (*DI* 265–7; 52)

Although Athanasius's argument generally remains on the level of God's maneuvers to bring us back to himself, the new recruits are also subliminally exposed to the very mechanisms God uses to lure us home. Athanasius appreciates God's cleverness in dealing with us so generously. God's empathy, compassion, and concern for our perceived needs enable us to attend to God over all the other concerns vying for our attention and leading us in other directions. Once God has our attention, we are confronted with his way of dealing with us, which becomes the standard for our own behavior. It is neither healing as such, nor self-sacrifice as such, nor resurrection as such, that are specific behaviors to be imitated. Rather, the teaching that is pressed home is God's exclusive concern for our welfare and happiness, and the recognition that we are not able to devote ourselves to the welfare and happiness of those in our charge simply by being told to do so; we must be led to do so by having our own needs met first. Once our immediate anxieties are quelled, we are secure enough to lift up our eyes and perhaps begin to deal with one another as God has dealt with us. Although Athanasius never says this explicitly, he comes close to this important aretegenic insight: "This is the indication of the Saviour's divinity: what men were unable to learn from idols they have learnt from him" (265; 52).

ATHANASIAN CHRISTOLOGY

So far we have followed Athanasius's narrative portrayal of human restoration, which is rhetorically poised to transform minds. But no treatment of Athanasius would be complete without addressing the more strictly dogmatic side of his work, often pointed to as a foundation of Nicene orthodoxy. In his mature writing Athanasius championed the Nicene *homoousios*, the insistence that Christ was of the same substance or essence as the Father. The question that jumps out at the reader is how Athanasius's rhetorical and pastoral concern about renewing the reader by having her know the Father through the events of Christ's life and death fit with his later "essentialism." Athanasius comes out with what R. P. C. Hanson called a "space-suit Christology": that Christ had a divine mind and soul inhabiting a human body (448). Does this talk of eternal essences fit with the historical-event character of the narrative of Christ actively restoring the creation? Or was Athanasius co-opted by static Greek categories in a struggle to have his way against the Arians?

I shall argue that, indeed, the essentialism of the *homoousios* follows from the theology of the earlier materials. The foundation for the later christology in *Ar. III* is poured in the *CG*, suggesting that Athanasius always distinguished how Christ is related to God (by nature or essence) from how we are related to God (by grace, adoption, or participation) in order that once we are restored to incorruption and immortality we not become confused about where the line between God and us is drawn.

The essentialist relationship between the Father and the Son is hinted at in the constantly hammered Johannine theme that Christ reveals the Father. The term *homoousios*, meant to capsulize this theme, is suggested in the last section of the *CG*, where the divinity of the Son is inferred back from the function he fulfills in the ordering and restoration of the universe.[6] Athanasius's point is that only God can stabilize the world, which on its own would be torn apart by opposing forces. The Logos "is other than created things and all creation; he is rather the sole and individual Word of the good Father, who has ordered all this universe and illuminates it by his providence. He is the good Word of the good Father, and it is he who has established the order of all things, reconciling opposites and from them forming a single harmony" (111–3; 40).[7]

This distinctive status of the *Logos* both assures the identity of Christ and enables believers to take full advantage of their own "sonship" without danger of confusing their status with Christ's. In the *CG* Athanasius does not use the word *homoousios;* he differentiates the nature of Christ's Sonship from ours without a technical term.[8] Apparently at this point he lacked a specific word to mark this distinction between Christ's natural relationship to God and our status as children of God by participation.

The essentialist relationship between the Father and the Son later expressed in *Ar. III* is a logical extension of the claim that Christ discloses the Father.[9] Christ is

God's Son eternally (*diaionizein*, *CG* 130; 47). This is not an acquired but a constitutive status. We, by contrast, are graced with intelligence [*logismos*]. Our thought and speech reflect what Athanasius considered our participation [*metochen*] in the divine capacity, but our participation is qualitatively different from the way the *Logos* is of God. Ours is a functional relationship bestowed by grace. As Christ leads us back to God, we become children of God by participation: "those who live in obedience to [Christ] have eternal life as reward" (133; 47). The restoration of immortality and the promise of resurrection are the core of *theosis* characteristic of eastern theology. The famous dictum "For he became man that we might become divine" (*DI* 269; 54), however, appears only once in these treatises, and only incidentally, near the end. It is elaborated more fully in *Ar. III*.

Ar. III defends Nicene scriptural interpretation, which supports the full divinity, eternality, and ingeneracy of the Son and his unity with the Father against Arian (or putative Arian) scripture interpretation. The Arian view is that God was not always Father because the Son was created by an act of the Father's will. Christ became the Son, advanced in virtue, or achieved the status of Sonship at a specific point in time, much as we participate in God. God became Father and Son through development.

The tone of *Ar. III* is combative and clearly written in the midst of struggle, whereas the two early treatises are hortatory in tone, seeking to persuade by pointing to the wonderful things that God has done. Rather than attempt a complete analysis of *Ar. III,* this discussion will highlight expansions and reinforcements of the Athanasian aretology.[10]

As we have seen, throughout both *CG* and *DI* Athanasius insists that the Son reveals the Father to us. This idea, supported by passages like John 10.32 and 14.10, are elaborated in the later polemical treatise (*Ar. III* 395–7; xxiii, 3–6).

According to Athanasius, our coming to know God is the reason for God's rescue mission on earth. In exegeting John 17.3 ("And this is eternal life, that they may know you, the only true God, and Jesus Christ whom you have sent") *Ar. III* repeats that the point of the whole divine initiative is the overthrow of paganism, "that He may make men renounce falsely called gods, and that they may recognise Him the true God instead" (397; xxiv, 8). From this evangelical end Athanasius infers that no one who himself is adopted by God can possibly give this knowledge. The *homoousios* handily clarified what must be the proper relationship by saying clearly that Christ does not simply point to God but discloses God. And it is the utter beauty, goodness, and truth of God that we need to know in order to reorder our minds and then our lives and communities.

Charles Kannengiesser finds *Ar. III*'s interpretation of the contended Johannine verses abstract, static, impersonal, and moralistic (1984, 326–35). He so dislikes the theology implied therein that as I already noted, he argues for its spuriousness. Robert Gregg and Dennis Groh, in their book on Arius, see the same theology (1981). They recognize it as Athanasian but equally dislike it, seeing it as fearful of change, development, and instability (161–83). They seek to rehabilitate Arian christology, which focuses on relationship, will, and becoming in Christ, perhaps to render Christ more human. The "moralism" that Kannengiesser dislikes and that Gregg and Groh do not take into account, however, is the aretegenic motive lying behind the term *homoousios*. It is significantly more than simply a Greek-inspired antipathy to change. Understanding the oneness of the Father and the Son teaches us to understand our own likeness to God in a properly qualified manner. Only then can we model our own behavior on the very reality of God:

> [The Son] says, "that they may be one as We are," whose oneness is indivisible; that is, that they, learning from us of that indivisible Nature, may preserve in like manner agreement one with another. And this imitation of natural conditions is especially safe for man, as has been said; for, since [the Father and Son] remain and never change, whereas the conduct of men is very changeable, one may look to what is unchangeable by nature, and avoid what is bad and remodel himself on what is best. (*Ar. III.* 405; xxv, 20)

Distrust of change in God arises not from fear of change and development *per se,* for *Ar. III* strongly insists on growth and change in us. Rather, it is the truth that we are to imitate that cannot be subject to growth and change.

The point of the *Logos*'s taking on a body turns out to be more than simply destroying the fear of death. Christ not only reveals the Father to us; he also teaches us through the intimacy of their relationship itself. By imitating them we find a standard for our relationships with one another. Social harmony, breaking out among new Christians, spoken of in the exhortation of the *DI,* stems from becoming one with the Lord, "having the one Lord in ourselves," not by "identity or equality" but by imitation (*Ar. III,* 406; xxv, 22). The Johannine oneness of the Father and the Son is recreated in those who imitate them. Deification, begun by the destruction of permanent death, is fully achieved by modeling ourselves after the relationship of the Father and the Son.[11]

Distinguishing Christ's relationship to the Father from ours was, however, paramount in this undertaking; otherwise, "hearing again from the Saviour, 'that they may be one as We are' they deceive themselves, and are arrogant enough to think that they may be such as the Son is in the Father and the Father in the Son" (403; xxv, 17). "Essentialism" is Athanasius's way of saying that we "become partakers *[koinonoi]* of a divine nature" but not as Christ does (415; xxvii, 40). In short, the practical concern about clarifying how God actually transforms us controls how the relationship of the Son to the Father is to be articulated; aretology authorizes christology.

Another way of putting the distinction the Nicenes made between Christ and us is to say that Christ is related to the Father "from above," while we are related to him "from below," although the end point is not the same. This forced Athanasius to defend the ingeneracy and eternality of Christ against the Arian interpretation that scripture teaches that Christ's divinity happens in time and space, as ours does. If

Christ received grace as we do—the Arian position—he could not reveal the Father or be able to effect our restoration to immortality. For only God can restore us to our proper selves. The Arians, in effect, have the aretology backward:

> For if the Word Himself, considered as Word, has received and been glorified for His own sake, and if He according to His Godhead is He who is hallowed and has risen again, what hope is there for men? For they remain as they were, naked, and wretched, and dead, having no interest in the things given to the Son. . . . But if [he came] that He might redeem mankind, the Word did come among us; and that He might hallow and deify them, the Word became flesh. (415; xxvii, 39)

The need to carve out a space between Christ's sonship and our own posed a linguistic conundrum that Athanasius fumbled to express. There must be continuity between God and what we become through genuinely knowing him. And there must be a way of talking about Christ's relationship to the Father that distinguishes that relationship from ours. Using the word "sonship" for both is confusing. Athanasius generally uses "equality of nature or essence" for Christ's sonship, and "participation" for ours, to avoid confusion. The word "*homoousios*" provided the needed conceptual clarity. But it was clarity in pursuit of a pastoral goal: that we be clear about who we are and the standards of excellence we pursue.

ASSESSMENT

Having worked through both treatises, we can now attempt to narrate Athanasian aretology. God, who is loving and beneficent, created the world in ordered harmony, and us as creatures capable of thinking clearly, by virtue of that same orderliness that we too possess. As a special gift, God graced us as godlike, capable of resurrection and immortality after death, thus promising us eternal happiness with God. But we spurned God and our own intelligence and fashioned gods for ourselves, producing social and personal degeneracy. God, having set a rule of obedience for us, had to withdraw the extra gifts when we turned from him.

God could not bear to see us languishing in our own depravity, however, and undertook to bring us back to himself, challenging the depravity we had taught ourselves by using deeds born of intelligence: love and compassion. The Incarnation of the Logos discloses our true belonging to God, and the ministry, death, and resurrection of Christ restore our immortality and incorruption, destroying the source of our anxiety, so that we experience God's power and wisdom rather than the jealousy and rivalry that pagan gods teach. When pagans realize that Jesus Christ is their true redeemer they savor a new way of life. When this happens they abandon idolatry and the debauchery it teaches and worship God. The consequence of this conversion is a rediscovery of the ordered life with which God gifted us at creation. Conversion to

Christ calls forth social arrangements and personal life based on peace and harmony and the tactics of love and compassion revealed in God's dramatic reclamation effort.

The aretology appears as follows. Despite our intelligence we are unable to direct our lives aright. But neither are we cured by threats, punishment, guilt, or any other form of suffering. There is no hint of anger, revenge, or contempt on God's part. God cures our weaknesses by teaching us himself of strength, dignity, and nobility of purpose. Yet we can only attend to these loftier thoughts if our immediate needs are met so that we are freed from craving transient pleasures. Athanasius does not portray the gift of resurrection as the completion of creation, as if God had left the creation unfinished the first time around. The promise of resurrection restores our true identity so that we return to God and take the unity between the Father and the Son as the model for our own relationships.

We have seen that living in accord with the beauty of God's creation and imitating God are central features of the Athanasian plan for our restoration. God is self-consciously teaching us how to live rightly. In this he has only the deepest respect for us. He is not interested in his own power, honor, or reputation. Nor does he demand obedience, remorse, or shame. He does not punish us or deprive us of anything. On the contrary, God seems to want to spoil us in the midst of our prodigality. In the end, God always appeals to our strengths, to coax them out of hiding, as it were, and make our nobility in him the foundation of our identity.

From this perspective, insistence on the *homoousios* becomes more intelligible. Christ breaks through our fear to reveal God. And since God wants us to model ourselves on him, it is paramount that the standard for our knowledge of dignity, compassion, and caring be indisputable and crystalline. Thus, the aretegenic function of the *homoousios* emerges. If the Son were not the very ordered goodness of God but became the Son at a point in time, he could not restore us to our true nature or provide us with the standard of human excellence. Athanasius wanted to be sure that neither the medium nor the message was lost on us.

Articulating the Christian doctrine of God was, for Athanasius, considerably more complex than insisting that any description of Christ conform with philosophical notions of eternality, immateriality, and immutability. Knowing God himself was necessary, he believed, in order for us to come to our senses, return to God, and flourish as God intended. In this sense, Jaroslav Pelikan cited a fine psalm text to sum up Athanasius's theology: "In your light we see light" (1962, 95).

Notes

An earlier version of this chapter appeared under the title "The Case for Concern: Athanasian Christology in Pastoral Perspective," *Modern Theology* 9:265–83.

1. Kannengiesser questioned the authenticity of *Ar. III* (1983). But his argument for the spuriousness of *Ar. III* is challenged by Michael Slusser (1985), Christopher Stead (1985), and

R. P. C. Hanson (1988). For our purposes, even if *Ar. III* only reflects Athanasian claims, its testimony is still helpful in understanding some of the issues that Kannengiesser and others, like Robert Gregg and Dennis Groh, found troubling in Athanasian thought.

2. "Through [the sign of the cross] all demonic activity is put to flight, and only Christ is worshipped, and through him the Father is known" (5; 1); "had they consulted their inner reason, they would not all have fallen headlong into these errors, or denied the true God the Father of Christ" (26; 71); "let us now . . . contemplate the ruler and creator of the universe, the Word of the Father, that through him we may come to an understanding of his Father, God" (81–3; 29); "when we see the power of the Word we form an idea of his good Father" (123; 45).

3. The theme of our superiority to animals recurs in *Ar. III* (404a; xxv, 18).

4. The *Logos* principle is not simply God's order, or intelligence. It is also divine beauty, which pervades creation. It also uplifts us as we come to understand ourselves as God's handiwork. In classical thought truth, beauty, and goodness were one.

5. I have already noted several points at which the *CG* mentions that Christ brings knowledge of the Father or more generally of God. In the *DI* this function of Christ is mentioned numerous times.

6. In their book on Arius, Robert Gregg and Dennis Groh criticize Athanasius's rejection of Arius's "voluntarist" relationship between the Son and the Father in favor of the "essentialism" of the *homoousios* (1981, 170–83). But essentialist language about the nature of the *Logos* and his relationship to the Father is significant for the aretegenic thrust of the argument as a whole, as I shall propose below.

7. The consubstantiality of the Son with the Father implies that Christ is the dispenser, not the recipient, of grace. *Discourse III Against the Arians* (413–6; xxvii, 35–41) works hard to refute Arian readings of passages that support the idea of development, growth, or receiving power, wisdom, or command from the Father, such as Matt. 11.27; 28.18; John 3.35; 5.30; 10.18.

8. R. P. C. Hanson argues that Athanasius did not begin defending the term *homoousios* until about 356 (1988, 418).

9. "Everything was created through him and for him, and that being good offspring of a good Father and true Son, he is the power of the Father and his wisdom and Word; not so by participation, nor do these properties accrue to him from outside in the way of those who participate in him and are given wisdom by him, having their power and reason in him; but he is . . . absolute light, absolute truth, absolute justice, absolute virtue, and indeed stamp, effulgence, and image. In short, he is the supremely perfect issue of the Father, and is alone Son, the express image of the Father" (*CG* 131; 46).

10. This should not be taken as suggesting a judgment one way or the other on Kannengiesser's argument against the authenticity of *Ar. III* (1983). Kannengiesser himself notes many Athanasian themes in *Ar. III*.

11. "For as, although there be one Son by nature, True and only-begotten, we too become sons, not as He is in nature and truth, but according to the grace of Him that called, and though we are men from the earth, are yet called gods, not as the True God or His Word, but as has pleased God who has given us that grace; so also, as God do we become merciful, not by being made equal to God, not becoming in nature and truth benefactors . . . but in order that what has accrued to us from God Himself by grace, these things we may impart to others, without making distinction, but largely towards all extending our kind service. For only in this way can we anyhow become imitators, and in no other, when we minister to others what comes from Him" (*Ar. III* 404; xxv, 19).

5

Drinking in the Majesty and Grace of God

Basil of Caesarea

Basil of Caesarea, a theologian-bishop like Athanasius, helped forward the Cappadocian formulation of the doctrine of the Trinity by inferring that since the Holy Spirit transforms lives, he is as important as the Father and the Son. Basil wrote *On the Holy Spirit* in about 375, amid the protracted and complex trinitarian controversies of the fourth century, whose third quarter focused on the dignity of status of the Holy Spirit.[1]

To suggest that the issue was whether the Holy Spirit was a creature or God puts the question too sharply, for the Holy Spirit could be thought of as a *hypostasis* of God, originating from the Father and therefore eternal (and consubstantial), but also in some sense derivative. This gave the impression that the Spirit is less important than the other two *hypostases* of the Trinity because subordinate to them. A way of speaking of that which originates with God without implying creation began with Eusebius and was fully delineated by the Cappadocians. By using the word *gennetos* to mean "born" and *genetos* to mean "originating from" (Prestige 1952, 139), they created a new category, "begotten not made," to apply to the second and third Persons of the Trinity alone, a strategy that would respect the ordering but deny subordination. This was difficult, however, because common thinking organized beings along the lines of Plotinian emanationism, the view that all of reality is interconnected and stretches as a descending hierarchy of being, with pure "being" at the top and less and less "being" as one moves down the line from uncreated to created, animate to inanimate objects. Ordering itself implied subordination. The Macedonian party, perhaps specifically Eustathius of Sebastia, somewhat misleadingly dubbed *pneumatomachoi* [Spirit-deniers], seems to have resisted the Cappadocian compromise. They denied not the existence of the Spirit, nor even its divinity, but its parity with the Father and the Son, based on the implied decreasing value of the scriptural ordering: Father, Son, and Holy Spirit (Hanson 1988, 760–72).[2]

Basil's position in this debate is not clear-cut. He opposed the subordinationist implication of the trinitarian ordering because the Spirit is the instrument of sanctification. It must be accorded equality with the other two Persons, or else Christians would not look to the Spirit for sanctification. By inferring the parity of the Spirit from believers' experiences of spiritual transformation in baptism and subsequent Christian discipleship, Basil made an inferential case for theological experience as legitimate knowledge of God. To this end he argued that spiritual transformation testifies to the truth of orthodox trinitarianism. This *a posteriori* argumentation is the sort that moderns have rejected for theology, primarily because of its imprecision, as I argued in chapter 1.

While on one hand he fought subordinationism, Basil nevertheless seemed to tolerate it, too. He linked his defense of the Spirit with an argument for the catechetical power of liturgy that makes clear who God is, because only when believers understand their faith will they look to God for guidance, indeed for their very identity. Basil explained the internal relationships and processions among the trinitarian Persons in order to press two pastoral concerns that flow from proper trinitarian doctrine. One was that liturgy assists worshipers in knowing God and so must be precise to be salutary. To this end he argued for the innovation and development of the tradition, notably in the liturgy, under careful episcopal supervision. Specifically, he defended the use of nonscriptural liturgical formulations, on the grounds that liturgy is an instrument of catechesis and edification.[3]

Basil's position may look confused, because on one hand he argued for the parity of the Holy Spirit with the other trinitarian Persons, while at the same time he defended two liturgical doxologies that seemed subordinationist. I will argue that this in-between position that Basil carved out can best be understood when viewed in light of his pastoral aims. The issue was not the logic of the doctrine but its salutarity.

The baptismal formula of Matt. 28.12 was the traditional doxology used in worship. It seemed to support the dignity and parity of all the trinitarian Persons because it links the *hypostases* with the conjunction *and* ("Glory to the Father and to the Son and to the Holy Spirit"). The contended doxologies that Basil defended used several nonscriptural prepositions that nuanced the relationships among the Persons considerably ("Glory to the Father *with* the Son, *together with* the Holy Spirit," and the more common but still nonscriptural "*through* the Son *in* the Holy Spirit"). Clearly, more is going on in Basil's grammatical analysis of the doxologies than a straightforward defense of orthodox trinitarianism. I shall argue that Basil was making a case for the transforming power of knowing God, so that the laity would give glory and gratitude to God and be piously shaped by that knowledge. As a master of rhetoric Basil realized that prepositions are fluid parts of speech that render a language supple and deft. Although these scriptural departures were not Basil's innovation, their defense, as agents of Christian piety, fell to his watch.

Another dimension of the case for liturgical innovation is Basil's argument for the authority of tradition in addition to scripture. As a whole, the treatise argues for the development of Christian tradition and, by implication, doctrine, for the sake of forming believers in the truth of God. In essence, Basil argued for the pastoral responsibilities of theology, as one might expect from a sitting bishop.[4]

This discussion will highlight Basil's pastoral concerns: to stimulate his flock's growth in Christian piety, especially as effected in worship, through engaged understanding of the Trinity; to use the experience of spiritual transformation in support of the equality of the Holy Spirit with the Father and the Son; to legitimate episcopal authority to develop church practices that promote proper knowledge of the truth and goodness of God; and to set forth the pastoral responsibilities of theology.

With Athanasius we noted that patristic understanding of Christian vocation is assimilating oneself to God in a gradual process of illumination and purification, spurred by the assumption that in order to become good one must know goodness. Thus, salvation is linked with Christian discipleship, for which knowing God the Holy Trinity and assimilating oneself to God are central. Two requirements for progress in the Christian life immediately present themselves. One is sapiential knowledge of the triune God, for without illumination, how can one participate in the divine life? The other is the desire to be transformed by this knowledge, or else it would be to no avail. In short, theology that renders God accessible to believers is essential to spiritual formation.

REMEDYING SOCIAL DYSFUNCTION

The argument will proceed in four steps. First, it will identify research on Basil's letters that illustrates his aretegenic concerns. Then it will examine points in the treatise at hand that directly relate knowing God to holiness. Next, it will examine the treatise's scriptural arguments for the legitimacy of patristic innovation. Finally, it will examine trinitarianism as an effective instrument of Christian virtue.

Basil's defense of patristic innovation demonstrated the importance of worship in the pursuit of Christian holiness. Public worship, the primary public nourishment of the Christian life, demanded careful attention to the nuances of words. Basil defended the use of two doxologies because together they conveyed more precise and clear knowledge of God to believers and thus were pastorally salutary. Two forms were needed because one taught the majesty of God, while the other taught the graciousness of God (Basil 1980, chap. xxxiii: para. 16). Together they provide handholds for seekers of truth and righteousness because they orient Christians to both realities simultaneously. In short, Basil's grammatical discussion addresses an aretegenic concern.

Since thinking about the classical trinitarian debates in pastoral perspective is not the usual first line of approach, it will be helpful to point to Basil's pastoral concern as revealed both in his other writings and through specific points made in the text at hand. There is support for highlighting Basil's pastoral motivation from historical research on his life and times. In her 1939 dissertation, Mary Margaret Fox offered a portrait of the educational, social, judicial, and moral issues that concerned Basil, the pastor, drawn from his letters. And according to R. P. C. Hanson, her work has withstood the test of time (1988, 679). Basil, himself a highly educated and successful rhetor, staunchly supported education. He provided educational opportunities for youngsters—both female and male—in a monastic setting (Fox 1939, 85). He viewed discipline as an edifying exercise in character development that would overcome a child's fault, not simply as a punitive instrument, as was common in the ancient world. Instruction was both scriptural and to the end of promoting moral conduct. Fox cites a Christian teacher, Libanius, who corresponded with Basil. Libanius refers to Basil's educational philosophy as attending "to sobriety and moderation [more] than to learning, and . . . he deterred souls from dishonorable pleasures" (86). Fox goes on to quote Basil's exhortation to his audience thus: "Give due consideration to both body and soul: To the one, what is necessary for its maintenance, food, and clothing; to the other, instructions in piety, a good education, practice in virtue, and victory over your passions" (86).

The eagerness to master the passions was no puritanical rejection of healthy emotions. Drunken revelries that took place after feast days disturbed Basil. When Christians, both women and men, participated in drinking contests, the result was licentiousness and debauched behavior that his preaching failed to curb. Along with drunkenness, Basil criticized his flock for several forms of gambling and being negatively influenced by licentious music (95). Such undisciplined behavior mocked pious religious observance and rendered his preaching pointless. Yet rather than react to his powerlessness with anger and a punitive attitude toward his charges, Basil consoled himself by regarding his preaching as prophylactic medicine to "fortify the healthy" (93). His dismay at the ineffectiveness of preaching alone may in part account for his focus on liturgy as an additional support for proper catechesis.

There is no reason to think that Basil distinguished sharply between issues of personal morality and the social dysfunction of rowdy drunkenness that tends toward violence and debauchery. While he worried over his parishioners' personal behavior, he was no less concerned about social corruption and exploitation of the poor by government administrators and justices (117). He complained about the crushing burden of taxation levied against the poor. He established and supported almshouses and hospitals and endeavored to inculcate Christian hospitality, a belief in the dignity of physical labor, and active participation in dispensing charity on the part of his clergy (151). But he took social justice to be grounded in holy living and theology to be the means by which his parishioners might be led to lift themselves up above the constant temptations that surrounded them. Holiness cannot be legislated; it must be cultivated. And Basil's means for cultivating holiness was knowing God. It is not surprising that his argument for trinitarian orthodoxy would seize on Origen's teaching that the Holy Spirit is the instrument of Christian perfection.

With Basil's concern for the moral character of his parishioners in mind, we may turn to the treatise under examination, where he argued that patristic innovation, like scripture itself, is an aretegenic agent. The treatise undertakes a rather tedious syntactical analysis. Perhaps before diving into it, it is worth recalling that I have selected the most apparently theoretical works to argue for their pastoral concerns.

THE VIRTUE OF KNOWING GOD

The treatise was written to those who "press forward to perfection." And the author warned his readers in advance that instruction in perfection would, in this instance, require tedious syntactical exegesis.

> those conscious of the goal of our calling realize that we are to become like God, as far as this is possible for human nature. But we cannot become like God unless we have knowledge of Him, and without lessons there will be no knowledge. Instruction begins with the proper use of speech, and syllables and words are the elements of speech. Therefore to scrutinize syllables is not a superfluous task. (16; chap. i: para. 2)

The treatise argues that proper speech—in this case, liturgical language—teaches correct knowledge of God, and knowing God is the only way to reach the goal of human life: to become as God-like as possible. As we have seen with both Paul and Athanasius, conformation to God is the source of human dignity, happiness, and excellence. Basil's Platonic assumptions stress knowledge as the root of goodness. His training in rhetoric taught him the power of language in service of knowledge. His defense of liturgical innovation rested on the insight that language shapes the mind, which in turn directs attitudes and behavior. The bishop took pains to sort out the linguistic confusion that fueled the theological struggles of his day because only correct language about God would arouse the awe and trust that enable Christians to achieve sanctity.

Basil tells his reader not only that the purpose of knowing God is righteousness but also how this knowledge is obtained. And here he breaks with the Platonic method of dialectic: one learns not through intellectual deduction, but gradually, over a long period of practice, as an apprentice learns a trade. The Christian life is a tutorial in the art of holiness. The author invites readers to open their minds to a new degree of understanding to assist them in their quest for perfection in the Christian life, by knowing God truly. Dogmatic exegesis is the means to this practical end. Basil's explanation of the Trinity, worked out through detailed defenses of the doxologies, is meant to persuade believers that God is capable of taking them to himself, so that their identity stems from the work of God.

The argument for the Son's aretegenic power anticipates Basil's argument regarding the Spirit. When scripture speaks of Christ as the Way, it means "the road to perfection, [by which we advance] step by step through the words of righteousness and the illumination of knowledge, always yearning for that which lies ahead and straining toward the last mile, until we reach that blessed end, the knowledge of God"

(37; viii:18). And note the multiple use of verbs denoting cognitive understanding to describe the process of spiritual transformation in those whom the Spirit indwells:

> finally [they] become spiritual themselves, and their grace is sent forth to others. From this comes knowledge of the future, understanding of mysteries, apprehension of hidden things, distribution of wonderful gifts, heavenly citizenship, a place in the choir of angels, endless joy in the presence of God, becoming like God, and the highest of all desires, becoming God. (44; ix:23)

Knowledge is the starting point of *theosis*, the goal of the Christian life and the ground of human dignity.

The importance of gradual growth in piety extends to understanding the faith properly as well. The theme of God as teacher returns in the context of a seemingly arcane discussion of the typological interpretation of scripture (54–6; xiv:32–3). Basil presents Moses as the mediator between God and the people, a type of Christ. A proper grasp of the typological relationship between the Old Testament and the New sheds light on the divine pedagogy. God revealed the mystery of salvation in digestible increments, first by "baptism" into the law, and later through the gift of regeneration through Christ.

> Education progressed gradually; the school of righteousness attempts to bring us to perfection by first teaching us easy, elementary lessons suited for our limited intelligence. Then God, Who provides us with every good thing, leads us to the truth, by gradually accustoming our darkened eyes to its great light. . . . He spares our weakness, and prescribes a gentle treatment. He knows our eyes are accustomed to dim shadows, so He uses these at first . . . so that we could make an easy transition to the secret and hidden wisdom of God. (56; xiv:33)

Basil agreed with Athanasius (and as we shall see, Augustine and Anselm followed their lead) that the divine pedagogy is gentle, not punitive. And the obscurity of some lessons Christians are to learn is tailored to the limits of their educability.

This theme returns in paragraph 66, where Basil argues that the secret and hidden wisdom of God for regeneration may not be in scripture; it will only be disclosed through the work of theologians like himself. Here we see the responsibility of the theologian as a midwife of the divine pedagogy. Christians resist God and need theologians to render divine guidance plain. Pastoral responsibility even authorizes the theologian to develop the "secret" traditions of the church, those that are not evident in the plain text of scripture. Theology's task is to ensure that believers are formed by a proper understanding of God—in this case, a proper understanding of God as he is in himself and as he is for us.[5]

Basil argued that nonscriptural customs like signing catechumens with the cross, praying facing east, and nonscriptural Eucharistic language were not included in scripture in order to guard them from becoming trite through overfamiliarity! He defends this reasoning by pointing out that Moses himself set this precedent, restricting entry into the Holy of Holies to but once a year, and then only for one priest, and only for a short time.

Now the curiosity of this argument is that Basil is using scripture to overcome scriptural authority. And the argument from scripture is not even analogous, because the customs for which he argues were not guarded in secret, as was the Holy of Holies. On the contrary, they were established customs familiar to all baptized Christians. What is "secret" is their source, rationale, and aretegenic value, which the bishop himself supplies. Basil, however, seems unaware of these incongruities in his argument. His point was to persuade his readers of his episcopal right to authorize change by linking Moses' rationales for secreting away the sacred spot with his own rationalization of nonscriptural additions to Christian practice. In both cases, secrecy is a pedagogical device to counter the human tendency to take the familiar for granted, so that awe is sustained. One can hear Basil's experience with his congregants' resistance to his preaching, their pressing him to legitimate his doxologies and perhaps other nonscriptural rites and customs, by aligning himself with Moses' and the others' psychological acumen.

> Moses was wise enough to realize that triteness and familiarity breed contempt, but the unusual and the unfamiliar naturally commands [*sic*] eager interest. In the same way, when the apostles and Fathers established ordinances for the Church, they protected the dignity of the mysteries . . . [with] unwritten tradition so that the knowledge of dogma might not become neglected and scorned through familiarity. (100; xxvii:66)

Basil, aware of the controversy over the *homoousios*, realized that the absence of scriptural grounding for these customs makes it difficult for some to admit the legitimacy of the doxologies. But his episcopal responsibility is to make that plain. Religious practices such as standing and kneeling for prayer are neither courtesies toward God nor expressions of one's humility and piety, as they came to be interpreted in the Middle Ages in the West. Rather, they represent instruction in piety, shaping believers and directing them toward God. Now the connections Basil draws may seem a bit strained to moderns. Standing for prayer on the day of the resurrection, he writes, reminds us of the graces we have been given, and of the age to come and our own anticipated resurrection. Standing during Pentecost reminds us "to focus on the future instead of the present" (101; xxvii:66). The continuous gesture of kneeling followed by standing reminds us that "through sin we fell down to earth, but our Creator, the Lover of Mankind, has called us back to heaven" (101; xxvii:66).

In short, customary prayer postures do not indicate holiness; rather, they induce it. While to the modern mind Basil may be reaching to justify existing customs, his point is that the customs have educational and aretegenic import. Constant behavioral reminders shape humility, give hope, and keep the point of the Christian life clearly in view. The theologian-bishop's task is to ensure that Christian practices forward Christian virtue and piety.

In its broadest scope, Basil's treatise is designed to authorize the theologian's responsibility for catching the faithful up in attending to their life with God. As worked out in this treatise, theology explains both the majesty and grace of God. The question of the dignity of the Holy Spirit is pressing because believers must understand how the whole Trinity works in their lives. Basil defended the dignity of status of the Holy Spirit in the service of educating worshiping Christians (17–8; i:3) about the nuances of the words they heard and uttered so that they might "embrace the fullness of wisdom" (16; i:2) and not be misled by false religion, which would teach them a bad understanding of God and thereby impede their spiritual development.

The doxologies Basil favored had probably been in common usage for quite a while (Kopecek 1979, 98). They were now being criticized for two reasons. One objection was that these phrasings are nonscriptural (Matt. 28.12 is the only biblical trinitarian formula), an objection which Basil met late in the treatise but which the general argument for responsible augmentation of liturgy and religious gesture is also designed to combat. The other objection was more strictly theological and reached to the heart of trinitarian faith. Subordinationists were trying to co-opt the doxology of grace in support of their own misleading theology. The subordinationist controversy, which had been raging for sixty years, involved different perceptions of existence implied by different philosophical frames of reference. Here we come to the narrowly theological agenda, and the most obscure part of the treatise.

The trinitarian conflict concealed two questions. One was whether the Matthean ordering of the *hypostases*—Father, Son, Spirit—already implied successively decreasing divinity. To this concern Basil argued that contrary to a casual reading, the alternative doxology refutes subordination even better than does the biblical formula itself. First of all, the doxology of glory, "Father with the Son together with the Holy Spirit," in no way changes the meaning of the scriptural text. And it has the advantage of expressing more clearly what later theologians would dub the essential Trinity, the "eternal communion and unceasing cooperation" among the *hypostases* (91; xxv:59). "With" demonstrates that persons mutually share a common act more clearly than "and," thus undercutting subordinationism (92; xxv:60). It has the additional advantage of combating the Sabellian mistake of identifying the divine persons indiscriminately. And it deters an Arian interpretation that the Son and Spirit are temporally separated from the Father, suggesting that they are created entities. In other words, "with" specifies the unity, cooperation, and equality of the *hypostases* more clearly than does "and." Basil insists on the doxology of glory because by understanding the internal relations of the divine Persons, believers are better able to understand the dynamics of *theosis*. Understanding how the divine Persons are related to one another teaches the bidirectional dynamics that enable God to take us to himself (Bobrinskoy 1984, 56).

Understanding the "essential" Trinity shows believers how God can carry us up to himself, initially through the work of the Holy Spirit, and, conversely, how the goodness and dignity of God may descend to us so that believers' illumination and *theosis* are possible. Basil described the bidirectional movement this way: "The way to divine knowledge ascends from one Spirit through the one Son to the one Father. Likewise, natural goodness, inherent holiness and royal dignity reaches [*sic*] from the Father through the Only-Begotten to the Spirit" (74–5; xviii:47).

The key to becoming divine is knowledge of God: knowledge of who he is, of the connection between God and us, what his expectations are for us. This knowledge confronts the reader with just how wrapped up in us God is, how intent on bringing us to himself, and where one's true identity is to be found. It is all designed to turn the reader's head from distractions with lesser pursuits to the one goal worth pursuing.

Unfortunately for Basil, scripture does not use "with the Spirit" but prefers "in the Spirit" not only of the grace of God but also sometimes when giving glory to God (89; xxv:58). This was apparently being used by subordinationists to argue for decreasing degrees of divinity, so Basil stretched to argue the reverse. To circumvent this impediment to his argument Basil claims that in 1 Cor. 2.12, Ps. 104.37, Ps. 43.9, and "countless" other citations, "in" really means "with." This defense of "in" is misleading, however, because it obscures another central plank of Basil's pastoral argument: that the doxology using "through" and "in" teaches the grace of God by distinguishing among the *hypostases*. This suggests that he interpreted the two doxologies as theologically equivalent. This is not the case, however, for throughout the treatise he energetically defended the distinct import of understanding both the majesty and the grace of God, or, as later theology would put it, the essential and economic Trinities.

The other trinitarian issue was how to express individuation among the three persons without implying that they are separated from one another in the work of salvation. That would be tantamount to paganism, because it implies three gods. In this regard Basil believed that the doxology of grace, using "through the Son" and "in the Holy Spirit," better conveys how grace works in God for us: the "abundant blessings [God] has given us, and how He has admitted us as co-heirs into God's household, [so that] we acknowledge that this grace works for us *through* Him and *in* Him" (33; vii:16). By delineating the mechanism of how the Persons work together, this doxology distinguishes their discrete functions; thus the patristic doxology is more edifying than the scriptural wording.

The doxology of grace teaches a proper understanding of the Son's saving power for us by the preposition "through" because "sometimes He carries these good gifts of grace from the Father to us, and other times He leads us to the Father through Himself" (34; viii:17). By teaching the beneficence of God's dealings with us, the doxology of grace evokes gratitude, thus humbling believers. A doxology of glory is needed because it teaches the structural unity of the Trinity, calling forth praise and evoking awe. And awe and humility are foundational Christian virtues. While Basil himself expressed the need for both formulae, he devoted most of his treatise to exe-geting the doxology of grace (*through* the Son and *in* the Holy Spirit), perhaps be-cause it was being co-opted by subordinationists, but also because it packed more pastoral punch, so to speak. It arouses love and devotion in the believer, who is stopped by the grace of God.

How can one best teach about the distinctions within God without implying di-minishing godhood? The subordinationists argued that the Holy Spirit "is different in nature and inferior in dignity from" the Father and the Son (45; x:24). The notion that difference implies inequality may hark back to Origen. In the Latin version of the *De Principiis* (1989, 252; bk. I: chap. 3), in the section on the Holy Spirit, Origen argued that creation derives from the Father, rational beings (angels and humans) derive from the Word, and holiness of the saints is from the Holy Spirit. This suc-cessive narrowing of functional spheres of action from general to specific could be interpreted as implying the inferiority of the more restricted functions of the Son and Spirit. Neoplatonism reinforced this view. Basil, however, took it upon himself to oppose this view by suggesting that increasingly specific nouns in a series, like essence, living, and human, while growing more specific, are not parceling out things into successively lesser or inferior parts (68; xvii:41). On the contrary, each increas-ingly specific thing partakes fully of the whole and is more spiritual, not less. On a nonaretegenic reading of this treatise, the need to designate the successive but not inferior relationship among the trinitarian Persons begs for an answer. But Basil's seeming residual subordinationism is in the service of commending the sanctifying power of the Holy Spirit.

An aretegenic reading goes behind the simple desire not to insult the dignity of the Spirit, on principle so to speak, to ask what is at stake in that dignity. An analy-sis of inner-trinitarian relations that would permit believers to ignore the work of the Spirit in their transformation would lead them away from the truth and destroy the faith, as far as Basil could tell. He has separated function from nature so that the scriptural order, which seems to imply subordination, does not impugn the power of the Spirit for Christian formation. Basil was defending Origen (and himself) against the charge of subordinationism because the aretegenic work of the Spirit was essential to the Christian life. The doxology of glory makes the equality of the Spir-it explicit, while the doxology of grace specifies the discrete functions of each divine Person in salvation—functions that the doxology of glory might obscure. For only by understanding both how God is structured internally and how he works for us may believers come to know and love God both without us and for us.

Basil interpreted the doxology of grace through a stoic understanding of exis-tence that held that differentiation of function did not suggest different substances, so as to hold to both individuation of function and unity of substance in the Trin-ity. On this view, relations among the trinitarian Persons show only how they inter-act, not what constitutes them. Basil's opponents, however, took a rationalistic ap-proach to the role of relations, arguing that differentiation of function suggests discrete existents.[6] An Aristotelian interpretation suggested that the Persons are variously constituted and thus separate from one another. And if they could be thought of as three gods, then the Holy Spirit cannot sanctify. The spirit-deniers brought an analogy from carpentry describing tools *by* which, materials *from* which, and a design *through* which a chair is made, for example. And to them these distinctions were independent of one another. This reading strained divine integrity, because by stressing individuation over unity of substance, it suggested three gods. To Basil, however, using "through" and "in" implies different functions but not different natures, so that the sanctification wrought by the Holy Spirit is genuinely from God.

The issue of cooperation among the *hypostases* is not an academic matter, for Basil's goal is to teach believers that they have already begun to participate in the divine life by virtue of their baptism. The question of cooperation and individuation within God is not a speculative conundrum but an issue of practical import for how Christians understand and conduct themselves. Only if the divine Persons are one God does baptism by the Holy Spirit mean participation in the being of God.

As noted above, Basil expends most of his energy on the doxology of grace. It is designed not simply to arouse gratitude but also, on the strength of the demonstration of divine love, to cajole believers into allowing that grace to transform them, to "make us into vessels fit for the Master's use, the use of our free will being made ready for any good work" (2 Tim. 2.21). As Basil hones in on the aretegenic function of this doxology, he recalls the goals he set for his readers at the outset: slowly growing in knowledge of God to the end of sanctity. Here he makes that goal concrete by pointing the reader to the title of Christ as "the Way to be the road to perfection, advancing in order step by step through the words of righteousness and the illumination of knowledge" (37; viii:18). In short, "our way up to God [is] through his Son" (37; viii:18).

The rhetorical movement of the argument is as follows. The doxology of glory impresses upon the believer the majesty and power of God. The doxology of grace at least hints at the goodness of divine providence, so that worshipers may "be struck with amazement at [the] Savior's mighty power and love for mankind [in that he] patiently endured to suffer our infirmities with us" (36; viii:18). It encourages believers to reach up to God through understanding. And as we saw with Athanasius, there is no hint of intimidation of believers through the threat of punishment or cancellation of reward. The whole is thought through on the basis of love and encouragement. On the strength of trust in Christ's power and love, one embraces Christ's authority over one's life and turns Godward.

The syntactical argument for the doxology of grace is that scripture itself sets the tone for patristic innovation by its own varied prepositional usages, which engage worshipers in the majesty and benefactions of God. The variability of scripture's use of prepositions in relation to the doings of God is, like the doxologies, to a practical end. Scripture itself endorses multiple use of prepositions in regard to the interaction among the *hypostases*. "From" is used of the Father in 1 Cor. 8.6 (22; v:7) and of the Spirit in 1 John 3.24, Luke 1.20, and John 3.6 (25; v:9). "From" and "through" are both used of the Father in Rom. 11.36 (23; v:7). And "through whom" and "by whom" are used of all three persons or simply of God: Rom. 6.4; 1 Cor. 1.9; 2 Cor. 1.1; Gal. 4.7 (26; v:10). "In" is used of both God and the Holy Spirit. By the time this treatise was written there was general agreement that scripture neither subordinates the Son to the Father, separates the Son from the Father, nor conflates the Son with the Father. This doxology enhances believers' understanding of the majesty of God and the benefits accruing to them from the interaction among the Persons. It should not be inappropriate, therefore, to reinforce scriptural teaching with liturgical adaptations patterned on scriptural practice.

In the course of making the syntactical point that scripture does not prepositionally straightjacket the doings of God, the treatise takes the reader on a tour of the magnificent works of God on our behalf (paras. 9–11). These sections offer verse upon verse of God's gracious gifts toward us and review the salutary effects these gifts of grace have upon us: we have fellowship with Christ, we are heirs of God through Christ, we are entrusted with truth and wisdom by the Holy Spirit.

This rehearsal carries the reader from the pedestrian portrayal of the Trinity as an artisan, which Basil attributes to his opponents, to an inspiring panoramic view of God's beneficence spread invitingly before the reader's eyes. Philosophical scrupulosity appears flat by contrast. It constricts or ignores the goodness of God, while scripture unfurls the depth, range, and complexity of divine involvement on our behalf. Although Basil doesn't put it quite this way, the objectors, limiting themselves to the use of Aristotelian categories to exegete the controverted doxology, cannot see beyond the philosophical technicalities to the far more uplifting testimony to divine grace expounded in scripture—testimony that calls forth praise and thereby promotes humility, gratitude, and love for God. This later explanation suggests what Basil meant by labeling his opponents' philosophical speculation "vain and empty distinctions." Metaphysical speculation proffers little practical benefit for believers. Pointing worshippers to the majesty and goodness of God, however, as scripture does with its multiple uses of prepositions, is salutary because it promotes proper knowledge.

Liturgical innovation takes its cue from scriptural usage. God builds us up into the body of Christ, abides in us by the gift of the Holy Spirit, and adopts us as children rather than treat us like slaves. He raised Christ, which gives us hope, and entrusts us with truth. In short, the flow of the argument suggests that the liturgical innovations are useful in describing the variegated gifts God showers on us. Basil portrays his opponents, on the other hand, as having a narrow and rationalistic understanding, restricted to a sketch of the divine topography alone, which is of scant practical value.

The soteriology behind the doxology of grace does not come until after the pneumatology. The claim that the Holy Spirit "perfects reason-endowed beings" means that He is present *in* them in the same way as form is present *in* matter. Indwelling by the Spirit is not to be understood concretely, however (44, ix:23; 94–5, xxvi:62). Basil goes out of his way to foreclose any suggestion that "in" be understood as referring to a location. "'*Place*' is contemplation in the Spirit" (95). The place of the Spirit is the working of divine grace in us. Nor is the indwelling of the Spirit to be understood materially. Rather, it "is similar to the action of reason with*in* our souls, which sometimes moves our hearts to think, and at other times moves our tongues to speak" (94; xxvi:61). The proper analogy for the Spirit's presence in the believer is that of an artist whose skill is always present, even when dormant.

Having whetted his reader's appetite for God, Basil lays out a practical prescription for spiritual direction. He assumes, with the Origenist tradition, that the Christian life is undertaken freely and that transformation is restorative. One must begin by ceasing from evil and "return to his natural beauty" so that the image of God may be restored. Once purified, one may approach the Paraclete, who will reveal himself and assist those who come to him toward spiritual perfection. "Through Him hearts are lifted up, the infirm are held by the hand, and those who progress are brought to perfection. He shines upon those who are cleansed from every spot, and makes them spiritual men through fellowship with Himself" (44; ix:23). Excellence is contagious. Those "Spirit-bearing souls, illumined by Him, finally become spiritual themselves, and their grace is sent forth to others" (44; ix:23). Salvation and sanctification are closely linked here. The believer is indwelt by God, as the process of restoration both nourishes believers in goodness and fans out from believers into the world. Evangelism involves the "contagion" of righteousness.

While the Holy Spirit is the general agent of sanctification, Basil pays particular attention to its role in baptism, revealing the full aretegenic force of his theology. God desires to reclaim us after the fall.[7] He does this through the Incarnation. Christ's passion and resurrection are undertaken "so that man might be saved through imitation of Christ and receive his original birthright. If we are to be perfect we must not only imitate Christ's meekness, humility, and longsuffering, but His death as well. . . . How can we become like Him in His death? By being buried with Him in baptism" (57; xv:35). And now we see the soteriological function of the Holy Spirit outlined above.

Paul recognized that Christian vocation requires severing oneself from one's old life. It must die for a Christian to be born. "How can we accomplish this descent into death? By imitating the burial of Christ through baptism" (58; xv:35). The water symbolizes the death of the old life. And Basil, taking a cue from Paul, uses dramatic language to arrest believers with attention to the serious business of Christian living, made possible by the Trinity. One can hear Basil the pastor preparing catechumens for baptism on Easter as he describes the new life in which they will participate, with their minds, hearts, and wills directed toward God. The baptismal water

> receives our body as a tomb . . . while the Spirit . . . pours in life-giving
> power, renewing in souls which were dead in sin the life they first pos-

sessed. . . . [T]he water accomplishes our death, while the Spirit raises us to life . . . with divine knowledge. . . . The Lord describes in the Gospel the pattern of life we must be trained to follow after the (baptismal) resurrection: gentleness, endurance, freedom for *[sic]* the defiling love of pleasure, and from covetousness. (58–9; xv:35)

The Holy Spirit is the believer's point of entry into intimacy with God through baptism (76–7; xix:49). Basil, like other Eastern theologians, speaks of knowing that one has been joined to God through the Spirit as "illumination." Illumination by the Holy Spirit leads to focusing one's attention on the Son, who in turn "gives true worshippers the knowledge of God in Himself. The way to divine knowledge ascends from one Spirit through the one Son to the one Father" (74–5; xviii:47). The trinitarian dynamic of Christian formation from the Spirit to the Son to the Father—perhaps developed out of the Johannine emphasis on Jesus as the way to know the Father—reveals how essential proper knowledge of the Trinity is for Christian formation. Through it believers are "inseparably joined to the Spirit of knowledge," a knowledge to which the Holy Spirit leads them personally (74). This joining of the believer to the Spirit of knowledge suggests the existential dimension of divinization. The believer is joined to the Trinity through knowledge imparting the goodness of God, which the believer is then able to disseminate in the world.[8]

As noted previously, the believer's ascent to the Father has parallel descending benefits. "Likewise, natural goodness, inherent holiness and royal dignity reaches *[sic]* from the Father through the Only-Begotten to the Spirit" and undoubtedly to us (75). Throughout, Basil carefully knits together the bond between truth and holiness established at the outset. The Holy Spirit is equal to the other trinitarian persons because he is holy, as they are; because he is intimate with them, and because he makes possible our intimacy with God. His mission is not only to ferry God's goodness to us and our attention up to the Son and Father but to endue us with gifts: the ability to avoid evil and persevere in goodness, to drive out the devil and remit sin, and to resurrect us from our death in sin into a converted life of holiness, "refashioning our souls in the spiritual life" (77; xiv:49). Because of all these works, the Spirit is to be accorded equality with the Father and Son.

Despite his profuse praise for the works of the Spirit, Basil, always the pastor, is keenly aware that the fruits of the Spirit are not always evident in the faithful. So, like a physician encouraging a patient to continue a course of therapy that is slow to take effect, he notes that like the skill of an artist at rest, the grace of the Spirit is not continuously operational in the faithful. It may be dormant, yet indwelling believers all the while (93–4; xxvi:61).

According to Basil, the Holy Spirit binds us into the goodness and wisdom of God. Belonging to God is the foundation of personal identity and the source of dignity. Basil is no theological literalist. He insisted that both creation and resurrection be understood as moral and spiritual rebirth. The grace of God is not a substance squeezed onto or into believers at baptism like toothpaste. It is, rather, personality-transforming insight that sets the goodness of God as the paradigm and norm of Christian integrity.

Sapiential knowledge of God is saving knowledge in Christian Platonism. It is not limited to deductive knowledge or information about God, but is divine wisdom that informs a person's identity by engaging one's attention and emotions, refocusing interests and thoughts and indirectly influencing behavior. At least this seems to be Basil's hope. His understanding of the pastoral function of theology is subtle and nuanced. Cognitive assent to a set of correct ideas is only a small piece of the knowledge that renews the believer. There is no hint of a set of moral rules to follow or rigid practices to repeat. Rather, the notion of formation in goodness is a direction for life that comes from knowing goodness, of becoming loving by being loved. Basil trusts God enough to act on the view that virtuous persons are produced not by beating people over the head, or ordering or threatening them to be good, but by gently and gradually helping them become good by imitating the source of goodness, whom he helps them to understand, love, honor, and experience through proper teaching, prayer, study, and meditation and in recalling their baptism.

The objective and subjective dimensions of salvation, so carefully separated in Western theology, are fully integrated here. God is clearly the agent of saving knowledge, but the consequence of this knowledge is a process in which the believer actively participates by desiring God. Boris Bobrinskoy, in discussing this treatise, puts it well: "The Holy Spirit indwells human existence in such a deep and intimate way, that we cannot discern the frontier between his presence and our own autonomy. In him is solved the antinomy of divine grace and human freedom. Does he pray in us or do we in him? We cannot say. He alone knows" (Bobrinskoy 1986, 12–3). But this synergy should not lead to a renewed round of debates about the freedom of the will and works-righteousness. Although Basil lived before the Western debates on Pelagianism, there can be little doubt that he viewed the desire for God as itself a consequence of the gracious gifts of God, who arouses the believer's desire to imitate him by means of the goodness he bestows upon us.

In sum, Basil argued that theology must disclose the pastoral intent of scripture to deepen believers' apprehension of and openness to God. The doxologies do this, the doxology of glory by expressing the parity of the *hypostases,* and the doxology of grace by focusing on "the abundant blessings He has given us, and how He has admitted us as co-heirs into God's household" (33; vii:16). Now the earlier rebuttal of his critics assumes a broader shape. They miseducate Christians both with their rationalistic interpretation of the doxology and by insisting on only scriptural language. Unless educated to grasp God's majesty and grace, we should fail to understand God properly and be moved to virtuous living as a consequence. Liturgical innovation, following the spirit though not the letter of scripture, discriminates the nuances necessary to lead the faithful to true knowledge of God, the key to excellent living.

In concluding this aretegenic reading of Basil's treatment of the knowledge of the Trinity, it is appropriate to note that like Athanasius's argument for the divinity of Christ, Basil's method is inductive, and he says so explicitly. "But from visible things we are able to construct analogies of invisible things. . . . When you consider creation I advise you to first think of Him who is the first cause of everything that exists: namely, the Father, and then of the Son, who is the creator, and then the Holy Spirit, the perfecter" (62; xvi:38). Since the Holy Spirit is the agent of Christian perfection, it is rude and unseemly to deny the Holy Spirit the glory and honor accorded to the Father and Son. The moral and spiritual renewal of believers points to the unity of the Spirit with the others.

The Spirit is the busiest *hypostasis* of the Trinity. The name alone, "Holy Spirit," is aretegenic, directing believers' attention to holy and spiritual concerns (42–4; ix:22). He is the source of Christ's anointing, healings, miracles, and resurrection (65–6, xvi:39; 88, xxiv:56). He is the agent of baptism, the source of renewal and enlightenment, the life-giving power of righteousness for Christians (88; xxiv:56). He also authorizes and empowers the church and distributes gifts for its proper and harmonious functioning (65–6; xvi:39). The Spirit directs our thoughts to divine attributes—incorporeal, immaterial, indivisible, uncircumscribable (42–4; ix:22)—that inspire awe and wonder, as we have seen. And the Holy Spirit will be present at Christ's return, and with those who endure in righteousness to the day of final judgment (66–7; xvi:40).

> All things thirsting for holiness turn to Him; everything living in virtue never turns away from Him. He waters them with His life-giving breath and helps them reach their proper fulfillment. . . . He is the source of sanctification, spiritual light, who gives illumination to everyone using His powers to search for the truth—and the illumination He gives is Himself. His nature is unapproachable; only through His goodness are we able to draw near it. He fills all things with His power, but only those who are worthy may share it. (43; ix:22)

Chapters 10 through 13 specify the soteriological role of the Holy Spirit. Since catechumens are transformed from pagans into Christians by the trinitarian confession and baptism, it would be fraudulent for them to claim to belong to God if the agent of their elevation to God were not appropriate to the task. Since Basil takes his readers to be sympathetic to his assumption of the integrity of their faith, he can conclude that anyone who distorts the baptismal profession by separating either the Son or the Spirit from the salvific action holds an empty faith.[9] Just as Paul argued for the resurrection of Christ based on the salvation of Christians (1 Cor. 15), and Augustine would later argue for original sin based on the practice of Christian baptism, Basil subtly flatters his readers by assuming their agreement with his argument for trinitarian orthodoxy, based on their experience of transformation following their own baptism. Would Christian readers dispute their own regeneration by denying the Holy Spirit as its agent? Or, on the other hand, would they be so bold as to attribute their transformation to their own efforts by denying this to God?

Here is precisely the inferential reasoning disallowed to theology by David Hume, discussed at the outset. Knowledge of the Holy Spirit is pointed to in scripture, received through the testimony of the tradition, and confirmed by personal experience. It is circumstantial rather than scientific evidence. Yet there is no reason on principle why hard evidence—"smoking guns," so to speak—should be the only evidence admitted in theological court. Inferring the dignity of the Holy Spirit and its responsibility for sanctification from theological evidence is like inferring a fine education from well-prepared graduates. The causes may be a good deal more complex than this, and a causal connection may be unwarranted, but there is no reason to doubt the probability that good students did have good teachers. It is not clear that Basil means to suggest anything more scientific than this.

Basil, like his brother Gregory of Nyssa, eschewed speculation on the nature of God and urged his opponents to reconcile themselves to pious ignorance about the divine nature (Haykin 1988, 350–2). The kind of knowledge the Cappadocians valued is of this circumstantial sort. It is like the knowledge a child has of a parent: it is many-sided and imprecise and changes over time. It is dependent on what the parent chooses to disclose of herself to her child and is filtered through the child's maturity and experience. Yet there is nothing to disqualify the child's knowledge as genuine simply because it is not objective. The knowledge of God that Basil believes scripture, doctrine, and liturgy yield is of this sort: imprecise, yet adequate to the believer's needs.

Calling Forth a Reader's Best Self

Basil wrote his treatise to catechize his flock. On one level he was pointing out the errors of his opponents in order to justify his own practices to his people and thereby maintain control of his see. But more than a simple desire for ecclesiastical authority is going on here. Basil assumes that his readers crave God and that pastoral teaching provides the means for satisfying that craving. That is, he dignifies his readers by treating them as people of integrity who yearn for the excellence that produces happiness; the bishop calls on their best selves. Whether that simply reflects the moral rectitude of the Caesareans, or whether it is a pastoral strategy to call people to their full moral stature, is pure conjecture, although the latter interpretation is supported by Fox's notation of Basil's frustration with his flock's penchant for drinking contests and the rowdiness it bred. For our interest in understanding theology, it is noteworthy that Basil aligns his people with himself in the pursuit of holiness, the goal of truth. By treating them as high-minded persons he calls forth their best.

The treatise binds the members of the church together in the pursuit of the knowledge the bishop expounds by reinforcing their baptismal covenant. The Holy Spirit has already begun the work of regeneration in them, for they have already placed themselves under the direction of the Son and Holy Spirit. Acceptance of the false teaching of the subordinationists would imply that these Christians had erred in their acceptance of the trinitarian faith at baptism, and surely none cares to admit to mistakes in such matters. Or it might tempt them to abandon the striving for *theosis* that occupies their energies as a community. So Basil appeals to their pride, and perhaps to their vanity, in enlisting their support for his pastoral and theological leadership.

The Son and Spirit both carry our attention up to God, who is the proper locus for moral and spiritual formation. The Son brings down to us specific traits modeled in the Incarnation, and the Spirit empowers and perfects the strength of character revealed by the Son. In other words, while Basil appeals to the integrity of his parishioners, he does not fail to acknowledge that they cannot achieve their goals on their own. The Trinity provides both a precise model of what they are to become and the means for its achievement. Basil's rhetoric is subtle and worth noting. He simultaneously dignifies his readers, complimenting them on their good intentions, and provides them with the divine guidance they lack. He never slips into berating or belittling them. On the contrary, he cherishes them, that they may in turn cherish the work of Christian excellence to which they have been called.

Basilian trinitarianism is a rhetor's episcopal exercise in pastoral theology. It balances the integral unity of the *hypostases* within the divine being with the individualization of their functions in God's dealings with the world in order that his flock will be adequately and accurately apprised of God's majesty and goodness. The trinitarian *hypostases* both cooperate with one another and are individuated from one another. Although Basil only touches on the horizontal implications of this dynamic, perhaps it is not stretching the text too far to suggest that awakened and regenerated Christians are encouraged not only to pattern themselves after Christ, as the text specifies, but to take the model of the whole Trinity, with its unity of purpose and majesty and its individuation of functions and gifts, as a model for understanding church membership. The unity of purpose in the Christian life unites all members so that by worship and mutual support in the pursuit of righteousness they reinvigorate one another with constant reminders of their common task. The distribution of various gifts of the Spirit, like the cooperation among the Father, Son, and Spirit, fosters mutual respect and cooperation in pursuit of their common goal.

Notes

1. The divinity of the Spirit was endorsed by the First Council of Constantinople in 381, for which Basil's language was definitive (Haykin 1988, 343; Bobrinskoy 1984, 59).

2. One must be chary of positing too clear a distinction between the proponents and opponents of the dignity of the Spirit at this time. Both Cyril of Alexandria and Basil hesitated to say overtly that the Spirit is God, although Basil did so in his eighth letter, written perhaps fifteen years before his treatise on the Holy Spirit.

3. It is possible that the argument for nonscriptural practices and language both reinforces and extends the Nicene use of the *homoousios*, a word that does not appear in this treatise. Karam suggests that bypassing this inflammatory word "was for the sake of the weak, making himself weak for them," in order to regain unity among the churches (Karam 1979, 143).

4. The more usual academic approach to examining classical theological treatises is exemplified by de Mendieta (1965).

5. This aretegenic interpretation of Basil's insistence on secret tradition contrasts with de Mendieta's view that Basil supported spiritual elitism (1965, 42–3).

6. Catherine LaCugna has illuminated this aspect of the dispute by pointing out that in Stoicism, connectedness of something to other things does not inform about the object's *existence* as an object. She cites J. Rist: "'Relative dispositions are the relations of an individual thing to other individual things that are associated with it in the world, but on which its continuing existence as an entity does not depend.' In the case of the father-son relation, if the child dies, the man ceases to be a father but he does not cease to exist. By contrast, in . . . Aristotelian philosophy, a father is *constituted* as father by his son, and vice versa" (LaCugna 1991a, 59).

7. There is a dislocation from chapter 13 to chapter 15. Earlier Basil followed Paul in that salvation means transforming pagans into Christians by virtue of their adoption into the household of God. Here he follows patristic tradition, most recently seen through Athanasian theology, that salvation is the overcoming of alienation from God caused by sin. Basil, like theologians after him, seems unaware of the tensions between these two positions.

8. For an excellent discussion of the existential dimension of Christian "personalism" in contrast to speculative theology in regard to this treatise, see Bobrinskoy (1984, 54ff).

9. Michael Haykin (1986) argues that Basil based his trinitarian theology on the baptismal formula in opposition to his former friend Eustathius, who argued that the baptismal formula did not suggest the co-equality of the Spirit.

6

Dwelling in the Dignity of God

Augustine of Hippo

THE STATE OF THE TRINITARIAN QUESTION

Augustine of Hippo decisively shaped Western Christianity's discussion of the doctrine of God through his *De Trinitate* (*DT* 1991b), a mature work of his episcopate. It is a complex and difficult work, written over a long stretch of time with many interruptions. It is readily given to multiple interpretations, so the eye of the beholder becomes particularly important in its assessment.

Symmetry was important in classical antiquity. *De Trinitate* is written in fifteen books divided into two seven-book halves, with book VIII pinning them together and books I and XV acting as bookends. The first explains the work's purpose: to cure diseased minds of seekers "who conceive of God in bodily terms" (65; bk. I: chap. 1: para. 1) and to purify them so that they may "contemplate and have full knowledge of God's substance" (66; I:1:3). It also offers a plan of the whole: to explain the missions of the Son and Holy Spirit in the context of the unity of God as a course of therapy for a happy life in God. In the last book, Augustine restates the pastoral goal and plan of the entire work: "In pursuance of our plan to train the reader in the things that have been made [e.g., Christ] (Rom. 1.20), for getting [the reader] to know [H]im by whom they were made, we came eventually to his image. . . . [T]his is what is called mind or consciousness" (395; XV:Prologue:1). The reform of the mind is necessary for knowing God.

Books II through IV begin the treatise with revelation, the point from which faith departs, by discussing the sendings or missions of the Son (the Incarnation) and Holy Spirit (at Pentecost) into first-century Palestine. These inform us of God's deeds in history and represent a sure source of knowledge of the Trinity. Books V through VII explain the church's doctrine of how the distinct Persons of the Trinity, made known in revelation, are the one eternal God, so that the discrete missions are not misunderstood as suggesting distinct gods. In other words, the first half of *De Trinitate* shows how revelation and church doctrine fit together. Book VIII bridges to the second half of the treatise, which argues that one must be poised to take advantage of scripture and tradition. The second half of *De Trinitate* is a treatise on growth in the Christian life—on knowing God at a deeper, more spiritual level than scripture and tradition alone can reach. Books IX through XI unfurl Augustine's psychology, which we moderns might see more as epistemology, because they try to explain how we can know God immediately. Books XII through XIV generally urge the reader to press beyond knowledge of God gained from historical or material sources (i.e., scripture, tradition, and nature) to knowing the essence of God: sapience, goodness and blessedness, the source of the good life. In other words, the second half of the work aims at growth in self-knowledge by knowing God. So while it is necessary to train the mind to know God, it is also necessary to know God in order to develop the mind or, more simply, the self—the process is reciprocal.

Over the past few decades, several prominent theologians, wanting to reclaim the doctrine of the Trinity for Western piety, have criticized Augustine's trinitarian theology. The main protagonists in this discussion are Fr. Karl Rahner, followed by Catherine LaCugna, Lutheran Robert Jenson, and Anglican Colin Gunton (Rahner 1989; LaCugna 1991a; Jenson 1982; Gunton 1991). I will try to state their objections succinctly, then discuss their respective arguments, and finally present responses to their objections in order to locate the present discussion.

As I noted earlier, Augustine treated the sendings or missions of the Son and Spirit in history (referred to as the economic Trinity because they express the economy of salvation) in books II through IV, and their relations or processions—that is, what might be called the structure of the godhead (known as the essential or immanent Trinity)—in books V through VII. He did this to be sure that speaking about the activities of the divine Persons in history would not be misconstrued as talking about different or lesser gods but the one God. Setting up the discussion of the doctrine of God in two parts, one about what God does and the other about who God is, became standard in medieval scholasticism: Aquinas, for example, first discusses the unity of God, *de deo uno*, and then the threeness of God, *de deo trino*, actually the reverse of Augustine's order.

In the *DT* Augustine suggests that salvation is dwelling in the fullness of God. Later Western soteriology, however, as noted in chapter 1, construed salvation as forgiveness of sins rather than participation in the divine life, as had been the case until the rise of monasticism. This focused the West's attention on the saving work of Christ in the economy: God as he relates to that which is not God. But as the West came to look to the economy soteriology became separated from theology: human salvation was detached from the being of God. That which is soteriologically relevant (Christ) appears as "theologically" empty—that is, not disclosing real knowledge of the being of God. This has created the Western anxiety that we really do not know the God who saves us, because there is a gap between God as he is with us and God as he is in himself.

It must be noted at the outset that this problem is only meaningful in post-Augustinian theology. To lay the problem at Augustine's feet is anachronistic because for Augustine salvation is dwelling in the being of God, not just reaping the benefits of the Incarnation, as came to be the case in subsequent Western theology.

The mystery of the intradivine life—theology proper—became separated from soteriology after Augustine. The medieval church, as we shall see, located salvation in the Cross, rather than in the sapience of God. With the Reformation, Protestant Christianity hunkered down on one version of the doctrine of justification, a sub-doctrine of christology. Although the modern loss of the Trinity probably began in the seventeenth century (Babcock 1991), by the time of Friedrich Schleiermacher it was relegated to an appendix to doctrine (Schleiermacher 1986)—a practice sustained by Paul Tillich (1963). This ever-narrowing focus for Western, especially Protestant, theology has truncated Protestant piety. It is ironic that Augustine, whose soteriology was grounded in theology in the proper sense of the term—that is, in the being of God—is blamed for the loss of the very doctrine he championed. History can be cruel. Were he here he would be tempted to offer his own doctrine as the remedy for the problem his critics present!

A second but related objection is that the Western doctrine of the Trinity has been burdensomely individualistic. God is seen as an isolated individual constituted by his internal relations, with which we identify. Analogously, the psychology of the second half of *De Trinitate* focuses on the solitary individual, retired from the world, in glorious and intimate seclusion, contemplating God. The complaint is that this teaching has led to contempt for the world.

Karl Rahner has mounted one of these contemporary criticisms of the Western doctrine of the Trinity. His argument is that the New Testament teaching on God is not of the attributes of God but the love of one person for another, the Father giving himself to us through the Son: to say that God is love is to speak of not "the emanation of a nature but the free bestowal of a person. . . . [I]t is the ceding and the unfolding of one's inmost self to and for the other in love" (1961, 123). The biblical teaching is better expressed by the Greek than the Latin view of the Trinity, which focuses on the unity of the divine nature that is revealed to us for purposes of contemplation in the next life, although in this life it has little to do with us. The mystery of the Trinity, Rahner argues, is a mystery of salvation, but it has not functioned salvifically in Christian piety, as has the doctrine of the Incarnation (1966, 87). The economy rather than the mystery of the Trinity became the locus of Western Christian piety.

Rahner's solution to the problem reverses Augustine's doctrine of God. Rather than seeing the being of God as the locus of salvation, Rahner recognizes that "the economy of salvation *is* the immanent Trinity" (1966, 1987). Since the Incarnation is the revelation of the second person of the Trinity, there is no reason not to say that the divine nature is not communicated freely in a person. It is not just that God designates created things through which to communicate his love to us; it is his very self that is given in Christ (90). Rahner's solution is to have the doctrine of God follow piety.

Phillip Cary, in responding to Rahner, summarizes Rahner's objection to the doctrine of God well (1992). To participate in salvation means (or certainly ought to mean) to be drawn into the divine life. Thus the missions of Christ and the Holy Spirit in first-century Palestine must be genuine communications of the divine being, for it is through historical events that graced believers are saved. If the missions are only accidental to the identity of God—that is, if they themselves do not constitute God, but only the internal processions of the Son and Holy Spirit from the Father do—then we are excluded from genuinely knowing and participating in God *in se.* Rahner's axiom, "'The 'economic' Trinity is the 'immanent' Trinity and the 'immanent' Trinity is the 'economic' Trinity'" (as quoted by Cary, 367), weakens or even abolishes the distinction, thus solving the problem that in the economic Trinity—that is, in knowing Christ and the Spirit—we do not know God.

Rahner is especially disturbed by the Latin doctrine of appropriations grounded in Augustine's *De Trinitate,* books II through IV. This doctrine, later stated as *omnia opera Trinitate ad extra indivisa sunt,* argues that any work in history assigned to one member of the Trinity belongs equally to the other two. This points to the unity of God so that we grasp all his attributes. To designate forgiveness of sins as exclusively the work of Christ would weaken the fullness of God that dwelt in him, undercutting divine unity. Rahner wants to close the gap between the being of God and salvation, not by rethinking salvation along Augustinian lines, which would have solved the problem as he stated it, but by bringing the doctrine of God in line with later Western soteriology. To this end he opposed the doctrine of appropriations because it weakens the distinctions among the Persons and suggests that God's self is really found in the common "substance" or essence of the godhead and not in the economy. To put it another way, Rahner believes that the work assigned to each trinitarian Person in his missions *are* what they *seem:* each is what he does, so to speak. There is no being or essence or "substance" of God hidden from view behind the Trinity we know from creation, Incarnation, and Pentecost. God is *constituted* by his Incarnation and the gathering of disciples at Pentecost (371). God is what God does. There is no reality of God behind historical revelation.

Catherine LaCugna agrees with Rahner's criticism and with his suggestion for doing away with the distinction between the essential and the economic Trinity in the name of Christian piety and practice. Stress on the being of God apart from the economy is unhelpful because it does not enable us to understand how God helps us, or, in more technical terms, it separates theology from soteriology. LaCugna and others want to argue for the soteriology of the economy because it is socially useful (1992, 679) and liturgically grounded (1991b, 162–5). She defends this position by saying that it is the economy, not the mystery of God that constitutes God.

LaCugna faults Augustine for claiming that God is constituted by self-relatedness rather than relatedness to us. If God is God apart from us—that is, if the Incarnation does not make God God—then God's relationship to us is incidental to God (*God for Us* 86). LaCugna's point seems to be that we are the center of divine concern. She criticizes what has been called the psychological model of the Trinity—Augustine's teaching that we can understand God through analogy with the workings of human consciousness. This implies both that God and the self are complete when enclosed within themselves rather than when in relationship with others, and that salvation is achieved through a vertical relationship between God and the soul that excludes the social dimension of relatedness to other persons. According to LaCugna, this psychological model has promoted individualism, which sidesteps the social responsibilities that constitute human life. Augustine's Platonic anthropology portrays a self that finds its identity by reintegration into the image of God, from which it has been sundered by sin and to which it seeks to return (103).

LaCugna's problem with Augustine is that according to him, human personhood is perfected by knowing and loving God, rather than through properly ordered social and interpersonal relationships. Construing salvation as a private relationship between God and the individual soul has had serious consequences for women and other marginalized groups throughout history, and perhaps also has something to say about the class and economic divisions that plague the churches. Again, LaCugna's answer to the problem is to suggest not that we are constituted by our relationship to God as Augustine does, but that God is constituted by his relationship to us. She and others turn to Gregory of Nyssa for support because he argued that we cannot know the divine nature and that the "Godhead" refers to the economy (Nyssa, 1954).

Robert Jenson, another critic of Augustine who also wants to reclaim Cappadocian trinitarianism, approaches the problem not from the perspective of social and interpersonal relationships but from the perspective of historical consciousness characteristic of biblical religion as compared to Greek philosophy (1982, 60–3). Jenson, equating salvation with the work of the cross, and reinforced by Karl Barth's insistence on revelation as event, identifies Augustine's failure as his inability to break decisively with the atemporality characteristic of Greek theism in favor of the Hebrew focus on God's involvement in time. Cappadocian trinitarianism made the break, but Augustine was unable to grasp the point and so left the West with a "blighted trinitarianism" that separated the being of God from human salvation. Jenson's way of putting the problem carries him farther than Rahner and LaCugna toward neoclassical theism, but the force of the criticism is related. The Western (i.e., Augustinian) disaster stems from the fact that direct knowledge of God by the soul obviates knowledge of God through the sendings of Christ and the Spirit to the world and the church. Knowledge of God comes through the inner life of reflection and discernment and scorns historical events (129).

LaCugna might agree with Jenson's paraphrase of Philip Melanchthon that to know Christ is to know his benefits (131). The contemporary critics have adapted the idea to read: to know God's benefits is to know God. Jenson finds the Western doctrine of God inordinately Platonic; Hegel came closest to historicizing it (134–5), but that is finally not close enough. In short, the chief exponent of the Western doctrine of God stood in quicksand, seeking to understand God in Greek rather than Hebrew categories, thus making the Christian doctrine of God unitarian (focused on the being of God) rather than trinitarian (focused on the saving work of God).

Colin Gunton does not add anything substantial to the arguments already presented—he too faults Augustine for never having thrown over Neoplatonism—but he does single out Augustine's intellectualism and spiritualizing as themselves problematic. Augustine, embarrassed by too close an association between God and the world, flattens out the distinctions within God that imply relationality (Gunton 1991, 35–6) and insists that the good life takes place within the self rather than in relationship with others. This establishes a distorted doctrine of the human person who is constituted by relationships (38–9).

Apparently none of these writers has stepped back from Western theology enough to see that Augustine did not belong to the soteriological, atonement-driven tradition they assume. Augustine's soteriology was patristic, not medieval, and it was ontological, not functional. But understanding these important nuances of the discussion probably would not matter. Rahner, LaCugna, Jenson, and Gunton are the most recent voices in the liberal movement to liberate Christian theology from residual Platonic thought, with its talk of essences and eternity, which has tended to remove Christian piety from the realm of action. Like Gregg and Groh, who, as we saw in the discussion of Athanasius, desire to rehabilitate Arius, these thinkers advocate a modern understanding of personhood that embraces growth and change and views personhood as constituted by action, not character. This fits with the theological judgment that salvation is constituted by God's acts in Jesus Christ, not by the being of God. God is best served not by reforming ourselves to be in harmony with the beauty and goodness of God, as Athanasius taught, but by doing, on the model of God's own intervention on our behalf. A slogan for this approach might be "We are what we do."

Augustine, like Athanasius and Basil before him, worked from a different model, an ontological model that began with the reality of God, to which we are morally, aesthetically, and socially accountable. This makes patristic theology public and universal in a way that is out of sync with modern thought, which distrusts leaving the historical-temporal world. I shall return to this point in the conclusion of this chapter.

Of course, Augustine has supporters as well as critics, and several of them should be noted before we examine the debate from the perspective of the aretegenic function of doctrine undertaken in this study. Of the three defenders of Augustine to be considered here, two take their point of departure from the objection raised by Rahner. Edmund Hill (1973) and François Bourassa (1966) argue that reconnecting the essential to the economic Trinity is unnecessary because Augustine's theology already does this. They deny that the epistemic gap between the essential and economic Trinity is true to Augustine's intent, although Bourassa defends the medieval practice of having separate treatises on the unity and Trinity of God. Phillip Cary, on the other hand, defends the importance of maintaining the so-called epistemic gap between the doctrine of the Trinity itself and the economy of salvation in order to protect the freedom of God (1992).

Hill makes the point (and Bourassa would agree with him) that Augustine was in continuity with the ante-Nicene economic theologians (e.g., Hippolytus, Tertullian, and Novation) but corrected their apparent subordinationism by insisting on the equality of the divine Persons on the grounds that it is impossible to tell from specific scriptural texts which of the Persons is involved in a specific event (285). Augustine's intent, Hill suggests, is to stress that the mystery of God is revealed but not constituted by the economy, because the sendings themselves do not constitute redemption, but lead us to know and love the wholeness of God (286). This is precisely the contended point.

Bourassa argues that the purpose of revelation is to lead believers to enjoy and love God; talk of God's self *is* for us, in that Augustine shows how the Trinitarian mystery really is accessible to human consciousness; the Incarnation, though it helps us grasp how God is for us, is not the end of spiritual growth (1966, 255–7). Augustinian soteriology argues that God is spiritual and we are too. Bourassa takes the position (correct, I believe) that for Augustine happiness (read salvation) is knowing God—that is, not just God's doings in history but God as an infinite source of charity and goodness before creation and the first-century missions in Palestine (265). Creation and creatures make God known but themselves constitute neither God nor salvation (267). For Augustine, salvation was not constituted by historical events, as later Western theology would have it (for example, locating salvation in Christ's death). Rather, such historical events are aids to lead us from a material to a spiritual understanding of God as goodness and wisdom so that we come to understand ourselves spiritually rather than materially.

Perhaps, then, the disagreement is not with Augustine but with the nature and locus of salvation. For Augustine the point is to use historical events and material things to go beyond them to help us enjoy the goodness they express or indicate. But moderns are not so clear about the reality of wisdom and goodness, so there is a real disagreement between Augustine and his modern critics that must be acknowledged. It is a disagreement that stems from living in two different worlds, one in which revelation leads seekers to wisdom and goodness, and another focused on history and action.

In a two-part essay on Augustine's trinitarian theology, Bourassa undertakes to defend Augustine against the charge of rendering knowledge of God available to reason apart from faith. He argues that the first half of *De Trinitate* is an apologetic defense of the faith of the church grounded in scripture, while the epistemology of the second half of the treatise explicates the dogmatic theology of the economy presented in the first part (1977, 688–96). Here again we see where the Augustinian doctrine of salvation differs from the modern. As Bourassa puts it, the goal of human life is the vision of God, or eternal life. This is achieved by knowing God, or, more precisely, by contemplating the Father. But this goal requires transformation, which is inaugurated by faith in Christ, through whom those who believe and live in that faith are led to contemplate the Father (703). For Bourassa, the mind is the proper locus for understanding the Trinity itself, as long as the economy is the instrument of the self's transformation. Had he synthesized his argument fully he might have held together the three poles of Augustine's trinitarian theology—the mystery of the Trinity itself, the economy, and the psychology—by concluding that the economy is the instrument by means of which the self first comes into contact with the mystery of the Trinity itself, and thereby into the enjoyment of God and self.

From this perspective, faith is not obviated by the psychology. Rather, the point is to demonstrate the close connection between the nature of human consciousness and the being of God (Bourassa 1978, 404), by indicating that humanity can discover itself to be in the image of God, where it finds happiness. This is because the missions themselves demonstrate that the economy is the Trinity who is God; Rahner, in effect, is in agreement with Augustine's intention. The problem arises from looking for Augustine's soteriology in his presentation of the missions, without seeing the soteriological power of the Trinitarian mystery itself. The criticism illustrates the very problem Augustine said he wrote the *De Trinitate* to address: the inability of people to understand God (and themselves) in other than material terms.

Of the commentators on Augustine examined here, only Phillip Cary engages the challenge being raised to the Western tradition's separation of the essential from the economic Trinity. Augustine's other defenders believe the point to be well taken but the reading of Augustine to be misguided. Cary burrows into Rahner's argument and offers a thought-provoking rejoinder to both critics and supporters—indeed, perhaps even to Augustine himself—by arguing that the objection to classical trinitarianism is informed (infected?) by what Cary calls a romantic expressivist anthropology that wants to "read-off" the identity of God from God's actions (393). This anthropology comes from a modern liberal understanding of the self that craves intimacy above all else, requiring complete self-disclosure as the standard of genuine knowledge of the other. Cary argues that total self-disclosure is not possible in knowing another person, and not desirable in knowing God, for "to know *any* person is (at least in part) to know them in the way that they freely choose to give themselves to be known" (395).

Cary defends the epistemic gap between God and us because it secures the freedom of God from curious seekers. We should be satisfied with what God chooses to disclose to us. Cary reveals himself as a thoroughgoing Barthian in his insistence that Rahner's pastoral goal, to draw believers into the divine life, is itself incoherent (398–9) because it assumes a knowable inner life of the other which, given the freedom of God that Cary presupposes, does not exist. And even if it did, to suppose that crossing the ontological divide between God and us is the only way for God to be really accessible to us is contrary to the Christian doctrine of creation, which assumes an unbridgeable gap between creator and creature. Cary counsels a more modest participation in the divine life, one that rejoices in the gifts of the economy, knowing oneself to be a creature and adopted child of God (403).

Cary offers a useful reminder about the virtue of theological humility, but he may be more faithful to Barth's way of thinking about knowing God than to Augustine's. For although Augustine adopted the Christian distinction between creator and creature, and insisted on the imperfect knowledge and vision of God, it is clear that he offered true seekers genuine knowledge of God.

From the cursory review of the works undertaken here, despite the fact that Augustine's defenders are sympathetic to Rahner's concern, it seems that the two groups arrayed against one another are not engaged in the same conversation. The closest they come to one another is a shared concern that the soteriality of the doctrine of God be preserved or perhaps reclaimed. As I suggested earlier, one way of stating their division is to say they are working with different notions of salvation. I suggest that it is time to reexamine the patristic understanding of happiness grounded in who we are in God—an understanding that died sometime in the Middle Ages, when salvation became narrowed to the question of how God forgives sins, and, specifically, whether he has forgiven mine.[1]

Learning to Savor God

For Augustine, the goal of life is knowing and enjoying God. Knowing God occurs on two fronts. One is the sphere of God's works in history: creation, the Incarnation, and so forth. The other is the spiritual sphere—a proper understanding of the qualities of God. In order to enjoy God it is necessary to know who God is based on what God has done and to understand ourselves in a certain way, a way that takes pleasure in the qualities of God and of ourselves as participants therein.

In the medieval period, when the Western church developed an extensive and powerful penitential system, the understanding of salvation shifted dramatically, or one might say narrowed, from knowing and enjoying God to the remission of sins. With Anselm's *Cur Deus Homo,* to be examined below, soteriological interest bore down on the Incarnation (i.e., the cross) as the locus of forgiveness. But it was one thread plucked out of Augustine's *De Trinitate* from a broader soterio-logical tapestry. Late medieval theologians wrestled with the role of grace in the remission of sins, but the locus remained the cross. Luther's reclamation of the gospel out of the tangle of medieval theology, especially the sacrament of penance, construed trust in God's mercy rather than the penitential system as the means of grace but maintained remission of sin as the soteriological juggernaut. Subsequent Protestant distrust of reason in favor of faith rendered Augustine's trust in the soteriological power of knowing the divine qualities anathema to the Reformation churches.

Today, in the absence of a unified doctrine of the atonement, scholars still argue the merits (or more likely the demerits) of various sacrificial theories—the penal substitutionary model, or the so-called dramatic model—but these are all only a hair's breadth from one another. Throughout the Western church, enjoying God was gradually marginalized to become the province of sporadic mystics who claimed to dwell in the presence of God in this life. One result of this loss is that it is virtually impossible for Western Christians to see the social and ethical implications of formation through the enjoyment of God. In short, Augustine's theology and psychology are unintelligible to the modern churches that no longer appreciate his Platonic moral philosophy.

Recognizing the loss of the soteriological and psychological paradigms Augustine shared with the Greek Fathers helps us better understand the dynamics of the contemporary argument. Augustine disappoints his Western critics not because his doctrine of God is nonsoteriological, as they suspect, but because they are not sympathetic to the Neoplatonic cast of his soteriology, which grounds human formation in knowing God and in basing self-understanding on that knowledge. Hill and Bourassa correctly argue that the economy, by leading believers to contemplate or dwell in God joyously, is not the end but the means of salvation. But this argument is confronted by the sheer weight of post-Augustinian Western theology's conviction that formation in God in Augustine's sense is not necessary. Ironically, Rahner and the others are not really opposed to the notion of knowing God. Indeed, they think Augustine complicated or obscured knowing God. Their interest in knowing God is through history alone, however. While Augustine recognizes an important role for revelation in history, he nevertheless urges believers to press beyond history so that in enjoying God's goodness and wisdom one comes to embrace these virtues for their own sake and not because they bring ulterior rewards. This is a gap across which it is difficult for Augustine and later theology to converse.

It is also a point at which Augustine differs from the Greek Fathers, whose apophatic theology might have been difficult for him to appreciate—unless, of course, embracing wisdom, love, justice, and goodness by knowing God, so central to Augustine, turns out on closer inspection to unify Augustine and the Greek Fathers. For despite Greek insistence that we cannot know the divine essence, we can know the divine attributes and the reality of God; indeed, *theosis* is the dominant paradigm of Eastern soteriology. Dwelling in God, found both in Paul and in John's Gospel, is as central to Augustine as to Greek theology.

Augustine's critics are disappointed because they see his theology as otherworldly, ahistorical, abstract, and impractical. They are not focused on the virtues that were so important in Augustine's world. Augustine's trinitarian theology is designed to enhance human dignity through virtue with God as its source and goal. *De Trinitate* is as much a treatise in moral as dogmatic theology. Bourassa, for example, sees that Augustine insists on the equality among the divine Persons in order to convey to us the unity of God. But he sees this, as all academic theology does, only as a dogmatic thrust against Arianism, subordinationism, or paganism. He misses the aretegenic point that the practical import of the unity, against which the distinctions among the Persons fade slightly, is to teach us that wisdom, truth, power, and righteousness—the qualities that constitute the spiritual "substance" of God—constitute our dignity as well. And the economy is the means of leading us into that spiritual realm. Augustine's point is that the economy disclosed in scripture gently transforms us, so that we come to understand ourselves afresh in, through, and as the image of God.

Even as the controversy about the Western doctrine of the Trinity rages, a fresh view of Augustine's trinitarian theology has been forming. Here, in the works of Gerhart Ladner (1967), Andrew Louth (1981), and Isabelle Bochet (1982), an aretegenic reading finds companionship.

In *The Idea of Reform*, Gerhart Ladner argues that reformation of the human being to the image-likeness of God is central to both patristic and medieval construals of the Christian life. His discussion of Augustine discriminates shades of difference between the Western Father and his Greek predecessors. He argues that for the West, renovation of the Christian surpasses paradisal innocence, while for the East, renewal is no more than restorative.

Ladner points out that Augustine combated the spiritualistic depreciation of the creation that survived in Christian Platonism. "The aim of reformation," he writes, "is not spiritualization pure and simple, but rather an order in which spirit and matter both have their place though that of spirit will always be higher" (173). Christian reformation is a process of becoming more and more similar to God, a process of deification accomplished by grace, not an adoption by nature. "The soul must turn toward God who has made it, and thus become consciously aware of its character as divine image; to be with God is to realize fully this image relation: to remember Him, to know Him, and to love Him—it is in other words, the reformation of the image of God in man" (200–1). My reading of *De Trinitate* supports Ladner's conclusion as long as the return to God accomplished by grace is recognized as a process of transformation of self-understanding. The process of coming to remember, know, and love God is simultaneous with the process of coming to one's senses—or, rather, becoming more and more like God is a process of coming to one's senses.

In a more recent work, Andrew Louth treats *De Trinitate* as a work of mystical theology designed as a search for God through introspective self-scrutiny. Louth sees Augustine as following a Plotinian model, yet differing from Plotinus by insisting on the doctrine of grace: the soul finds God only because God deigns to disclose himself both in history and to the mind. Louth argues that the craving for a return to God requires the seeker to reclaim and perfect the image of God in herself. Augustine assists the seeker in this process by disclosing love as a chief (and trinitarian) function of the mind, so that through awareness of how it loves itself the soul comes to love the qualities of God disclosed by the economy and move beyond the image into God himself.

Louth notes (correctly) that "Augustine is less concerned to illustrate the doctrine of the Trinity from his understanding of man, than to discover the true nature of man by means of the doctrine of the Trinity that he believes by faith" (148). Recognizing one's likeness to God is requisite for ascending to God. It is perhaps unfortunate that Louth used the term "mystical" to describe the dynamic of self-discovery through faith, however, since the term has been reserved for exceptionally gifted believers, rather than the thoughtful pious to whom Augustine wrote. It has come to imply an elitism that is foreign to Augustine's thinking. Growth in loving God repairs the deformed self. The point is not that a proper understanding of self leads to finding God but that a proper understanding of God is the only way to come (gradually) to a purified self—that is, a happy self.

Isabelle Bochet responds to a Jansenist reading of Augustine that insists on a static and dualistic notion of reality. She argues that such a reading is simply not true to the work of the master, whose trinitarian theology is dynamic and not overly spiritualized. Her book *Saint Augustine et le désire de Dieu* argues that the transformation of the reader is Augustine's primary task in *De Trinitate*. Although she does not directly address the Rahnerian challenge to the relationship between the mystery of the Trinity and the economy of salvation, she takes the discussion quite close to an aretegenic interpretation of Augustine. Her work is particularly useful because she develops the anthropological side of Augustine's trinitarian theology.

Augustine sought to correct and transform human desire. Natural human desire is corrupt because, in searching for happiness, the self grasps at carnal objects—those that it knows best. But these desires cannot be sated, for the carnal objects themselves carry one away from the proper object of happiness and truth, indeed the authentic source of itself—God. The result of misplaced desire is lust, evil, and sin born out of ignorance and pride at thinking one can find happiness in self and transient pleasures. Bochet correctly notes that Augustine's autobiography provides the foundation for his philosophy. He based his anthropology on a generalized version of his own struggle between the Manichees and the Catholic faith chronicled in the *Confessions* (hereafter *Conf.*) (9).

The distorted self is spiritual but starved, ill, and dying (23, 34). So God, realizing that creaturely things that lead away from God in the first place can just as easily lead back toward God (59), sent the Son and Holy Spirit into the created order. For the desire for truth and happiness is irrepressible, and consequently, the repair of desire is possible (231–3). The theological virtues are essential to the soul's recovery, for faith rectifies desire, and hope fortifies it, with *caritas* as the principal result (239). But creaturely things, notably Christ, our servant in his human aspect, combats evil and ill-begotten desires by refashioning them (339). Bochet has put her finger on the crux of Augustine's intent as he summarized it at the close of the work, cited at the outset of this chapter. Historical events such as Christ's humility and obedience teach spiritual truths by countering human pride and despair, which keep us from knowing God spiritually. The soul is slow to make war on wrong desire and to change, but Christ is the key creaturely instrument by means of which sin may be left behind and union with God achieved (236) in a process of transformation in heliotropic motion. A little epigram sums it up: the self is formed by creation, deformed by sin, and reformed by Christ (228).

Ladner, Louth, and Bochet pave the way for an aretegenic reading of the *De*

Trinitate, one that illustrates how the doctrines constructed and elaborated therein, including the anthropology, the soteriology, and the epistemology, are linked in a self-conscious plan of reform of self through the economy of salvation, which discloses the beauty, truth, and goodness that are the being of God. Those who want to confine the being of God to the economy of salvation have set aside Augustine's basic point that while God acts in history as a piece of the plan of salvation, salvation itself is not constituted by those acts but happens as one matures through love and divine companionship.

As Bochet argues, Augustine encourages his reader's life with God by pointing out God's power to transform and thereby heal their desires. The two halves of *De Trinitate* cannot be understood apart from one another. The explanation of the scriptural story of God's dealings with us in the Old and New Testaments, and the explanation of how the historical events express the truth and goodness that constitute the being of God, correct a distorted understanding of both God and self. A materialistic doctrine of God, like the one Augustine had learned from the Manichees, valued things wrongly. Augustine's mature (and now widely distrusted) preference for spiritual over physical goods arises from a conviction that goodness and wisdom make us happier than food and sex.[2] *De Trinitate* undertook to persuade citizens of late antiquity that they would be happier on these terms than on any other—as difficult a case to make now as then. Because by the time he wrote *De Trinitate* he was persuaded of our inability to realign our value system simply by knowing intellectually that we ought to, Augustine took pains to show that God has taken on this task himself. Augustine is of one mind with Athanasius on this point. In effect, the treatise on the Trinity, like Athanasius's treatises, is a handbook for spiritual healing.

The second half of the treatise painstakingly works out a psychology or epistemology to heal the believer who gropes to experience herself as a homologue of God. The self derives its dignity and values from the essence of God that can be expressed simply as wisdom (400–1; *DT* XV:2:8–9). In this process one gradually comes to value one's intellect as the key to truth and happiness. This is the reason Augustine's psychology is grounded in epistemology. It is not that Augustine prefers "reason," philosophy, or arid speculation over faith and feeling as an independent source for knowing God—as if believers of a more philosophical bent could avoid revelation. Such a reading is a total distortion of Augustine, and perhaps even a distortion of Anselm and Aquinas. Augustine locates moral and spiritual reform in becoming wise. What we think about and desire, whether and how we act on these desires, and how we envision ourselves involve both intellect and affect. In fact, the division would not even make sense to Augustine. His point was that proper self-esteem is based on the wisdom of God, not the skills of the self.

A second reason Augustine chose the mind as God's therapeutic tool was, as he told us in book XV, to demonstrate that God uses precisely the corporeal things that deformed desire misuses to lead us to their proper use. The point is not to shun corporeal realities but, as Bochet argues, to teach us to value them properly. It is a clever irony of Augustine's rhetorical method that he constantly points out how God uses corporeal things to heal us spiritually. This departure from Platonism probably stems from the Christian insistence on the doctrine of creation and is reinforced by the Incarnation. God embraces created existence, so it must be good. Material things must be used properly to benefit us well.

A central goal of Augustine's treatise is to persuade the reader that revelation and doctrine work together to reshape our minds and affections and thereby our identity. In this sense, the mechanisms by which God chooses to convey himself to us are agents of spiritual cleansing that allow us to arrive at our true destiny: enjoyment of God and ourselves. It is, however, important to note that Augustine distinguishes knowledge *(scientia)* from wisdom/love *(sapientia)* as separate instruments for learning God in *DT* XII–XIV (Charry 1993, 91–5). *Scientia* is laid out in the first half of the work and *sapientia* in the second. Both are necessary, but *sapientia* is where the payoff comes. *Scientia* is factual knowledge upon which one makes rational judgments. In the case of knowing God, the content of judgments are the deeds of God made known in scripture, the foundation of faith. Faith, in Augustine's terms, is not trust that God loves me in the face of my sinfulness, in the Protestant sense. It is belief based on historical information that one accepts on the testimony of the apostles and the leadership of the church. It is factual knowledge, much like the knowledge we glean from history books, which we consider trustworthy because the author is trustworthy.

Modern academic theology has largely limited itself to *scientia*. While it is essential for pointing seekers in the right direction, in Augustine's view, *scientia* alone is unable to heal us. The goal of *scientia* is to move the seeker to *sapientia*, wisdom. *Sapere* in Latin originally meant "to taste or smell things" and was carried over into the cognitive realm to mean "to discern, think, or be wise." In the ancient world, knowing something implied tasting it—indeed, participating in it—which we saw was a central principle of Pauline theology. Augustine pressed Christians not just to celebrate what God has done for them but also to taste and enjoy God. And since the "essence" of God is justice, wisdom, love and goodness, participation in these qualities *is* eternal life with God. Becoming good and wise through healing by God must begin before interpersonal relationships can be life-giving. This is one reason why Augustine's soteriology no longer makes sense to modern Western thought: the latter pays scant attention to formation by God.

Among the writings of Augustine's maturity, no work has more frequently lent itself to speculative interpretation than *De Trinitate*.[3] The work was undertaken shortly after his elevation to the episcopate and encompassed his years of controversy with the Donatists and Pelagius. By that time, trinitarian doctrine was officially settled, although still argued. His trinitarian theology, while reinforcing orthodox decisions made earlier, weaves his aretegenic concern into the fabric of doctrinal exegesis.[4] One of his dogmatic efforts, to explain the procession of the Holy Spirit without using the terms "son" or "grandson," ended in a stalemate.[5] It raises a question not only about whether Augustine adequately treated the processions but also about whether elucidating them was his primary intent. For why would he undertake such a task if he had no solution to the problem of the procession of the Holy Spirit? Indeed, books V through VII, on the processions, are really about the relations among the divine Persons set against the Cappadocian teaching. Edmund Hill, who believes these books are not so much about the Trinity as they are linguistic analysis for talking about the Trinity, reinforces the critics' view that Augustine was playing logical and linguistic games (1973, 281–4). Hill has missed the sapiential punch of the discussion. These books, often presented as an example of Augustine as abstract and disinterested in God *pro nobis*, actually show Augustine as concerned with making an aretegenic point.

With books V through VII we move from revelation to a discussion of doctrine—the church's way of talking about God—that derives from Tertullian's way of putting the Trinity: one substance, three Persons. This moves the discussion away from the concrete—a fatal step, as far as Augustine's critics are concerned. But the move is crucial for the development of Augustine's argument, because it begins the reader's spiritual ascent. Augustine focuses on the relationships among the divine Persons in order to show that although distinguished by the relations, "this three is one only God, good, great, eternal, omnipotent; his own unity, godhead, greatness, goodness, eternity, omnipotence" (197; V:3:12). Moving from the material to the spiritual level confronts the reader with the eternal "substance" of God, which will turn out to be the basis of the believer's self-understanding as well, although to a lesser degree.[6] And these eternal qualities are meant not to suggest that change is bad, as they have so often been interpreted, but to convey to believers that God's love and goodness endure the fickleness of human caring and righteousness, thereby offering the proper model for the reader (201; V:4:17).

The dense discussion of the processions or relations is designed to establish the contended doctrine of appropriations: that anything predicated of one Person of the Trinity applies equally to the others, although it is perfectly acceptable to designate the Persons using scripturally based language. So, for example, 1 Cor. 1:24 teaches that "Christ the power of God and the wisdom of God" applies wisdom and power to the Son, but in discussing this passage Augustine is at pains to show that these attributes, along with justice and love, suffuse or more precisely *are* the essence of God (206–10; VI:1:3–7). The intent here is not to downplay the distinctions among the Persons or the authority of the economy but to help readers move from the actions of God to the sapience of God: to let go of a material existent or thing that is God. Augustine notes repeatedly how difficult it is for us to move from material realities that we readily grasp to this spiritual notion of God.

The fear that Augustine's God has escaped our knowledge is a testimony to the intractability of the problem he tries to solve. He constantly reminds the reader that although we may say God is wise, just as we may call a person wise, this is a misleading analogy. God's truth, wisdom, greatness, and blessedness are identical with himself: "with him being blessed is not one thing, and being great or wise or true or good, or just simply being, another" (211; VI:2:8). These qualities, not a hazy material substance that holds them together, constitute the being of God. The doctrine of appropriations prevents readers from supposing that love, justice, or wisdom can be nailed down by pointing to one Person of the Trinity and so avoiding their moral force. For as the seeker turns out to be a homologue of the Trinity, these spiritual qualities become the ground of the seeker's new godly identity.

The aretegenic force of the doctrine of appropriations escapes moderns like Rahner because the virtues and attributes seem to dissolve into a blur of abstractions rather than to effect moral transformation, as Augustine intended. Indeed, it is not clear that academic theology has been sympathetic to the aretegenic intent of the doctrine. But the message in Augustine is explicit, not hidden. He puzzles over why scripture uses both "begotten" (implying eternality and the inner life of the Trinity) and "made" (of the Incarnation) when speaking of wisdom, the divine quality that Augustine most longs for his readers to enjoy (222; VII:2:4). The Word is identified as the Wisdom of God, implying eternality, as orthodox doctrine put it, while John 1.14, "the Word was made flesh," suggests that "Christ is made wisdom because he was made man" (222; VII:2:4). Was the Son the eternal wisdom of God or made wisdom at the Incarnation? The resolution of the paradox lies in seeing the apparent contradiction as intentionally *pro nobis.* "Is it perhaps to commend to us for our imitation the wisdom by whose imitation we are formed, that wisdom in those books never speaks or has anything said about her but what presents her as born of God or made by him, although the Father too is wisdom itself?" (222; VII:2:4). The whole purpose of the Incarnation is "in order [for us] to abide with him for ever" (223; VII:2:4).

Augustine waxes passionate about the wisdom of God, which becomes the foundation for the reader's recovery of her self. By means of this wisdom one draws close to God—that is, conforms the self to his image. By copying the model of Christ, by loving and clinging to him, one becomes sapient, one tastes God, "that we may be refashioned to the image of God; for we follow the Son by living wisely" (223; VII:2:5). And with sapience we become our truest and best selves. Discussion of both the missions and the processions, then, base the reader's transformation in *scientia* while setting the stage for the epistemology of books XI through XIV.

A bit further on in book VII, Augustine makes another try at inviting the reader to approach God so as to overcome the recidivism into corporeal thinking. Approaching God, he explains, happens not in spatial terms but by imitation or approximation. We are the image of the Trinity in approaching God's likeness, through the qualities God advocates. We are exhorted to this imitation, he says, by Rom. 12.2, "Be refashioned in the newness of your mind," and again in Eph. 5.1, "Be therefore imitators of God as most dear sons" (231; VII:4:12). Citations of both these verses recur regularly throughout the work. Transformation of the mind from the desire for immediate pleasure to desire for God is a transformation from self-imposed indignity to proper dignity and power. The reader is invited to wade ever deeper into the risky business of becoming God-like.

The themes of imitation and participation in God, prominent in Paul, the Johannine literature, and Eastern theology, have been viewed with skepticism in the West, especially in Protestantism. This harks back to the shift in Western soteriology from enjoyment of God to forgiveness of sins, as I discussed earlier. Stronger language refers to deification or *theosis,* although Augustine does not use the term. This theme has generally been ignored by Augustine scholars perhaps because it seems to suggest salvation by works. Gerald Bonner argues that deification is a category of Augustine's thinking, but he interprets it in a Protestant manner, not unlike Phillip Cary's approach to participation in the divine life, discussed earlier (Bonner 1986). Bonner thinks that Augustine, in interpreting Galatians, means being adopted as God's own through Christ (377). But we have not seen this theme at all in *De Trinitate.* Rather consistently, on the contrary, Augustine's view is that Christ is the model whereby the divine traits of justice, love, wisdom, and so on are taught to believers so that they taste and enjoy God directly and thereby are transformed or conformed to God intellectually, emotionally, and morally.

Augustine's view of participation in the divine life should not be mistaken for the Pelagianism against which he strove at about the same time that *De Trinitate* finally appeared (419 C.E.). Influenced by the Platonic tradition, Augustine was interested in the transformation of his reader from the inside out, or from the mind "down," so to speak. He believed character development to be, like Wayne Booth's coduction, the product of insight and reflection undertaken over a long period of dwelling in God and honing memory and judgment. Based on his own moral and intellectual struggles, Augustine was also persuaded of one's complete dependence on God's grace because our minds are distorted by false pleasures. In the *DT* prevenient grace does not appear as magic, however—some sort of special power added to strengthen a weak will; instead, it seems to work through scripture and church teaching on one who waits patiently for God.

If Augustine set the tone for modern insight-oriented psychotherapy, Pelagius may be likened to a behaviorist. Change comes from changing, not from thinking about changing. Desire follows doing, not the reverse. He is impatient of the gentle life with God that Augustine cherishes. From his letter to the virgin Demetrias, we know that Pelagius believed that the human being knows good and evil and is capable of acting on this knowledge with or without God (1981). He also believed that one can easily act on the good it knows it should undertake. He is not taken with the slow, patient teaching that Augustine commends.

Both Pelagius and Augustine believed that in order to change, seekers need to be encouraged, assured that success is possible and that grace is available. The difference between them is that Augustine put prayer, revelation and the necessity of church teaching at the head of that process of transformation, arguing that there is no going around it, because human desire is warped when left to its own resources.

Pelagius had greater trust in the power of the will to see clearly what Augustine, from his own experience, knew that he saw in a fog. To put it slightly differently, while Augustine believed that holiness was achieved indirectly, through an enjoyment of God that gathers up the believer's energies to love justice and goodness, Pelagius believed that holiness could be achieved directly, through sufficient self-control and discipline.

God's task, therefore, was to transform or, more precisely, to train his reader's mind to persuade her that he destined us for happiness; we need to know and love God in order to become our best selves. Augustine's energy for this arduous task is immense. It appears in two of his greatest works, the *Confessions* and *De Trinitate*. His great treatises on the human mind—particularly the role of memory, which is the primary means of processing what the Incarnation as well as the being of God itself have to teach—explain his vision of the power of the mind to discern goodness, and enjoy God, and be transformed.

It may be disappointing to modern romantics that Augustine selected the mind as the seat of human dignity and personhood. This should not, however, be construed as Augustine's preferring the intellect over the emotions. In late antiquity, ratiocination was not split off from affect, as is sometimes thought, because civilized life prized self-control. Thought and emotion were recognized as two important aspects of consciousness, just as Freud recognized what he called the id and the ego as two aspects of consciousness. In Freud's terms, violent emotions need control by the ego and superego. This concept was important both for Freud and for Augustine, who would never separate the heart from the head. The passions are far too labile to be on their own without control. Emotions are not to be stamped out.[7] Rather, they are to be redirected aright, and this responsibility can only be properly fulfilled when we rightly understand the power and dignity of our minds in the image of God. Augustine assigns this task to the will. Bochet translates it into French as *désire*. Augustine describes the well-ordered will as an act of deliberate choice toward acquiring excellence (244; *DT* VIII:2:4).

The goal of understanding is to train the mind to enjoy goodness itself—in short, to enjoy God—so that "by participation in the good, you can perceive good itself by participating in which these other things are good—and you understand it together with them when you hear a good this or that—if then you can put them aside and perceive good itself, you will perceive God. And if you cling to him in love, you will straightaway enter into bliss" (244–5; VIII:2:5). Enjoying God becomes us.

The Practical Task of the Catholic Faith

Bochet points out that Augustine's own experience structured his understanding of the spiritual quest evident in both the *Confessions* and *De Trinitate*.[8] Yet he did not countenance individual experience as theologically authoritative. On the contrary, he insisted that relying only on one's experience, thought, and judgment leads one deeper into the mire of blind spots and impure loves, especially when the mind is corrupted by false teachings (*Conf.* 61–2; IV:x:15).

On the basis of his experience, Augustine concluded, first, that clear thinking requires assistance, in the form of the church's teaching (94; VI:iv:5). This may account for his explaining church teaching, in books V through VII, before engaging the psychology. Still, his own experience of growing up in the church wandering off into Manichaeism for nearly a decade, and returning to the Church, became the prism through which his teaching on knowing God was refracted. His own life recapitulated the biblical story of a pristine creation and life with God, followed by a fall into sin and spiritual death, and eventual reversal by Christ the Mediator, who carries purified souls back to God to know and enjoy him. The struggle and eventual enlightenment and personal liberation Augustine experienced in re-embracing the Catholic faith modeled his teaching on how others should and could come to enjoy God. The biblical story and his own experience exemplified the Platonic paradigm of separation and reunion. Yet this is no self-conscious Neoplatonizing of Christian faith. The three testimonies merge unselfconsciously into a powerful tool of Christian formation.

Second, Augustine's spiritual journey is at once intellectual and moral: a search for truth and goodness. To sever mind from life would be unthinkable to him, for he trusted that the mind guides action. And he understood that one's actions are guided by one's conceptualizations of the world, shaped by norms of thought and behavior. It is no coincidence that the journey home to the Catholic faith created an equal and inverse distress about his sexual behavior (98–103, VI:vii–x:11–6; 111–32, VIII). And it is surely significant that it was scripture, and specifically Paul, that enabled him to break the bonds of addiction to sex, accepting both baptism and celibacy in virtually the same breath. But the way he links receiving the Catholic faith with receiving celibacy is no reason to conclude that he despised sex, as R. A. Markus points out (1990, 61). Augustine's point is that lusting after sex, or wealth, or power, or fame all distract one from seeking God, a point he felt qualified to speak to. Separating understanding from the spiritual and moral life would render the former pointless and the latter incoherent. The very essence of religion is to hold thought and action together because the human person is whole.

Third, Augustine's conversion came after he had lost hope that he could think his way out of his spiritual quagmire. And while he never denied a continuing role for reason in knowing God, he concluded that the Incarnation starts the process of amendment for life with God. Healing the mind is altogether the work of God effected by the Mediator as interpreted by the Catholic faith.

Augustine was convinced (perhaps with himself as the paradigmatic example) that those on the path to true knowledge that brings genuine happiness must first confront their own self-degrading behavior. Each must come to see that lasting happiness requires a transformed self-consciousness. As the modern self-help movements might put it, one has to hit bottom before being willing to risk change, even change for the better. Augustine was psychologically astute enough to realize that motivation for change requires two insights: one must recognize that one has a problem, and one must not despair of success. The former requires humility, which has little to do with the extreme self-denigration seen in some forms of monasticism and later medieval piety. The latter requires trust, provided by a proper grasp of revelation and doctrine.

"First we had to be persuaded how much God loved us, in case out of sheer despair we lacked the courage to reach up to him. Also we had to be shown what sort of people we are that he loves, in case we should take pride in our own worth, and so bounce even further away from him and sink even more under our own strength" (*DT* 153; IV:1:2). Augustine realized that in order to submit to divine guidance we had to be persuaded of God's good intentions. In an earlier treatise, *Of True Religion (TR),* he observed that God "did nothing by violence, but everything by persuasion and warning" (1958, 239; xvi:31), so that we might draw near to God out of love rather than fear.

The economy of salvation carries out this prodigious task. Creation itself, and, more important, the Incarnation, are part of a concerted pedagogical strategy to transform our thinking by bringing us to enjoy God. Augustine takes rain as a simple example. When we understand it as a gift of grace, rain, which freely nourishes both the just and the unjust, persuades us of God's generosity toward us, thereby simultaneously showing us that we can improve, all the while humbling us so that we trust God instead of ourselves (*DT* 153–4; IV:1:2).

In *Of True Religion* Augustine points out that Jesus is a better teacher than rain, for he severs people from their superficial joys and toys. God has sent a "bearer and instrument of the wisdom of God on behalf of the true salvation of the human race" (227; iii:3), the Word of God, "in order that men may receive the Word, love him, and enjoy Him so that the soul may be healed and the eye of the mind receive power to use the light" (228; iii:4). In his ministry Jesus speaks a word to the greedy (Matt. 6.19), the wanton (Gal. 6.8), the proud (Luke 14.11), the wrathful (Matt. 5.39), the belligerent (Matt. 5.44), the superstitious (Luke 17.21), the curious (2 Cor. 4.18), to *everyone,* in order to turn them from frivolity (1 John 2.15) (228; iii:4). The reason for sending the Incarnate Word is to get our attention, to recall the mind from unsightly thoughts and deeds and thereby reshape the character of believers. The Wisdom of God made known in Christ is the moral life, which is the enjoyment of God.

Sending Christ to us is the most potent cure for pride. For Christ teaches the eternal truth that humility is superior to pride when, by divesting himself of power and taking on weakness, he gains our allegiance and persuades us to do likewise (*Conf.* 128; VII:xviii:24). And the fact of the Incarnation itself as God's chosen design, far from denigrating God, increases our sense of our own dignity and deepens our respect for our bodies.

For thus he showed to carnal people, given over to bodily sense and unable with the mind to behold the truth, how lofty a place among creatures belonged to human nature, in that he appeared to men not merely visibly—for he could have done that in some ethereal body adapted to our weak powers of vision—but as a true man. The assuming of our nature was to be also its liberation. And that no one should perchance suppose that the creator of sex despised sex, he became a man born of a woman. (*TR* 239; xvi:30)

Not only does the Incarnation teach us by example to honor and respect our bodiliness and sexuality; by example, Jesus' life also teaches us how to conduct ourselves in relation to one another. Jesus' commending his mother to the care of the beloved disciple, his poverty, his refusal to be crowned king, his scorn for dynastic power, his bearing of insults and injuries, "all the things which [we] sought to avoid and so deviated from the search for truth, he endured and so robbed them of their power over us. . . . His whole life on earth as Man, in the humanity he deigned to assume, was an education in morals" (*TR* 240; xvi:31–2).

De Trinitate carries forward the exposition of the aretegenic goal of the Incarnation. Spiritual blindness prevents us from grasping the truth, so we need to be intellectually and morally purified. Although the purification remains incomplete in this life, the Catholic faith is the only means by which we experience God's grace. By holding the Catholic faith "in things done for us in time for our sakes," we approach the truth:

> *This is eternal life, that they should know you the one true God, and Jesus Christ whom you have sent* (John 17.3). . . . Now until this happens and in order . . . to prevent . . . faith . . . from clashing with the truth of contemplating eternal things which we hope for in eternal life, truth itself, coeternal with the Father, *originated from the earth* (Ps. 85.12) when the Son of God came in order to become Son of man and to capture our faith and draw it to himself, and by means of it to lead us on to his truth [emphasis original]. (*DT* 170; IV:4:24)

Christ's mission is to penetrate our minds and hearts and turn us to God, "in order that, when we come to sight and truth succeeds to faith, eternity might likewise succeed to mortality" (169–70; IV:4:24). Eternity or immortality begins by dwelling in the eternal truth of God in this world. Augustine offers a fuller explanation of eternal life later on (352–3; XIII:3:12). Immortality is happiness achieved through dwelling in God, which we do when we become children of God by grace—that is, when Christ transforms us from misery to happiness. Bliss begins in the spiritual life and is perfected for the saints in the world to come (*CG* XXII:29).[9]

Christ's death and resurrection are also designed to humble the reader. His death, no less than his Incarnation, exemplifies humility (*Conf.* 219; X:xliii:68).[10] And in *De Trinitate* IV.5–6, Augustine wrestles with an apparently logical question: how the single death and resurrection of Christ cancels the complex death of humanity.[11] Christ's death does double duty on the moral front. It slays sinfulness and calls the reader to a life of righteousness, then encourages her by offering hope of resurrection. The "logical" problem, however, screens an aretegenic agenda:

> To this cry [of dereliction on the cross] there corresponds what the apostle says, *knowing that our old [self] was crucified together with him, in order to cancel the body of sin, that we might no longer be the slaves of sin* (Rom. 6.6). By the crucifixion of the inner [self] is to be understood the sorrows of repentance and a kind of salutary torment of self-discipline, a kind of death to erase the death of ungodliness in which God does not leave us. And, thus it is by this sort of cross that the *body of sin* is *canceled* (Rom. 6.6), so that we should no longer *offer* our *members to sin as the weapons of wickedness* (Rom. 6.13) [emphasis original]. (*DT* 156; IV:1:6)

Sinless behavior cancels out godlessness when the cross impresses itself upon us and repentance and self-denial fill us with godly attitudes and actions. In other words, the cross is a gift that leads the believer to repentance and abandonment of sin.

Augustine provides an extended account of the practical function of the cross in the middle of the epistemology (bk. XIII). Here the intellectual problem is the same one with which Anselm of Canterbury would struggle six centuries later in the *Cur Deus Homo* in order to stress mercy. The death of Christ seems to imply that God was powerless to overcome the devil (who held humans in thrall) any other way. Again, we see that Augustine's answer is purely practical, although the issue is presented as if it were purely theoretical. That is, the therapy of choice was to use righteousness first (in the cross), and then power (the resurrection), for the following reasons. First, as an example of how to conduct our business, since on our own we are most likely to

> neglect or even detest justice and studiously devote [our]selves to power, rejoicing at the possession of it or inflamed with the desire for it. So it pleased God to deliver man . . . so that men too might imitate Christ by seeking to beat the devil at the justice game, not the power game. Not that power is to be shunned as something bad, but that the right order must be preserved which puts justice first. (*DT* 356; XIII:4:17)

Second, righteousness is a virtue to be cultivated, and right living creates happiness. But the vulnerable person needs personal power first in order to become righteous. Yet God realizes that "men hardly ever want to be powerful in order to overpower these [faults], they want it in order to overpower [others]" (*DT* 357; XIII:4:17). The divine strategy put justice before power to the following end: "Let a man will to be sagacious, will to be brave, will to be just, and by all means let him want the power really to manage these things, and let him seek to be powerful in himself and in an odd way against himself for himself" (*DT* 357; XIII:4:17).

Christ's death, an instrument of grace, convicts believers to exercise self-control and commit to righteousness. The difference between Augustine's understanding of the Incarnation and how it leads to eternal life, and the later Western focus on forgiveness of sins or election, is striking. This is not to suggest that Augustine lacks an objective theory of the atonement. Indeed, the teaching on the virtues as a consequence of the Incarnation occurs in the midst of it. But it is not the central focus of the chapter. Perhaps Anselm unwittingly exaggerated the technical side of the atonement when stressing mercy where Augustine had stressed justice. At any rate, Augustine taught, "This is how we are said to be justified in the blood of Christ. This is how that innocent blood was shed for the forgiveness of our sins. That is why in the psalms he calls himself *free among the dead* (Ps. 88.5); he is the only one who ever died free of the debt of death." And after citing other scripture texts he concludes, "And he proceeds straight from there to his passion, to pay for us debtors the debt he did not owe himself" (357; XIII:4:18).

Immediately following this note on justification, however, Augustine goes right back to the aretegenic import of Christ's deed. His voluntary suffering should not be interpreted to mean that Christ lacked power (and so was not really God). He did this intentionally. "In this way the justice of humility was made more acceptable, seeing that the power of divinity could have avoided the humiliation if it had wanted to; and so by the death of one so powerful we powerless mortals have justice set before us and power promised us. He did one of these two things by dying, the other by rising" (357; XIII:4:18).

THE SALUTARITY OF SAPIENCE

Recognizing the aretegenic drive of the doctrine of God is an important step in understanding how Augustine retrains the disordered minds of his readers. But it does not yet tie together the various strands of the argument woven through *De Trinitate*. Several questions persist. How is the soteriology of knowing, explained in the second half of the work, related to the soteriology of the divine economy, inserted in books VIII and XIII? What is the aretegenic function of the carefully developed doctrine of the *imago Dei?* What is the import of the conundrum of loving the unknown?

Rather than treat these questions separately, I will develop the picture of the second half of the work to show that Augustine's response to these issues constitutes a Christian corrective and criticism of Neoplatonic moral philosophy of his day. Though Augustine is in sympathy with philosophy's goal of moral reform and contemplation, he decisively Christianizes it on aretegenic grounds.[12]

Both the *City of God* and the *Confessions* criticize pagan philosophies. Book VIII of *CG* traces true religion in the history of philosophy from Thales to Plato, who went astray in not recognizing the world's creator, revealed through created works (*CG* 312; VIII:10). Plato also erred in countenancing polytheism, though Augustine gave him credit for holding that the gods are good and honorable, so that those who worshiped them would at least be well influenced (316–7; VIII:13). But the moral power of polytheism failed after Plato, especially with Augustine's fellow African Platonist philosopher Apuleius, who believed in evil demons and led people astray by connecting these ethereal creatures with terrestrial animals (321–2; VIII:16). But Apuleius failed to include "the qualities of virtue, wisdom and felicity" (321–2; VIII:16) that would have justified belief in demons. So when humans began worshiping demons, true religion, which should free people from vice, was crushed. Instead of being resisted, vices were reinforced. True religion should assist adherents to control anger, shun bribery, respond to people and events not impulsively but with calmly considered decisions, even to love enemies, and to quell emotional turmoil in the soul (323–4; VIII:17). Yet these are precisely the vices exemplified by the demons whom Apuleius establishes in the air. And to add insult to injury, he condoned magic. Again, one hears echoes of Athanasius: a morally harmful religion must be false.

Augustine criticizes other philosophies that promote bad religions, which degrade and debilitate their adherents. He contrasts these with Christianity, which, while it may appear to share some superficial commonalities with these religions, is true while they are false. For example, the belief in angels and the Christian cult of the martyrs do not encourage worship of themselves but only emulation of their goodness (341; VIII:27). So even though Plato had insights close to Christianity, the heirs of his thought led people badly astray, so that they are hindered rather than helped by their religion. The gateway for Augustine himself to rectify these errors seems to lie open before him.

The *Confessions* contains a second hint about the relation of Platonism and Christianity. As taken as he was with Platonic philosophy, especially Cicero's *Hortensius,* now lost to us, Augustine believed a central element in philosophy to be missing. "One thing alone put a brake on my intense enthusiasm [for Platonic literature]—that the name of Christ was not contained in the book. . . . Any book which lacked this name, however well written or polished or true, could not entirely grip me" (*Conf.* 39–40; III:iv:8). And a bit later on, he justified leaving both the Manichees and the philosophers; to any "who were without Christ's saving name, I altogether refused to entrust the healing of my soul's sickness" (89; V:xiv:25).[13] The upshot of this discussion is that even though Platonic philosophy aimed to heal the self, it failed because it lacked historical grounding; it failed to teach through material things. It stands to reason, then, that one should read *De Trinitate* in light of this dilemma: what is the best way, indeed the only true way, to heal the self?

De Trinitate book VIII turns from the scriptural and dogmatic exegesis of the first half to the task of helping the reader perceive truth and goodness apart from material things through material things. For the self is healed by becoming true and good. Augustine does not suggest, however, that truth is discernible apart from knowing God. He has taken pains to tell us that deformed minds corrupt our desires. So the truth and goodness we seek must be outside ourselves, yet something we can partake of, indeed taste, enjoy, participate in, and love (*DT* 244–5; viii:2:5). Happiness is not an ontological state of being but an epistemological state of understanding: a breakthrough in consciousness, a radically changed state of mind that results when one dwells in God rather than in falsehood and evil. Perhaps modern psychotherapy partly understands this. I say partly because psychotherapy, like theology and philosophy, has left God and its responsibilities for moral formation behind.

Augustine's problem in recommending clinging to truth and goodness arises from his Christian commitments. Both his experience and the church's teaching persuaded him that there is a gap between creator and creature that the creature cannot bridge. Augustine concluded that the sapience that would make him (and his reader) happy is not to be found within himself unaided. Since it is outside us, how can we even want it, let alone achieve it?

Plato had taught that we become sapient in a process of discovery through dialogue rather than through either didactic or experiential learning. Wisdom is not gained directly, the way information for baking a cake is gained or as in a classroom lecture. It must come through insight, reflection, discernment, and inspiration as a result of thinking and guidance from a higher source.[14] As Karl Jaspers put it, for Plato, knowledge requires desiring to know, purification, openness to correction (humility), and developing a taste for such things (1962, 21–8). Augustine follows Plato in this. Recall that at the outset of book IV, and consistently thereafter, Augustine reminds his readers that the economy teaches these spiritual virtues of purification (humility and trust) necessary for healing. But even all this is not enough for Augustine. And so he spends half of book VIII and books IX through XI wrestling with the problem of how one can love the unknown. For without an answer to the problem he could grow in virtue with the help of the economy but not achieve sapience through love (*DT* 245–8; VIII:3:6–8).

The partially successful epistemology of these books aims, on one level, to develop an answer to the problem of loving the unknown. But its subtext pivots around Augustine's carefully crafted psychology, built on the concept of the *imago dei* that became the standard Western doctrine, if in somewhat truncated form. He constructed this doctrine in two parts, one having to do with Christ, in book VII, and the other having to do with human beings, in book XII. The first part of the doctrine is that Christ is the power and, particularly, the wisdom of God (1 Cor. 1.24) (217–22; VII:1:1–3, 2:4), so that sapience is found in him. Immediately following this concept Augustine adds the notion that since Christ is "in the form of God and equal to God" (Phil. 2.6) but emptied himself to become our servant, he is the model and example through whom we perceive the sapience of God and live according to it: he is "the model which the image who is equal to the Father provides us with that we may be refashioned to the image of God; for we follow the Son by living wisely" (223, VII:2:5; cf. 156, IV:1:6; 164, IV:3:17).

The second element in the psychology is, of course, that we are made in the image of God, Gen. 1:26–7 (325; XII:2:6).[15] Early on Augustine associates the image of God in human beings with the Trinity, which he believes is implied in Gen. 1.26, "let us make," so that he starts out with the conviction that "Man is the image of the Trinity; not equal to the Trinity as the Son is equal to the Father, but approaching it" (231; VII:4:12). Finally, in book XII, Augustine connects the *imago Dei* with the mind, an association made in Pauline theology (Eph. 4.23; Col. 3.9). Being in the image of God means being renewed of mind. "If then we are being renewed in the spirit of our mind, and if it is this new man who is being renewed for the recognition of God according to the image of him who created him, there can be no doubt that man was not made to the image of him who created him as regards his body or any old part of his consciousness, but as regards the rational mind, which is capable of recognizing God" (329; XII:3:12).

The last element of the psychology takes place in the midst of a discussion on sin, which he views as an abnormal state. He puts these elements together to create a theological psychology in which the being of God—God's wisdom—is the true dignity of the human person. One discovers and become one's true self by conformation to this wisdom of God, discerned through Christ.[16]

Thus, the search for the unknown itself turns out to be the means for arriving at one's proper self, for exercising one's God-given destiny—enjoying God. But even as the subtext becomes visible, the main line of the plot becomes more complex. For in the search for the unknown, self-knowledge, the first resort, turns out to be a dead end. The seeker finds that the dignity of truth and goodness requires reconstructing a dignified and refined self, one whose identity stems from loving and participating in God. The search seems to end in a stalemate that is necessary in order for one to press forward.

Inference and discerning judgment, gleaned from known examples to unknowns of similar type, are the first steps in the ascent to the unknown (248–51; VIII:4:9). Genuine learning of this sort (Booth's coduction again), which transforms the learner by expanding her repertoire and honing her judgment, is the contribution of faith through revelation. In the work of faith, heroes (saints for Christians) are especially important because they promote emulation of good character traits, as our literary critics Booth, Nussbaum, and Eldridge point out. Of course, the greatest figure we have is Christ, who cries "learn of me" (Matt. 11.29), giving both hope of success and a model for loving one's neighbor (251–5; VIII:5:10–4). Admiration for the right sort of people is an essential preliminary step in preparing the self to know and love God.

In book IX, amid the epistemology that yearns to figure out how one can love the unknown, Augustine takes up the second question, that of the function of the *imago Dei*, which turns out to be the solution to his problem and our proper link to God. Scripture provides the key to overcoming the gap between creator and creature and adumbrates the proper source of personal identity. He struggles with the tangle of these issues through book XI, leaving the pathway strewn with trinities that finally will not advance the reader to the desired goal of sapience because they are limited to temporal considerations and so provide little hope of secure happiness. In the process, however, he introduces another subtext: enjoyment of the life of the mind for its own sake. He points out the pleasurableness of using one's mind adroitly—at the self-improvement that accompanies discovering one's likeness to God. At the same time he continues to warn the reader of the inevitable pitfalls on the path of self-examination, pitfalls that can end in self-degradation.

While it may appear that the dogmatic teaching of the church has been left behind, this is not really so, for it remains the backdrop before which the interior quest for God is played out. The triunity of God—that is, one substance, three persons—is not only the correct understanding of God but the model for self-understanding. The pleasure gained from the various mental trinities Augustine tries out—memory, understanding, will; lover, beloved, and love; mind, its love, knowledge; sight, vision, and interpretation of what is seen, and so on—all contain a good deal of truth in that they all support the teaching that the human mind is a unified trinity, as God is, and so builds the case for the dignity of the *imago Dei*. They even bring genuine pleasure at the joy of understanding, the powers of imagination, and creativity. But as pleasurable as the life of the mind is for its own sake, the true seeker presses on, because these trinities, while true, fail to carry the seeker beyond the material objects that give rise to them to a permanent source of happiness.

The search of books IX through XI fails because self-understanding based on self finally ends in a circle. Self leads only to more self, and Augustine is sated with self. But the mind as the chief instrument of transformed understanding cannot be abandoned, for it is the best tool we have. And so he makes one final attempt at addressing the problem, setting up the challenge of knowledge all over again in books XII through XIV.

Book XII distinguishes *scientia* from *sapientia,* as already noted; XIII focuses on knowledge, while XIV is devoted to the final goal, genuine sapience. Book XII makes an eloquent appeal for the life of the mind as the locus of the image of God. The mind distinguishes us from animals and is the source of dignity and righteousness. A mind, he proclaims, is a terrible thing to waste. One maximizes being in the image of God when dwelling on God, the most sublime of human pursuits. But the dignity of the image carries over into quotidian activity as well, even when the activity is not focused on God (328; XII:3:10).

The notion that the image of God resides in the rational capacities of human beings has become so commonplace in Christian theology that its power as the seat of human dignity has faded from view. Augustine is, to my knowledge, the first to state the value of human personhood in such a positive, powerful, and persistent manner. As we have seen, Paul argued that human dignity arises from being taken into the drama of salvation; Matthew located human dignity in one's ability to hold fast to goodness, made known through divine teaching, despite persecution; Athanasius located the norm for human relationships in conformation to the Johannine unity that obtains between the Father and the Son. But only Augustine says that we experience the nobility and truth of God whenever we use our minds rightly. Human dignity is becoming ourselves by knowing God. Yet without Christ to teach us we would not even know of it. This is the aretology underlying the whole work.

Book XIII answers our initial question as to how the Platonic soteriology relates to the Incarnation—or how Augustine Christianizes Platonism. Given what he said about Christ in the *City of God* and the *Confessions,* it should not be surprising that Christ is the key to knowing both God and ourselves: "Our knowledge therefore is Christ, and our wisdom is the same Christ" (363; XIII:6:24). To those who trust him, Christ teaches knowledge about temporal things, including the development of virtues and piety, especially the priority of righteousness over power, a moral orientation which Augustine inherited from Plato but which Plato could not accomplish because he lacked Christ. Augustine concludes the book on faith with "the admonition that *the just man lives on faith* (Rom. 1.17), and this *faith works through love* (Gal. 5.6); in this way the virtues, too, by which one lives sagaciously, courageously, moderately and justly, are all to be related to the same faith" [emphasis in original] (365; XIII:6:26). Augustine's final word about the virtuous life desired by the philosophers is that it only happens through Christ.

As wonderful as the benefits of faith are in this life, the benefits of sapience are greater, for they finally enable the seeker to rest permanently in God, to achieve immortality by gazing on God. Having begun with the church's teaching on the Trinity, and finding personal identity to rest therein, Augustine turns at last to the reason the self was made, "to use reason and understanding in order to understand and gaze upon God that it was made to the image of God" (374; xiv:2:6). Prayer and piety are the way to rest in God, and resting in God is finally the way to a wholesome self; resting in self brings at best happy moments. The goal of life is rest in God. Once the soul understands itself called to "remember its God to whose image it was made, and understand[s] and love[s] him [it is] able to share in him. . . . [I]t will reign in happiness where it reigns eternal" (383; xiv:4:15).

In sum, God longs for us to be happy, and we are only happy when we are our best selves, and our best selves are our most dignified selves, who find their home in God. The economy, made known through the scriptures, church teaching, and perhaps Augustine's own work on the powers of the mind, all bend to that end.

Assessment

Although the difficulty of the *DT* mitigates against strong claims for any single interpretation, I have argued that Augustine's aretegenic goal was to present the doctrine of the Trinity so that it establishes the seeker's identity as arising from the being of God. He gets his reader's attention by shaming, embarrassing, and exposing her weaknesses, as well as by encouraging, urging, and reassuring her that a new and better self is both called for and possible, in order to focus her energy on the search for self in God. The chastisement is persistent though never punitive. God means to form us by leading us gently to himself.

The divine pedagogy starts from the missions or sendings of the Son and the Holy Spirit in the economy, leads the seeker to their procession from the Father, and finally ends at the divine "substance" or "unity" or God. Scripture *(scientia)* captures our attention by explaining the economy; dogmatic exegesis explains how the processions of the Son and Holy Spirit ground our identity in the identity of God; and "contemplation" enables us to glimpse the divine "substance"—*sapientia*—goodness, truth, and justice.

The discussion of the processions of the divine Persons, while awkward and inconclusive, suffices to invite the seeker to recognize herself as the *imago Dei*—homologous with the threeness of God—the springboard from which she will be able to dwell in the sapience that is the divine "substance," or unity, of God. The doctrine of appropriations teaches that regardless of the point that arrests our attention in the economy of salvation, its purpose is to lead us beyond the material realm of *scientia* to the spiritual realm of *sapientia,* the divine unity.

Augustine's theology becomes more accessible to those who agree that spiritual formation is necessary for a happy life. The sapience of God is the core of human happiness, as far as Augustine was concerned. But Western theology focused on the economy—whether and how sins are forgiven. This constriction had the effect of obscuring the aretegenic function of the doctrine of God, and especially of the unity of God. But for Augustine, formation through the economy, the mystery of the Trinity, and the unity of God is the only firm foundation for social and interpersonal relations. The loss of sapience as central to personal identity has alienated the modern world from Augustine's teaching.

Augustine's current critics argue that his theology is unhelpful on several counts: it does not support social action; it does not support interpersonal skills as a standard of sociality; and it does not support the modern norm of growth and change. It short, it is unhelpful because it strains toward "contemplation" rather than action. None of these criticisms is precise, however. Augustine would support these modern values as long as they arise from and tend toward divine sapience. He would object to the division between the active and contemplative life because everyone's life must be guided by sapience. He would hesitate at the contemporary emphasis on interpersonal relationships that are not grounded in sapience, because an identity constructed by relationships and actions can easily lose sight of its spiritual grounding. Indeed, staking one's identity on relationships with others is far too precarious for Augustine, both morally and emotionally. We are far less vulnerable if our dignity and self-worth come from being planted in goodness and righteousness than if we try to sustain relationships on any other basis. He, like Athanasius before him, would certainly support growth and change, if we agree that there are divine standards of goodness and truth pointed to by the economy for which growth strives.

This is the point at which moderns object to both Athanasius and Augustine. It is no longer evident that sapience is a reality, that goodness and righteousness have the independent validity and clarity that these Fathers attributed to them as the divine "substance." This makes the apophatic teaching of Gregory of Nyssa very appealing, for if we cannot know the divine nature we can at least grasp the social relationships and actions into which God enters. Pressing actions and relationships "back" to the divine nature seems too speculative and abstract, even empty for those who live in the world of change and becoming. But Augustine is insisting that actions and relationships be grounded in the being of God because we are too unstable to act or love on any other terms. In essence, by teaching that our identity is to be found in the divine nature rather than in God's actions and relationships alone, he is offering us a safety zone to protect us from our own failings and those of others.

Augustine is concerned with strengthening the nobility and dignity of human personhood by pointing us to the spiritual truth that is God's nature. This approach to human dignity, cultivated through virtue ethics and dedication to an unswerving norm of goodness learned from the actions of God, is only now being retrieved for theology. Despite the often dour view of Augustine conveyed by his teachings on original sin and predestination, here we find a different approach: self-esteem and happiness stem from the most exalted source. God's respect for us extends so far that he reaches to bring us to himself in order to reform us. His whole struggle in the *DT* is to bring us from a material to a spiritual concept of both God and ourselves, so that we formulate what we do based on who we are as homologs of the Trinity.

Theology, if one judges it from the works examined here, is the art of persuading people of the wisdom and goodness of God so that they may better understand themselves and God. Augustine, anticipating Calvin, insisted on the interdependence of knowledge of God and of ourselves, using his own experience as a beacon to light the way. Interpreting scripture and doctrine is in the service of this therapeutic and pastoral end. Theology encourages intellectual and emotional maturity—to be able to use one's mind for one's good and that of others; that is, it promotes wisdom.

Augustine lived at a time of tremendous social upheaval. And his work was pivotal in providing a theology that would both link people to God and provide the moral foundation for a new society in a culture sated with the degrading aspects of popular paganism. That foundation, poured by God himself and made real to us through the Incarnation, is wisdom. It fell to Augustine to persuade God-seekers that they and posterity would be better served if we understand our selves as echoes of God than as any other reality they could desire or pray for.

Notes

1. In chapter 8 I shall suggest that the replacement of the ontological view of salvation with the functional view began with Saint Benedict.

2. Reading from this that Augustine lived in abstractions and despised the body is in-

creasingly recognized as a misunderstanding, as Bochet has argued. She is joined in this by R. A. Markus (1990) and Paula Fredriksen (1988), with specific reference to the role of sex in Augustine's thought.

3. Viewing *DT* as an ascetical work is unusual, as it is generally viewed as a dogmatic and highly speculative work. In his important biography of the bishop, for example, Peter Brown does not treat *DT* extensively and considers it a speculative work of little importance (1969, 166, 277).

4. Edmund Hill, in the introduction to his new translation of *DT*, assessed its dogmatic contributions, although he is one of a growing number of scholars to recognize the work's spiritual goals. Here it will suffice to note Hill's observations that the dogmatic purpose of Augustine's trinitarian exposition was to eliminate all traces of subordinationism from treatments of the "economic" Trinity, by reassessing scriptural passages traditionally interpreted as supporting the submission of the Son to the Father (45–9). Augustine does this by asserting that the sendings of the Son and the Spirit do not imply their inequality with the Father but, rather, reveal one sent on a mission. It is the missionary character of the second and third Persons of the Trinity that, I will shortly argue, reveal the apparently dogmatic concern of undermining heresy as an essentially pastoral one. Hill concludes that one of Augustine's lasting contributions to western trinitarian theology is the distinction of the Persons based on their relationships to one another.

5. Insistence on the full divinity of the Holy Spirit, and the difficulty of demonstrating why the Holy Spirit is not called a son or grandson nor spoken of as begotten, are recurrent themes throughout *De Trinitate*. At the conclusion of the whole, the author admits that he has not been successful in the latter endeavor. "So great has this difficulty been, that every time I wanted to bring out some comparative illustration of this point . . . I found that no adequate expression followed whatever understanding I came to; and I was only too well aware that my attempt even to understand involved more effort than result" (430; XV:6:45). Each time he demonstrated the third moment of another mental trinity he added that it is inappropriate to speak of it as either parent or offspring. Yet this is more assertion than argument.

6. Augustine remarks, and I would agree, that the word "substance," as a translation of *substantia*, may not be the best, and that "quality" may be better (190; V:1:3). "Substance" is a particularly poor choice in English because it leaves the impression of an underlying material substrate beneath the Persons of the Trinity, when what he is wanting to say is that the being of the godhead is these qualities. The use of the word "substance" has fed western anxiety that, on Augustine's view, we do not, cannot, really know God, when Augustine's hope is that we come to see that in knowing God's wisdom and goodness we genuinely know God. Sadly, his use of the word "substance," which no doubt has changed connotations over the centuries, focused subsequent theology on precisely the materialist understanding of God that he sought to overthrow.

7. Bochet has an excellent discussion of Augustine's break with Stoicism on this point (70–7).

8. Several years before writing his autobiography he inserted a snapshot of his experiences of being lost and found into his treatise on *The Usefulness of Belief*: "If, therefore, your experience has been of this kind, and you have been similarly anxious about your soul, if now at last you see you have been sufficiently tossed about and wish to bring your toils to an end, follow the way of the Catholic discipline which has been derived from Christ himself and has come down to us through the apostles, and by us will be passed on to posterity" (307; viii:20).

9. Augustine's treatment of the Christian life in *DT* and *Conf*, encouraging seekers to

dwell in God as the means to happiness and immortality, appears to contrast markedly with the doctrines of original sin and predestination developed in *CG* and the anti-Pelagian writings. Rowan Greer, noting that the *DT* and the *CG* were written contemporaneously, suggests that the treatise on the Christian life only applies to those blessed with prevenient grace (Greer 1986, 85). Since no one knew their final destiny, all seekers would presumably be interested in the search for happiness developed in the *DT*.

10. This chapter contains both a speculative and a practical interpretation of the cross, with the objective reconciling act of the cross serving to shape believers who take its display of divine love to heart. Those who understand themselves to be loved by virtue of God's reconciling work on the cross experience their despair over their sins transformed into hope. By this reconciliation—which is objective, *extra nos*—those who understand themselves as occupying a new status as children of God, in Paul's sense, are strengthened and healed. Whereas apart from Christ they saw themselves as weak and unskilled, the wondrousness of Christ's death on behalf of all encourages a new self-understanding: self-respect based on God's love.

11. For Augustine death was a complex of events progressively distancing the individual from God. The first death begins with the death of the soul by separation from God at the Fall and is completed with the separation of the soul from the body at what we recognize as death. The second death is the reunion of the body and soul to eternal torment at the final judgment (*CG* XX).

12. The argument that Augustine's aretegenic soteriology is a Christian corrective of Neoplatonism and its derivative philosophies contrasts with, or perhaps nuances, that of John Cavadini. He believes that Augustine intentionally confuses readers, feigning to persuade them of the ability of Neoplatonic philosophy to lead in ascent to God (1992, 105). This goal, Cavadini argues, is a deliberate failure, because the success of the mission—contemplation— is impossible for the human mind and remains an eschatological goal. Faith, not the "introspective character of the soteriology of ascent" (108), turns out to be the hidden point of the work. Instead of a speculative work, Cavadini finds it a polemic against Neoplatonic views of salvation (110).

13. This last passage may also help moderns regain a bit more interest in Augustine's theology and soteriology, because it reminds us who have lost interest that philosophy was the ancient world's moral and spiritual therapy. The definitive work on this topic was Werner Jaeger's three-volume *Paideia*, published in the 1940s (1944). It was supplemented and expanded by Robert Cushman's *Therapeia* in the late 1950s (1958). Recently Michel Despland's work on Plato, *The Education of Desire* (especially chapter 6) (1985), and Martha Nussbaum's work on the Greek dramatists and Aristotle, *Love's Knowledge*, discussed in the opening chapter, reclaim the therapeutic task of their works. But perhaps it is worth noting again that modern philosophy and theology have suffered a similar fate. With the separation of aretegenic from intellectual activity, the search for "truth" in both fields became divorced from the search for goodness, and both disciplines were truncated into purely cognitive pursuits. This is a radical departure from both cognitive pursuit in the ancient world and from the purpose of philosophy and theology as classically conceived.

14. Socrates is always pictured by Plato in dialogue with small groups of close friends. While many people do think things through best in the presence of others, the more introverted will process their reflections internally, and only in solitude will they reach the insights called forth in Platonic dialogues.

15. An excursus in the text is worth noting here. Augustine spends most of book XIII chap. 3 of *De Trinitate* worrying over an apparent scriptural discrepancy between the de-

scriptions of being in the image of God in Gen. 1.27, the primary text, and 1 Cor. 11.7. The Genesis text suggests that women and men are equally in the image of God, while the Pauline text argues that this honor applies only to men, while women are to the glory of man. Augustine is exercised about this inequality and struggles mightily to resolve the problem. Finally, he cannot accept the idea that women are not in the image of God. So he introjects the Pauline inequality between women and men into the person of every individual, saying that since every person is liable to sin, the duality exists within each person.

16. In terms of Augustine's corpus, this work is striking for the complete absence of any doctrine of original sin. Sin is depicted as a fall from one's true self, a seeking of happiness in self or transient pleasures rather than in God. Sex is consistently depicted as good. One is forced to conclude that any construal of Augustine's anthropology as pessimistic, built around sex, or even misogynist is a partial reading.

PART IV

Medieval Piety

With the close of the patristic age, Western Christianity turned inward. No longer a persecuted minority, Christians turned their attention from evangelizing pagans to shepherding the baptized through life. The possession of power itself began to reshape Christian beliefs and practices.

Monasticism began as a movement to escape from the corrupting influences of the cities and from the religious laxity that accompanied the church's flush of power. Taking refuge first in the isolation of the desert, then in the solitude of the monk's cell, both eremitical and cenobitic forms of monasticism focused on prayer and self-control. Western piety turned from dwelling in God, or being indwelt by God to the anxiety-ridden question "How can I ever be certain that God loves me?" Perhaps most significantly, the assumption that God respects us because we are his own was replaced with the cultivation of humility in the face of God's anger at our sinfulness. Medieval theology made its home in the doctrine of the atonement and the practices that developed around it: recounting of sins, the means of their remission, and procedures for absolution.

Yet the alleviation of anxiety was not the whole story. The three theologians examined in part IV all sought to educe the salutarity of the Incarnation and death of Christ for the Christian life. With both Anselm of Canterbury and Thomas Aquinas we see the development of a theme earlier found in Augustine: we learn to love righteousness and pursue mercy by watching what God has done in Jesus Christ. While Christ had always been a model for pious Christians, his obedience and humility were now singled out for special attention.

Despite the work of theologians like Anselm and Thomas to focus attention on what we are to learn of God, the age was taken with the seriousness of sin and divine wrath. In a move that challenged the tenor and assumptions of the time, Julian of Norwich contributed a woman's voice to the theological mix. Julian frontally challenged the popular emphasis on the wrath of God. It is God's love, not his wrath, that enables us to love God and be "oned" with him.

7

Learning the Cross of Christ

Anselm of Canterbury

The history of theology is filled with stories of strife, contests for power and control, and political intrigue. In the face of all that, St. Anselm offered a fresh alternative. In a remarkable inversion of power politics, he "literally loved his enemies until they submitted to his rule, and there is no doubt that his love was sincere" (Vaughn 1987, 50). His biographer and disciple, Eadmer,[1] described Anselm as

> loved by all as a mild and gentle man to whom—in his own eyes—nobody owed anything. . . . [I]n Anselm [there shone forth] a wonderful and pure humility and simplicity which won all hearts (111). . . . [H]e knew how to possess his soul in patience; he was peacemaker among those who hated peace; to those who attacked him he spoke words of gentleness and peace, desiring to overcome their evil with good (82). . . . [H]e made himself all things to all men, helping everyone to the extent of his power, admitting to his conversation all who wished to hear him without regard to who they were, and satisfying each one with his kindness and affability whatever the nature of the subject they raised might be. (Eadmer 1970, 107)

As abbot of the monastery at Bec, Anselm became both mother and father to the youngsters in his care.

> For he bore with equanimity the habits and infirmities of them all, and to each, as he saw what was expedient, he supplied what was necessary. . . . It was, in fact, Anselm's custom to spend time in the infirmary, making careful enquiries about the illnesses of all the brethren, and bringing to each of them without hesitation or unwillingness whatever his illness required. And so, while he was a father to those who were well, he was a mother to the sick: or rather, he was both father and mother to the sick and the sound alike. Hence any of them with any private trouble hastened to unburden himself to him, as if to the gentlest of mothers. (22–3)

His generosity extended beyond the oblates in his charge to whoever asked for his help, including lay people (72). He was so dedicated to the cultivation of kindness that even as Archbishop of Canterbury, he was criticized for poor judgment and excessive mildness in ecclesiastical discipline (79).

As abbot, Anselm perfected his irenic disposition into a mature management and leadership style. He was convinced that mildness and gentleness are the proper instruments for the correction of faults, especially the character development of the oblates. Anselm was a self-conscious teacher who summed up his pedagogical strategy by way of a simile.

> He compared the time of youth to a piece of wax of the right consistency for the impress of a seal. "For if the wax" he said, "is too hard or too soft it will not, when stamped with the seal, receive a perfect image. But if it preserves a mean between these extremes of hardness and softness, when it is stamped with the seal, it will receive the image clear and whole." (20)

Eadmer illustrates Anselm's pedagogical method with the frequently cited story of a bright young man named Osbern whose "difficult character" (expressed as hatred for Anselm) the abbot undertook to tame in order to develop the youth's intellectual abilities. Anselm reached out to the boy by indulging and flattering him. The anecdote is quite long, but worth repeating because Eadmer captures Anselm's penetrating grasp of human psychology and his deft pedagogical strategy.

> The youth rejoiced in these favours, and gradually his spirit was weaned from its wildness. He began to love Anselm, to listen to his advice, and to refashion his way of life. When Anselm saw this, he showed a more tender affection to him than to any other; he nursed and cherished him, and by his exhortation and instruction he encouraged him in every way to improve. Then slowly he withdrew the concessions made to his youth, and strove to draw him on to a mature and upright way of life. Nor was his pious care in vain: his holy counsels took firm root in the youth and bore fruit. When therefore he saw that he could confidently rely on the firmness of the young man's good intent, he began to cut away all childish behaviour in him, and if he found in him anything worthy of blame, he punished him severely not only with words but also with blows. And how did he stand it? He bore everything patiently, he was strengthened in every religious endeavour, he was eager to learn every form of religious exercise, he patiently endured the reproaches, the insults, the detractions of the others, and preserved towards all an attitude of unfeigned love. (16–7)

Anselm used love and discipline (in that order) as the instruments of choice in character-training. The point was to win the pupil's trust and loyalty before imposing discipline. And he taught others to do so as well. Eadmer tells how Anselm corrected a brother abbot who misguidedly preferred rigorous discipline to love. The abbot complained to Anselm that he was at the end of his tether with the "incorrigible ruffians, the stupid brutes" entrusted to his care, because repeated beatings did nothing to cure them. Anselm observed that the abbot had succeeded in raising beasts instead of men and helped his peer to understand why through the use of analogy:

> Now tell me, my lord abbot, if you plant a tree-shoot in your garden, and straightway shut it in on every side so that it has no space to put out its branches, what kind of tree will you have in years after when you let it out of its confinement?" "A useless one certainly, with its branches all twisted and knotted." "And whose fault would this be, except your own for shutting it in so unnaturally? Without doubt, this is what you do with your boys. At their oblation they are planted in the garden of the Church, to grow and bring forth fruit for God. But you so terrify them and hem them in on all sides with threats and blows that they are utterly deprived of their liberty. And being thus injudiciously oppressed, they harbour and welcome and nurse within themselves evil and crooked thoughts like thorns, and cherish these thoughts so passionately that they doggedly reject everything which could minister to their correction. Hence, feeling no love or pity, good-will or tenderness in your attitude towards them, they have in future no faith in your goodness but believe that all your actions proceed from hatred and malice against them. The deplorable result is that as they grow in body so their hatred increases, together with their apprehension of evil, and they are forward in all crookedness and vice. They have been brought up in no true charity towards anyone, so they regard everyone with suspicion and jealousy. (37–8)

Seeing that the abbot still did not grasp the point, Anselm spelled out his own educational philosophy: "the weak soul, which is still inexperienced in the service of God, needs milk—gentleness from others, kindness, compassion, cheerful encouragement, loving forbearance, and much else of the same kind" (39).

Anselm used every opportunity to set forth gentleness and compassion as the choice instruments of character-formation, often using analogies to point out that in practicing benevolence and compassion we emulate that which we seek from God. Eadmer recounts an incident on the road in which Anselm and his party came upon a group of boys chasing a hare. The frightened animal sought refuge beneath Anselm's horse. Anselm reined in his animal, who guarded his little charge from the pack of dogs. Anselm, seeing the horsemen round about laughing at his protection of the animal, seized the teachable moment:

> You laugh, do you? But there is no laughing, no merry-making, for this unhappy beast. His enemies stand round about him, and in fear of his life he flees to us asking for help. So it is with the soul of man: when it leaves the

body, its enemies—the evil spirits which have haunted it along all the crooked ways of vice while it was in the body—stand round without mercy, ready to seize it and hurry it off to everlasting death. Then indeed it looks round everywhere in great alarm, and with inexpressible desire longs for some helping and protecting hand to be held out to it, which might defend it. (89)

Anselm's earliest biographer testifies that Anselm's virtues informed his pedagogy; love and compassion set the stage for the rigors of monastic life.

TESTIMONY FROM ANSELM'S LETTERS

Anselm's strategy of love and friendship, evident in his correspondence and conversation as well as in Eadmer's anecdotal record, has provided recent historians with a rich vein of ore to mine. The letters written between 1070–93, the years as prior and abbot at Bec, express in his own words the pedagogy of love and encouragement reflected in Eadmer's later reconstructions. Letters from this period are effusive in their outpouring of love and desire for union with the addressee. They include the language of physical love and devotion to such an extent that a scholarly controversy has broken out in the past two decades as to whether Anselm was a homosexual (Boswell 1980, 218–9). While an answer to this question is not directly germane to this inquiry, the ardent love expressed in his letters to prospective monks and nuns does tell us something about his relationships with people and clearly contributes to understanding his pedagogy: how he got people to take up the monastic life or to lend their support to those who did. A summary of the highlights of the recent conversation about Anselm's personality follows.

In a lengthy article, Brian P. McGuire applies twentieth-century psychological categories to Anselm in a rather mechanical way (McGuire 1974). He assumes that Anselm's "Meditation virginitatis male amissa" is an anguished lament for sexual sins of his youth, against which the monastic life acts as balm (119–21).[2] McGuire notes that Anselm's love letters to specific monks—Gundolf, Maurice, and Gilbert Crispin—are initially effusive but gradually taper off or cool in ardor over the length of the correspondence. McGuire concludes that "Anselm is afraid of loving anyone when that love ... means a personal relationship in daily life" (140). Although McGuire does not conclude that Anselm is terrified of a sexual relationship with a man, which he very well may have been, he does say that "for him the individual was only a stepping stone, and a fragile and dubious one, to the much more dependable world of unchanging ideas and truths" (143). McGuire interprets Anselm's self-distancing from the hyperbolic and passionate letters of earlier years as a neurotic fear of involvement, deriving from a homoerotic orientation that did not necessarily find sexual expression (150).

This conclusion, however, is anachronistic, for it assumes norms of intimacy in relationships that simply did not exist in Anselm's world. It may just as readily be the case that Anselm's passionate rhetoric misled the letters' designees into thinking Anselm felt more personal involvement with them than was the case, so Anselm appropriately withdrew in order to protect both himself and his friends from untoward intimacy. And even if fear of a sexual relationship with a man was at work, in Anselm's world there would be nothing neurotic about that. Despite his unnuanced conclusions about Anselm's personality, McGuire believes that Anselm's intimate writing style constituted "a breakthrough to a new world where individual emotions are decisively important. . . . The old stiff world is dying, but the new world of personal feeling is only on the way to being born" (151). He sees Anselm as a transitional figure who presaged the birth of romantic love that would soon sweep across Europe.

Sally Vaughn, recounting the relationship between Anselm and Robert of Meulan, recognized Anselm's uses of love and kindness as contributing to a new doctrine of the monastic life developed at Bec. She cited an article by Christopher Harper-Bill that characterized Bec's spirituality as one "in which the positive value of charity replaced penitential mortification for the sins of the world as the prime purpose of the life of the monk" (73). Vaughn recognized that Anselm's use of kindness, affability, and hospitality, while genuine expressions of his personality, were also tools for enriching the abbey, protecting the monks, and building up the monastic vocation to which he was totally dedicated. He advised his successor at Bec, William of Beaumont, to continue his benevolent and beneficent policies because they genuinely expressed Christian love and because they rebound to the benefit of the giver. "And so I tell you this: use money, tainted as it is, to win you friends, and thus make sure that when it fails you, they will welcome you into the tents of eternity" (73) Anselm's spirituality of love as the foundation of monastic life expanded and deepened monastic life in Europe and suggested a new bent for the notion of the Christian life in general that would flower with the Cistercians in the following century.

Walter Fröhlich has written on Anselm's prolific correspondence as an important contribution to "the art of letter-writing, a newly revived feature of the intellectual life of the eleventh and twelfth centuries" (1990, 489). Fröhlich argues that Anselm intentionally organized and edited collections of his letters three times with an eye toward both posterity and a cultivated image of his administration at Bec and Canterbury (490, 492, 493).

Contained in Anselm's correspondence over the thirty-year period at Bec are numerous letters detailing his philosophy of monastic education and training, based on love of God and neighbor as both the motivating factor in the Christian life and the bond of brotherhood around which the monastic community cohered. His expression of love and adoration to prospective adult monks is Anselm's strategy to win souls for the life of spiritual perfection and happiness as he had found it in the monastery (506). And his ethical will to the whole community at Bec, on his accession to the see of Canterbury, summed up the practical dimension of his spirituality:

Remember why I was always accustomed to acquire friends for the church of Bec. Make haste to follow my example by exercising the virtue of hospitality and showing kindness to all; and, when you have nothing else to offer, at least offer the grace of friendly words to all. Never think that you have enough friends. Bind everyone, both rich and poor to you in loving fraternity, for the good of your church and the salvation of those whom you love. (qtd. in Southern 1990, 160).

R. W. Southern was careful to locate the function of monasteries in society at the time. They were, as he put it, "central points of cohesion in the social order" (1990, 182). They were sanctuaries in times of trouble, homes for the elderly, and refuges for widows, unmarried daughters, and children who could not be supported on family lands. They represented the spiritual vanguard of the society, and their upkeep and support enabled the aristocracy to support those who put their lives on the line for God. Thus a social harmony cohered among several social classes. And this description does not even mention the educational role played by monasteries both in the formation of external schools and in the education of the professed. From this perspective, Anselm's pedagogy of encouragement and gentleness takes on broader social implications than perhaps even he imagined.

Returning now to his letters, it seems that Anselm was crafting a new type of spirituality that transformed the rigorous formalism characteristic of Benedictine spirituality of his day into a spirituality that lifts the individual to the love of God by being loved by other monks and spiritual guides and, significantly, by cultivating loving behavior on the part of neophytes and prospective recruits. His letters professing love and spiritual union with monks from whom he is geographically separated, and even to people he does not know, suggest, as Mary-Rose Barral has argued, that these "were not really personal relationships, but rather a general attitude toward his fellow religious [and others] . . . who fell in some way within the scope of his religious or pastoral care. . . . Friendship . . . was one way of reaching the hoped-for blessedness. Friendship, begun in this world[,] . . . was of its nature everlasting" (1988, 175). Common monastic profession was the essence of friendship. Anselm established love and friendship in the context of humility and obedience as the cornerstones of the Christian life, practiced in its perfected form in the monastery.

Southern reviews and synthesizes the work of previous scholars and provides a richly flavored interpretation of Anselm's life and thought in the context of his day. Like McGuire and Barral, Southern rejects Boswell's contention that Anselm was homosexual, agreeing with Barral's position that Anselm's espousal of spiritual friendship was part of his theology as well as a natural expression of his irenic personality.

Southern locates Anselm's emphasis on friendship in relation to the classical typology of friendship, transmitted to him, most probably, by John Cassian. Anselm introduced elements of romantic love into an understanding of male friendship based on groups of persons coming together to pursue a common purpose or set of ideals. In Anselm's case, the common purpose was the pursuit of life with God. The romantic dimension stressed joy over duty, mercy over justice, and passion over reason (Southern 142).

Southern also locates the physical expressions of spiritual love—found in Anselm's references to kisses and embraces, and passionate sense of loss at separation from his soul mates—within the context of contemporary religious ritual and civic ceremony. He finds Anselm's common reference to these completely appropriate, although perhaps disconcerting to the recipients of his letters (153–4). Additionally, Southern notes that Anselm took care to preserve his correspondence, so that his letters, containing what sounds to modern ears like intimate expressions of sexual passion, could be shared among the monks in a given community. Southern concludes, "These letters were not intended to convey private emotional attachments, still less forbidden yearnings. They were public statements about the rewards of the life dedicated to God" (147). Anselm and his soul brothers bonded together in their dedication to live in the kingdom of God; "in speaking about friendship, he was making statements about eternity" (159).

The scholarly consensus is clear at several points. First, Anselm is an innovative spiritual guide and teacher who revitalized monasticism through a deep commitment to compassion, gentleness, love, and encouragement as the chief means of promoting rigorously disciplined monastic practice, which for him embodied freedom and happiness in the pursuit of life with God. This passion for tenderness challenged rigorous and formal penitential discipline as the chief instrument in the cultivation of piety. Second, he revitalized the medieval tradition of letter-writing and introduced elements of romantic love into his conversation and writing in the service of his monastic reform program. During his archepiscopacy, Anselm recommended the same behavior and attitudes for civil rulers.

As is evident in the anecdote about Osbern, Anselm did not shrink from imposing punitive discipline when necessary. He reacted with horror and took punitive measures against those who engaged in sodomy and effeminate behavior. Southern noted the contrast between his generally mild temper and his harshness on this particular issue, concluding that this uncharacteristic attitude may signal a previous struggle around this issue himself (152).

Testimony from Anselm's Prayers

Another source for assessing Anselm's pastoral theology comes from his prayers.[3] These, we shall see, support the general picture drawn from his letters. But they also disclose Anselm's enduring struggle to understand the relationship between the justice and mercy of God, trying always to hold fast to the latter.

René Roques has examined the prayers, which he sharply delineates from the philosophical treatises for which Anselm is better known (Roques 1970).[4] The latter rely on logic and rigorous reasoning to disclose revealed truth, while the prayers appeal to the reader's affections and are designed to prick the conscience (122). The distinction is not quite as rigid as Roques suggests, however, since only 3 out of the 26 chapters of the *Proslogion* are philosophical, while the remainder constitute a prayer to God. Roques himself softens his distinction between the two types of writing, finding traces of Anselm's use of logic and reason in the prayer to St. Nicholas (149) as well as at the conclusion of the *Meditation on Human Redemption* (158).

The prayers were created on requests from correspondents, supporters of the monastery, or other notables who sought Anselm's spiritual direction.[5] They are inspirational pieces designed to stimulate personal devotion through meditation and to cultivate self-examination and the fear and love of God.[6] Anselm sent the prayers to his patrons with instructions that they be read in segments as short or lengthy as the petitioner finds useful. The prayers adopt a generally standard format and, like the letters, were intended for general use and circulation, although they were written in the first-person singular.

The testimony of Anselm's prayers, more than half of which are addressed to biblical characters, suggests that his pedagogical philosophy informed the theology of the prayers as well.[7] His long personal intercessory prayer-poems to key New Testament figures follow a common pattern. The prayers begin by extolling the character for his/her righteousness, piety and, above all, intimacy with Jesus. Then they contrast the greatness and virtues of the saint with the sinfulness and inadequacy of the supplicant. The rhetorical point is to induce compunction, self-examination, and a heightened consciousness of sin in the reader (Anselm 1973, 53–6; Roques 1970, 138). This cultivated unworthiness leads to petitioning the saint to intervene with God on the supplicant's behalf by virtue of his or her goodness, generosity, love, mercy, and/or close relationship to Jesus or God. The prayers appeal both to the saint's virtues and to his/her responsibility and faithfulness, exhorting (almost extorting) the saint into interceding with God (Roques 1970, 145).

The supplicant is moved beyond self-castigation, however, as each prayer/poem explores intimacy with Jesus. And as each prayer reaches its climax, the supplicant prays to both the saint and Jesus together on the strength of their relationship to one another. This effectively encourages the reader to reach toward both the protection and the stature of the saints. Despite the heavy emphasis on what Vaughn identifies as the topos of humility, which played such a prominent role in medieval piety and in Anselm's own life, the progression in the prayers is from self-abasement to being lifted up to the mercy of God through the goodness of the saint. This echoes Anselm's tireless invitation to women and men to be bound with him to God through monastic profession. The cult of the saints encourages sinners—by implication, not directly—to emulate the saints' virtue, dedication, and service performed for Jesus and for them, and to hope that Jesus' love and compassion might extend to themselves. Each prayer concludes with thanksgiving for all that God has done and promised, an exhortation to repentance, and a resolution to piety. The topos of self-abasement does not in any way cut the supplicant off from the goodness of the saints or God.

Indeed, the biographical testimony suggests that Anselm's assessment of human psychology called for encouragement and reinforcement of positive behavior. It required positive models for emulation, with Anselm himself acting as the chief testimony to gentleness and compassion. The prayers to biblical saints focus on the interaction of each character with Jesus according to scripture. This includes Saint Paul, even though he did not know Jesus in the flesh. By suggesting an intimacy between the suppliant and the saint, the prayers enable one to become intimate with God through the character who knew Jesus on earth or was totally dedicated to him (e.g., Saints Paul and Benedict). Mary, his mother, empowers us to call Jesus brother (*Prayers* 123). John the Baptist, who baptized Jesus and revealed him to believers, encourages the suppliant to ask Jesus for healing and forgiveness (132–3). Paul, who treats his converts like a nurse and mother, as Anselm himself treated his charges, reveals Jesus as a mother who gave birth to us on the cross by kindness and mercy (155–6). John the Evangelist, Jesus' beloved friend, emboldens us to think that Jesus might love us, too (160–2).

Of the prayers just referred to, that to St. Paul reveals most clearly Anselm's pedagogical commitments as Eadmer described them in his biography. This prayer picks up scripture's references to Paul as a mother and nurse (following Gal. 4.19 and 1 Thess. 2.7) and to Jesus as a mother hen (Matt. 23.37). Anselm presented his contemporaries with an accessible Jesus who loved and was loved in return. On the strength of repeated evidence of God's love, gentleness, and compassion, contemporary Christians, far removed both in time and virtue from Jesus' intimates, may also seek refuge under his "wings."

While the proper posture for the suppliant is humility and fear of God, even the lowest sinner can petition God's "loving dealing with me" (91; line 25) and "powerful kindness" (93; line 14). In the Prayer to Christ he asks to be dealt with "not according to my deserts but out of your kindness that came first to me" (94; lines 33–4). This same prayer acknowledges that love is enkindled by the good things God has done and recalls God's mercy and patience in waiting for the suppliant's amendment (lines 40–52). Amendment of life is stimulated not by fear of punishment but by recollection of God's goodness, just as Anselm himself trained Osbern through love and compassion. The prayer concludes with a passionate petition for the presence of Christ, which in tone and style is not unlike the letters that cry for reunion with geographically distant monks.

Anselm, whose imagination enabled him to teach through animals and trees, addressed one of his prayers to the Holy Cross almost as if it were an animate object that understands the prayer. Southern dates it around 1082 (110). Here one might expect to hear adumbrations of Anselm's soteriology as it later solidified in the *Cur Deus Homo*. But there is no hint of the so-called satisfaction theory of the atonement. There is not a word about the justice or dignity of the honor of God, which must be appeased in order for us to be ransomed. Rather, we find attributes of what Gustav Aulén characterized as the classic or dramatic theory of salvation (1969), in which Christ defeats the demons that hold humans in thrall, restores the creation, raises the dead to life, and establishes the kingdom (*Prayers* 103; lines 46–55). The role of the cross is "that by you I may come to those good things for which man was created, by the might of the same Jesus Christ our Lord who is blessed for ever and ever" (105; lines 98–101).

In the second of three Marian prayers (Southern dates them at 1073–4, p. 107), the theme of the quaking sinner accused before a stern judge does appear, along with the delicate topic of whether God will decide justly to punish or mercifully to pardon the accused (*Prayers* 110; lines 13–28). Though in fear of divine wrath, he calls on the goodness and mercy of the mother and Son, and still there is no mention of features of what Aulén called the "Latin theory" of satisfaction. Indeed, in the third Marian prayer (he wrote three because he found the first two unsatisfactory), the Athanasian themes of Christ's triumph over the demons and restoration and reconciliation of the world by the creator prevail throughout the main body of the piece (118–20; lines 101–87). Through Mary's maternity, idolatry is overturned, demons are trampled, creation is redeemed for those who confess God, and creatures are made green again (120; line 159). The themes of healing, return to innocence, and promise of future incorruptibility, all reminiscent of the Athanasian doctrine of redemption, appear in the prayer to John the Baptist as well.

The so-called Latin motif of exacting justice owed to God appears in the third Marian prayer, only to be rejected when Anselm addresses Mary and Christ together. "Lord and Lady, surely it is much better for you to give grace to those who do not deserve it [t]han for you to exact what is owing to you in justice? The first is praise-worthy, the other is wicked injustice" (125; lines 323–6).

The same hope of deserving God's justice, but pleading for and expecting God's mercy, recurs at the conclusion of the prayer to St. Peter:

> I deserve to suffer because I have sinned of my own free will, I do not deserve to be heard because I have disobeyed. Ah, how bitter it is to be without hope! That, surely, is the sentence of justice, not of mercy, and who calls on justice in my cause? My talk was of mercy, not of justice. In the wretched tribulation of my soul I beg of you, my God, the bread of mercy. (140; lines 167–75)

The transfer-of-merits theme typical of Anselmic soteriology does appear, however, in the second prayer to St. John the Evangelist (pp. 163–71). After the requisite obeisance to his own worthlessness, Anselm beseeches, "[G]rant to me, Lord, by the merits of him from whom you have honour, that I may be made worthy out of my unworthiness" (164; lines 57–9). The payment metaphor appears in the next paragraph according to the following logic: if the evangelist can get God to love us because he is the beloved disciple of Christ, we are indebted to the saint. And John himself repays our debt to him by bringing us nearer to loving Christ. Anselm's point is that John brokers our relationship to Christ and thus repays the debt we owe John for restoring a soul to God (165; lines 73–92). The master motif of the *Cur Deus Homo*—paying the debt owed—appears here as payment for the brokerage services the saint provides. The dynamic of the cult of the saints is that the saint's grace is so great that it "will count for so much before God who loves you that he will forgive my sins and by loving me will make me his beloved" (166; lines 109–11). If a profane and modern image be not offensive, one might also say that although the insurance policy is taken out in the name of the saint, the policy also covers the suppliant, so to speak.

The debt-payment topos is closely tied with channeling love for God, as suggested in the earlier segment of the prayer just cited. Anselm's logic repeats itself here. God loves John because of John's goodness, which envies no one. On the contrary, the saint wants everyone to share in his goodness. Additionally, like all human beings, John owes God all his love. Anselm asks John to love the petitioner in exchange for the love that he (John) owes God, "so that you may set free for him even my love with yours" (166; line 120), thus bringing ever more love to God, thereby fulfilling his own obligation. As Anselm sees it, at least at this point in his theological development, "no one is able to give to God before he is in debt, [and] no one can give back more than he is in debt for" (166; lines 125–7). So no matter how many people John brings to love God, they will not suffice to pay the debt. Anselm asks John to include him among those John brings to love God because it is in John's long-term best interests to do so.

In terms of Anselm's soteriology, which we will consider below, it is important to note that the debt-payment motif is not connected either to the wrath of God or to the capital nature of the crime. The issue is rather about love owed to God, love that would be impossible for us without the intervention of one who is already known to love God. The issue is not that the slightest dishonor due God is punishable by death, as it appears in the *Cur Deus Homo*. Rather, the concern is how to get us to love God as we ought.

The soteriological framework of God's mercy being extended to sinners by virtue of the meritorious overflow of the saints is also operative in the prayer to St. Stephen, where it is associated more with forgiveness than with love. Here the great number of the penitent's sins are matched and outweighed by the power of the grace of the first Christian martyr. Again, Anselm ingratiates himself with the saint, who will use the opportunity to show mercy to the suppliant in order to live up to a reputation for goodness and forgiveness rather than punishment, deserved though it may be. "But you and all the saints are so full of such wealth from the unending fount of all goodness, that you delight rather to free by your goodness those whom by justice you are able to condemn" (177; lines 111–4). Anselm not only appeals to Stephen's self-image as merciful; he also assures the saint that he will not be damaged by sharing his merits with others, for he has enough to spare. He encourages Stephen to approach God on his behalf on the same grounds. Anselm believes that God will listen to Stephen: "For he is merciful and my creator, I am wretched and his workmanship, and you are the beloved friend of him who is 'blessed for ever. Amen'" (177–8; lines 128–31).

The theme of the saint as intermediary, which would later serve as the basis of the soteriology of the *Cur Deus Homo*, recurs yet again in the prayer to St. Nicholas, and, as usual, on the grounds of the goodness and mercy of the saint. The basic topos of humility that undergirds the cult of the saints grows out of the love of symmetry characteristic of Christian theology at least since Augustine. Symmetry as right order conduces to positing humanness as the opposite of whatever is posited of God. This in turn leads to the topos of humility, which presses the contrast between the sinner's sinfulness and the saint's goodness. It is the ground upon which Anselm stands to invoke mercy. It would be surprising if this same dynamic were not operative when Anselm approached the central question of the atonement wrought by Christ himself.

The prayers express the important themes with which Anselm wrestled in the *Cur Deus Homo:* the role of the devil in salvation; the tension between the justice and mercy of God; and the possibility of excess merit being transferred from the saint to the sinner. The dynamic behind Anselmian prayer is the topos of humility. Modesty dictates that it would be presumptuous of a sinner to think that on the basis of one's own love for God one could either plead for forgiveness or love God sufficiently. Love does not arise out of fear of the wrath of God or the need to repair the honor of God in some absolute or objective sense; it arises in response to goodness.

TESTIMONY FROM ANSELM'S TREATISES

Proslogion

The *Proslogion*, written in 1077–8, while Anselm was prior at Bec, was a pastoral work written "from the point of view of someone trying to raise his mind to the contemplation of God" ([1965] 1979, Preface). Of its twenty-six chapters, only 2 through 4 present the ontological argument for the existence of God with which the name of Anselm will forever be linked. Chapter 1 and extended parts of the rest of the treatise take the contrastive doxological style characteristic of Anselm's other prayer-poems. The remainder exhorts the reader to piety by describing the benefits obtainable therefrom. Yet throughout, Anselm reflects on the problems posed by his conviction of divine compassion, as compared to the doctrine of the absoluteness of God. In both form and content, Anselm casts speculation in the wider context of devotion.

Chapters 9 through 11 explore the relationship between justice and mercy in God's dealings with us. This raises the question of whether God experiences emotion, specifically empathy and compassion. In George S. Heyer's article on Anselm's view of the relationship between divine mercy and justice, the author discusses these chapters of the *Proslogion* ([1965] 1979, 33–6). Although Heyer grants that Anselm is trying to argue the justness of God's mercifully sparing the wicked, he points out that

Anselm has juxtaposed and not harmonized justice and mercy (34). But because Anselm cannot admit that God experiences emotion as we do, in chapter 8 he argues that our experience of divine empathy has no counterpart in God himself. Heyer concludes that Anselm has driven "a wedge between God's being and his action. . . . God's acts of mercy make him appear compassionate when really he is nothing of the sort" (35). Heyer maintains that in both the *Proslogion* and the *Cur Deus Homo*, Anselm, hoping to prove that both justice and mercy are consonant with divine goodness, has done just the opposite—"grounded mercy in divine justice" (39) in the interests of the "passion for right order" that clearly surfaces in the *Cur Deus Homo* (40). With Heyer's work in mind, I shall proceed to examine this section of the *Proslogion*, asking what Anselm was hoping to accomplish.

Again, Anselm holds that God acts compassionately without feeling empathy, distinguishing divine action from divine nature, as Heyer pointed out, in order to protect the impassability of God, which was unquestioned in his day. But do we not do the same when, for example, we acknowledge that a child can commit a wrong action and yet not identify the child as "bad" because to label a child would undermine motivation to improve? Like Anselm, we too want to separate the act from the "nature": one can make mistakes and still be considered a "good person." In fact, we should find it strange to identify human nature with every act committed by a human person. We maintain a freedom of action apart from universal attributes we might posit about human nature; people are generous, petty, selfish, curious, and so on, yet we do not believe that any such group of traits or attributes confine the range of one's behavioral possibilities. We allow for change and spontaneity. Anselm faced a similar quandary regarding the nature of God, although he could not say so explicitly.

Anselm sought to harmonize the attributes of justice and mercy, for God sometimes punishes and sometimes forgives.[8] Forgiveness seemingly betrays the righteousness of God; punishment seemingly impugns the goodness of God. There is nothing particularly arresting, however, about the observation that compassion expresses divine goodness. The issue is how to understand how compassion expresses righteousness or justice. And the still more problematic question is whether to complete the symmetry of justice and mercy by suggesting that punishment of sinners expresses divine goodness. Compassion, Anselm argues, must be just, because if God were unjust he would not be entirely good but only good when he justly rewards and not when he forgives and transforms the wicked into good. This would be the same as saying that it is wrong for God to have compassion on the wicked and to transform them into good. But it is clearly wrong to say that God should not be compassionate, because God is good. Therefore, "it is right to believe that you have compassion on the wicked with justice" (Anselm 1973, 252, chap. 9, lines 382–3).

Lest the reader mistakenly infer that God always pardons, Anselm added that it is also right for God to punish wickedness (252; chap. 10). Punishing comports with divine justice: "when you save those whom with justice you might have deserted, you are just not because you give us our due, but because you act in accordance with your nature as being entirely good" (ibid., lines 398–401). The important point here is what Anselm does not say next. He does not say that God is also good when he punishes; punishment reflects only the attribute of justice, not goodness. Mercy is a form of or consonant with justice, although justice is not a form of or consonant with goodness. Heyer concludes from this form of argumentation that Anselm has not shown how God's mercy flows from his justice but has posited two senses of divine justice, "one with a view of man's deserts and one with a view to God's nature" ([1965] 1979, 34). This is not entirely correct, however. Anselm believes that God's justice is universal whether expressed as mercy or as punishment. Divine mercy, however, is not absolute. It is only expressed through forgiveness, not through punishment. What Heyer has not taken into consideration, because he can examine Anselm from only a strictly logical perspective, is the pastoral motivation behind Anselm's position. Anselm refuses to say that punishment of the wicked—or of the righteous, for that matter—expresses divine goodness, the logical extension of the position that divine goodness and justice are coterminous in God.

Anselm wants believers to be able to turn to the goodness of God in hopes that this goodness will express itself toward them in admittedly undeserved mercy. The pastoral need subordinates the rational argument for two reasons. First, Anselm wants to encourage his readers to believe that they really can trust in divine mercy, as we saw in the prayers. But he also wants to rid them of the fear either that they could be unjustly punished or that God's "goodness" expresses itself in punitive action. This pastoral concern arises from his own pedagogy of compassion, encouragement, and tenderness. Were he to insist on the coterminousness of divine justice and mercy, he would have provided theological grounds for punitively oriented powerholders, like the brother abbot he chastised, to justify their deforming pedagogical methods. Anselm may think that he has demonstrated that God is entirely good and entirely just. He has only shown that God is just when compassionate, because compassion transforms sinners more effectively than does punishment. Perhaps it is fortunate for us that he did not completely equate divine justice and mercy.

Why God Became Human

Perhaps Anselm was not fully satisfied with the answer he gave to the question of the justice and mercy of God in the *Proslogion*. Two decades later, when writing his most important theological treatise, *Cur Deus Homo,* he made another stab at the issue in the context of a discussion of christology (1969). *Why God Became Man* is usually read as the definitive statement of what Gustav Aulén calls the Latin theory of the atonement (84–92). In the context of the medieval penitential system reaching back to Tertullian and Cyprian, penance is just or requisite payment of a penalty for fault. Excess payment may be stored up as merit, and Christ (or the saints, as we saw in Anselm's prayer to St. John the Evangelist), who has an excess of merits by dint of having voluntarily given his life freely as a gift, may apply them as payment against the price owed by others to satisfy the requirement of divine justice. The payment necessary to restore God's honor must be made by the one who has damaged that honor: the human being. But humans are unable to make restitution because they are all sinful. Thus God must do it for them. The only answer is the God-man Jesus Christ. This is the crux of the logic of the *Cur Deus Homo*.

The treatise is usually read as a rational demonstration of the necessity for the Incarnation, apart from knowing anything of Christ through revelation, as Anselm himself tells his readers in the preface to the work. The apologetic function of doctrinal exegesis, as Anselm remarks at the outset, is to support believers against the objections of unbelievers who ask why God had to become a person and die in order to "restore life to the world" (64; bk. I, chap. 1). There is some legerdemain here, however. Anselm does not proceed to offer a purely rational demonstration; instead, he cites or interpolates scripture verses sixty-nine times. So we are advised to take his overt purpose with a grain of salt.

One issue of the treatise is the dignity and omnipotence of God; why did God "[take] on the lowliness and weakness of human nature, to restore it?" (65). Humanness, defined as the opposite of divinity, seems to degrade God. The purpose of *Why God Became Man* is to demonstrate that the indelicacy of the Incarnation and the cross do not really impugn the propriety of God. While both Heyer and Southern accurately focus on right order *(rectitudo)* as the central issue, Anselm presses upon his reader that right order includes not only symmetry and righteousness but also the mercy of God. The Incarnation and cross seem to impugn these attributes of God as well. Anselm takes on a formidable task. The Incarnation and cross are problematic from two points of view. They are degrading to God if instruments of choice, and unnecessary if God is really omnipotent.

Anselm mounts a defense of the power and mercy of God. Putting one's innocent son to death is, on the face of it, neither merciful nor just. The Christian claim that the Son of God died on the cross to save humankind suggested to skeptics that God either was powerless to redeem humanity without brutality, didn't know what else to do, or is vengeful (because he demanded Christ's death on the cross as payment). Anselm's treatise is usually read as a response to these objections in support of the claims that God is all-powerful, all-knowing, just, and merciful. Yet a close reading of the work suggests that while this intellectual defense of the traditional attributes of God was certainly high on his agenda, Anselm also had a practical interest.

Anselm was doing more than answering contemporary questions here. He was, as he said in his cover letter to Pope Urban II, correcting the Fathers (stemming from Augustine's account of these matters in *De Trinitate* XIII), who "were not able to say all that they could have said, had they lived longer" (59). Such modesty masks the delicacy of Anselm's taking on the master. Anselm lived in a world that prized the past and suspected innovation. Humility and respect, not independent thinking, were expected. And Anselm's penchant for flattery to cultivate supporters should prepare his readers for a subtle presentation of his disagreement with accepted theological tradition.

Augustine, as we saw, was eager to establish justice instead of brute power as the principle of social morality by showing that although God could have rescued humankind from the devil simply by willing it, he chose an act of justice in order to teach that power is to be used in the service of justice. Anselm, whose pedagogy cultivated compassion, was not satisfied with Augustine's hierarchy of virtues and sought to nuance it in two ways: by strengthening the role of the hero through the elimination of the villain, and by stressing voluntary obedience, motivated by a love for justice rather than submission to justice out of duty alone.

Boso hints at the weakness of Augustine's position—that God dealt with the devil in terms of justice rather than power—and introduces the foundation on which Anselm's own soteriology will be built: the devil had no right at all to hold humankind in bondage; humans sinned freely and either should not sin or should be punished, "*unless* mercy spares the sinner and liberates and restores him" (74; bk. I, chap. 7, italics added). By eliminating the devil from the soteriological scheme, Anselm highlights the great qualification that Christ's sacrifice introduces into ordinary thinking that justice must be satisfied. Christ puts his body between human sinfulness and the demand for punishment. Thus, Anselm's first step in correcting Augustine's soteriology was to focus exclusive attention on Christ without the diversionary effect of the devil, which might leave readers with the impression that their salvation was tantamount to watching a gladiatorial contest between Christ and the devil. In Anselm's accounts, Christians witness not a display of power between the forces of good and the forces of evil but a display of mercy and compassion that breaks forever the assumption that force and power are the only tools for dealing with sin and injustice.

The second step in the correction comes from Christ's willingness to give his life to restore creation to its proper state (74–83; I:8–10). Emphasizing that Christ volunteered for the suicide mission offered Anselm's readers a fresh perspective on the cross. If Christ was compelled by the Father, the reader might conclude that God hated his own Son. But if Christ volunteered, attention shifts to his love for us. In book I, chap. 10, Anselm, following Heb. 5.8, argued that God engaged Christ to teach us obedience to both justice and mercy in employing power. Anselm takes pains to demonstrate that willingly taking on human lowliness displayed God's mercy, which satisfies yet finally overshadows the divine demand for justice (67–8; I:3). And so to him fell the task of showing not only that God's mercy and justice are harmonized but also that Christ, through the Incarnation (Phil. 2.8–9) and the cross (Heb. 5.8), is the supreme teacher who volunteers for obedience to justice out of love for righteousness and for us.

For Anselm, the Incarnation, cross, and resurrection are not separate actions of God. They are one complex divine action to teach us humility and obedience to righteousness, motivated by compassion and displayed by Christ's example. Two

texts that Anselm twice quotes in tandem reveal the aretegenic message of the Incarnation, cross, and resurrection in his thinking. These were Heb. 5.8, "Although he
was a Son, he learned obedience through what he suffered," and Phil. 2.8–9: "he humbled himself and became obedient to the point of death—even death on a cross.
Therefore God also highly exalted him and gave him the name that is above every
name." Anselm first conjoins these two texts in book I, chap. 8, to point out that the
Hebrews text suggests that the Son was compelled to suffer, while the Philippians text
suggests that he volunteered for the mission. What appears as confusion about
whether Christ went to the cross willingly or under compulsion is actually God's
means of demonstrating that the Son of God voluntarily humbled himself in order
for "just plain folks" to be reconciled to God. And his deed was rewarded with resurrection and fame. This is our knowledge of God.

In chapter 9 Anselm conjoins the two texts a second time. He suggests that the
Hebrews phrase "'He learned' means either that 'He made others learn' or that He
learned by experience what He was not aware of through infused knowledge" (78).
The argument is at pains to demonstrate that taking on human lowliness should not
be misconstrued as a sign of divine impotence. Rather the Incarnation/cross should
be viewed as an intentional decision on God's part to teach us that justice can be satisfied (in this case through Christ's death) without mercy, the reconciliation of the
world to God, being abandoned as the primary norm. The theologian's task of
demonstrating the harmonization of justice and mercy in the Incarnation and cross
is not, however, simply to defend God. His task is also to show that Christ, the
supreme learner of obedience, is the supreme teacher by example.

God's task is to restore a languishing creation (64–6; I:1). Now, since God could
have chosen any number of ways to accomplish this, Anselm probed for a particular reason why God selected the Incarnation/cross. His conclusion, that it was to
give powerful expression to divine love so that we would focus on it rather than on
power and justice alone (70–1; I:6), countered the rescue-from-the-devil motif. The
Son's voluntary obedience unto death exemplifies submission to justice in order to
save God's human children (74–83; I:8–10). Its voluntary character reveals it to be an
act of self-sacrifice undertaken in love, not simply to satisfy the objective need to re-
quite just demands for payment or punishment. God himself lives out the norms of
humility and obedience, distilled from Phil. 2.8–9 and Heb. 5.8, in order to show us
the realization of justice and mercy, even when the price is dear. "'*He learned obedience by the things which He suffered*,' that is, to what extent obedience must be observed" (77–8; I:9).

Certainly, in teaching that we are to learn to embrace righteousness, Anselm
follows Augustine's lead regarding theology's role in maintaining civic order. But
note that the voluntary submission to justice on Christ's part is in the service of the
larger goal of displaying divine mercy—the salvation of the human race. So the fuller
teaching is that obedience to justice ought to be based not on fear of punishment but
on the desire to become an instrument of mercy.

Anselm's pedagogical interest in his reader's moral character becomes clearly evident in the discussion of sin (84–91; I:11–5). He reminds us that human sin has besmirched the honor of God, which must be restored. But then he admits that we can neither honor nor dishonor God (90–1; I:15). All that our sinfulness does is create an aura of disorder in God's perfectly symmetrical world, leaving us, perhaps, with diffused anxiety at our clumsiness. Thus, what began as an expression of divine mercy, to repay on our behalf what we are unable to pay, turns out to be payment for a sin (dishonoring God) that we are not even able to commit. By the end of book I, the reader is led to wonder, "What, then, is the point of the divine humiliation, if we are unable to damage God's honor in the first place?"

Book II opens with an abrupt shift of concern from the interplay of justice and mercy in God to a discussion of the human capability of knowing and acting justly, hinting that the two are not unrelated and that Anselm is, as previously noted, interested in the divine modeling of these character traits. But this theme is quickly set aside for the central issue of the treatise: explanation of the God-man who redeems us, and the efficacy of his death. This discussion has largely been examined for its exposition of atonement through satisfaction of the debt paid by the Son on our behalf. But a key aspect of the divine strategy of restoring us to a state even more miraculous than our original creation, in Anselm's thinking, is to teach us to focus on our true destiny and purpose: the enjoyment of God through willing obedience.

Anselm admits that the instrument of restoration is an offering of God to himself for the sake of his own honor, which we can neither defame nor restore (155–9; II:18). The point, therefore, is to establish a concrete model of what constitutes our true happiness: dedication to righteousness, which Anselm has already noted we are capable of knowing and following. He acknowledges that

> when He bore with generous patience the injuries and outrages and death on the cross in the company of brigands . . . He gave to men the example of never turning away from the justice they owe to God, no matter what disadvantages they can experience. . . . He would absolutely not have given this example, if, by using His power, He had escaped the death inflicted on Him. (156; II:18)

And to be sure that the reader grasps it, Anselm presses the point home once again: "So He gave us a far greater example to influence every person not to hesitate to give back to God, in his own name, when reason requires it, what he is sometime suddenly going to lose" (156; II:18). The cross graphically thunders what we are to learn is true happiness: self-sacrifice for the rescue of others.

Meditation on Human Redemption

Anselm's last meditation was written at Lyons in 1099 as a summary of *Why God Became Man* (1973). The purpose of the Incarnation/cross is for the restoration of the human race "to that for which it was made."[9] Anselm specifically says that "God was not obliged to save mankind this way" (*Prayers* 232), for God does not need it, nor can God be humiliated, presumably either by sins committed by humans or by partaking of finitude. Anselm repeats over and over that the need for human rescue necessitates the divine "humiliation." One misunderstands the Incarnation/cross if one only sees in it the humiliation of God and not the exaltation of human nature by the mercy of Christ. Again the emphasis is on the "perfect and free obedience of human nature . . . without any compulsion" (234). And Anselm repeats the divine rationale behind this tortuous salvific design.

> This man . . . gave his life of his own accord to the Father, when he allowed his life to be taken from him, for the sake of righteousness. This gave an example to others not to reject the righteousness of God because of death, which of necessity they would all at some time have to undergo. . . . He did not submit to violence, but freely embraced it out of goodness, to the honour of God and the benefit of other men. (233)

The theme of imitation returns once again as Anselm muses on how to overcome the guilt at being the one on whose behalf God endured the cruelty of those who crucified the Lord and yet deplored the cruelty committed. If their cruelty were required for the rescue of the human race, one might infer that cruelty may be a justifiable means to a higher end. Here, as we saw in the *Proslogion,* Anselm explicitly draws back again, one suspects because his own pedagogy and aversion to cruelty for any reason pressed him in another direction. One may not rejoice in one's own rescue if it is won by virtue of cruelty as an instrument of instruction. "Thus I must condemn their cruelty, imitate your death and sufferings, and share them with you, giving thanks for the goodness of your love" (235). Anselm was entranced with the aesthetics of righteousness and honor, which morally balance the world. And the free act of God on the cross restores the symmetrical beauty of the moral world in which God would have us live. But Anselm's commitment to compassion and his disdain for cruelty in cultivating the Christian life are fresh thoughts for medieval Christian pedagogy. They assume a place as an integral dimension of that symmetry and rectitude.

Assessment

With Anselm, humble obedience becomes the signature of Western piety in response to the fearsomeness of justly deserved divine wrath. The person and work of Christ rivet our attention on the question of our orientation to God the Father and the Son, the models for our edification. Christ's Incarnation and death are a humble offering of God to God, a strategy by which we are to learn humility and obedience from the one who lowered himself to us and himself "learned" obedience in order to rescue us.

Although it is never explicitly stated, one suspects that this model of divine justice and mercy also provides a standard of how justice and mercy are to be executed on the horizontal plane. We not only rejoice in the Son's courage to rescue us by his death; we also learn obedience to justice in order to rescue one another. When in positions of authority, we are to imitate justice subordinated to mercy as shown by the Father; when subordinate we are to imitate the obedience, humility, and devotion to the restoration of justice on behalf of others modeled by the Son.

Anselm relied on the emotional power of the stunning example set by God in the Incarnation/cross to stop us in our tracks. The objections to the Christian story—that the Incarnation impugns divine power and the cross impugns divine mercy—turn out to be defenses critics erect against the high standards of justice and mercy God has set for us. The whole complex of redemptive events is a spectacular display of the divine strategy to gain our love for and obedience to God, thus arousing our own ability to live justly, obediently, and humbly. Anselm's mimetic approach to character education is one we have met before: we become what we know.

The relationship of Father and Son is the model for our imitation. We are caught up into the story on three levels: as observers of parental behavior, as observers of filial behavior, and as interested observers whose fate hangs in the balance as the events unfold between the two main characters in the drama. Anselm develops two models of filiality: one in which the earthly child is unable to meet the stringent parental demands, and another in which the divine child complies with an extreme demand for the sake of God's weaker offspring. The Father sets standards of behavior and respect that the earthly child cannot meet. But his love overwhelms his standard of justice, and he devises an alternative way of having the divine child meet those standards and thus let his earthly children off the hook. As earthly children, we rejoice at this reprieve and pattern ourselves after the courage and love of the divine child; as parents, we learn to gauge our demands according to what the child can handle.

Anselm's express statements that Christ became human and died as an example to us mean that we are pressed beyond assimilating behavior that befits the earthly children of God toward imitation of the Son of God himself. His primary motive was the salvation of others, regardless of the cost to himself. This and no less is the highly exalted standard God has set for us. The focus on sin as dishonor, ability or inability to pay what we owe, satisfaction, and substitution are all parts of a strategy to lead us to the true standard God has set for us: the rescue of others for the sake of justice and mercy working in tandem. God leads us from what we think we can do (honor God and pay our debts) to what we really know we are unable to do: save others when our own safety is at risk. Ironically, just when we think we have gotten away free and clear, we turn around and realize that God has pitched us a fast ball.

Notes

1. Sir Richard Southern, in his masterful biography of Anselm, tells us that Anselm met Eadmer, an English monk, in 1079, on Anselm's first visit to Canterbury in the first year of his

abbacy (1990, 319). But they did not develop a working relationship until Anselm chose him as a close companion and member of his staff after his elevation to the archepiscopacy in 1093 (318–21). Beginning in 1101, Eadmer began keeping an anecdotal record of the archbishop's activities and some sermons. He provided Anselm with "the sedative of spiritual conversation" when he got out of sorts, and eventually became Anselm's spiritual director (243). For seven years Eadmer kept his log of events as well as incidents and stories of Anselm's earlier life at Bec as the archbishop told these to him. Eadmer decided to organize his notes into two books, one on Anselm's public life *(Historia Novorum)* and one on his private life and character *(Vita Anselmi).* In the latter he tells us that upon reflection, Anselm ordered Eadmer to destroy the biography, which, fortunately for us, Eadmer did only after making a copy of the work, which he completed after Anselm's death (409–13).

2. McGuire is supported in this contention by C. R. Walker and, to a lesser extent, Southern (105). René Roques does not remark on a biographical underpinning to the piece (132).

3. Anselm's prayer-poems, like his letters, introduced a new form of devotional literature into European spirituality. After Anselm's death, imitators practiced his style. Anselm himself had encouraged this in his cover letter to Countess Mathilda of Tuscany (Anselm 1973, 90).

4. Southern does not draw such a rigid demarcation, suggesting that *cognitio* and *meditatio* "are different modes of the same mental operation" (79, 103) and noting that both the *Monologion* and the *Proslogion* are in the form of meditations.

5. Southern dates the composition of the prayers and meditations over a period of thirty-five years, from shortly before 1070 (with a collection of nine prayers sent to Adelaide, daughter of William the Conqueror in 1072) to 1104 (with the Prayer to God and "for the communicants at the Eucharist") (106–11).

6. Southern argues that Anselm's contribution to devotional literature lay in his fully detaching it from corporate worship, infusing a sober tradition of meditation inherited from the Carolingian period with extreme fervor of expression and personal anxiety through horror of self (104). He concludes that the goal of Anselmian theology is knowledge of God, which begins with self-abasement and introspection.

7. This point will be substantiated by analyses of and citations from the texts. In a discussion of how Anselm dealt with the justice and mercy of God, George S. Heyer cited a few excerpts from several prayers and meditations. He sees Anselm as unable to navigate between the justice and mercy of God, keeping the suppliant off-balance as to which aspect of God's character may jump out at him at any moment (1965, 32–3). René Roques, on the other hand, although he does not address that question directly, sees mercy and love as the characteristic attributes upon which the sinner relies when approaching saints and God.

8. Perhaps the criticism Anselm himself received for being too lenient with disobedient monks hides behind this justification of the absolute goodness of God.

9. The first issue Anselm tackles in this Meditation is the question of the divine humiliation of the Incarnation/cross. He arouses the reader's interest by suggesting that there is "surely something hidden by this weakness, something concealed by this humility. There is something mysterious in this abjection. O, hidden strength" (230; *Meditation on Human Redemption,* lines 23–6). This "hidden power" of God on the cross anticipates Luther's *deus absconditus.*

8

Learning Love and Justice

St. Thomas and Dame Julian

THE CLIMB TOWARD HUMILITY

From the perspective of the late-twentieth-century desire to enhance self-esteem, cultivate assertiveness, and seek personal fulfillment, fourteenth-century piety and devotionalism appear frankly bizarre. From the perspective of the fourteenth century's stress on obedience, humility, and patience, the late twentieth century's focus on self appears frankly barbaric. While in a way both centuries might be said to be seeking perfection of the self—one by abolishing it, the other by cultivating it—late medieval devotion and late modern values are, nevertheless, like ships passing in the night. They face in different directions, one anchoring happiness in knowing and loving God, the other seeking to investigate the world by using the self as the fulcrum. Indeed, the whole modern period, beginning with the seventeenth century, may be viewed as a protest aimed at shifting from one worldview to the other. In this chapter we will examine the deeper foundation of these virtues to see if we cannot open up a genuine conversation with an age that, in many ways, is alien to us.

The Middle Ages, as we have seen from St. Anselm, were inspired by the values and practices of monasticism. Western monasticism took clear shape when Benedict of Nursia, drawing strength from the monks of the Egyptian desert and John Cassian, wrote a rule for his monks that established humility, along with its extensions, patience and obedience, as the foundations of monastic discipline (Benedict 1975). St. Benedict authored twelve-step spirituality on a ladder of humility by which the monk climbs to God.

Ascent in humility reveals a central dynamic of the Christian life—the motive for obedience to God shifts from servile fear to filial love.[1] According to chapter 7 of Benedict's *Rule*, piety begins when the monk obeys God's commandments out of fear that the angels will tattle on him, because there is nowhere to hide from God. In step 2, the monk seeks to follow God's will instead of his own. By step 3, the monk's motive has advanced from fear of punishment to love of God, and he accepts spiritual instruction from his superiors "in imitation of the Lord" (Benedict 1975, 58). The fourth step influenced later Christian piety more broadly.

The fourth step of humility is reached when a man, in obedience, patiently and quietly puts up with everything inflicted on him. Whether these are painful, unjust or even against his nature, he neither tires nor gives up. . . . To show that the faithful must suffer all, no matter what, for the Lord's sake, the psalmist says, "For you we suffer death all day long; we are considered as sheep for the slaughter" (Ps. 44.22). Secure in the hope of Divine reward they rejoice, "But in all things we overcome by the help of Him Who has loved us" (Rom. 8.37). . . . They fulfill the Lord's command in the midst of adversity and injustice—by the patience with which they obey. (59)

Next, the monk confesses evil thoughts and acts. Sixth, the monk "contentedly accepts all that is crude and harsh and thinks himself a poor and worthless workman in his appointed tasks" (60). Seventh, he actually believes that he is an inferior wretch. Eighth, he obeys all rules of the monastery and elders. The twelfth rule sums up the last four degrees of humility. Whatever he does, the monk "must think of his sins, head down, eyes on the ground and imagine he is on trial before God" (61). The assumption seems to be that as one thinks less of self and less of oneself, the more and better one will think of God, and the better God will, in turn, think of one. To put it directly, the teaching appears to be that God wants us to hate ourselves, and the more we do, the better we will be.

Bernard of Clairvaux's *On the Steps of Humility and Pride* (1980) portrays the shadow side of the Benedictine ladder for the Cistercian reform movement in the twelfth century. Bernard takes his monks on a sophisticated, if by modern standards somewhat harsh, psychological excursion into the craftiness of pride, as it steals into the monastery, taking over the affections of even the most devoted recruits to the intentional Christian life: nursing jealousy and contempt for others, being saddened by the goodness of others, rationalizing one's faults, distinguishing oneself by starvation, or secretly believing oneself to be holier than others. Bernard understood from experience the insidiousness of vanity, its traps and temptations, and reinforced the biblical warning that the devil prowls around like a roaring lion, seeking someone to devour (1 Pet. 5.8b).

Yet Bernard was not primarily interested in denouncing the deceitfulness of the human heart. He blends growing interest in romantic love into the Benedictine teaching on humility, thus loosening—though not severing—the link between humility and self-hatred and reinterpreting humility as love rather than fear of God. Even before detailing the intricacies of the stubborn heart, Bernard offered a therapy for growth in excellence—that is, growing into the truth of Christ, which is love—in three stages grounded in the humility and urged by the Beatitudes (chap. III). One begins with an honest self-assessment in which one confronts the truth about oneself. While honest self-assessment may lapse into self-hatred, self-knowledge, if achieved carefully, should stimulate empathy with others—fellow-sufferers who are also miserable over their own weaknesses, as well as the sick and hungry.

Christ is the standard of this self-knowledge, the model for this process. And Bernard, following Anselm, singled out the Hebrews passage that teaches that Christ "willed to suffer so that he might know compassion; to learn mercy he shared our misery" (35). Compassion is learned, even as our great High Priest learned it, by becoming one of us.

The point of Christ's learning empathy is not, Bernard insists, "to remain with them in misery, but to raise them from it by his mercy" (40). Christ's mercy confronts Bernard's monks with their proper calling: "If he submitted himself to human misery . . . how much more ought you not make any change in your condition, but pay attention to what you are, because you are truly full of misery. This is the only way, if you are to learn to be merciful" (41). Monastic discipline aims to help others and not judge them; to instruct gently, and without anger; to be unburdened of self-righteousness and filled with compassion. Bernard turns humility outward, toward the cultivation of mercy.

Bernard completes his teaching on the Christian life as a life of love in *On Loving God* (1980) and in his extensive sermons on the *Song of Songs* (1971; 1976). Cistercian ascesis craves an ever-deepening and maturing love of God that gradually dignifies and ennobles the God-seeker, who lives into the uplift of enjoying God. First, one loves God because of the gifts he has bestowed: the physical world and the spiritual gifts of the human mind, freedom, and virtue. Later the seeker loves God for himself, realizing that God is the only source of true happiness and rest. In *On Loving God* Bernard argues that eventually, in the light of the self-knowledge that comes from deepening humility, one comes to love oneself only in God. Christian excellence takes shapes with growth in love. And to grow in love is to grow in happiness. As Etienne Gilson put it, "The displacement of fear by charity by way of the practice of humility—in that consists the whole of St. Bernard's ascesis, its beginning, its development and its term" (Gilson 1990, 72).

Those not naturally given to compassion should seek a master for help. Since God is the goal of life and God is love, proper human desire seeks to achieve union with God by conforming one's will to the divine will. Obedience to God is therefore not so much to subdue the self as to remake it to be as loving as God is. Medieval Christians, led by the Franciscans, meditated on Christ's life and especially his passion, the example *par excellence* of humble love, in order to cultivate love and mercy. But it is easy to slip from the humility-as-compassion that the passion calls forth to humility-as-suffering as implied by Benedict's *Rule*. According to the psychological dynamic driving popular medieval devotion, the human being justly deserves divine wrath and judgment for sin for not being as loving and patient as Jesus. Even on this more moderate view, self-hatred is not an unseemly virtue.

By the fourteenth century the craving for self-abasing humility reached virtuosic heights. Renunciation of sex, property, and family, especially among a growing number of women, was strong, both inside and outside monastic enclosures (see Bynum 1987). What our century would label self-destructive behavior in the forms of sleep-deprivation, voluntary starvation, and self-flagellation were viewed by their adherents as perhaps eccentric, even crazy, but still as expressions of devotion, because love for God and care for self were thought to be polar opposites (see Kieckhefer 1984). Saintliness became tied to selflessness, especially among women, who gained a moderate amount of control over their own lives through pious scrupulosity (Lynch 1992).

Late medieval piety was dominated by the crucifix. The perplexity of the earliest followers of Jesus at his degrading death was transformed by what would become one of Christianity's more offensive teachings. What looked to many like a local lynching to placate the Roman authorities became, in Paul's hands, the salvation of the world. With Paul's theology of the cross, as we have seen, this politically and religiously inspired violence became the reconciliation of the world to God.

Whether Paul's theology of the cross was rightly or wrongly understood, it was received in the Middle Ages as a teaching of salvation based on divine displeasure. Similarly, whether rightly or wrongly read, Augustine's teaching on self-control was perceived to hold the flesh in contempt. Again, Anselm's treatise on the Incarnation left the impression that God demanded that his honor be restored by Christ's death. The late Middle Ages would ride the crest of this tidal wave of what our own century might regard as dismay at rather than acceptance of human frailty.

Yet a simple and concrete interpretation of the cross that called for its imitation by bearing the "little" crosses that afflict each of us in the natural course of life, or by volunteering for or seeking mortification, was not the intent of most thoughtful interpretations of the cross of Christ. Paul expected moral behavior but did not tie it to self-inflicted suffering. Augustine stressed that the cross teaches obedience to the demand for righteousness—in the sense that evil must be redressed—and Anselm followed him in this, adding the need to temper righteousness with mercy. Cistercian piety turned the interpretation of the cross back toward another central Augustinian theme: the cultivation of love. Eventually, meditation on the passion of Christ and the variety of devotional practices and artistic expressions that grew up around this meditation became detached from love and righteousness. Many in our own day bristle at forms of Christian piety that mistake self-hatred for love and righteousness.

A blatant and potentially dangerous message does indeed emanate from the center of the cross: suffering pleases God. Jesus is depicted as patiently enduring and knowingly allowing himself to become the innocent victim of unjust suffering and death at the hands of his enemies in order to meet the demands of righteousness. His disciples are urged to follow his example in all things. In popular medieval devotion, being a follower of Jesus meant imitating his virtues quite concretely, thus encouraging sufferings as like to the master's as possible. St. Francis was reported even to have received the stigmata. But more subtle minds had a vision of Christian excellence grander than a mind paralyzed with the fear of divine wrath could imagine.

Two of the ablest medieval theologians who set to work on the meaning of the cross for the Christian life were Saint Thomas Aquinas (1225–74) and Dame Julian of Norwich (b. 1342). St. Thomas's treatise on the passion, found in part III of the *Summa Theologiæ*, not only synthesizes the various images commonly applied to Christ's work on the cross but also balances teachings on love and righteousness (1965). Mother Julian, a fourteenth-century English theologian, had a bolder and more independent voice. She took a clear and uncompromising stand on the love of God, daring the church to unreservedly embrace the transforming power of love.

THE PASSION ACCORDING TO ST. THOMAS

The chapters of Aquinas's *Summa Theologiæ* are presented as questions on the topic under investigation.[2] Questions 46 through 49 of the treatise on the passion, which open up Thomas's discussion of soteriology, fall neatly into two halves. The first two questions explain the meaning of details of the biblical narrative that appear theologically ambiguous or perplexing on a casual reading. The second two questions specify the mechanisms of salvation, including its effects, by treating the various images commonly used to describe how the passion saves the human race. The remaining two questions of the treatise, 50 and 51, deal with Christ's burial and descent into hell. Here we will focus on questions 46 through 49 because they illustrate how Thomas understood the relationship between love and anger behind the divine pedagogy.

Thomas's questions on the passion of Christ immediately reveal the common and enduring perplexities surrounding the claim that Jesus' death was the most fitting instrument of human salvation. The passion appears unseemly precisely because it grounds salvation in divinely caused or at least divinely tolerated suffering and suggests that God authorized this strange means of redemption. There is also the question of precisely how Christ's passion effects salvation, given the variety of atonement theories prevalent in the church. And there remains the elusive task of pinpointing the precise content of salvation: freedom from sin, release from the power of the devil or from punishment, reconciliation with God, and so forth. While Thomas includes all of the major images for explaining the atonement that were common in the church, it is not at all clear that "systematic" theological questions drive the treatise, since he makes no attempt to harmonize or prioritize the various images (O'Callaghan 1986).

Thomas wants the reader to understand what God hopes to accomplish with each detail of the story, why it was carried off just this way rather than some other way, and this to a pastoral end. Questions 46 and 47, in particular, present an aretegenic interpretation of the passion story, one that explains that salvation is far richer than forgiveness of sin alone. Rhetorically, Thomas presents to his readers the demands of righteousness and the power of love made graphically clear by the passion of Christ. That is, the objective work accomplished by Christ on the cross has aretegenic effects, just as we saw with St. Athanasius's teaching on the Incarnation.

Thomas suggests that Christ's suffering was God's instrument of choice for our salvation (5–7; *Summa Theologiæ* part 3a: question 46: article 1). If God had merely canceled the effects of sin without the intervention of Christ, which certainly was an option, we would not have been confronted by the demand that wrongdoing be redressed; neither would we have seen God's mercy so starkly, or grasped his faithfulness to scriptural testimonies and prophecies. In other words, Thomas's first point is that without the passion we would not be adequately taught to love righteousness and trust God.

Thomas presses the view that God did not choose the most efficient or the "cleanest" means of getting the job done, because an act of divine will would only have addressed the issue of forgiveness of sins and not the "many things having to do with man's salvation over and above liberation from sin" (13; 3a:46:2). In the *responsio* of article 3 of question 46, Thomas says that "perfection of salvation" consists both in being forgiven and in perfecting our character in five ways: by understanding how much God loves us; by teaching us the virtues of obedience, humility, constancy, justice, and so on; by meriting for us justification and blessedness (as distinct from forgiveness); by encouraging us to refrain from future sin because we now stand in awe of the high price paid for our release; and by increasing human dignity through the knowledge of God's having overcome the deceits and evil of the devil. The justness of defeating the devil through an act of such lowliness reinforces the power of the cross to teach virtue (15; *ad* 3). In short, Thomas believes that discovering oneself to be the recipient of goodness and the overcoming of evil *in themselves* dignify believers and thereby carry them up the ladder of excellence.

Thomas follows Augustine in justifying God's choice of the cross itself because he believes, like Augustine, that it gives us symbolic examples of how we should live: not in the fear of death but in hope, with patience, and with gratitude for divine grace freely given. Thomas deepens what could be a dry teaching by viewing the passion as a model for human conduct and the development of virtue. Explanations of the depth and breadth of Christ's suffering—bodily injury, plus insult and abandonment by friends as well as enemies and strangers—are not demonstrative but rather didactic. Such explanations elicit the spiritual implications of the circumstances surrounding Christ's passion for those who would otherwise miss them.

Reflecting on the pastoral lessons taught by the passion gives meaning to small and seemingly insignificant details of the narrative. Christ died at a young age and in good physical health in order both "to draw attention to his love" and to show "what bodies will be like after the resurrection" (43; 3a:46:9). He died in Jerusalem, "the center of the habitable world," so that his teaching would spread globally. He died between two criminals in order for his victory to overcome wickedness (51; 3a:46:11).

Thomas, while a man of his age in accepting the value of suffering, did not countenance suffering as a good in itself (77; 3a:48:1). Christ's deliberately taking on suffering for a moral end reveals his nobility and greatness (27; 3a:46:6). The virtue involved lessens the sadness, though not the physical pain. Indeed, Christ enjoyed the bliss of bringing human salvation to fruition even in the midst of bodily and emotional suffering (37; 3a:46:8). By distinguishing the higher from the lower powers of the whole soul in articles 7 and 8, as Julian also would, Thomas helps the reader to develop a self-observing ego—the strength to draw back from the immediacy of pain and suffering—and to reflect on the unique ability of the human being to be conscious of nobility of purpose and moral ends as guides to action. Christ is in no way a victim, because the passion is under his control, undertaken deliberately and to a virtuous end.

Many in our own day are troubled by a type of Christian piety that finds suffering redemptive and approves of blind obedience to authority, possibly exemplified by Christ's obedience to the Father. And the notion that the Father handed the Son over to death seems to condone cruelty on the part of God and, by extension, on the part of persons in positions of authority. As we have seen, earlier Christians, such as Augustine and Anselm, also worried about these implications. Thomas devotes articles to each of these concerns in question 47 of the treatise on Christ's passion.

Thomas makes clear that while it was appropriate for Christ to be obedient to his Father in going to his death, the motive was not simple obedience to authority. The Dominican unpacks a rich notion of obedience that lesser minds of any age are apt to reduce to automatic compliance with an order or command. The pastoral nuances that cropped up repeatedly throughout question 46 are also evident in question 47. Christ may be said to have suffered out of obedience, if obedience is understood as needing to make amends for wrongdoing (59; 3a:47:2). Further, in Christ's case, death constituted a victory over death, indicating that his obedience, like the suffering, was virtuous not in its own right but only as it served a higher end.

The nub of the objection to obedience is this: the obedient one complies with a command against his natural will simply for the sake of fulfilling his duty or avoiding punishment. Thomas carefully argues that while Christ did fulfill a divine mandate in his passion, he did so willingly and out of love both for his Father and for his neighbor (61). That is, the Son agreed with the Father on this means of effecting human salvation: he did not simply obey the Father's will. As with Anselm, love, not fear, grounds Thomas's treatment of obedience. Neither Anselm nor Thomas counsels blind obedience as a virtue.

Closely allied to the issue of obedience is the delicate question focused by Rom. 8.32: the viciousness suggested by the Father's handing the innocent Son over to death. The issue is not clear-cut, Thomas maintains. First, since Christ went to his death willingly, it is not fitting to say that the Father handed him over to his enemies (63; 3a:47:3). And Christ's willingness was not a willingness to suffer *per se*, but a willingness to suffer *for us*, because he was filled with charity (63; 3a:47:3). In *ad* 1 of article 3 Thomas acknowledges God's severity in requiring that sin be requited but insists that because the Father inspired the Son with love for us, so that he willingly undertook his act of martyrdom, the crucifixion "also illustrates God's goodness, for man was unable to make sufficient satisfaction through any punishment he might himself suffer" (63; 3a:47:3). It was not from cruelty or wrath but "from love that the Father delivered Christ, and that Christ gave himself up to death" (65), in order that evil not go unredressed.

There is little to suggest that Thomas intended to use guilt and fear of divine wrath as a motivating strategy. Divine wrath is tied to the motif of righteousness that threads its way through this treatise. God must be placated, not because we are hateful but because we violated the canons of righteousness. God is disappointed that the human race did evil, as symbolically represented by various biblical characters: Adam and Eve chose to serve the devil rather than God; the Jewish leadership killed Christ instead of following him. These and presumably other misdeeds demand redress, not because God is personally offended but because a society that does not establish clear standards of right and wrong and hold people responsible for those standards cannot long endure.

While our own society may take the rule of law for granted, in the Middle Ages the rule of law was only gradually taking hold. Attempting to persuade an entire populace to internalize the very notion of the rule of law over the temptations of brute power, medieval theologians insisted that the issue for God is more the principle of righteousness than the personal slight involved in having ungrateful children. The notion that righteousness demands punishment for wrongdoing suggests how important internalizing standards of righteousness is for maintaining social order. The fact that God does not exact the punishment due, but absorbs it himself, tells us a lot about the divine pedagogy, and perhaps something of a Christian norm of parenthood.

Thomas and the Christian tradition behind him continually reflect on how to balance the demands of righteousness with the power of love to motivate and transform. Thus, the talk of placating God is but one perspective on the work of the atonement as Thomas interprets it. The suffering of Christ on the cross, while it points out the seriousness of wrongdoing, also expresses and explains God's goodness and the love God has for us. God's love is the matrix within which we confront the seriousness of wrongdoing and the need for moral order.

Questions 46 and 47 examine how the various elements of the passion narrative provide a well-rounded picture of what God was up to. Questions 48 and 49 discuss the major frames of reference used to explain how Christ's passion meets the demand for righteousness necessitated by human sin. Thomas discusses four "theories" around a common theme of vicarious atonement: a sign of Christ's love is that he does for us what we cannot do for ourselves. The first is the view of vicarious merit. Although Christ was highly meritorious by virtue of his sinlessness, the voluntary nature of his death was so abundantly virtuous that it sufficed for the goodness lacking in the members of the church. The merit that we could not earn by ourselves accrued to him and is "pour[ed] out from him upon his members" (77; 3a:48:1). Next is the satisfaction theory, based on a contractual model and usually associated with Anselm. Humankind owed a debt to God, caused by sin, that it could not meet. Christ's death more than suffices to pay the debt on our behalf because he himself has no debt to pay, being sinless (art. 2). Third is the idea, which Thomas credits to Augustine, that Christ's death is the perfect sacrifice, modeled after Old Testament animal sacrifices. It pleases God and unites us to him in holiness. (art. 3). Fourth is the view, also found in both Augustine and Anselm, that humanity was in bondage to the devil and that Christ's death defeats the devil and frees humanity from the devil for service to God (art. 4).

Christ's vicarious intervention on our behalf implies that we are quite helpless to make amends, whether by accumulating sufficient merit to outweigh our sins, paying the debt we owe for sin, remaining united with God, or freeing ourselves from service to the devil. The bottom line—that we are not up to what is required of us but that one who cares deeply for us is—calls forth awe and love in the faithful. Seeing Christ's overflowing love for us develops our gratitude. Our circumstance is no cause for despair. On the contrary, we ought to be filled with joy and gratitude and love for God, *and* with awe and honor for the one who gave his life for our freedom (77; 3a:48:1). The force of the scenario is to enhance human dignity without weakening our dependence on God.

We have seen that most of Thomas's treatise on the passion construes the problem dealt with by the cross as amendment for wrongdoing. Still, there is one article that casts the issue in interpersonal terms. Question 49, article 4, following three biblical texts (Wisd. of Sol. 14.9; Ps. 5.7[6]; and Sirach 12.3), asks whether Christ's passion really reconciles us with God. Thomas's first objection is that since God has always loved us, reconciliation cannot be what is needed. And the very next objection is that God's love is the reason behind the passion, so it cannot be that God had ceased to love us because of sin and begins loving us anew with Christ's deed. In the third objection Thomas notes that those who put Christ to death gravely offended God in the vileness of their sin, so the passion itself could be understood as promoting God's wrath rather than placating it.

Thomas's reply to these three objections reveals the broader matrix of love within which the teaching of righteousness is placed. He advocates what modern psychology might recognize as loving the sinner but hating the sin. Thomas distinguishes the human nature that God created, and loves without ceasing, from the sins that we commit (107; 3a:49:4, *ad* 1). Human sin, an impediment to God's love, is removed by the compensation made by Christ's offering of himself, with all the goodness attached to it that is discussed throughout the treatise: "the love of the suffering Christ outweighed the wickedness of those who slew him. His passion therefore was a greater reason for God's being reconciled with the entire human race than it was for his being moved to wrath" (107; 3a:49:4, *ad* 3). Christ's love, made evident in his willingness to suffer, speaks of God's love for us as he created us and effectively cancels the wrath aroused by the injustice of putting Christ to death, of becoming a servant of the devil, and so forth. Thus, while the believer dwelling on his or her insufficiencies could be filled with dread and guilt, Thomas declines to commend such dreary remorse to the faithful. He sees divine anger restrained within a broader commitment of love. By emphasizing the broader context of divine love, he strengthens the move begun by St. Bernard to assuage the fear of divine wrath that was set in motion by Benedict's *Rule.*

Although Thomas is usually interpreted as a rationalist, in this treatise he pursues another agendum.[3] For he is deeply interested in what happens to the reader as she wends her way point by point through the work. The rhetorical effect of Thomas's presentation of atonement theories and of his exegesis of the passion narrative is certainly to strengthen the believer's conscience, or what modern psychology would call her superego, by focusing attention on the importance of dealing properly with wrongdoing, whether by punishing the evildoer or, as God chose, sparing the one responsible and making amends himself. Another purpose may have been to establish firmly that Christ, not the saints or the priesthood or the papacy, is the fountain of salvation and the head of the church. In addition to both of these aims, Thomas draws a portrait of God's character for the reader. The treatise peers into God's heart and mind so that one can see the care he took with every detail of the story. The treatise can arouse a variety of emotional responses in the sensitive reader: awe at the greatness of Christ's deed, gratitude that someone has intervened on her behalf, relief that the threat of punishment has been mitigated, resolve to keep sin under tighter rein because of the enormity of the deed that had to be called forth to make amends, love for Christ because of his bravery and the depth of his love, and perhaps some guilt at having called forth such dramatic events to counter the effects of sin. Anxiety can also play a role in the believer's working through the issues, and perhaps, in order to rouse the conscience, this is appropriate.

Thomas wants the reader to engage the issues in order to grow in self-understanding, to know God more deeply, and to grasp the power of love, the need for humility, and the importance of righteousness. The reflective reader will be led to self-examination by Christ's virtues, by both the love and the righteousness of God, and by the power of God as well as the anger of God, because an example has been set before her, a man lifted up upon a cross, who willingly gave his innocent life that she might be spared. Although Thomas never explicitly invites the reader into the story, by alighting on each detail and each symbolic interpretation of its efficacy, he extends Jesus' own invitation as stated in Matthew: "Take my yoke upon you and learn from me; for I am gentle and humble in heart, and you will find rest for your souls" (Matt. 11.29).

THE WORK OF CHRIST OUR MOTHER

Thomas is the consummate scholar. One imagines his study filled with books. As Thomas writes (or dictates) each article of the *Summa* one can see scripture at his right hand, Augustine's great corpus at his left, Aristotle's philosophy on a table near-by, the works of the Fathers piled up on the floor, and the questions and perplexities of the monks he taught and lived with written on scraps of parchment and arranged in the order of topics as he would tackle them. One sees secretaries and research assistants scurrying to find the precise wording of the citations he has requested, and copyists awaiting the finished manuscript. And one can hear the clucking of those who criticized the new synthesis of truth and knowledge as it appeared.

Compared to the excitement that whirled around Thomas, the situation of Mother Julian is plain indeed. She is alone in her anchorhold, a small set of rooms attached to the Church of St. Julian in Norwich, where it is probably cold and damp. Her book *Showings* starts off as a memoir of her nearly fatal illness when she was thirty years old (1978). The intimate tone with which she recounts the "revelation of love" that she received during that illness remains throughout her explanation of the sixteen "showings" or revelations based on the passion of her beloved Jesus. Julian opens her mind and heart to us, or, rather, allows us to overhear each encounter in her love affair with God over the twenty-year period in which she recollected the visions and moved ever more deeply into the theological and psychological insights that were granted her as a result of her vivid visions of Christ's suffering and death. The long text, in which she elaborated the retelling of the showings with her acute theological insights, contains only four visions of the passion. The other twelve showings are theological reflections gleaned from recollecting them.

At first Julian appears to be precisely the type of fourteenth-century woman whom moderns distrust. She begins her book by telling us that she regretted terribly not having been present at the crucifixion and asked God for a "bodily sight" of Jesus' suffering so that she might deepen her own compassion (178; chap. II). Allied to this is her request for physical illness, including "every kind of pain, bodily and spiritual . . . every fear and temptation from devils," so that afterward she could live more to Christ's glory and be purged by God's mercy (178; chap. II). And finally she asks to be wounded by true contrition for sin, loving compassion, and longing for God. She sought pain and suffering as a way of learning empathy and growing closer to God; all her desires were granted.[4]

Yet surprisingly, instead of telling her story in order to encourage others to do likewise, Julian sounded a new note for theology, a note that would lead her so near the border of the church's teachings that one wonders why she was not suspected of heresy.[5] The Holy Church seemed to Julian to be ambivalent on the matter of grace and mercy, an issue of crucial importance for those of sensitive conscience. Early on, Julian tells the reader that her having received revelations from God on the subject of divine love is itself evidence that God is not far off and to be feared, but "familiar" and "courteous," stooping down to bring revelations even to herself (181–2; IV; cf. 188, VII).

Julian's signature phrase appears in the first chapter of her book, where she lists the sixteen showings, and continues unabated. God reveals to her that his love is the basis of the Christian's love and hope: "I shall make all things well which are not well, and you will see it" (176; I). And she trusts that those doctrines which seemed at odds with her conviction that God is all compassion either will become clear eventually or are not fitting for her to know in this life. In the meantime, she contents herself with, and counsels us to rest content in, the teachings of Holy Church (235–6; XXXIV). Indeed, although Julian disagrees with much that is going on in the church, her theology builds on an orthodox foundation. But Julian is both patient and trusting. God has only good in mind for her and for us, and equanimity of spirit is the only path to this truth.

Julian's refrain, "all will be well, and all will be well, and every kind of thing will be well" (225; XXVII), is unexpected from one whose theology focuses on Christ's passion. Her graphic visions of his suffering, the profuse bleeding and gashes to the head, the scourging, the rapid discoloration of his face, the deep drying and shriveling of his body as he died, are among the most vivid in Christian literature. Yet from all this suffering, which she sought to recapture in her own life, she came to the startling, and some might argue heterodox, insight that there is no anger in God. All the pain of sin and the suffering of body and spirit will be turned to blazing joy by the mercy of the Holy Trinity. How does Julian come to this hopeful yet controversial conclusion, knowing, and professing as she does to abide by Holy Church's teaching, that not all will be saved and that purgatory and hell are real (233; XXXII)?

Julian's gentle yet firm temperament and circumstance themselves are part of the answer. She thoroughly understood and grasped the theological and pastoral implications of Catholic doctrine but was either bold enough or isolated enough not to allow them to constrain the trust in God's love and mercy that she received through the visions. The experience of direct revelation itself authorized her demurral from received church teaching. In a sense, she stands at the head of English theology's tradition of direct illumination, later to become the touchstone of the theology of both George Fox and John Wesley, although Wesley's understanding of experience was that it reinforced church teaching. Julian used the authority of her showings and "touchings" to counter both official teachings and popular beliefs that instilled fear and guilt with teachings that foster hope and love. And she drew all this from orthodox Catholic doctrine.

Julian had the gift of patience and encouraged it in her readers. She referred to herself as a "simple, unlettered creature" (177; II), although she also tells us that she was theologically "instructed and grounded" (258; XLVI). God sent her these visions and the theological understandings that flowed from them in order to assist those faithful and sometimes unquiet souls who sought her advice as a spiritual director and confidant.[6] Perhaps her calmness is revealed by the very fact that she chose to retire into an anchorhold. Her solitude shows that she realizes that theological problems, like the problem of theodicy to which she regularly returned, are not easy of resolution. She allows God's showings to mature in her before setting them down to assist others. Fortunately, our own day recognizes her not only as a mystic but also as a first-rate theologian (Palliser 1992) who carefully worked through central Christian teachings for the well-being of believers well beyond her immediate acquaintance.

As a result of her understanding of the spiritual life, gained from recollecting the visions over a long period of time, Julian criticizes church doctrine. Her theology of divine compassion challenges both teachings and popular devotional practices that based piety on God's wrath and thereby encouraged self-hatred, fear of God and the future, or guilt. As she puts it, the church taught her to see herself as a sinner who sometimes deserves blame and wrath (257; XLV). But Julian's anthropology is more nuanced than this. She sees what she calls a "godly will which never assented to sin nor ever will, which will is so good that it can never will evil, but always constantly it wills good and it does good in the sight of God" (283; LIII) The godly will, a most controversial point in Julian's theology, is not necessarily visible to human judgment but is the basis on which God judges those who will be saved. Julian believes that we want to do right and that God sees this.

Julian's anthropology is so positive that she must take the need for human redemption on the faith of the church (283; XLIII). Humankind is the noblest thing God has made (284). "Our soul is created to be God's dwelling place, and the dwelling of our soul is God, who is uncreated. It is a great understanding to see and know inwardly that God, who is our Creator, dwells in our soul, and it is a far greater understanding to see and know inwardly that our soul, which is created, dwells in God in substance, of which substance, through God, we are what we are" (285; LIV).

In contrast to St. Thomas, for whom God's judgment and righteousness rightly point out the distance between us and God, Julian departs strikingly from the standard view that God's wrath comes from his judgment and leniency from his mercy. Julian argues that God's judgment of our "natural substance" is from his "own great endless love," not his anger, and so it always keeps us "whole and safe" (256–7; XXXV). Human judgments are mixed—sometimes harsh, sometimes lenient. But Jesus takes hard judgments, "reforms [them] by mercy and grace through the power of the blessed Passion, and so brings [them] into justice" (256–7; XXXV). Instead of seeing righteousness as the judgment of anger at our failing, as St. Thomas and the rest of the tradition had, Julian teaches that God's mercy intervenes and transforms harsh judgments as an act of righteousness! God's righteousness judges us based on our godly will, not our fallenness, as we see it.

At the same time, Julian knew that at least by human standards, we sometimes do deserve wrath and blame. But since this was not shown to her in her revelations, she could not reconcile the knowledge from her revelations with the teaching of the church to forsake evil and understand oneself as deserving "pain, blame and wrath" (258–9; XLVI). With Julian the link between piety, fear, and self-hatred, which began with St. Benedict and was progressively challenged by St. Bernard and St. Thomas, is finally broken. She rebels against the use of fear as an instrument of character-formation. But as we shall see with Calvin, Julian's alternative to the more severe traditions of Western piety was not widely received.

Julian concludes this particular chapter by taking refuge in the "many hidden mysteries" to which we are not privy, leading the reader to think that she "submit[ted] myself to [her] mother, Holy Church, as a simple child should," and left the conundrum unresolved. In fact, she did resolve it, and in favor of her revelation that "it is against the property of [God's] power to be angry, and against the property of his wisdom and against the property of his goodness" (259). Anger is against the divine nature. God knows us better than we know ourselves, so his judgment is more trustworthy than our own. And only when we know ourselves fully and truly, either in the last moments of our life or in heaven, may we trust our own self-judgment. In the meantime, we are to distrust the harshness of human judgment and rest in the leniency and mercy of divine judgment (259). This position harks back to St. Bernard's fourth and highest degree of love, "where one no longer even loves [one]self except for God" (Bernard 1980, "On Loving God," 19; chap. X.)

Julian's theology of compassion did not emerge directly from her visions, however. Like every clear-thinking theologian, she began from a fixed point and let the rest of her theology flow therefrom. She took her stand in the Christian doctrine of providence after "experiencing" the force of the doctrine while holding in her hand a small unnamed object about the size of a hazelnut (Julian, 183–4; V). This insignificant piece of God's creation reinforced an important foundation of Catholic doctrine and taught her all she needed to know of God: God is the creator, who loves and preserves his creatures. From this vantage point, the idea that God hates us, so we should hate ourselves, makes no sense. From this experiential reinforcement of orthodox doctrine she leapt forward into St. Augustine's great pastoral insight. If God protects and loves us, "until I am substantially united to him, I can never have perfect rest or true happiness" (183–4; V). These two planks of classical theology—that God keeps us in his love as part of his commitment to creation, and that we find true happiness in being, as Julian put it, "oned" with God—are the building blocks of her whole theology. She will seek to render the rest of Christian doctrine consistent with these theological building blocks in order to overcome fear, guilt, and distress in believers.

Julian's project corrects the knowledge of God on which punitive piety was based. God created us for knowing himself and his truth, wisdom, and supreme love. But we must live into this love if we are to realize the goal of our life. Julian makes clear to believers that God rejoices in us, so that we are united to God by rejoicing in him. The point is not only to persuade the reader of God's love but thereby also to discern one's purpose as part of God's creation. The corollary of knowing God's love is that we, like God, also exist through love (256; XLIV).

Julian is both a theologian and a pastor. We know that anchoresses acted as spiritual directors for laypersons in their towns. And we know that Julian counseled

Margery Kempe, an eccentric and spiritually distraught lay woman whose search for suffering was most disturbing (Kempe 1985, 77–9). It is as if in the twenty or more years since the initial revelations, Julian had been working as a spiritual counselor and finally wrote this book as the fruition of her advice and counsel to the Margerys of the world. Julian begins her book with the evidence of God's love from creation and her own experience, so that when she turns to Christ's suffering, her frightened reader will already feel safe enough in God's love that the fear of divine wrath may be set aside (190; VIII).

When Julian wants to be sure that the meaning of a point she has been developing is crystal clear to her "even" Christians, she turns and directly addresses her reader: "This revelation was given to my understanding to teach our souls wisely to adhere to the goodness of God" (184; VI). Ignorance of this love—or, more precisely, fear of God—sends people to pray to intermediaries, as if they could help. She reminds her readers (gently as always) that praying to the passion, or the cross, or St. Mary, or the saints is not really helpful, but only insofar as it reminds us of God's goodness in everything, "which comes down to us in our humblest needs. It gives life to our souls and makes them live and grow in grace and virtue" (185). In this passage Julian rebukes not only the church's practices but its pastoral strategy, too. God's goodness, not God's threats of punishment or damnation, help us grow in grace and virtue, because love is stronger than fear.

Julian warns her readers, her pastoral charges, that seeking happiness in created things leads to unhappiness, because safety is only found in God. Compared to God, one is to despise "as nothing all things which are created" (184; V). Julian does not mean to suggest that created things are evil or worthless, only that they are worthless in comparison to the true prize, union with God. Indeed, in the very next chapter she sees God's love for us displayed in the human digestive system (186; VI)! John Calvin would begin his theology from this same trust in God's commitment to creation. And as Calvin too would conclude, this evidence of God's goodness has a naturally humbling impact on the faithful. The whole of the Christian life follows from acceptance of this basic doctrine: "contemplating and loving the Creator make the soul to seem less in its own sight, and fills it full with reverent fear and true meekness, and with much love for its fellow Christians" (187; VI). Julian has already set a clear path for herself. Reverent or filial fear or awe for God and proper self-knowledge come not from the fear of punishment but from clinging to God's love and mercy.

Julian has built on Bernardian love theology, strengthening its foundation by stating strongly that the love is initiated from the divine side, finally severing the link between divine wrath and humility. Only when this is clear does she impress upon her reader that God's love is to be requited and that this is the foundation of the moral life. In chapter IX she again turns and addresses her reader directly, to be sure that she is not misunderstood. "I am not good because of the revelations, but only if

I love God better; and inasmuch as you love God better, it is more to you than to me. I do not say this to those who are wise, because they know it well. But I say it to you who are simple, to give you comfort and strength" (191; IX).

Although her book takes its theological stand on the doctrine of providence, Julian's literary strategy casts the whole as a sustained reflection on the passion of Christ, the most frightening of Christian images. She posits that God is not a distant and fearsome judge whose hatred for us is placated by our suffering or alms but a loving and compassionate mother under whose care all will be well.

Julian is perhaps best-known for her extensive use of the image of Christ as mother, which dominates the fifteenth revelation. We do not know whether in fact she was a mother, nor do we know anything of her relationship with her own mother. For our purposes, calling Christ our mother is a key element in the larger project of her theology: to teach that love is more salutary than anger. It is important to note that Julian never ceases to use Father language of God also. She has no interest in pitting a loving mother against an angry father, for there is no anger in God at all. But she does identify motherhood with "tender love" (262; XLVIII). And this property of God transforms fear and dread into consolation (263), and consolation is the foundation of moral strength.

Julian assumed that her readers' suffering, whether physical or spiritual, came from an inner life that was misformed as a result of dwelling overly much on their sins, real or imagined. And she admitted frankly that she did not understand why God allowed sin in the first place (224; XXVII). For anguish over sin and the desire for punishment or suffering to relieve it would more likely make a person want to avoid God than cling to him. In other words, Julian saw that the pain caused by sin could be pastorally counterproductive, not motivating, as Thomas and perhaps other male theologians held. It is difficult to love someone who disapproves of you. One must rely on a strong sense of duty and discount one's feelings. Contrary to many theologians who believed that in thinking less of ourselves we think more of and cling more dearly to Christ, Julian realized that it is difficult to follow a parent or leader who is full of negative judgments and anger (225; XXVII).

As we have been seeing, in order to soothe tender souls, Julian says boldly, and contrary to church teaching, that "in God there can be no anger" (201; XIII). That God means no ill for us, or at least those who serve him (even only a little and even if badly), means that God does not want us to suffer, and for the tender souls for whom she wrote, Julian knew that the greatest suffering came from sin. If Thomas may be said to have written to those whom he believed had weak consciences, Julian may be said to have written to those Christians whose superego was strangling them with guilt and fear.

Julian lived in a dangerous and anxiety-ridden world. War, disease, and political and ecclesiastical instability were constant companions in the fourteenth century (see Jantzen 1988, 3–14; Lynch 1992, 303–14). It was a time of troubled spirits as well as troubled bodies. It is not difficult to imagine how readily the subtlety of a teaching like St. Thomas's, which countenanced obedience, suffering, and humility only in the context of the pursuit of righteousness and compassion, could be lost.

As we have seen, on a popular level, self-destructive and self-hating behavior were not uncommonly thought of as penitential and virtuous. As Richard Kieckhefer put it, "In the late Middle Ages, the obsession with the cross led to a widespread, overwhelming, and quite explicit desire to share in Christ's agony through self-imposed ascetic practices. Not content merely to bear up patiently under sufferings sent to them by God and their fellow human beings . . . they took matters into their own hands" (119). Julian objected strenuously to the view that our suffering placates God, for if that were true it would undermine her ability to trust God. She wrote, for example, of having alternating experiences of consolation and desolation, times when she felt "powerfully secured without any painful fear" even though she did not deserve such feelings of joy, and times when she felt "oppressed and weary of my life and ruing myself" although she had committed no sin (Julian 204; XV). Both extremes, she says, express God's love, for sometimes we need to be left to ourselves. But God desires that we should "do all in our power to preserve our consolation, for bliss lasts forevermore, and pain is passing, and will be reduced to nothing for those who will be saved. Therefore it is not God's will that when we feel pain we should pursue it in sorrow and mourning for it, but that suddenly we should pass it over, and preserve ourselves in the endless delight which is God" (205).

On a popular level, the suffering and ugliness of Christ's passion were used to frighten believers into being good, either out of awe or guilt at what Christ suffered for us, or because by sinning after baptism we open up the problem of deserved punishment all over again. Julian, however, went in a different direction. Taking the classic Neoplatonic Christian position that sin "has no kind of substance, no share in being," she argued that the pain of sin is real, and in this sense sin can have didactic value if understood properly (225; XXVII). The embarrassment caused by sin, just like Christ's suffering on the cross, was passing pain. In Christ's case, the pain of his suffering was turned to joy because of the benefits it brought us. Similarly, the pain of sin "purges and makes us know ourselves and ask for mercy" (225; XXVII). But because Christ's love is the sign of the promise that this pain will cease, and we will be comforted, in Julian's mind there is no place for anguish. In other words, God does not blame me for my sin; I blame myself. God is full of compassion and mercy.

From the perspective of God's love for us, the passion enables the sensitive soul to gain control over embarrassment and anguish over sin and to find consolation instead of a spur to mortification. The proper understanding of Christ's suffering is as a gift of grace: "if we well contemplate his will in this, it keeps us from lamenting and despairing as we experience our pains; and if we truly see that our sins deserve them, still his love excuses us. And of his great courtesy he puts away all our blame, and regards us with pity and compassion as innocent and guiltless as children" (227; XXVI-

II). Christ's having set our sin right is the basis for hope that all else will also be set right.

Medieval devotionalism had learned to manipulate fear. The penitential system extended into every aspect of life. And, of course, fear is always a firm basis for economic gain. Pilgrimages, traffic in relics, the sale of indulgences, the building of shrines, and the cult of the saints were all directed toward the alleviation of guilt stirred up by vivid teaching and preaching on hell and purgatory, divine wrath and human failure. Popular piety and psychology held that guilt and shame could be controlled through strenuous penitential disciplines: if one suffers voluntarily, one will eliminate the guilt by paying for one's sins. This was the approach followed by Catherine of Siena, for example, whose confessor protested that she was inventing sins that she had not committed in order to justify more severe ascetical practices (Kieckhefer 124). Catherine also exhorted her readers to delight and share in the sufferings of Christ, as if the suffering itself would be of salvific value: "Be a glutton for abuse—for Christ crucified. Let your heart and soul be grafted into the tree of the most holy cross—with Christ crucified. Make his wounds your home" (qtd. in Kieckhefer 109).

Julian rejected this whole approach. The way to control anguish is neither alms, pilgrimages, nor mortification, but trust in God's love and mercy, which give hope of salvation. Julian's eschatology is undaunted by the teaching that not all will be saved. Although the Church holds that some will be lost, and she accepts this teaching (at least in theory), she believes that God will perform an "honorable, and wonderful and plentiful" work of salvation on behalf of those who "do nothing at all but sin" (238; XXXVI). Salvation begins on earth and continues through the eschaton in heaven. And God made this revelation come to her in order to provide hope to those anguished about their salvation on account of their sins. On this basis Julian herself must stop worrying about the ultimate fate of each individual, for "we ought to rejoice in him for everything which he reveals and for everything which he conceals; and if we do so willingly and meekly, we shall find great comfort in it, and we shall have endless thanks from him for it" (239).[7]

Julian, like Thomas, wanted her readers to know themselves and God better as a result of her writing. What she wanted the reader to take away, though, was a bit different. She was one of the first Christian theologians to examine Christian doctrine for the cumulative psychological effects it was having on a popular level. Her theology assumes a basic aretegenic principle that we have seen at work regularly in the readings we have undertaken: we become what we know. Julian believed that love begets love and mercy begets mercy, and that fear begets fear and anger begets anger. Being good comes from believing oneself to be God's noblest creature, who belongs to God himself. Basic human dignity is God-given, and, Julian says, God never turned aside from this original decision. Who are we to question God's eternal judgment?

It is tempting to suggest that Julian's theology of compassionate motherhood and divine goodness bring a long-awaited and refreshingly feminine perspective to Christian theology. Her strong opposition to divine anger and vengeance and her insistence on gentleness and mercy certainly suggest a new foundation for pastoral guidance. But it is important to keep in mind that other women of her day—we have pointed to Margery Kempe and Catherine of Siena—did not share her antipathy for standard teaching. Still, her insistence on the unconditional love that characterizes both the motherhood and the fatherhood of God do hold up classically feminine virtues as truer to the reality of God than images based on anger and harsh judgment, images that were common in her day. Certainly her being a woman was not incidental to her theology. The norm of love she holds up for us may exceed the grasp of both women and men, in her day as well as our own. And the church, too, may shrink back from the denial of any anger at all in God, as Julian insisted. Still, Julian has given theology much to think about.

ASSESSMENT

In the work of St. Thomas and Mother Julian on the passion of Christ, we see two different versions of the divine pedagogy. St. Thomas believed that in the story of human redemption, through the vivid and offensive reality of the suffering and death of Jesus, God speaks to us of love and righteousness in order to have us reflect deeply on the standards of right and wrong to which we are called, and on the power of love to draw us close enough to God to be able to hear the more painful message about standards of morality that we might prefer to avoid. Christ's atoning sacrifice brings home to those who would naturally seek to escape from the consequences of their actions that "the piper must be paid." God is disobeyed, and our misdeeds cannot go unpunished. Yet at the same time, the classic Christian view of the atonement is that we are in fact not asked to pay. Like Abraham rescued from sacrificing his son, we are paid for by God in an act of love and mercy, and we live to learn the lesson and tell the tale.

In the view of Thomas, representative of the normative Western tradition, the means of human redemption, which in many respects looks quite odd, brilliantly synthesizes God's love and anger, teaching us that anger is to be tempered by love. In the end, God stands as the great master noble character. For God is able to control his anger at being disobeyed and return the insult with love, teaching us infinitely more through self-restraint than he ever could through punishment.

Mother Julian offers a different aretology. Unlike St. Thomas, who agreed with the tradition that God undertook to save us because we could develop a strong conscience and self-control no other way, Julian speaks to those of tender conscience who are scrupulously nervous about themselves, or who have developed such a negative self-image that by mortification they abuse God's beautiful creatures: themselves. Julian is, in a way, demanding a higher moral standard than Thomas. For Thomas allows for the reality of anger, if in God, then certainly in us. The issue, he says, is how we handle anger, and for that we need God. Julian, on the other hand, admits no anger at all. God is nothing but love, compassion, and mercy. It is God's love for us that enables us to love ourselves, God's compassion that commits him to holding onto those whom he loves no matter what they do, and God's endless well of mercy that models who we are to become. Only by moving into the reality of divine presence and substance for which we were created do we fully understand ourselves and, by extension, how we are to live with others.

The passion of Christ, in Julian's theology, teaches God's love for us. Although she shies away from discussing the classic interpretations of the atonement, her position seems to be that our salvation depends on knowing and loving God. And when we do, then all manner of thing shall be well with us. Although she does not put it quite this way, the atonement is necessary because without it we would have only our own judgments to rely on, and we are notoriously bad at judging both ourselves and others. In the passion, Christ our mother has shown us that we must trust God's judgments more than our own, for he sees the good in us even when it is visible only to himself. And this teaches us to love God graciously and with equanimity.

In conclusion, it looks as if a choice must be made. Is there anger in God or not? Do we follow God because we need to develop a superego or to escape from one that is strangling us? Do we learn to love under threat of punishment or by being loved? Christian theology has generally proposed univocal psychologies to account for the human condition. All human persons have been assumed to be similarly constituted, to work under the same psychological dynamics, and therefore to respond to the same pedagogical strategies. But perhaps St. Thomas and Mother Julian are inviting us to nuance these generalizations. At least from a human point of view, it does seem that there are temperaments that need to know of God's anger and of the standards of right and wrong that do not seem to have a strong hold on them. And certainly we see, as Julian saw, those of tender conscience, whose timidity and fearfulness debilitate them. And perhaps with the help of theologians like Thomas and Julian, latter-day Christians may see that God selects the pedagogy that we most need to heal us of infirmities, so that we may truly find our rest in him.

Notes

1. The first elaboration of the distinction between relating to God as a servant and as a legitimate child comes from Galatians 3.16–4.7. The distinction between servile fear, based on law, and holy or reverential fear, based on God's kindness, appears in Augustine's *City of God* (1984, 1006; book XXI: chap. 25).

2. The *Summa Theologiæ* is the most perfected form of medieval dialectics. Each question or topic is divided into articles or subquestions. Each article begins by stating the question at issue and then gives several objections raised in opposition to the question as it has been framed. The objections are followed by an opposing statement, the *sed contra*, brought from a highly respected authority, often Augustine, Aristotle, or scripture. After this comes Thomas's own reply *(responsio)* to the question. Each article concludes with specific answers

(introduced by *ad*) to each objection raised at the beginning of the article to round out the whole.

3. In an essay on Thomas's passion narrative Aidan Nichols notes that here Thomas is interested not in deducing a set of systematically interested truths from the articles of the Creed but, rather, in demonstrating the convenience and fittingness of the passion. He does not, however, draw the aretegenic conclusions from Thomas's treatment (Nichols 1990, 447–59).

4. It is the testimony and experience of women like Julian that today's feminists seek to overturn on the grounds that such women were victims of systemic misogyny. The slip from regret for sin to a desire for suffering illustrates a self-hatred that Judith Plaskow, and feminists following her, consider the greatest sin of all: denial of self. Feminists object to the ideal of selflessness cultivated by monasticism. Since the ideal of self-hatred, if it can be called that, was designed for monks (women asked to be included by setting up parallel orders), it may be more precise for feminists to direct their concerns at medieval monastic ideals rather than hierarchical forms of social structure per se (1980). Of course, ideals of self-hatred are easily manipulated by those given to abuse authority in any case. We have already noted points at which late medieval monastic piety could fall into self-hatred. This essay argues that at least in the cases of St. Thomas and, as we shall see, Julian as well, a highly sophisticated understanding of sin and its relation to suffering was actually at work. Julian herself, while casting her theology in terms of the culture of her day, sought a way to correct the abuses to which sensitive souls—like Margery Kempe, who sought Julian's counsel—were prone.

5. In a sensitive and beautiful rendering of Julian's theology, Grace Jantzen entertains the question of whether Julian's insistence on divine love led her into pantheism (1988). She suggests that while Julian insists that God is the "source and substance of all reality," she allows for the individuality of creatures such that they are distinct from God. Richard Harries discusses two doctrines that led Julian to the edge of orthodoxy: her teaching of divine mercy and her idea of a godly will seem to contradict the church's teaching on original sin (1987).

6. For a discussion of the life of anchoresses at the time, see Grace Jantzen (1988).

7. In her helpful discussion of Julian's doctrine of sin, Sr. Margaret Ann Palliser makes a useful distinction between the moral and ontological levels of sin in Julian's mind. Morally—or, one might say, pastorally—we experience our sin as separation from God. But ontologically—that is, from God's side—we are still in God's keeping, and sin in no way interferes with God's love for us (99). That is, sin has a pedagogical function but no absolute power to harm us.

PART V

Sixteenth-Century Reform

The reform movements of the sixteenth century, both Protestant and Catholic, sought to educate the laity, stabilize the clergy, and reform ecclesiastical practices and popular devotionalism. While Catholics and Protestants were more combative than co-operative in these renewal efforts, it would be a mistake to think that the Protestant side was completely discontinuous with the medieval heritage. The central question remained the acceptance by God of sinners. The twist Protestants gave to the answer, however, did make a difference. Rather than stressing devotion to God, as many of the medieval mystics and monastic orders did, the Protestants settled on faith. One can only trust that in his mercy God finds one acceptable.

While these were the dominant themes of the day, we shall see that even in a magesterial reformer like John Calvin, and perhaps more so in him than in any other thinker examined in these studies, the aretegenic agendum is in the forefront. Perhaps aroused by the violence and social disorder wrought by the Reformation, Calvin turned back to the authority of divine law as the primary tool of obedience to the divine will. Yet he went still further back, picking up a theme central to both Athanasius and Augustine: moral personhood is shaped by knowing God. Theology's task is to facilitate that knowledge for each individual Christian believer.

9

"By the Renewing of Your Minds"

John Calvin

THE TASK

Had Saint Thomas and Dame Julian discussed their differing assessments of the needs of the human temperament in John Calvin's presence, he would have agreed with Thomas. Like his predecessors, he was concerned with engaging Christians in understanding God deeply and personally. With Thomas, he believed that Christians need moral strengthening and that God is the proper agent of reform. Training in godliness is the purpose of his *Institutes of the Christian Religion,* stated in the opening paragraph of his prefatory address to King Francis I, which accompanied the first (1536) edition: "My purpose was solely to transmit certain rudiments by which those who are touched with any zeal for religion might be shaped to true godliness" (1960, 9). And in the prefatory note to the final (1559) edition, Calvin repeats that he had "no other purpose than to benefit the church by maintaining the pure doctrine of godliness" through his "zeal to spread [God's] Kingdom and to further the public good" (4). Calvin begins by identifying himself as an aretegenically oriented teacher of the church who understands the implications of theology for public life.[1]

If we take doctrine and piety as belonging to two separate fields, one academic and the other pastoral, we will never understand Calvin. For Calvin, the purpose of treating articles of religion is to enhance godliness. If that treatment is comprehensive, so much the better. The modern academy eliminated spiritual and moral formation from scholarly inquiry, rendering the modern disciplines of marginal use to the church. Calvin would stand down from this decision.

Lacking a vocabulary for the aretegenic program, modern scholars have noted Calvin's pastoral concern variously, some attributing it to different aspects of his background, training, or temperament, others identifying it in terms that come from the commentators' own time or discipline. In his classic work on the duplex knowledge of God in Calvin's theology, written at the height of the influence of religious existentialism, Edward Dowey pointed out that Calvin, who eschewed speculative philosophy for theology, was not primarily interested in formulating correct propositions about God. Rather, he was concerned with the existential effects of revelation, "existential" meaning "knowledge that determines the existence of the knower" (Dowey 1952, 26). For Calvin, knowing God defines the self, as he hints at the opening of the *Institutes* (35–8; bk. I: chap. I: paras. 1–2). While existentialism may have been an understandable vocabulary for describing Calvin's project in the early 1950s, it neglects the moral and ethical dimensions of godliness.

In "John Calvin's Doctrine of the Christian Life," John Leith noted that "Calvin wrote his theology to persuade, to transform human life" (1989, 17). He argued that even Calvin's (in)famous doctrine of election "provides the true motivation for moral living" (130). And Leith concludes that these themes conflict with the long-honored tradition of considering Calvin a systematician. Not only do glaring inconsistencies or paradoxes suffuse the *Institutes,* but for Calvin, the truth of God is grasped as "the personal and deeply mutual relationship of humankind to God," not as the sort of static and impersonal truth that Calvin associated with scholasticism (220). The result is to set Calvin against Calvinism.

In an article published in 1973, Quirinus Breen attributed Calvin's rejection of scholasticism and speculative philosophy to his deep commitment to Renaissance humanism: "faith in the Erasmian ideal of virtue through knowledge" (1973, 33). The classical ideal for which the humanists strove, "betterment through knowledge" (34), captures the aretegenic heart of the *duplex cognitio dei* that Dowey had earlier delineated. Breen winsomely summed up his comments on both Erasmus and Calvin with the help of Werner Jaeger's work on ancient Greek literature: "all of it expressed a persistent thrust toward . . . finding clarity on what it means to be human" (39). Again, as long as the moral dimension of "betterment" and "means to be human" is understood, this description fits Calvin well.

An astute student of Reformation history also locates Calvin's theology in the tradition of Renaissance humanism and the knowledge gained from experience. William Bouwsma roundly rejects the notion of a systematic Calvin, arguing that Calvin was a humanist who used rhetorical discourse adroitly "to stimulate human beings to appropriate action. . . . The central motive force of Calvin's life was not to set forth a true theology for the ages but to remedy the particular evils of his own age. He aimed not so much to state truths—he rarely made truth claims—as to galvanize other human beings to appropriate action, to induce activity, to obtain results" (1990, 35). Calvin's was "a dynamic rhetorical theology with characteristically humanistic epistemological, anthropological, and other implications" (36). Bouwsma put well the case for an aretegenic reading of Calvin: "The doctrines he discovered or uncovered in scripture are not so much truths as they are statements about how the spiritual world operates: in this case, how God's energy is communicated or transfused into human beings and what the consequences of this transfusion should be. Such practical knowledge was, for Calvin, the only kind accessible to human beings" (37). The rhetorical task was to "induce love, action, obedience, and service" (38).

Of course Calvin believed himself to be expounding the truth of God and was making theological claims that he held to be true. And since God never changes, corrections for his own age would, he believed, be relevant to future generations as well. But Bouwsma located the existential task in the context of the experiential knowledge of the Renaissance, although he, like Dowey, failed to recognize how persistent the moral content of experience is. Knowing God is the key to moral transformation, which is closely allied with salvation. It involves the affections and arises from experiencing the moral despair that turns us to God (Bouwsma 1988, 158–9). In an important sense, Bouwsma put his finger on the pulse of Calvin's aretegenic program. Calvin's scriptural exegesis and his theology have the same sustained pastoral goal, articulated quite bluntly in his commentary on 2 Corinthians: "even the saints need to be threatened by a complete collapse of human strength, in order that they may learn from their weakness to depend entirely upon God alone" (Calvin 1964, 12). "We have to look at death before we can be brought to God" (13). Theology comments on ideas in order to bring people to God.

Calvin's practical interests call for an aretegenic reading of his theology, a reading that seeks the pedagogy God uses to bring us "to glorify God and enjoy him forever."[2] In such a short compass, however, it will be impossible to present this achievement fully. Since the *Institutes* is Calvin's most comprehensive presentation of the faith, it seems appropriate to concentrate on it—and, within it, on books I and II, which are organized around the knowledge of God—since, as Calvin persuasively argues (echoing Augustine), it is impossible to glorify God unless we know him. Perhaps lack of adequate attention to Calvin's commentaries will stimulate readers to delve into them: there is rich ore to be mined there.

Before proceeding to our task, however, a note on what Calvin means by "doctrine" is in order, to prevent our slipping into a modern mode that separates systematic from pastoral theology. Despite demurrals as to Calvin's commitment to coherence and consistency, several of the writers mentioned above, especially Dowey and Leith, perhaps lacking an alternative paradigm for Calvin's *oeuvre*, speak conventionally of how Calvin laced or failed to lace doctrines together. Dowey, for example, laments Calvin's having separated the doctrine of scripture from the exposition of the doctrine of faith (1952, 88). Leith laments the separation of predestination from providence (1989, 107–45). While registering these disappointments speaks to each writer's appreciation of Calvin's pedagogical interests, both writers still function within the modern systematic theological paradigm that attends to the rationality or coherence of ideas apart from their moral power. But if Calvin could not conceive of what we would designate as academic systematic theology, in ordering (and reordering) his *magnum opus* he may have attended more to whether the reader cooperated with the pastoral program than to how well ideas fit. If this is correct, examining the ideas without regard for the larger aretegenic purpose is bound to lead us away from understanding Calvin's project. For example, it may seem logical to locate the discussion of predestination next to the teaching on providence, following scholastic theology; but it may also be that putting the discussion of election with the doctrine of providence, which comes relatively early in the 1559 edition, would have undercut Calvin's constant exhortation to righteousness.

Another example of Calvin's "odd" placement of a doctrinal discussion is his much-debated doctrine of the authority of scripture, as Dowey has suggested. The scholarly debate has focused on whether Calvin subscribed to a doctrine of inerrancy or dictation or would allow for historical criticism. Dowey finds the pertinent chapters in the *Institutes* (I:vii–ix) to be a mislocated excursus to chapter vi.[3] Since the Holy Spirit authorizes scripture, Dowey argues that that discussion really belongs (i.e., more logically fits) with the discussion of the doctrines of Christ's benefits, faith, and the Spirit, which do not come until book III (1952, 88). And from this observation Dowey mounts an extended discussion of the state of the question on Calvin's doctrine of inspiration at the time he was writing (90–124).

Yet as he began this excursus on the authority of scripture, Calvin himself twice (*Institutes* I:vii:1, 4) tells us why the discussion of the authority of scripture is located where it is: scripture must have authority beyond that given by the church in order to be taken seriously. "Credibility of doctrine is not established until we are persuaded beyond doubt that God is its Author" (78; I:vii:4). This is part of the general polemic against "traditions of men" and in favor of the Word of God. Calvin made the same point in a Pentecost sermon on Acts 2:1–4 (1975, 561). The question there is why the Holy Spirit appeared as tongues of fire to the Jews gathered in Jerusalem. Calvin's answer reveals his aretegenic drive. Since we are so inclined to unbelief, we need a visible sign that the apostles' writings were actually "approved and authorized" by God (1975, 561). Otherwise we might think that the scriptures are just the opinions of the writers. The authorization of the apostles by the Holy Spirit indicates that these writings are God's way of leading us onward, "and that the teaching which is preached to us is His pure and infallible truth" (1975, 561). The Pentecost episode affirms scripture's credibility. Calvin was emphasizing that the apostles have more authority than the papacy, a major plank of the evangelical protest at the time.

The treatment of the authority of scripture may appear to be an excursus, but its early placement is essential to the work's aretegenic goal of shaping Christians for true godliness. The substitution of scripture for the traditions of the church is not simply the replacement of inauthentic with authentic authorities. Rather, by "see[ing] manifest signs of God speaking in Scripture . . . the majesty of God will immediately come to view, subdue our bold rejection, and compel us to obey" (*Institutes* 78–9; I:vii:4). The point is well placed because it marks the transition from knowledge of God the creator, gained by observing the creation, which is common to Christian and non-Christian alike, to knowledge of God known to Christians alone from special revelation. The point of explicating a "doctrine" of scripture is not to defend scripture's rationality but to establish scripture's authority so that its readers will flee to its pages to learn of God.

This brings us to a further question of how Calvin viewed his own task and responsibilities within the church. Calvin understood ecclesial vocations to be five in number, following Eph. 4.11 ("that some would be apostles, some prophets, some evangelists, some pastors, and teachers, to equip the saints for the work of ministry, for building up the body of Christ"). He located himself in the last category—responsible for "Scriptural interpretation—to keep doctrine whole and pure among believers" (*Institutes* 4). Theology is a form of proclamation that aims particularly at interpreting God's Word to assist Christians in living a godly life. It is telling that Calvin's *Institutes* contains no prolegomenal statement but instead plunges directly into the core concern: how does God make himself known to us, and what is to be the tangible fruit of that knowledge? While this directness speaks to the fact that in the sixteenth century, revelation was not yet problematic, it also sets Calvin apart from Saint Thomas, for example, who began the great *Summa* by laying out the parameters of the discipline in which he was engaged.[4] Calvin makes no apologies for his calling as a pastoral theologian.

Allied with his vocational self-understanding is how he distinguished among doctrine, doctrines, and articles of religion, and the role each played in his project. To my knowledge, Calvin did not explore this question, so this discussion is a working hypothesis of what he might have said. He used the word "doctrine" in the usual sense of the whole teaching or instruction of God, whose end lay beyond itself. He uses phrases like "sum of doctrine," "the perfection of the gospel doctrine," "the received doctrine of the gospel," or "the sum of necessary doctrine," or (when defining faith) the "sound doctrine of godliness" (this last, 558; III:ii:13). Calvin also refers to doctrine as a virtue, characterizing certain church councils as displaying "insight, doctrine, and prudence" (1172; IV:ix:8). Doctrine is scriptural teaching in a composite sense, closely allied with the teaching of the Law, the Prophets, and the Gospel of Christ (93–4, I:ix:1; 495, II:xv:1; 496; II:xv:2; 1041, I:ii:1) While it has clear and unambiguous content, doctrine is important not because assent to cognitive claims constitutes salvation but because it is necessary to understand who God is and what God has done for us in a comprehensive sense and with historical perspective.[5] It may be necessary to believe specific claims, but the cognitive act of believing itself is not efficacious. The reason for believing correctly, and therefore for explaining doctrine carefully, is that good teaching enables believers to know and trust God. And these two are the bases of a godly life. This is the reason Calvin rejected the medieval notions of both implicit and unformed faith, and required explicit, formed faith—heartfelt faith based on understanding—of all Christians (547–8, 551–5; III:ii:5, 8, 9, 10).

Calvin mentions specific doctrines only rarely, and these instances refer to what we moderns would call practices rather than doctrines. For example, he uses "doctrines" when admonishing the church that councils are not authorized to formulate nonbiblical practices (1219–21; IV:xi:8), or when criticizing their having done so, as in withholding the cup from the laity and prohibiting clerical marriage (1178; IV:ix:14). He does not divide up interpretation of specific aspects of Christian teaching into discrete doctrines.

What we refer to as doctrines (e.g., a doctrine of Christ, or the church, or sin) in Calvin's day and long after were sections of the Creed referred to as articles of religion. The proper function of councils is to adjudicate contested articles of religion, as the Councils of Nicaea and Ephesus did (1176–7; IV:ix:13). Calvin engages in sharp refutations of interpretations of contested articles of religion that he believed would lead believers astray, like those of Michael Servetus and Andreas Osiander.[6] The reason for rebuttal is that these heterodox interpretations fail to promote godliness profitably. It is not so much that a teaching is profitable because it is orthodox but that it is orthodox because it is profitable, since God only does for us that which is profitable for us.

Though these distinctions are drawn more tightly than Calvin himself did or would, this brief look at his use of the terms suggests that he probably distinguished among the totality of knowledge of God ("doctrine"), specific but nonessential practices ("doctrines"), and "articles of religion on which all believers ought to agree" (1041; IV:ii:1). "Doctrine" in the broad sense refers to the general force or sum of teaching that guides believers toward God. Presenting it clearly is the task he set himself as an interpreter of the Creed: he structured the *Institutes* into four books, each corresponding to an article of the Creed, with the last article divided in two, following the Creed itself. Calvin, then, was commenting on the Creed, which he took to be the gist of scriptural teaching.

Of course, since God's Word and the Creed are of a piece, even if disclosed incrementally, Calvin discerned a unity among Mosaic, prophetic, and dominical teaching that moderns suspect. While he did puzzle over apparent contradictions in the texts, he did not permit such infelicities to mar the glorious vision of the whole, which he set himself to open to us in a clear and orderly fashion. He treated the articles of the Creed because they state the material content of Christian teaching in summary fashion.

What is missing in Calvin's understanding of his office as a teacher of the church is any hint that theology is either an academic or a constructive undertaking in the modern sense. He was persuaded by what he knew of scholasticism that an academic presentation that sought to be rational and objective would fail to assist sinners be transformed by the grace of God. And he would have abhorred the constructive task as well as the academic task, because both tend to highlight the cleverness of the theologian and suggest that the wisdom of God needs to be retouched or is nonexistent. For Calvin, theology finally cannot be separated from proclamation and exhortation. All five biblical offices of the church tend to a common end.

In sum, Calvin was a teacher of the church. His calling was to let God be known, clearly and with passion—for God is enough. As Calvin himself put it in a preface to the French edition of 1560, "Although Holy Scripture contains a perfect doctrine, to which one can add nothing, since in it our Lord has meant to display the infinite treasures of his wisdom, yet a person who has not much practice in it has good reason for some guidance and direction, to know what he ought to look for in it, in order not to wander hither and thither, but to hold to a sure path, that he may always be pressing toward the end to which the Holy Spirit calls him" (*Institutes* 6). This is the task Calvin set himself in the *Institutes*. Our task is to follow the rhetorical argument of the *Institutes* in order to lay bare Calvin's understanding of how God transforms us to glorify him and enjoy him forever.

Now we will turn to the main work of this chapter: eliciting Calvin's aretology. We will proceed first by identifying the human need as he diagnosed it, then by examining the goals God set for the therapy, and finally by following, or rather narrating, the rhetorical and pedagogical strategies that both God and Calvin use for getting the job done. The final section of the chapter will assess Calvin's achievement.

Diagnosing the Problem

Calvin's view of the human condition is unambiguous. Given who we are and who God is, we ought to glorify, worship, and obey God. But we don't. Why we don't and how God tries to rectify the situation is the Christian story that Calvin explains in the *Institutes*. As a psychologist he is clear-eyed, if somewhat stern, sobered by his own observations of human behavior and shaped by the Augustinian vision of the human plight: estrangement from God, in whose image we were created.[7] Missing in Calvin is the trend we observed from Bernard to Julian that edged Christian theology away from piety based in fear and self-hatred, found in St. Benedict, and toward piety grounded in pure love. Calvin holds tenaciously to the view that God requires that we come face to face with the worst that is in us. We must throw ourselves on God's mercy knowing that we deserve nothing but wrath and condemnation.

Calvin knows that any defects in us reflect poorly on God (183; I:xv:1). Our proper state is "original nobility, which [God] had bestowed upon our father Adam" (244; I:ii:3), and so we "ought to be thought the reflection of God's glory" (189; I:xv:4).

> [T]he likeness of God extends to the whole excellence by which man's nature towers over all the kinds of living creatures. Accordingly, the integrity with which Adam was endowed is expressed by this word, when he had full possession of right understanding, when he had his affections kept within the bounds of reason, all his senses tempered in right order, and he truly referred his excellence to exceptional gifts bestowed upon him by his Maker. (188; I:xv:3)

Original integrity or nobility, however, has long since passed away, even though we do not always grasp this sad truth. Paul teaches, and surely empirical evidence suggests, that we are corrupt and do not reflect God's glory. The Apostle teaches "that none of the soul remains pure or untouched by that mortal disease . . . but [he] especially contends [that] the mind is given over to blindness and the heart to depravity" (253; II:i:9). "Our destruction, therefore, comes from the guilt of our flesh, not from God, inasmuch as we have perished solely because we have degenerated from our original condition" (253; II:i:10). Despite this severe deformity, however, "we grant that God's image was not totally annihilated and destroyed in [man] yet it was so corrupted that whatever remains is frightful deformity" (189; I:xv:4). It is "so corrupted that it needs to be healed and to put on a new nature as well" (253; II:i:9). The basic Platonic dynamic of *exitus-reditus* is in place. We have lost paradise and spend our lives seeking to reclaim it.

The phrase frequently used to describe Calvin's view of fallen humanity is "total depravity." The word "total" can be misleading, however, for it fails to make clear that the *imago Dei* remains the foundation of Calvin's psychology and pedagogy. Total depravity is pedagogically unsound because it could engender hopelessness, which Calvin would want to avoid at all cost. There must remain in us mechanisms through which our restoration can take place.

To appreciate Calvin's teaching, it may help to recall that he believes that the *imago Dei,* while utterly deformed, is still present in us. This enables us to distinguish between our capacity for renewal and our ability to be renewed. Since our renewal is the reclamation of the *imago Dei,* the capacity remains. It is our ability to act on that capacity that is utterly gone. Knowing that the image of God remains in us undermines the hopelessness that would result from grasping the full impact of human inability to love God adequately. Calvin holds that despite all our problems, God never ceased to love us, even though he can only love the faint glimmer of himself that remains in us. That "out of his kindness he still finds something to love" makes God's mercy even more poignant (505; II:xvi:3).

In order to carry his aretegenic interest forward from psychology to soteriology—from how God made us to how God saves us—Calvin emphasizes the subjective side of the work of Christ. Calvin harmonizes scriptural passages that suggest that God began to love us only with the death of Christ (John 3.16, Rom. 5.10) with passages that suggest that God's love is eternal and unchangeable (1 John 4.19; Eph. 1.4–5; Rom. 5.8), citing Augustine as his authority. The reason for harmonizing the passages is deeper than that scripture must be shown to speak with one voice. Calvin quotes Augustine's balanced view that "he loved us even when he hated us. For he hated us for what we were that he had not made; yet because our wickedness had not entirely consumed his handiwork, he knew how, at the same time, to hate in each one of us what we had made, and to love what he had made" (507; II:xvi:4).

The position enables us to see the pedagogical effects of Christ's saving work on the cross. In the following discussion of the work of the cross, Calvin does not say that Christ's expiatory sacrifice soothed God's wrath. Rather, the change that takes place is in us: "Christ was offered to the Father in death as an expiatory sacrifice, that when he discharged all satisfaction through his sacrifice, *we might cease to be afraid of God's wrath*" (emphasis added). While there is no doubt that the transference of guilt from us to Christ constitutes our acquittal, the impact of that acquittal is pastoral: "we must, above all, remember this substitution, lest we tremble and remain anxious throughout life—as if God's righteous vengeance, which the Son of God has taken upon himself, still hung over us" (510; II:xvi:5). The aretegenic goal is to encourage sinners by showing that while they deserve only wrath, God's love prevails. This way they will focus on God's love rather than his wrath and will be encouraged in virtue.

Total depravity is a bit misleading also because Calvin knows that there must be tools by which the therapy God provides may be appropriated. Since sin arises in the mind, regeneration also arises in the mind. Reason is not completely wiped out; though it is in twisted ruins, sparks still gleam. "These show [man] to be a rational being, differing from brute beasts, because he is endowed with understanding. Yet, secondly, they show this light choked with dense ignorance, so that it cannot come forth effectively" (270; I:ii:12).

A general denunciation of human corruption does not suffice. Calvin specifies a psychology that suffices "for the upbuilding of godliness" (193; I:xv:6). The basic bone structure is in place; the muscle, sinews, and skin are missing. Among all the desires and capacities of the self, the most important for theological purposes are understanding and will. The former makes judgments of approval or disapproval. It is "as it were, the leader and governor of the soul" (194; I:xv:7). The latter chooses to follow the things approved by the understanding and awaits its judgments. "God provided man's soul with a mind, by which to distinguish good from evil, right from wrong; and with the light of reason as guide, to distinguish what should be followed from what should be avoided" (195; I:xv:8). Originally, reason, understanding, prudence, and judgment all worked well together to control emotions. And there was freedom to "make the will completely amenable to the guidance of reason" (195; I:xv:8) But the Fall changed all that. Adam fell because "his will was capable of being bent to one side or the other, and was not given the constancy to persevere" (195; I:xv:8). Until beset by a weak will, "man by free will had the power, if he so willed, to attain eternal life" (195; I:xv:8). Why God did not sustain Adam by the virtue of perseverance has not been disclosed to us (196; I:xv:8). The fact is that before the Fall we were in good shape; now we are alienated from God. The goal of the Christian life is to regain control of ourselves with God's help.

The problem created by the Fall is that despite considerable powers of understanding, Adam could not persevere in doing the right thing, and we have been doing the same ever since. Calvin put it this way:

> But man does not choose by reason and pursue with zeal what is truly good
> for himself according to the excellence of his immortal nature; nor does he
> use his reason in deliberation or bend his mind to it. Rather, like an animal
> he follows the inclination of his nature, without reason, without delibera-

tion. . . . [M]uch as man desires to follow what is good, still he does not follow it. There is no man to whom eternal blessedness is not pleasing, yet no man aspires to it except by the impulsion of the Holy Spirit. (286–7; II:ii:26)

Sin arises when reason loses its grip on the emotions. After the Fall, strength to persevere in goodness is lost. "Let this then be agreed: that men are as they are here described not merely by the defect of custom, but also by the depravity of nature" (291; II:iii:2).

Calvin's diagnosis is that we are sick: on one hand we are arrogant and ambitious, on the other we are dull and listless (368; II:viii:1). He usually speaks of the effects of sin in terms that we moderns would recognize as a character disorder, a sociopathy that makes us inevitably lean away from integrity of character and toward weakness of character: ambition, pride and, worst of all, ingratitude to God (245; II:i:4). Although he does not quote it, he frequently alludes to Ps. 32.9, which captures his dour assessment of human corruption: "Do not be like a horse or a mule, without understanding, whose temper must be curbed with bit and bridle, else it will not stay near you." Calvin often uses the word "bridle" as both noun and verb to express his view that we are like horses needing to be broken (and perhaps to describe the rhetorical challenge that lay before him).[8] Breaking us in is the beginning of the cure, the first step in regeneration. Our pride and passions need to be reined in so that we can come to our senses.[9] Less frequently, but still noticeably, he uses words like "goad," "incite," or "prick" to depict our mulelike need for arousal from dullness, stupidity and sloth.[10]

That we owe everything to God and ought to cleave to him, honor him, "break forth into praises of him" (55; I:v:4), be "kindled to heed the law" and "captivated to embrace the Lawgiver" (381; II:viii:15), and "yield him willing service" (41; I:ii:1) is self-evident to Calvin. Equally evident, to his chagrin, is that without help we simply don't do this at all. Once we "hold God's Word in contempt" and "shake off all reverence for him," we are overcome by "ambition and pride, together with ungratefulness" (245; II:i:4), and "are actually puffed up and swollen with all the more pride" (55; I:v:4). In our own failure to focus on God, we have lost our way, become terribly confused and, as Athanasius had long since pointed out, shaped idols for ourselves that better conform to our limited vision. As Calvin put it, "Daily experience teaches that flesh is always uneasy until it has obtained some figment like itself in which it may fondly find solace as in an image of God" (108; I:xi:8). Here already is adumbrated where the true therapy will be found: the true image of God—Christ.

Calvin operates in a very narrow space. He wants to protect both the goodness and the power of God. At the same time, the reader must understand her dependence on God for doing anything good yet still strive for godliness. In short, he needs a rationale for the church's moral authority. He does this rather fitfully throughout the Institutes, however, here stressing the importance of striving for perfection, there denouncing any thought that we can do anything at all in this regard.[11] This is the great inconsistency that Dowey, Leith, and others have pondered in Calvin.

Without digressing too far afield, I will just note how Calvin solves this problem in II:iii of the *Institutes*. While Calvin has been noted for dividing the world into elect and reprobate, his position is really more subtle. Calvin discerns four classes of people: the regenerate elect who are cured by supernatural regeneration and so do not really have to work hard at godly living; those who are restrained by shame and fear of the law, even though they still sin; those who at least aspire to observe the law and be good, even though they have even less ability than do those in the second category; and, finally, leaders who by virtue of their own example seek to keep the rest obedient (292–3; II:iii:3). And later, in the treatise on faith, Calvin admits that the difference between the elect and the reprobate is the firmness with which they trust God's love for themselves and can act on their experience of God's goodness. The reprobate are confused about their adoption as children of God, because they experience God's mercy only fitfully or fleetingly (555–6; III:ii:11).

The bottom line seems to be that the elect simply have an easier time of living righteously because they trust and fear God more. But the distinction doesn't really matter to Calvin. He preaches equally to the elect and reprobate, for the former always need encouragement and the latter must be exhorted to do their best. For righteousness is dependent on trusting God, and trusting God is only possible for those who know the goodness, righteousness, justice, and mercy of God. In at least two places, Calvin himself lets us know that the distinction between elect and reprobate is really irrelevant to his aretegenic undertaking by saying that everyone should fear God and live righteously even if there were no hell (43, I:ii:2; 572, III:ii:26).

This space for exhortation is the grounds on which Calvin brings Melanchthon's third use of the Law into play and of course is also the space into which he insinuates his own responsibilities as a minister of the gospel. He spells out the rationale for exhortation more clearly when rebutting the objections to his teaching on the bondage of the will (316–40; II:v).

The crux of the argument—that we are both fully dependent on God's grace to do any good at all and fully responsible for our own sins—comes with Calvin's distinction between necessity and compulsion (294–6; II:iii:5). Here Calvin, following Bernard of Clairvaux, argues that despite sin, we still will the things we do. What has happened is that when we will ill it is understood as the result of our corrupt nature. When we will well, it is a gift of grace. If we look at God as the model for doing this (since it is of God's nature to be good), when we speak of God's goodness, we impute it not to compulsion but to his free and boundless goodness. Similarly, the Fall was not compelled; disobedience came from "the eager inclination of [Adam's] heart, not by forced compulsion; by the prompting of his own lust, not by compulsion from without" (296). That is, the soul is both enslaved and free. It is enslaved because its nature has turned to evil instead of good. Yet in performing acts, the self is still willing the things that it chooses, and so in another sense it is free, or at least not compelled from without. Perhaps Calvin put it better in the discussion on perseverance. We can see the good we should do, but lack the willpower. We are weak-willed, though willing all the time. Romans 7 lurks in the background here. If God is to be held responsible, which Calvin would never concede, it can at best be only indirectly—for the evil will that we have had since the Fall is wholly our own.

THE WAY BACK

Calvin, like Athanasius and Augustine before him, attributes the lack of moral integrity he sees around him to confused knowledge of self and God. Since we have gotten off the track, we must be reformed. Reformation is called "conversion" or "regeneration" or is described simply as "lift[ing] up the minds of the people . . . [to] arouse them to ponder the happiness of the spiritual life to come" (447; II:x:20). Regeneration gradually clears a confused mind. It is the only solid foundation for a comprehensive program of character-strengthening and reform accomplished through deep self-reflection in light of who God is and what he has done and continues to do for us. This therapeutic process is built up gradually from several sources.

Understanding God is first gleaned from observing his creatures. From them we infer that God is kind, good, merciful, just, and true. This can be stated as knowing either who God is or what God does. But Calvin does not distinguish divine attributes from a doctrine of providence or the economy of salvation. The point is not to specify ideas but to encourage "gratitude of mind for the favorable outcome of things, patience in adversity, and also incredible freedom from worry about the future" (219; I:xvii:7). "This same knowledge will drive us to put off rashness and overconfidence, and will impel us continually to call upon God. Then also he will buttress our minds with good hope, that, with confidence and courage, we may not hesitate to despise those dangers which surround us" (222; I:xvii:9). Scripture reinforces these conclusions. Together they "invite us first to fear God, then to trust him. By this can we learn to worship him both with perfect innocence of life and with unfeigned obedience, then to depend wholly upon his goodness" (98; I:xi:2).

Scripture, of course, is the most direct means for knowing God. But Calvin does not recommend what we might call its "raw" application. Scripture's utility must be solicited. For example, in Calvin's hands the Decalogue ceases to be a list of do's and don'ts and becomes an extensive aretegenic treatise whose purpose is "the fulfillment of righteousness to form human life to the archetype of divine purity" (415; II:viii:51). This perfection of holiness comes under two headings: love of God and love of neighbor. It is not merely the "rudiments and preliminaries of righteousness by which men begin their apprenticeship" but aims at perfect piety, "to join man by holiness of life to his God, and, as Moses elsewhere says, to make him cleave to God" (415; II:viii:51).

Scripture's pointing to our lack of moral integrity has a pedagogical purpose: "that we should not rely on any opinion of our own strength, however small it is, if we want God to be favorable toward us" (268; II:ii:10), for as Chrysostom taught, "the foundation of our philosophy is humility" (268; II:ii:11). The modern rule of real estate—that it takes three things to sell a house: location, location, and location—is adapted from the adage in rhetoric that the chief rule of eloquence is delivery, delivery, and delivery. Calvin adapts the rule to his own end: the first, second, and third precepts of the Christian religion are humility, humility, and humility (268–70; II:ii:11).

Christian experience and scripture are like a multifaceted mirrored ball. Each tiny mirror radiates a fresh insight, and all sparkle together to lead us back to God by distancing us from our deformed self and constructing a refreshed and refurbished self once the corrupt self has been left behind. While the path may be clear, the journey is painfully incremental, made up of two steps forward, one step back, and sometimes one step forward, two steps back. Like Augustine, Calvin believed that the problem of sin lay in a disordered and confused mind.[12] While in the *Confessions* Augustine speaks of healing the eyes of the mind, Calvin speaks of knowing God, and of aids to knowing God—the "spectacles" that are scripture. And like Augustine, Calvin believed that this knowledge was learned by looking both inward and outward and by taking advantage of the extra-biblical aids that God provides, two of which are angels and devils. Angels, if we understand their job, "lead us by the hand straight to him, that we may look upon him, call upon him, and proclaim him as our sole helper" (172; I:xiv:12). And scripture's depiction of devils aids formation in godliness by calling forth courage and perseverance to prevail against "their stratagems and contrivances," building our character like a well-disciplined soldier or athlete (172–3; I:xiv:13).

Calvin spurns purveying knowledge about God, an approach he associated with the scholastic philosophies, which lack edificatory effect. "[W]e are called to a knowledge of God: not that knowledge which, content with empty speculation, merely flits in the brain, but that which will be sound and fruitful if we duly perceive it, and if it takes root in the heart" (61–2; I:v:9). Knowing *about* God is not the point; knowing God is. Calvin repeatedly distances himself from seeking knowledge of God's self. Although he discusses divine attributes, he never lists abstract attributes of divine simplicity, perfection, and immutability for their own sake, as that which is to be assented to or recognized as constituting saving or correct information because it is authorized by the church or even by scripture. What is wanted is knowledge of God "as he is toward us: so that this recognition consists more in living experience than in vain and high-flown speculation" (97, I:xi:2; 549, III:ii:6). Calvin does, of course, want to inform us about God, but the believer has to work to gain the knowledge. Calvin followed Augustine's teaching that only when the believer infers God's sterling qualities from his works, so that she becomes vulnerable to God, will her knowledge be activated by love and trust. Love and trust cannot be commanded by an ecclesiastical authority; they can only develop organically from the believer's experience and growth in understanding.

Calvin was fighting on several fronts simultaneously. He reacted against speculation in theology because it did not engage the whole person but seemingly only appealed to the intellect. For the same reason, he objected to religion as a set of ritual observances that can be acceptably performed without touching the heart. And he refuted other reformist positions that failed to uphold the evangelical faith. The reformers, like many before them, sought to internalize religion (537; III:i:1). This is the existential dimension of Calvin's program that Dowey and Leith recognized. For Calvin, religion is more than a set of rules or practices, although these remain central. The deeper issue is who you are, who God calls and enables you to be(come); religion is a matter of character. Calvin is interested in the kind of people we are, or rather ought to be, and he says so forthrightly:

> Now what is to be learned from the law can be readily understood: that God, as he is our Creator, has toward us by right the place of Father and Lord; for this reason we owe to him glory, reverence, love, and fear; verily, that we have no right to follow the mind's caprice wherever it impels us, but, dependent upon his will, ought to stand firm in that alone which is pleasing to him; then, that righteousness and uprightness are pleasing to him, but he abominates wickedness; and that, for this reason, unless we would turn away from our Creator in impious ingratitude, we must cherish righteousness all our life. For if only when we prefer his will to our own do we render to him the reverence that is his due, it follows that the only lawful worship of him is the observance of righteousness, holiness, and purity. (369; II:viii:2)

True piety requires that we "lift up our minds higher than our eyes can reach" (163; I:xiv:3)—up above the earth, above the elements of this world—while at the same time going into ourselves, so that the work and Word of God affect us truly. Calvin's aretegenic program undergirds his objection to the medieval understanding of faith, which had higher standards for clergy than for laity. Luther and Calvin insisted on the higher standard for all, in essence democratizing the church through a single norm of faith for lay and clergy alike.

Calvin's great treatise on faith in Book III of the *Institutes* exemplifies this single standard by repudiating various points of medieval teaching, summarized in Aquinas's treatise on faith in the *Summa Theologiæ*. Whereas Aquinas recognized cognitive assent as a central feature of faith (*ST,* vol. 31, 61–5; II:II:q2:1), Calvin focused faith around "certain knowledge of God's benevolence toward us, founded upon the truth of the freely given promise in Christ, both revealed to our minds and sealed upon our hearts through the Holy Spirit" (*Institutes* 551; III:ii:7). The knowledge of which Calvin speaks should not be confused with seventeenth-century empiricism; it is emotionally charged, not scientifically objective.

Saint Thomas held that both educated and uneducated were required to understand the Incarnation, passion, and resurrection of Christ, as well as the mystery of the Trinity (*ST,* vol. 31, 87–97; II:II:q2:articles 7, 8). But he prefaced these articles with a disclaimer that vitiated them: "just as the higher angels who illumine the lesser have a fuller knowledge of the divine . . . so too those of higher rank, whose office it is to instruct others, must have a fuller awareness of the contents of faith and a more explicit belief" (*ST*, vol. 31, 85; I:II:q2:6). Calvin, by contrast, repudiated the distinction between implicit and explicit faith entirely,[13] citing Paul, who "requires explicit recognition of the divine goodness upon which our righteousness rests" (*Institutes* 545; III:ii:2). Again, the point is not assent but internalized understanding of divine goodness. And finally, Thomas accepts unformed faith—that is, faith held as a duty, distinct from heartfelt faith, which is grounded in reverence for God—as an adequate expression of faith (*ST*, vol. 31, 127–31; II:II:q4:art4). Calvin, on the other hand, rejects any hint that faith out of duty suffices, for faith without love and devotion is no faith at all: it has no roots (*Institutes* 551–5; III:ii:8–10).

The theologian's task, therefore, is not separable from catechesis and requires tremendous rhetorical skill. Her goal is to turn what could be dry propositions about God—for example, that he is just, powerful, and good—into inviting understandings of God gleaned from experience, scripture, and the Creed.

> We should not merely run over them cursorily, and, so to speak, with a fleeting glance, but we should ponder them at length, turn them over in our minds seriously and faithfully, and recollect them repeatedly. . . . [Readers are] not to pass over in ungrateful thoughtlessness of forgetfulness those conspicuous powers which God shows forth in his creatures, [but] learn so to apply it to themselves that their very hearts are touched. (180–1; I:xiv:21)

THE DIVINE PEDAGOGY

As hinted in the previous section, the divine plan works slowly and indirectly. God discloses what Calvin calls the "covenant of his mercy" incrementally, beginning with Adam and culminating with Christ (446; II:x:20). The plan also works indirectly—that is, inferentially. Of course, God could have undertaken human restoration by an act of will. But he chose to do it by a gentle program of education that does not simply cut to the chase but instead wakes us up, so that we actually change as God chips away at our self-concept. The whole program of character-reform happens through reflective discernment.[14] Moral and spiritual maturity develop in response to experiences that deepen one's understanding of God, "his fatherly favor in our behalf," and teach us "how to frame our life according to the rule of his law" (277; II:ii:18).

Calvin recognized that we have a short attention span along with great powers of denial and forgetting: "such is our stupidity that we grow increasingly dull toward so manifest testimonies, and they flow away without profiting us" (63; I:v:11). And even though he posited a "seed of religion in all men[,] . . . yet all degenerate from the true knowledge of [God]" (47; I:iv:1). We have moments of clarity, but we lose these insights, and old patterns of thought and rationalizations for bad behavior return (64; I:v:11). "And so it happens that no real piety remains in the world" (47; I:iv:1). Calvin's exasperation with human defensiveness and belligerence seeps into his writing. He is frustrated that getting us to attend to God is so difficult. Yet getting angry at us is to no avail. The problem is not that we are stubborn but that we are deformed.

God bombards us with evidence of himself at every turn so that we should continually trip over these learning aids and be stopped in our tracks. Book I highlights, in serial order, the physical world, the human body, and the social structure of public order and governance, all prior to scripture, as sources that ought to suffice to teach us of God and turn our minds from ungodliness. These manifestations of divine goodness are initially helpful in awakening awe and reverence for God. But eventually they become familiar, we take them for granted, and their salutary impact wanes (46, I:iii:3; 161, I:xiv:2). And so God republished the history of creation, with its unfolding aesthetic, in Genesis.[15]

Since creation itself failed to set our minds on God, he issued the Law, sent prophets, and eventually became incarnate himself.[16] Although Calvin cannot keep his irritation with us to himself, it is evident that he believes that God tirelessly finds ever-fresh ways of getting our attention. Calvin's vision of the divine pedagogy follows the pattern established by Ps. 78, which likewise is designed to embarrass the reader into gratitude for all that God has done for Israel, although it perseveres in sin and idolatry.

The pedagogy of self-knowledge is similarly balanced: first we should understand the purpose for and gifts with which we were created, and then we should understand our own limitations (244, II:i:3; cf. 242, II:i:1). Calvin sees these learnings as mutually reinforcing, since they intersect at numerous points. The self-knowledge inferred from the Genesis story, for example, has several aretegenic purposes. Disclosure of our original nobility at creation provides us with an image of the ideal self to be regained.[17] The new godly self is, therefore, really our original self, and growth in holiness is really a return to self rather than the imposition of an alien self. Genesis 1 also teaches us of the goodness of God and of our constant dependence on him. Then Genesis 3 abruptly challenges us by pointing out our current miserable condition, "the awareness of which, when all our boasting and self-assurance are laid low, should truly humble us and overwhelm us with shame" (242; II:i:1). This passage illustrates one of Calvin's favorite rhetorical devices: contrast. From showing us what we ought to be alongside who we are "arise[s] abhorrence and displeasure with ourselves, as well as true humility—[from which] is kindled a new zeal to seek God, in whom each of us may recover those good things which we have utterly completely lost" (242; II:i:1).

Contrast provides a rule or straightedge (38; I:i:2) by which we can measure ourselves. Finding ourselves wanting, we have a standard to which we can conform (12; I:xiii:3). Contrast promotes self-displeasure, the first step in self-knowledge. It is the opening move of the *Institutes* and recurs throughout. The first paragraph argues that knowing God benefits us by compelling us to look upward. Seeing God, we realize that we lack wisdom, virtue, goodness, and righteousness, which rest in God alone. At this we become fearful and humble. This unhappiness is true self-knowledge, which "not only arouses us to seek God, but also, as it were, leads us by the hand to find him"(37; I:i:1). Calvin states his guiding principle of self-knowledge clearly: "we cannot seriously aspire to him before we begin to become displeased with ourselves" (37; I:i:1).[18] He sees it as a simple choice: God or ourselves.

Proper self-knowledge produces self-displeasure, the first step toward deconstruction of the self in preparation for the reconstruction of a new self. This basic dynamic of deconstruction and reconstruction re-enacts on a psychological plane the *exitus-reditus* pattern that the Christian story itself follows. Leaving the present self and returning to one's original self is the theo-therapy that God undertakes and Calvin abets through the *Institutes.*

We can only be broken of our pride by becoming alienated from ourselves, or realizing that "what in us seems perfection itself corresponds ill to the purity of God" (38; I:i:2). It is important that the deconstruction-reconstruction pattern not be thought of as sequential, however. The two movements occur simultaneously. General improvement is slow, since accumulated assaults on the self and practice in new ways of thinking and acting are needed to build up a new self.

We can only become self-reflective in this way and let go of ourselves, so to speak, when an alternative model or ideal is accessible. That is why we cannot possibly reform on our own. It is not only that we lack the perseverance, then, that we need the assistance of divine grace. We also need God to provide us with another way that we can see, taste, and touch in order slowly to make it our own. This other way, of course, is God himself.

The dynamic of self-displeasure, stimulated by contrast with an external standard, is also an exercise in unlearning. Calvin understood that the journey of Christian piety had to be gradual because there was much to unload. An especially difficult unlearning, for example, is the shedding of reliance on self, the major impediment to proper worship of God and therefore to righteousness. Those who are confident of their own righteousness will not seek conformation to God but will rely on themselves (357; II:vii:8).[19]

Calvin uses several rhetorical ploys for deconstructing the confused self, strategies designed to penetrate our dullness with the fact that something is amiss with us. In order to elicit shame and guilt he embarrasses the reader, pointing out our failure to praise and worship God. Sometimes he says the law condemns us outright, because it is the instrument of holiness. He writes so as to arouse the sort of fear, even terror, in the reader's heart that will act as a wake-up call.

Although he has no hesitation about pointing out how miserable we are, Calvin is also aware that too much chastisement can be harmful (356; II:vii:8). He strives to elicit just enough self-loathing to stimulate constructive change, recognizing that if he goes too far the sensitive soul may plunge into despair, and give up. He admonishes moderation to those who would follow his example (1964, 5, 29). Many, including his most famous pupil, Karl Barth, would argue that in this regard Calvin did not practice what he preached, as was noted in chapter 1. Calvin did not think of us as tender flowers, easily crushed by being walked on, perhaps as Julian did, but as stubborn weeds, inured to weed-killer. We resolutely defy God's teaching, eagerly jump to our own defense, and only slowly let go of any of these self-destructive stances.

In this aretegenic context, Calvin's antispeculative polemic takes on sharper focus. He is interested only in that knowledge of God and of ourselves which edifies, benefits, and profits us. By this he means that which has the potential to make us rethink ourselves. We should seek only what it is to our advantage to know and leave the rest to God (39–41; I:ii:1). For this reason revelation is more important than philosophy, which gets caught up in idle curiosity. Philosophers "are like a traveler passing through a field at night who in a momentary lightning flash sees far and wide, but the sight vanishes so swiftly that he is plunged again into the darkness of the night before he can take even a step—let alone be directed on his way by its help" (277; II:ii:18). Even if philosophy can provide correct information about God, it may be useless to the Christian seeking a godly life.

Although Calvin is well-known for his jaundiced view of human nature, his psychological insight into the reconstruction of a righteous self is just as acute. Whereas Luther focused almost exclusively on assurance for terrified consciences—and Calvin surely follows him in this—Calvin is also attuned to other emotional responses and reactions that upbuild the self in a more constructive manner. That is, Luther understood the gospel as an instrument of guilt-reduction that overcomes the terror wrought by the Law. Word and sacrament eliminate a destructively negative impediment to human well-being by substituting trust in God's mercy for fear of God's wrath. To put it in its most conventional terms, Luther focused on justification because the self had to be released from the structures of terror that popular church practices and teachings had constructed.

Calvin, the great theologian of sanctification, had a broader view. He is not concerned only about ridding us of fears of hell; indeed, he is not sure that that is an entirely salutary move. He wants to provide us with tools for relating expansively to the world in which we live. Although the treatise on faith that opens book III of the *Institutes* revolves around the question of whether one believes oneself to be loved by God, the overall plan of reform of the self formulates a three-part dynamic for reconstructing the self, a dynamic that is the core of Reformed piety. Regeneration is properly built on reverence, obedience, and gratitude.[20]

Reverence is built up both from awe and wonder at the beauty and orderliness of creation, and the considerable abilities of God's creatures, and from "'the fear of the Lord' . . . which in some places is called 'the beginning of wisdom'" (Ps. 111.10; Prov. 1.7 qtd. on 572; III:ii:26). The seed of religion, to which Calvin clings as the tender sapling that grows into a mighty tree by God's careful teaching, is not only innate conscience, the ability to distinguish right from wrong instinctively. It is also a natural ability to grasp the majesty of God (43; I:iii:1), to be "rapt in wonder" at the care God took with creation (160; I:xiv:1; 179–80, I:xiv:20). This natural sense of awe and reverence is not only for God but for art and science too, as well as for civil authority (42–3; I:ii:2). This is not a fear that strikes terror in the heart but a healthy respect that engenders trust in God and those in positions of responsibility, both within and without the church. Calvin explained the proper fear of God as "reverence compounded of honor and fear," which combines the honor due a father with the service due a lord, thus honoring both the filial and servile understandings of fear that trace back to Paul (572; III:ii:26), noted in chapter 8.

Reverential trust engenders proper obedience. This is not blind obedience to authority, although in his own area of jurisdiction Calvin proved himself to be somewhat rigid. Rather, we obey God because we trust and believe that he has our best interests at heart, being persuaded, as the pious are, that unaided we are unable to act in our own best interest. The pious mind understands the Law in this way, as help from a trustworthy source. This is the famous "third use of the law" (360–1; II:vii:12). Obedience is for Calvin, as it was for Anselm, an internalized understanding of and desire for righteousness accomplished by God in us. "God begins his good work in us, therefore, by arousing love and desire and zeal for righteousness in our hearts; or, to speak more correctly, by bending, forming, and directing our hearts to righteousness. He completes his work, moreover, by confirming us to perseverance" (297; II:iii:6).

Finally, underlying reverence, obedience, and humility is gratitude. If self-serving pride is the root of sin, then gratitude is the root of piety. Heartfelt reverence, obedience, and humility can only stem from genuine gratitude. Without gratitude, other virtues float free. It might not be an overstatement to suggest that Calvin's whole *oeuvre* aims at the cultivation of humble gratitude. Though he spoke much of self-denial and cross-bearing, and objected strongly to human clumsiness and confusion, he believed all would be well if only genuine humble gratitude dominated our thoughts and actions. And who but God is worthy of such gratitude?

Assessment

It is perhaps fitting that Calvin is the concluding figure in this series of studies, not only because the aretegenic motif is more difficult to discern—perhaps nearly collapses—once the Enlightenment gets going but also because Calvin is perhaps the staunchest of all the theologians we have examined. His aretegenic agendum is implied in almost every sentence he wrote. Perhaps he was disturbed—as was Luther—by the violence unleashed by the first wave of the Reformation and sought to do more than simply restate the authority of God's law by unpacking the psychology that made it necessary and effective. On the other hand, his stern temperament, and perhaps even his many illnesses, may have reinforced the strict standards of behavior he demanded of Genevans.

In any case, what becomes clear in reading Calvin is that he was a psychologically sophisticated pedagogue who exegeted Christian Creed and scripture and thought his way through the interstices of the human mind and heart for the sake of moral integrity. We live at a time that is skeptical of using guilt, shame, fear, and embarrassment as instruments of moral improvement. This makes it difficult for us to appreciate Calvin's aretology. For today's popular psychology is more likely to stress the psychological damage done by guilt, shame, and fear than to enlist them as means of achieving human excellence. Perhaps this is in response to some of the effects of Calvinism itself.

Calvin's aretology is, of course, based on a religious view of reality in which God is awesome and powerful and human beings stubborn yet vulnerable. They want to please God by being good and doing good. Calvin assumes that moral failure is, or at least can be, made to be bothersome, so that moral self-awareness stimulates reform. Even though all credit for transformation goes to the Holy Spirit, Calvin believes that Christians retain enough shreds of reason to be educable.

Although at times the result appears a bit unbalanced to modern ears, Calvin tries to offset fear with hope, despair with encouragement. The Christian life is, as John Bunyan later described in it *Pilgrim's Progress,* a series of episodes of falling down and being lifted up, or of getting off the track and getting back on track. The key to understanding the race to be won lies in the ability to learn from experience. What is to be learned is that God's displeasure does not cancel out his love and that trust in his mercy is the only sure-footed foundation from which to allow him to transform us into righteousness. On our own we have no clear image of what virtue is: goodness, wisdom, and justice are just words until God's works give us graphic testimony of the selves we want to become. Worship of God, then, is important not because God needs it, but because we need it—because it keeps God's Word and work ever before our eyes, which tend to wander far and wide.

A secular age, like our own, that is no longer sure that we need help, or, even if we did, what help would look like, will have difficulty with Calvin. It will have difficulty with the self-displeasure that is so central to Calvin's project, and it will have difficulty with the dependence on God that it assumes. Yet in another sense Calvin is deeply in touch with, or perhaps presaged, the modern sensibility precisely because his whole program is so interiorized, so privatized. The Christian life is lived between the individual and God. The church supplies trained teachers and pastors, but the work of reform happens between the Holy Spirit and the believer's heart. Calvin has taken Augustine's insistence on moral transformation through knowing God but left behind the nobility and dignity that come from being taken out of the self by participating in the being of God. The knowledge that Christ's death has made one a member of the household of God becomes in Calvin, and perhaps throughout the West, a means of stilling guilt and anxiety. In the process, God's respect for us and our sharing in the dignity of the divine life have been lost. Calvin's stress on being either elect or reprobate, a winner or a loser, rechanneled the fear and anxiety of medieval piety but did little to soothe it. In this he perhaps paved the way for modern psychotherapies devoted to self-esteem, assertiveness, and other forms of self-construction.

Notes

1. Two structural features of the *Institutes* support his determination to focus on righteousness. One is the heavy stress on the law. Christ is not really introduced until well over four hundred pages into the text, and two hundred pages into book II on "Knowledge of God the Redeemer." Also noteworthy in this regard is Calvin's putting the chapter on regeneration before the chapter on justification, reversing the traditional order.

2. From the *Westminster Shorter Catechism,* as quoted by Leith (1989, 40).

3. The McNeill/Battles edition of the *Institutes* assumes the correctness of Dowey's position on this point, which was also held by Warfield and Doumergue, two early and eminent Calvin scholars (Calvin 1960, 74).

4. *Summa Theologiæ,* Prima Pars, Q.1 (Thomas 1965, vol. I).

5. Calvin explicitly rejects "a common assent to the gospel history" in favor of the spiritually productive knowledge of God gained by embracing God's mercy in Christ (543; III:ii:1).

6. Calvin opposes Servetus's christology, which rejected the idea of Christ's preexistence, because it puts Christ's Incarnation on a par with the creation of other creatures. If Christ were preordained to become the image of God, and was compounded out of elements other than the eternal divine substance, Calvin believed Servetus "extinguished the hope of salvation. For if flesh were divinity itself, it would cease to be the temple of divinity" (493; II:xiv:8). In other words, there would be no need for the self to be conformed to the divine standard. Calvin argues against Osiander for conflating justification and regeneration because such an approach obscures God's grace, and displaying divine grace is essential to knowing God, which is the basis of transformation (732; III:xi:6). Now, in both of these examples the pastoral grounding for the criticism remains rather obscure. And Calvin may have done himself and posterity a disservice by appearing to lapse into an authoritarian imposition of the tradition for the sake of control and power. But the pastoral intention, muted as it is in these polemics, cannot be denied. For example, Calvin never states that Servetus and Osiander are to be rejected simply because their teachings are not orthodox.

7. "[T]he mind of man has been so completely estranged from God's righteousness that it conceives, desires, and undertakes, only that which is impious, perverted, foul, impure, and infamous. The heart is so steeped in the poison of sin, that it can breathe out nothing but a loathsome stench. But if some men occasionally make a show of good, their minds nevertheless ever remain enveloped in hypocrisy and deceitful craft, and their hearts bound by inner perversity" (340; II:v:19).

8. 50, I:iv:4; 102, I:xi:3; 117, I:xii:1; 176, I:xiv:17; 184, I:xv:1; 209, I:xvi:9; 220, I:xvii:8; 224, I:xvii:11; 246, II:i:4; 292–3, II:iii:3; 358, II:vii:10; 359–60, II:vii:11; 421, II:viii:57.

9. "God's Word . . . was the best bridle to control all passions: the thought that nothing is better than to practice righteousness by obeying God's commandments; then, that the ultimate goal of the happy life is to be loved by him" (246; II:i:4).

10. "The law is . . . like a whip to an idle and balky ass, to arouse it to work" (361; I:vii:12. Cf. 221, I:xvii:8; 309, II:iv:1; 328, II:v:10).

11. On one hand he writes, "God lays down for us through the law what we should do; if we then fail in any part of it, that dreadful sentence of eternal death which it pronounces will rest upon us. . . . But [it is] above our strength . . . to fulfill the law to the letter. . . . [T]here is but one means of liberation . . . Christ the Redeemer . . . if, indeed, with firm faith we embrace this mercy and rest in it with steadfast hope" (542–3, III:ii:1). And on the other hand, "Though all of us are by nature suffering from the same disease, only those whom it pleases the Lord to touch with his healing hand will get well. The others, whom he, in his righteous judgment, passes over, waste away in their own rottenness until they are consumed. There is no other reason why some persevere to the end, while others fall away at the beginning of the course. For perseverance itself is indeed also a gift of God, which he does not bestow on all indiscriminately, but imparts to whom he pleases" (320; II:v:3).

12. The word "mind" may be a bit misleading, because the rationalist tradition within modern thought has divided "mind" from "heart," cognition from affect. This dualistic psychology is unknown to classical Christian theology, where the self, while often referred to as *mens*, includes both cognition and affect. This is the holistic sense in which Calvin understood the work of regeneration to take place in the mind or self. This nuance is central for appreciating the rhetorical strategies Calvin employs, for they perhaps appeal more to the emotions than to some construct of pure cognition.

13. "Is this what believing means—to understand nothing, provided only that you submit your feelings obediently to the church? Faith rests not on ignorance, but on knowledge. . . . We do not obtain salvation either because we are prepared to embrace as true whatever the church has prescribed, or because we turn over to it the task of inquiring and knowing. But we do so when we know that God is our merciful Father, because of reconciliation effected through Christ" (545; III:ii:2).

14. "For even if God wills to manifest his fatherly favor to us in many ways, yet we cannot by contemplating the universe infer that he is Father. Rather, conscience presses us within and shows in our sin just cause for his disowning us and not regarding or recognizing us as his sons. Dullness and ingratitude follow, for our minds, as they have been blinded, do not perceive what is true. And as all our senses have become perverted, we wickedly defraud God of his glory" (341; II:vi:1).

15. The divine pegagogy is adeptly consolidated in the opening paragraph of the Westminster Confession of 1646: "Although the light of nature, and the works of creation and providence, do so far manifest the goodness, wisdom, and power of God, as to leave men inexcusable; yet they are not sufficient to give that knowledge of God, and of his will, which is necessary unto salvation; therefore it pleased the Lord, at sundry times, and in divers manners, to reveal himself, and to declare his will to the Church . . . to commit the same wholly unto writing" (Leith 1982, 193).

16. It is telling that Calvin's discussion of the law and the relationship between law and gospel and the two testaments all come in book II, under the heading of knowledge of God the redeemer. This is because for Calvin, Christ does not offer a qualitative break with the previously disclosed knowledge of God but simply confirms the former in a clearer and more decisive way. That is, knowledge of God through the law is knowledge of God the redeemer, the one who brings us to righteousness.

17. In this Calvin follows Aquinas and Augustine.

18. Contrast is also the means of seeing through counterfeit acts of righteousness (355; II:vii:6; cf. 367, 370; II:viii:1, 3).

19. In our own day, when self-esteem is touted as the way to happiness, Calvin's insistence on forsaking confidence in one's own virtue sounds a rudely discordant note (267–8; II:ii:9, 10). Indeed, Calvin is something of an embarrassment in our day. But how helpful is it really to fill youngsters with the myth of their own invulnerability?

20. This structure is spelled out in Calvin's explanation of the fifth commandment, to honor parents (401–2; II:viii:35). But its presence is evident on virtually every page of the *Institutes*.

PART VI

Conclusion

10

Sapiential Theology

The Salutarity of Christian Doctrine

Now that we have before us expositions of various Christian doctrines stretching over a period of sixteen hundred years, we are in a position to construct a brief narrative about the pastoral function of doctrine as it emerges from this study: doctrine as an aid in cultivating a skilled and excellent life. To do so, I will gather up the testimony from our nine expositors by questioning them about the nature and task of doctrine as they developed and refined it.

One might object that such a procedure is anachronistic, because not all of our classical writers conceptualized doctrines. But even those working within a preconceptual framework had operative doctrines as well as an implicit understanding of the function of doctrine. Eliciting the development of the function of doctrine, as well as the operative doctrines implied in the texts, may help us expand our own notion of doctrine—heavily influenced as it is by Protestant scholasticism and the Enlightenment heritage. Our goal will be to construct a narrative of the functions of doctrine into which our latter-day notion of doctrine fits. Thus, the questions use second-order terms, with which modern theology is more comfortable, in an attempt to enable us to converse with our theological forebears across the great epistemic divide posed by modernity.

Our theologians did not construct theories about the work in which they were engaged. They simply did what they thought needed to be done. But we are watching what they did, analyzing the process and principles they followed, even when these remained unarticulated. In this we have followed William Christian's distinction between primary and secondary doctrines. Primary doctrines are first-order assertions that teach about God and propose right courses of action, virtues, and a way of life in which members are to be nurtured by the community. Secondary doctrines are the rules and principles that maintain a community's authentic identity, assure the consistency of its teachings, and relate its authentic self-understanding to competing claims. We have been examining expositions of primary doctrines. Now it is time to extract from them the regulative or secondary function of doctrine. The questions posed are:

1. What understanding of theology is at work here? Who is its audience?
2. What is the function of doctrine?

3. What are the operative doctrines being articulated?

4. How does the author frame the issue he or she is working on?

I will put the questions to each group of writers by historical period and then elicit a narrative to get a better grasp of the principles they followed in the housekeeping of the theological life of the church.

New Testament Foundations

Let us begin with the New Testament writers. With what understanding of theology are Paul and the author of Ephesians working? Theology for them was the art of making sense of what God had done in Israel through Jesus Christ for the sake of Jews and Greeks. Pauline theology offered an account of who Jews and Greeks are, especially in light of Christ's death. Those interpreting the events that had taken place in Israel aimed to invite people into a new way of life that the writers believed was better than any other because it was a new path made straight by God.

The theological task is trifold. First, it must explain why the old ways of understanding God's promises, obedience to God, God's mercy, scripture, the Jewish people, and expiation for sin were no longer operative. Then it had to explain what the new understandings were. Third, it had to point out the implications of the new circumstance for an obedient life, since believers were often unable to make these connections themselves.

Paul exegetes several operative doctrines by drawing a picture of God's universal grace and authority that eclipsed all those that had preceded his own. And he is forced to upset the Israelology that failed to take seriously God's gracious outreach to pagans. Universalizing the Jewish doctrine of God and the doctrine of election and preaching against rabbinic tradition were necessitated by the new life God calls for in Christ Jesus. The standard notions could no longer contain or explain what God had done. In second-order terms, we might say that Paul's interpretive principle is that doctrines are revised as the fulfillment of divine promises become evident.

How do they frame the issue on which they are working? Paul's way of framing the issue perhaps derives from his own experience of suddenly realizing that God had done something decisive and that nothing was as it had been before. His theology takes its point of departure not from a belief but from an event: the event of Christ crucified. Since Paul's task is not to explain articles of religion but to invite people into a new community where they would be formed in a new way of life, beliefs were reframed to lead to the deeper goal. At one point Paul does this by explaining the message of the cross, at another the authority of faith, at another the significance of baptism, at another the demands of living in the new community, and at another the newly disclosed meaning of scripture, all in light of what God had done in Jesus Christ.

Paul never thought of himself as developing a soteriology, or an ecclesiology, or a doctrine of scripture. He is always telling people what the case is, now, and how they are to understand and live in its light, for all that has happened is for them, for their freedom and well-being. And to the extent that doctrines later came to be distinguished from one another and can be discerned *in nuce* in Pauline theology, Paul and his followers may be said to be firmly convinced of the salutarity of doctrine: that the work of God and the teachings about it that Paul received and handed on in expanded form would lead to abundant life.

Turning from Paul to Matthew's Sermon on the Mount, we begin by asking what theology is for Matthew. As it is for Paul, theology for Matthew is nothing less than a radical reinterpretation of Judaism necessitated by Jesus. This time the ethic is governed not by the death of the Lord but by his public teaching. The Sermon on the Mount presents a new law of righteousness given by God. The reason the law of righteousness must be tightened up is to challenge people to adopt the new ethic called for by Jesus. The Sermon's radical revision of Pharisaic purity confronts new and potential Christians with a fresh moral vision of personal integrity and honor: a new law of God that binds Jews and gentiles into one people of God through God's anointed savior. Matthew is constructing a countercultural community that lays bare the high cost of discipleship.

Matthew locates religious authority in Jesus rather than Moses. He frames the invitation to life in the new community essentially as a call to rigorous discipleship in response to Jesus' radical reinterpretation of scripture and tradition. Paul also reinterpreted scripture and tradition in order to authorize fresh thinking about the universal electing grace of God. Matthew undertakes a comparable task to impress upon his hearers the demand of discipleship. But Matthew is angrier than Paul. For Paul, Christ crucified makes all the difference. For Matthew, obedience to the new law determines who are the sheep and who will be the goats cast into eternal punishment for having failed to comply with the new terms of righteousness.

Matthew is pressed into constructing a new doctrine of election and a new definition of the Law by Jesus' teaching on purity construed in aretegenic rather than ritual terms. Jesus' teaching on what goodness is forces Matthew's attack on received tradition and lore. Matthew reasons that God has sent Jesus as the new teacher of righteousness, the new lawgiver, to correct received teaching and thereby raise us to a higher life. Again, as it is for Paul, Christian teaching—a better term than doctrine at this stage—better explains what the case is now that God has done this decisive new thing in Israel. The guiding principle is that God is good for us, and our thinking about things like the nature of the community, the criteria of election, the authority of the Law, and the call of discipleship must now be rearticulated so that we are directed aright. Of course, one must assent to the truth of these claims. Assent is logically prior to accepting the new terms of identity and guidance for spiritual development.

In short, for Paul and Matthew doctrinal reconstruction is a must; the old categories and principles no longer hold. Yet doctrine is preconceptual, operating at the level of implicit rather than explicit propositions. In light of the subsequent conceptualization of trinitarian and christological dogma—in order to standardize and unify the church in the fourth and fifth centuries—the tentative beginnings of definitive Christian doctrines appear as the articulation of a new vision of God and his people as these are being tested out in practice. In the case of Paul and the Sermon on the Mount, the fresh teachings on piety, the law, and the nature of the community are forced by the conviction that what God has done in Jesus is essential for our salvation. Had they had the conceptual tools at their disposal they could have put these teachings in the form of assertions. The fact that they did not does not mean that they were not working with an implicit set of doctrines. But their informal style may help us see that doctrine aims to shape a distinctive identity and way of life.

Patristic Voices

In turning to the Fathers, we moved into a self-consciously doctrinal age. We can put our questions to the three patristic bishops we studied as a group. First, how did they understand theology, and for whom was it done? The patristic age benefited from and built upon the New Testament foundation for the purpose of distinguishing what was now clearly the Christian tradition from other traditions. Doctrine that sets criteria for distinguishing between Christian and non-Christian beliefs was now necessitated by confusion about how to think about God, confusion caused by competing interpretations of scripture and variations in worship practices. At the same time, theology had to demonstrate the moral integrity of Christianity in order to invite those who sought life with God to join their ranks, as had Paul and Matthew before them.

The task of doctrinal specification was to sort through the various claimants for clarity and certainty in order for believers and potential believers to know what was expected of them as community members. The task of clarification was intimately related to the tasks of evangelism and subsequent Christian formation. Understanding was the foundation of them all.

Athanasius, Basil, and Augustine, as it happens, all worked on the doctrine of God from different vantage points. Since Christianity had made such rapid advances in the pagan world, these pastors needed to make clear to new Christians what this new faith, and specifically its strange-looking trinitarian explanation of God, was really about, what it held for them. And so they presented the mystery of the Trinity as a way of helping believers come to know God. That is why the trinitarian debates loomed so large in the fourth century. They were a fight for the hearts and minds of the masses of pagans who sought a new life through the church at that time.

Athanasius focused on the good life that resulted from coming to know God the Father properly. And since our knowledge of the Father is through the Son, articulating the relationship between the Father and the Son precisely became central to his argument, especially against opponents whose construal of this relationship would not lead to the proper understanding of God and thus to an excellent life. By Basil's day, knowing God fully also involved taking seriously the role of the Holy Spirit in leading people to righteousness. So he argued for the equality of status of the Holy Spirit with the Father and the Son as an extension of the earlier argument for the consubstantiality of the Son with the Father.

Augustine, writing after the roughest of the fourth-century trinitarian debates, wrote a spiritual guidebook for perplexed and serious God-seekers. Knowing God is, for Augustine, the key to mature and refined happiness. His attempt to render the doctrine of the Trinity transparent by appealing to a series of trinities in ourselves, was to help seekers over the mental gridlock that the doctrine invites. But in addition to the cognitive clarity he sought to provide, he also led seekers into the mystery of God. By linking God intimately with ourselves, Augustine brought his readers to a deeper self-understanding, by means of which they make their way to the good life.

From this vantage point we can see how ill-considered is the judgment of some later Christians that these Fathers were simply forcing Christian teachings into a Procrustean Greek bed. Scholars looked back on this period of consolidation and specification as ending the creativity and flexibility of the apostolic age, a retrogression from the dynamic and historical orientation of the New Testament writers to the rigid eternal essences of Greek philosophy. But we have seen a different side of these pastors. They were using Greek categories, and they did speak of essences. But Greek categories were not purely cognitive concepts, because the classical notion of truth and knowledge could not separate the cognitive from moral realms. Doctrinal exegesis was to the end of preserving the intellectual integrity of Christian teachings in terms of the dominant intellectual culture. But since truth could not be distinguished from moral power and authority, doctrinal exegesis was not a dry abstract undertaking. Nor was it simply imposing episcopal authority in order to put down dissenting voices and consolidate ecclesiastical power. Understanding God correctly was necessary in order for people to grasp their own identity as Christians and achieve true happiness in it. It is primarily from the vantage point of modern epistemology, which has divorced goodness and happiness from truth, that Greek thought patterns appear to us problematic.

This latter point calls for further comment. The reduction of truth and knowledge to their purely cognitive dimension has characterized both conservative and liberal Christians trying to make sense of Christian claims after the Enlightenment. The difference between them is not that conservatives cling to pre-Enlightenment epistemology while liberals embrace modern epistemology. Both have embraced modern epistemology, which requires assent to propositions that are coherent and intelligible. The difference between them is that liberals apply the criteria of credibility and intelligibility more stringently than conservatives usually do.

In the patristic age, theology constructs explicit doctrines and argues for their scriptural and moral integrity against challengers. This marks a change from the biblical task of reconstructing received Jewish teachings in light of God's new work in Christ. Now the theological task became to interpret and synthesize the scriptural witness and insights gained from liturgical practice, in order to render the whole accessible to believers both far removed from the events and perhaps confused by the plethora of prevalent interpretations. In this move from interpreting events to constructing, exegeting, and defending doctrines based on Christian scripture, we see Christianity's transition from a Jewish heresy to a world religion rapidly gaining tremendous strength and power. In light of such a changed situation for theologians, the enduring vivacity of the aretegenic dimension of doctrine is all the more striking.

Medieval Piety

We now turn to the medievals: Anselm, Aquinas, and Julian. Like the patristic Fathers, they are all working on the central topic of their age, a period that spans the full three hundred years that separate them. As the reinterpretation of scripture and tradition were to the New Testament, the Trinity was to the fourth century, and christology was to the fifth century, the central theme of medieval Christianity was the passion of Christ.

What was theology for them? By the end of the eleventh century, when Anselm was writing, Christianity was firmly established in Europe. The medievals inherited a large library of interpretation of the Christian doctrines formulated in the first six Christian centuries. Patristic theology had been thematic and occasional. Further interpretation resulted in a mélange of theological opinion that called for integration. Peter Lombard responded to this call, organizing theology by topic. St. Thomas transformed the Lombard's work from mere organizing to synthesizing theological knowledge with secular philosophy in order to demonstrate that all truth and knowledge come from and lead back to God. It is from them that modern theology derives its systematic urge, although the notion of truth toward which it drives is no longer understood in St. Thomas's holistic sense. In the West, theology was dominated by Augustine read with monastic eyes. There was by then a good deal of experience with church teaching, enough to bring to light the weaknesses of some interpretations and practices based on them. The time to understand the theological task as correction of the received tradition had arrived. It was from the medievals that we moderns inherited the tasks of systematic theology as both an exhaustive and synthetic presentation of the faith and a critical assessment of the tradition.

Here again, we see a significant change in what doctrine was up to. In addition to interpreting events or giving formal voice to liturgical practice, theology came into conversation with itself. Paul and Matthew were, of course, in debate with Jewish theology, largely (though not exclusively) as insiders. Now Christian theology came to debate the authoritative teachers of its own past and the hallowed teachings of a strong, centralized Holy Mother Church, with a very quiet eye toward doctrinal revision. Anselm has an *Auseinandersetzung* with Augustine, and patristic teaching more broadly; Aquinas puts scripture and theology in conversation with modern philosophy; and Julian takes on the monastic tradition.[1] Theology begins to engage in self-criticism and revision in a way that the debates and polemics of the formative patristic period did not. For the purposes of historical continuity, it is important to note that they did their work as insiders, committed to the truth of the Christian faith, yet admonishing it to be its best self.

The recurrent theme in the materials we examined, from Anselm's prayers to the saints to Julian's pastoral advice to distraught sinners, was how to hold to God's mercy when we know ourselves to be deserving only of his punishing justice. The medievals could barely stand under the weight of their sins. The problem in addressing this anxiety was as follows. If God simply forgives sin in order to calm anxiety, the believer might conclude that he or she was not, in fact, called to account before the bar of divine justice. But if the sinner was to be properly punished in order for God to encourage righteousness among his followers, God may appear vindictive. And if believers could not rely upon God's mercy for forgiveness, the whole penitential system could be undermined. Additionally, a God who sets justice above mercy does not endear himself to his followers. The epistemological task of the age was to synthesize all truth as God's truth; the theological task was to balance justice and mercy.

Still, in all three of our medieval representatives a further concern is evident. The question of the justice and mercy of God was central because it is to God that Christians themselves look for leadership and guidance in dealing with questions of justice. So although the teaching of the passion of Christ as Anselm and Thomas worked on it, is meant to "explain" the events so that they do not appear morally repugnant, at the same time the theologians are exerting moral leadership for the church. While the men recognize the pastoral need to provide assurance of forgiveness without undercutting motivation for righteous living, Julian takes a more radical position by stressing mercy alone: a wrathful God is not a loving God.

The medieval problem exposes the close relationship between doctrinal assertions and the aretegenic agenda. The concern with balancing justice and mercy pointed out tensions in the doctrine of God and of the atonement. Anselm saw that one of these doctrines had to be revised. He chose to revise the teaching on the atonement to balance these two virtues. He, like Julian, had simultaneously to honor and revise accepted teaching. Respect for the tradition may be the reason that the older teaching on the fallen angels and the ransom-from-the-devil motifs still show up in the *Cur Deus Homo*. In Anselm's hands, theology becomes a highly sophisticated art of simultaneous affirmation and criticism of the tradition, one that brilliantly explains the work of Christ as a synthesis of justice and mercy.

Sixteenth-Century Reform

Our last figure is John Calvin. As with our medieval writers, in Calvin's hands theology is an instrument of synthesis and revision of the tradition with an eye on its pastoral effectiveness. Because doctrine was in a flurry when Calvin lived he had to fight misreadings of the faith on both left and right. This lent a complexity to his work that makes it patient of many interpretations. Calvin sought to preserve the spirit of the apostolic tradition against the radical reformation while liberating it from the ecclesiastical stranglehold exerted by the papacy. Despite the polemical edge, it was still for the sake of enabling God to sanctify believers, or, as Calvin put it following Augustine, to restore them in the image of God.

The pastoral functions of doctrine, then, are to clarify and, when necessary, revise the teachings of the church in order to invite believers to be transformed by knowing God and giving him honor and glory. Calvin was a man of stern temperament who espoused the benefits of discipline for spiritual maturity. Because God is good for us, Calvin believed that obedience and gratitude constitute the only proper attitude for a Christian standing before God. Theology is to persuade believers to obey God's commands and the ordinances of the evangelical church. Because of the Reformation setting, Calvin could not argue that one should obey God in order to please him and thereby accomplish something for oneself. But as a person who prized order, he was probably nervous about the violence that the Lutheran Reformation had let loose. And so there sits uneasily in the center of his theology an unresolved conflict between an insistence on obedience to God and urging acceptance of the eternal judgment that God has determined for each, a fate of salvation or damnation known to God alone. Calvin held this together by implying that God is so great and good that we should strive for righteousness even if we should be consigned to the rank of the reprobate. Refurbishing the image of God is not tied to salvation. In this he seems to follow Augustine.

Calvin framed the project in terms set forth for the West by Augustine: knowing God—some would say knowing the sovereignty of God—is the proper foundation of Christian piety. In this Calvin harkened back to the sapiential understanding of knowledge of the Platonic tradition. Nevertheless, the element of dwelling in the divine mystery, so central to Augustine and the Eastern theological tradition—as well as its Western counterpart, beholding the vision of God—were gone. In their place, Calvin, following Luther, put faith. Trusting God, even against the odds, calls forth a life of thanks and praise, no matter how many obstacles God sets in one's path. Knowing God is the key to self-knowledge, and self-knowledge is the key to self-despair, and self-despair is the entry point for a sanctified life with God.

The centrality of self-despair and the emphasis on self-denial as the way of Christian discipleship in Calvin's aretology separate him and the medieval tradition that stood behind him from the patristic age generally, and Augustine specifically—particularly the Augustine of the *De Trinitate*. While Augustine despaired of his ability to be chaste, control his overeating, or quench his desire for honor on his own, his anxiety about these things did not lead him to think that God was angry about this and resented him for his failures. We have suggested, however, that after Augustine—we noted the Rule of St. Benedict—a deep anxiety enters the Western tradition that in the wrong hands seems to counsel self-hatred and suffering as a way of pleasing God or at least appeasing his wrath.

The Tasks of Christian Doctrine

This overview of theology throughout the classical period now allows us to draw some limited conclusions. I say limited because many important theologians and theological genres are not included in our sample. And even though, as noted at the outset, I chose the most difficult cases upon which to make the argument for the salutarity of doctrine, there are undoubtedly many influential treatises in which intellectual clarity alone may be the norm. It would, for example, be interesting to examine Cyprian's treatise "On the Unity of the Church," or Nyssa's treatise "On Not Three Gods," or Cyril of Alexandria's christology in this regard.

The argument here is not to suggest that all classical theology is aretegenic, for it is surely not. Rather, the point is simply that as these major shapers of the Christian tradition formulated, reformulated, and revised Christian doctrine, its moral, psychological, and social implications were uppermost in their minds. Even when refuting their colleagues or opponents who, in the writers' judgment, were distorting the tradition and falling into heresy, they never forgot that God was seeking to draw people to himself for their own good.

An immediate objection to this finding will be that a pragmatic and utilitarian understanding of doctrine is being advocated that challenges the notion that Christian doctrine is a matter of truth—the truth of God—and that Christian faithfulness depends solely upon assenting to true propositions about God, Christ, humanity, the church, and so forth. It will be objected that the aretegenic view renders theology vulnerable to the definition of salutarity in any age, of relativizing truth.

I have argued that the modern notion of truth only makes sense on modern evidentialist and rationalist terms for truth and knowledge. Our theologians would not understand the objection being made to their work, for they could not envision a notion of truth that is not salutary, or a notion of doctrine that is not interpreted along these lines. For if something is harmful to us, it must be false and certainly cannot be the truth of God. Indeed, a judgment that something is true and yet morally harmful would, from their perspective, impugn the goodness of God. This is precisely Julian of Norwich's argument against the wrath of God.

The tasks and issues for theology changed considerably over the centuries. This brief look at the development of the task of theology suggests the following regulative conclusion. In its axial age Christian theology sought to redefine the authority of scripture and tradition in order to provide a theological interpretation of the decisive events that took place in Galilee and especially in Jerusalem in the three short years of Jesus' ministry. Once religious authority was established, it became necessary to construct wholly new teachings to ground and nurture the new community. Because the biblical teachings themselves were not univocal, a period of refinement and focusing was necessary.

After six hundred years of formation, theology began to synthesize its body of doctrine and eventually, when it became evident that they were not doing their job properly, to revise specific teachings. The overarching regulative task of theology is to keep the Christian tradition resilient. There is no single method that theology employs in every age. Theologians are doing many things all at the same time. Yet we have seen in every case that each theologian sought to unfold the mystery of God in order to bring people to know and love him and to live accordingly.

Our studies have now brought us to a critical point. I have been arguing that before the seventeenth century, interpretation of Christian doctrine often aimed to elaborate the divine pedagogy in order to shape Christians as excellent persons. Tracing the history of how various theologians undertook this task has led us to see that although a theologian like Anselm strove to balance divine justice and mercy there has been a tendency in the West to emphasize divine wrath over divine compassion. Although we have not followed every step of this development, it may not be inappropriate to suggest that it is a theme that began with *The City of God*, took a personal turn with the Rule of St. Benedict, was sustained by medieval devotionalism, and recast by Calvin.

From our own vantage point in history, perhaps listening particularly to the testimony of Christian women, this stern interpretation of God's will for us has been damaging at least for some, rather than genuinely salutary. Perhaps we can conclude that Christians have suffered at the hands of theologians who lost sight of God's respect for us even in the midst of our sinfulness, and portrayed God as implicitly approving of our suffering and self-abasement. Those who have interpreted the cross as countenancing suffering as pleasing to God, rather than as teaching compassion, or who have encouraged God-seekers to hate themselves in order to cajole God into loving them, instead of building them up into the nobility of life with God, have misunderstood God's commitment to creation and respect for us taught by the Incarnation itself. Some may have lost sight of the aretgenic function of doctrine altogether, while others may have been unable to visualize the damage heavily punitive aretologies may bring in their wake.

This admonition is not meant as license for abandoning the centrality of the teaching on sin, or the aretegenic function of Christian doctrine. Nor does it countenance the revision or elimination of doctrines of the faith that constitute its integrity. Current suggestions to eliminate the maleness of God, the doctrine of the Trinity, or the doctrine of the atonement, it seems to me, offer radical solutions to the wrong problem. They judge that the doctrines themselves are at fault rather than specific interpretations of the doctrines. They jump over the fact that if some theologians and church bureaucrats failed to read the tradition carefully and allowed their own insecurities and frustrations with the intractability of human sinfulness to overcome them, the fault lies with them and not with God. Although the construction of doctrines themselves is the work of theologians, they were trying to articulate the being and work of God made known to Israel and in Jesus Christ. That there have been bad theologians or that there have been good theologians who wrote things that later turned out to lead the tradition away from God's grace and goodness should come as no surprise. Theology, like every other human activity is a human discipline.

This realization should call us back to doing careful doctrinal exposition that savors its past without sentimentalizing it and understands the nature and scope of proper theological self-criticism. Abandoning careful theological work and rejecting the tradition from which it draws will not relieve the problem; it will only cover it over. Those who conclude that the Christian tradition is useless or irredeemably harmful cannot in good conscience be Christian theologians. They must find another place to stand where their integrity can be respected.

One goal of this work has been to illustrate that the tradition of reinterpreting the tradition while being faithful to its theological integrity is long-standing. Indeed, the fallenness of theologians itself should be a caution to those who are called to the theological task of helping the tradition be its best self. This calls for the careful training of theologians who are willing to reinterpret the tradition because they know and love God and God's children.

The primary task of these studies has been to highlight the indivisibility of the intellectual and pastoral interests of classical doctrinal exegesis. These became separated in the modern period so that Christian doctrine and the theology that criticizes it have become marginal to the lives of many believers. It is to the repair of this breech that we now turn.

RENEWING SAPIENTIAL THEOLOGY

We have noted that the sapiential function of theology, nourished by a Neoplatonic outlook, underwent a slow and gradual change in the Middle Ages as Christians became worried about the wrath of God. Anxiety focused theology on understanding the mechanism of salvation so that the question "Does God love me?" became compelling. Fear of receiving a negative answer to this most central question quashed the joy of theology's invitation to seek God; the quest for certainty began to compete with the quest for sapience.

Still, the Platonic notion of truth managed to prevail. It held to the unity of beauty, truth, and goodness, with a participatory underpinning. That is, to know the truth was to be in the truth. To know the good, in Christian understanding, was to participate in it with God's help. Classical thought believed that truth, beauty, and goodness are affective: that is, that they change the seeker by bringing her into their orbit and under their influence. This is what Pauline and Johannine literature and the theology that followed them mean by dwelling in God and being indwelt by God.

The mystery of God takes up residence in those who meet it. All truth was both sapiential and aretegenic because dwelling in God and being indwelt by the wisdom and goodness of God help us. Coming to benefit from the wisdom and goodness of God is a gift of God's grace nurtured through prayer, reflection, and study of God's word. Getting the doctrines straight was essential to the classical task, but when in supple hands, the conceptual and historical work was ordered to the goal of what, from our modern perspective, we would call spiritual and moral formation. This is the model of theology through St. Thomas, even though medieval piety became grim at times.

Sapiential truth is unintelligible to the modern secularized construal of truth. Modern epistemology not only fragmented truth itself, privileging correct information over beauty and goodness, it relocated truth in facts and ideas. The search for truth in the modern scientific sense is a cognitive enterprise that seeks correct information useful to the improvement of human comfort and efficiency rather than an intellectual activity employed for spiritual growth. Knowing the truth no longer implied loving it, wanting it, and being transformed by it, because the truth no longer brings the knower to God but to use information to subdue nature. Knowing became limited to being informed about things, not as these are things of God but as they stand (or totter) on their own feet. The classical notion that truth leads us to God simply ceased to be intelligible and came to be viewed with suspicion.

Johannine talk of dwelling in God, or Paul's phrase "being in Christ," or Eastern theology's talk of deification were dismissed as types of mysticism that permitted a dangerous confusion between creature and Creator. The classical holistic notion of truth was deemed dangerous to piety, especially in the West, where the older notion came to be associated with Pelagianism, a fear that had a mighty and noble history as late as the famous Barth-Brunner debate of the 1930s. One consequence of this distaste for a broader notion of knowledge was suspicion between East and West, and later, in the nature and grace debate, between Catholic and Protestant. It also undercut the capacity of the Christian tradition to bring Christians to discover their proper dignity in God and to grow in the Christian life in the transformational terms that Paul understood it: being conformed to the image of Christ (Rom. 8.29) "by the renewing of your minds" (Rom. 12.2).

The judgment that a Platonic worldview leads inevitably to pantheism or a distorted view of human creatureliness is not, however, so clear. Athanasius and Augustine both constructed safeguards against this possibility (Athanasius via the *homoousios*, and Augustine through the doctrine of original sin). While distortions of any position may be inevitable, the conclusion of this study is that the decline of the Platonic perspective in the medieval period, coupled with the development of a sense of genuine and enduring enmity between God and us that replaced it, has been equally harmful in the long run, especially to tender souls. On the other hand, one would wish to know how many bolder souls were restrained from evil by the church's sterner teachings.

Eventually, the classical worldview was replaced by a modern counterpart that restructured philosophy in two forms, one British empiricism, the other German rationalism, romanticism, and idealism. On the empiricist model one could still be persuaded by knowledge, and perhaps influenced in that way. But the art of persuasion was now dependent on one's ability to bring empirical evidence in support of claims. Reasons and evidence came to serve critical second-order argument against Christian claims from a standpoint outside the Christian faith. If good argument brought people to God, all well and good. If it sent people away from God, at least the truth had been served.

On the German model, Christian doctrines were reinterpreted in terms of speculative philosophical principles. Leibniz, Wolff, Kant, Lessing, Fichte, Schelling, Hegel, and Schleiermacher all undertook to rethink theology in relation to these modern philosophical categories in one way or another. Some of them wanted to adapt theology to modernity by providing a philosophical foundation for Christian teaching, on the assumption that it could no longer stand on its own terms.

The secularization, elevation, and constriction of reason in the seventeenth and eighteenth centuries undercut the sapiential, aretegenic, and participatory dimensions of doctrinal interpretation. Although Protestant scholastics like John Gerhard insisted on the sapiential function of theology, the dominant goal became laying out the pattern of Christian doctrines so that Christians would assent to correct propositions. Now the church had always insisted on right belief, but as we saw with Thomas's teaching on formed faith, it was right belief in the service of devotion. With the Enlightenment, reason was used to free theology from church control, not to lead believers to know, love, and serve God better. From the perspective of classical thought, today's theology is abnormal, shrunken, and impoverished, because it is limited to science alone, whereas for Augustine science was preparation for sapience. From the perspective of modern thought, classical theology is imprecise, unscientific, and precritical because it fails to demarcate preaching from criticism, teaching from analysis, and guidance from systematization.

The preceding argument may be summarized graphically by an example from painting. The seventeenth-century French painter Georges de La Tour painted *Saint Sebastian Tended by Saint Irene*. It is a striking work, illustrating de La Tour's brilliant handling of light. The painting is perfectly balanced. The figures, the two saints and a woman holding a lantern in the center, bend toward one another to form an intimate circle that pulls the viewer into the action of the painting: St. Irene removing an arrow from Sebastian's thigh. The light from the lantern illuminates Irene, particularly her face, with a tear falling from her eye. Irene is dressed in pink, with a soft translucent head-covering that shimmers in the lantern light. The painting is elegant, refined, and perfectly executed. The observer will learn much about color, line, and light from studying it. And the issues of technique will be fitted into the history of art as an aesthetic discipline.

The preceding paragraph is an uneducated admirer's attempt to describe de La

Tour's painting in the categories of modern art criticism. It is analogous to the work of modern theology, which is critical in the sense of using second-order norms to describe and then evaluate doctrine. Line, color, balance, light, and so on correspond to the norms of coherence, intelligibility, and appropriateness.

Now let us look at the painting as a Christian seeker rather than as an art buff. For the Christian, the success with which the artist executes the norms of his discipline is of interest insofar as the use of color and light, and the balance and line of the design, help her grasp what the painting offers. The seeker is interested in the message that the skill of the artist is trying to convey. The observer will note that the painting's title is a bit misleading. The painting is really of St. Irene tending St. Sebastian. All the light falls on her. What is she telling us? The line of the light that falls on her as she prepares to remove the arrow runs from her face to her hands. She steadies herself by placing her left hand on Sebastian's knee as her right hand grasps the arrow, but a tear falls from her eye. She is tending Sebastian with compassion and calm determination. There is nothing unsightly about the scene. Indeed, it is beautiful. Christian ministry is beautiful, she seems to say.

The Christian seeker finds herself in the company of the saints, and their message is clear. Christians are called to take arrows out of other people's bodies. This is the truth of God. The viewer who seeks life with God will be taken into the sapience of God by de la Tour's preaching of the gospel, allowing it to reform and thereby beautify her. The thrust of my argument is that to interpret de la Tour as simply a painter and not also as a theologian is to fail to understand him.

What would be required for theology to reclaim its sapiential voice today? Given the postmodern criticism of Enlightenment rationality, perhaps some of the classical, especially patristic, interpretations of Christian doctrines may be more accessible now than at other times. This could spawn a renewed willingness to seek the wisdom of God in genuinely Christian categories. The purpose of such a return would not be to adopt the answers that any one thinker or age gave to the issues posed, but to reenter their conversation.

The first step in such a renewal would require theologians to reconnect truth and goodness. This means challenging the modern notion of truth that is amoral and aspiritual and forcing theology to stand on its own feet. This is a daunting task because, since the Enlightenment, theology has worked to be considered intellectually acceptable precisely on modern terms of rationality. Yet unless theology is willing to make such a bold move, it is difficult to see how it can again speak of God. The best it can do under the modern conditions laid down by John Locke is to speak of ideas of God and the power of faith.

Perhaps it would clarify matters to take a cue from St. Augustine and recognize that for theology, science is a necessary preliminary to sapience. This is the position that recognizes Georges de la Tour as a preacher of the gospel through painting. What science calls truth is only part of what theology calls truth, for theology insists that truth is salutary—that God is good for us. Rather than render sapience dependent on science, however, a truly liberated understanding of the truth of God must be bold enough to say that the wisdom of God made known in the story of Israel and in Jesus Christ stands as a norm of truth and goodness on its own terms, as Karl Barth pointed out.

In a culture in which moral categories are empty, to link truth and goodness seems precarious. If goodness has no clear content, how can one argue that goodness is a norm of truth? But scripture as a whole—and the Decalogue, the Sermon on the Mount, and the story of Jesus Christ in particular—should protect Christians against the moral neutrality of our day. Discerning theology will always test itself against the testimony of the great tradition, trusting that the wisdom of God is indeed good for us.

An adequate formulation of how truth might again be understood as sapience lies beyond the capacities of this writer. Various epistemic questions will need to be dealt with by those more adept at these considerations. The purpose of this exposition has been to point out that reclaiming the pastoral function of Christian doctrine for the church will require further attention to this matter. It is neither possible nor fully desirable to jump back over the Enlightenment. But certain blind spots to which the crafters of modernity succumbed are now coming to light. I have suggested that their notion of truth was truncated and that this realization provides an opportunity for Christians to reclaim a truly theological understanding of truth, which engages believers in the wisdom of God.

A corollary of this first point is that to revive the pastoral function of theology requires theologians to think of themselves as pastors helping people to find their identity in God. This is challenging, for not only does it require a change in thinking, it also means that theologians must think of themselves as spiritual directors. Sapiential theology offers spiritual guidance through the exposition of doctrine and encouragement in the repair of identity and character. The point, of course, is not to give theology over to preaching and psychology. The masters we studied never fell into this trap. But in order for believers to become sapient, theologians must be comfortable talking about the wisdom of God that makes for an excellent life. That is, theology must again become a normative and not simply a descriptive discipline. It must take a position on what an excellent life looks like.

Practicing the Theological Art

Up until this point I have focused the argument largely in terms of the modern truncation of truth and knowledge, which has shut us off from the fullness of Christian doctrine. But for Christians to benefit from the older view, we cannot just reread classic texts realizing that they are more sophisticated and complex than we thought. Reclaiming the beauty of life with God for the people of God will require attending to the practice of life with God. What is called for is not only expanding our grasp of what doctrine does but also attending to how Christians can best utilize it. Whatever the intellectual adjustments that must be made in order to do so, the reclamation of the pastoral functions of doctrine will fail unless theology is reconnected to devotional life. For theology is not just an intellectual art; it cultivates the skill of living well.

Friedrich Schleiermacher pointed out the importance of connecting the head to the heart when talking about Christian doctrine. Turning to the aretegenic and sapiential functions of Christian doctrine points out that doctrine has also been severed from the hands and feet, the eyes and the ears. The assumption of academic theology has often been that doctrine is the theory of Christian belief. It is to be understood, internalized, and acted upon in a purely cognitive procedure of assent and decision-making. Doctrine and practice are so separated, and their separation so reinforced by the divisions of the classical theological curriculum, that the idea of practicing Christian doctrine is an oxymoron.[2]

This book has argued that Christian doctrine can guide the Christian life because it forms identity and character. But it is not the only Christian instrument of formation, but the chief of several such tools. We started out by observing that insight and understanding are not the only way we are formed. We also come to understanding by doing: thinking is shaped by experience. Indeed, much cognitive learning remains aloof unless and until it is experienced. It is not only the case that we must know God in order to love him. It is also the case that in loving we learn what loving is—indeed, how difficult it really is.

Devotional life is traditionally spoken of under the rubric of ascetical theology. It is most often associated with monastics and visionaries, separating those who practice living to God rigorously through the contemplative life from the majority of Christians, who serve God in "the world." While some people do have extraordinary experiences that others miss, and perhaps a different temperament that facilitates them, for our purposes, the feature distinguishing these two classes of Christians is the intensity of the yearning for God that powers their devotional life. While a yearning for God is itself a gift of the Holy Spirit, once it is aroused it must be honed and channeled. In this we follow Augustine and Calvin.

While people are undoubtedly differently gifted, the distinction between specially talented and ordinary Christians ignores the fact that a major difference between the two groups is how they allocate their time. The issue of the use of time is the underlying principle that conventional Christian wisdom has used to distinguish the contemplative life from the active life. Today the intentional devotional life can be mistakenly thought of as a leisurely life that stands aloof from the great "rat race" of postindustrial society in the West.[3]

Together, these two traditional criteria of the intentional devotional life—a special charism and leisure to set "the world" aside—render a rich spiritual life inaccessible to many Christians. The monastic life may even appear to some Christians as self-indulgent, for it seems to renege on social responsibilities like child-rearing, even further discouraging many people from cultivating their yearning for God and readjusting their priorities accordingly. In an overwhelmingly secular culture, this presses the issue of "becoming a (serious) Christian" into the ranks of rescue from a self-destructive life of drugs, alcohol, or whatever. The assumption behind this catch-me-when-I-fall approach to conversion is that the culture has so alienated us from the norm of a God-centered life that one would only turn to God in desperation.

Modern thinking on the Christian life, however, generally assumes that a vigorous devotional life is best for everyone, of course, not only for those whose lives have spun out of control or who have a special calling as clergy or contemplatives. This is evident in the general reframing of devotional life that has been taking place over the past three decades or so, in what has been dubbed the Age of the Laity. I will review this development and then ask how the doctrines of the faith, along with other formative tools, can be practiced to form believers in Christian excellence.

The traditional distinction between the contemplative and the active life is probably of limited help today. A more useful model is the Benedictine integration of prayer and work, adapted to the demands of modern life. This is happening through many renewal movements and through the proliferation of literature on spirituality across the church today. The spirituality movement frequently helps people adapt their prayer life to the hectic pace of modern life. It is not unusual to see prayers being said, the Bible being studied, and devotionals being read on commuter trains and subways on the way to work. The retreat-center movement has burgeoned over the past two decades. The reclamation of liturgy and frequent communion in many traditions is another indication of the growing willingness to acknowledge that Christian identity is best shaped through Christian practices. It is now widely acknowledged that worship and study—perhaps even the practice of silence—are important supports in an increasingly frenetic world.[4]

All of these developments are signs that many Christians are beginning to reprioritize their time to allow for attending to God more carefully. This is all to the good. Prayer, study, and sacramental worship are essential for training one's thoughts, and the need for silence cannot be overemphasized. Attending to God requires quiet. The need to quiet the din of a busy life, however, should not be understood in opposition to Christian service (which can keep one very busy). The criticism that practicing doctrine has been severed from hands and feet is real.[5] One can grasp what our theologians are inviting us to consider through silence. But being in Christ can remain theoretical unless one meet Christ by caring for children, the elderly, the poor, the sick, and those in prison. Indeed, it may be that unless one meet Christ in the face of the dying, Julian's understanding of divine mercy will remain alien to us. Some Christians, like mothers who stay home with children, and those able to dedicate their work lives in Christian service both within the church and in the society, are fortunate. Others will need to develop other avenues for service. And perhaps those whose work is in tension with their Christian calling will have to seek redirection of their skills.

Framing the Christian life around the practices of prayer, study, and service suggests that a division between personal holiness and social justice is false and misleading. The life of prayer and study will ring hollow unless illuminated by service. And in service to children, the elderly, the poor, the weak, the sick, and the imprisoned, one worships and glorifies God and comes to know the Lord and perhaps to touch his wounds, so that doubt is stilled. With these three pillars of an integrated devotional life in view, we are ready to move on to suggest a three-stage process for undertaking it: awakening, catechesis, and sapience.

One's point of entry into a sapiential life is irrelevant. Any door will do. At the same time, any element can miss the mark. Rote prayer, perfunctory study, and mechanical restocking of the community food pantry can all become busywork rather than means of knowing God. With sufficient guidance, however, prayer, study, and service illuminate one another; together they open the door to a richer life with God. Perhaps we might reclaim the medieval distinction between formed and unformed faith. What Thomas called formed faith corresponds to what for us is reflective prayer, study, and service, while unformed faith corresponds to dutiful prayer and service. One should not shun beginning with dutiful practices, for these are the elementary levels of Christian training. But once one yearns for God, mindless practices will not do. One prays for the illumination of the Holy Spirit.

Few people start out looking for an intentional devotional life; it is simply too arduous. Something has to intervene in the person's life to awaken desire for another way. God must turn one's head from current pursuits to a new realm of possibilities. For Augustine, reading Cicero's *Hortensius* propelled him into the pursuit of the spiritual life. Occasionally the Holy Spirit will even use preaching, or simply the presence of someone in another's life. It may come through moral, social, or psychological stumbling or pain, or just out of curiosity. For some, as Calvin pointed out, complete self-despair is necessary. God must, however, make himself an object of desire.

For some people this will happen violently, in a dramatic act of conversion. For others it may be slow and not at all clear. Yearning may begin as no more than dissatisfaction with one's work or forms of entertainment, without God in the picture at all. That is why Christians must always be alert for opportunities to be of service to others in the Christian life, and to serve them without pressure or lock-step expectations, perhaps thinking of themselves as midwives. It is important that the struggle of coming to God be respected. That God breaks through to us at all is an awesome miracle.

Once one's yearning is awakened, tracks must be laid down all along the way in order for entering God's presence to be comforting rather than frightening or off-putting. No serious student would undertake to study the violin or painting alone. One studies under skilled teachers and begins with easy assignments. The same is true for training in the Christian life. One needs a guide, preferably a gentle and seasoned guide, as well as other spiritual confidants with whom one can converse as one gains basic competence in Christian understanding.

Nothing can replace basic catechetical training as undertaken by the Rite of Christian Initiation for Adults by the Roman Catholic Church, for example. The din of the secular world's ways is so loud that the ancient catechetical norm of a three-year preparation for baptism is not outrageous. For without lengthy socialization into the pacing of the Christian life, the turn to God will not be experienced as a homecoming but as entrance into someone else's house. The church is obligated to provide basic training for a skilled life with God and then to invite Christians to advance beyond this training to dwell in the sapience of God. Without a sturdy foundation the seeker may well fall into confusion. As Augustine so wisely pointed out, sapience is built on science.

Augustine realized that all three levels of Christian training, from the arousal of desire for God to entrance into the mystery of God itself, is a continuous process of the training of desire. Even though he concluded that yearning for God itself is a gift of grace, he still struggled with how that yearning is aroused. The literary remains of his struggle appear in both the *Confessions* and the *De Trinitate* in his long discussions of how we love God if we do not know him. As we have seen, he concluded that we can love God, whom we do not "know," because there is an abiding sense in which we are not cut off from God. We can intuit the beauty of God just as we can recognize just persons even if we ourselves are scoundrels or are surrounded by them. Christian growth in sapience, then, is a dialectical movement that at one turn nurtures insight or existential encounter with God by grounding them in scripture, doctrine, and tradition *(scientia)* and at the next enlivens that *scientia* with prayerful insight nurtured through reflective prayer and service.

Augustine also recognized that religious intuition, like a native aesthetic sense, must be cultivated to be useful. And he knew from experience that even bright people like himself need a teacher. The journey of life with God cannot, ought not, be undertaken alone. Augustine realized fully that the Manichees had led him astray only when he put himself into Bishop Ambrose's hands. The church is responsible for providing mentors and guides for less experienced Christians. It would be well for the church to take a lesson in moral pedagogy from Saints Basil and Anselm. They understood that discipline may sometimes be necessary. But they also knew that discipline will only be effective if it is administered in a safe environment. Indeed, the church should take a pedagogical lesson from God, who, as Augustine pointed out, first had to assure us of how much he loves us before we could allow him to teach us.

Since the modern church is far from insisting on extensive training for Christian discipleship, it may help to offer some comment on the suggestion. The untrained eye and ear, like untrained muscles and an untrained mind, are usually able to function adequately to provide the basic groundwork of an organized life. But training of these natural faculties improves the quality of life because it expands the range of awareness and opportunities one has. And training of one faculty through the cultivation of one discipline should slip over and expand one's freedom and opportunities in other fields as well. Bird-watching, for example, trains one to attend to the different colors and sounds of birds and, more broadly, to attend to detail, which is helpful in most areas of life. Training of the muscles through tennis or basketball should carry over into other areas of life that require endurance, coordination, and practice.

Indeed, proper training of any faculty enables one to appreciate the notion of training altogether. For without training of some faculty, one lacks the notion that training advances appreciation and opens up new and deeper levels of meaning. There is no way to tell someone whose faculties are untrained how much richer life can be, how much more control and power one has over one's life, with training. But training takes discipline.

We may liken training in enjoying God to growing in the enjoyment of Mozart's music: it can be enjoyed at face value, but the degree of enjoyment increases when one's ear is trained to pick out the harmonies and dissonances. The better one knows a piece, the more one can appreciate one interpretation or performer rather than another, recognizing that one is more faithful to the composer's intention, or one is more contemporary, and so forth. The more skilled the ear, the greater the reward.

It is possible to be a Christian without much training. Some would say it requires only acceptance of Jesus as Lord. Others would say it requires a warm heart and an outstretched hand. But to progress in Christian excellence beyond the basics requires training and cultivation of the skill of attending to God and of reexamining and reforming oneself in light of that attending. Becoming a sapient and excellent Christian requires development of the eyes, ears, muscles, and mind of the whole self. The more training, the deeper the involvement, and the deeper the involvement, the greater the enjoyment; and the greater the enjoyment, the greater the dignity and nobility of life. In short, sapience emerges with a deepened grasp of the tradition. In this regard we may note that it took Julian twenty years in an anchorhold to fully understand her visions as a teaching on divine mercy.

At an advanced level of training in the Christian life, help comes from almost anywhere because one is waiting for it. Connections appear that one never noticed before, and the distance between oneself and the great cloud of Christian witnesses begins to shrink. All the practices of Christian devotion offer the believer words and images that bring the mystery of God's goodness and beauty into sharper view.

Experiences of pain and suffering, especially watching the suffering of others, illuminate Christ's work on the cross. And God's bearing our pain on the cross also teaches that in our pain we are not alone but accompanied by God himself, so that the idea of following a crucified messiah is not a scandal at all but, rather, a relief. In John's gospel we meet Jesus washing the uncomprehending disciples' feet as he faces his own death. How much clearer an aretegenic text could there be? Each step forward in the mutual illumination of teaching and experience strengthens the self as one moves deeper into the mystery of divine wisdom.

As one matures in sapience, one is able to see more clearly what each one needs from the church. One person needs to see past the distortions of Christian teaching, or one's own pain and hurt blocking one from the goodness of God. Another becomes able to accept the discipline of the church for self-control. One gains the courage to let go of old resentments. Another gains the courage to cease from sin. Old patterns of thought and behavior are replaced as one gains confidence from the skills of the new life. In the end, submission to God and giving up oneself to his service are the means to true freedom.

Theology today lives on the margins of the secular culture, the margins of the academy, and the margins of the church. It could be that responsibility for this marginalization lies equally with a desacralized culture and with the field of theology itself. Perhaps the renewal of theology is not unlike the renewal of the Christians about whom our theological teachers worried, as a mother cares for a child who has lost her way in a confusing world. She must be healed with love before she can flourish again.

Notes

1. Aquinas is a special case within this generalization because he did not select the passion narrative for special treatment but treated it in the course of explaining the entire scope of Christian theology and doctrine. He is also exceptional in that his correction of the tradition is spurred not only by internal considerations, as were Anselm's and Julian's, but also by contemporary philosophy. Finally, he represents an alternative to the narrowing of theological concerns because he resists the urge to commend one interpretation of a doctrine over another that would take firm hold beginning with Luther. For example, in his treatment of soteriology (which we saw) and his treatment of the doctrine of justification (which we did not study) he presented all the options available without passing judgment on which one was correct. This pluralism was perfectly appropriate, since the church had not officially ruled on these questions. The Reformation forced a confrontation on justification, closing options off and dividing the church, leaving soteriology as one of the few doctrinal loci where diversity could be tolerated.

2. Edward Farley has stimulated discussion of this problem with his book on theological education (1983). He argues for theology as *habitus* and for theological education along these lines rather than as the professional training it has come to be in the past two centuries. My own recovery of this understanding of theology, however, comes not from Farley, and not even from reflection on theological education, but from reflection on theology in general and specifically from St. Augustine.

3. This is a misrepresentation of many religious orders whose ministry is education, hospitality, or medical service.

4. Worship here includes private prayer, liturgical prayer, and reception of the sacraments. Study includes study of the Bible as well as Christian spiritual writers and theological texts.

5. The fact that some Christians line up behind the importance of doctrine while others line up behind the importance of service as the central pillars of the Christian life, testifies to the confusion on both sides about what Christian doctrine is about.

Works Cited

Abraham, William J. (1987). Cumulative Case Arguments for Christian Theism. In *The Ratio-nality of Religious Belief,* ed. W. J. Abraham and S. W. Holtzer, 17–37. Oxford: Claren-don Press.

Adson, Martin A. (1995). "An Endangered Ethic—the Capacity for Caring." *Mayo Clinic Pro-ceedings* **70:** 495–500.

Allison, Dale C. (1987). "The Structure of the Sermon on the Mount." *Journal of Biblical Lit-erature* **106**(3): 423–45.

Alston, William P. (1993). The Fulfillment of Promises as Evidence for Religious Belief. In *Faith in Theory and Practice: Essays on Justifying Religious Belief,* ed. E. S. Radcliffe and C. J. White, 1–34. Chicago and La Salle, Ill.: Open Court.

Amand de Mendieta, E. (1965). *The "Unwritten" and "Secret" Apostolic Traditions in the Theo-logical Thought of St. Basil of Caesarea.* London: Oliver and Boyd.

Ameriks, Karl (1992). The Critique of Metaphysics: Kant and Traditional Ontology. In *Cam-bridge Companion to Kant,* ed. P. Guyer, 249–79. New York and Cambridge: Cambridge University Press.

Anselm, Saint, Archbishop of Canterbury ([1965] 1979). *St. Anselm's Proslogion with A Reply on Behalf of the Fool, by Gaunilo, and the author's Reply to Gaunilo.* London: Oxford University Press. Reprint Notre Dame, Ind.: University of Notre Dame Press.

———. (1969). *Why God Became Man & The Virgin Conception and Original Sin.* Albany, NY: Magi Books.

———. (1973). *The Prayers and Meditations of St. Anselm with the Proslogion.* Middlesex, Eng.: Penguin Books.

———. (1990). *The Letters of Saint Anselm of Canterbury.* Kalamazoo, Mich.: Cistercian Pub-lications.

Aristotle (1963). *The Philosophy of Aristotle.* New York: New American Library.

Athanasius, Saint, Patriarch of Alexandria (1971). *Contra Gentes and De Incarnatione.* Oxford: Clarendon.

———. (1986). Discourse III Against the Arians. In *Nicene and Post-Nicene Fathers,.* **IV:** 393–431. Grand Rapids: Eerdmans.

Augustine, Saint, Bishop of Hippo (1958). Of True Religion. In *Augustine: Earlier Writings,* ed. J. H. S. Burleigh, 218–83. Philadelphia: Westminster Press.

———. (1984). *City of God.* London: Penguin Books.

———. (1991a). *Confessions.* Oxford and New York: Oxford University Press.

———. (1991b). *The Trinity.* Brooklyn, New York: New City Press.

Aulén, Gustaf (1969). *Christus Victor: An Historical Study of the Three Main Types of the Idea of Atonement*. New York: Macmillan.

Babcock, William S. (1991). "A Changing of the Christian God: The Doctrine of the Trinity in the Seventeenth Century." *Interpretation* **XLV**(2): 133–46.

Balch, David L. (1981). *Let Wives Be Submissive: The Domestic Code in I Peter*. Chico, Calif.: Scholars Press.

Barral, Mary-Rose (1988). Reflections on Anselm's Friendship and Conversation. In *Anselm Studies: An Occasional Journal*, ed. J. C. Schnaubelt, et al., **II:** 165–82. White Plains, NY: Edwin Mellen.

Barth, Karl (1956). *Church Dogmatics* IV.1 *The Doctrine of Reconciliation*. Edinburgh: T. & T. Clark.

———. (1958). *Church Dogmatics* IV.2 *The Doctrine of Reconciliation*. Edinburgh: T. & T. Clark.

Basil, Saint, Bishop of Caesarea (1980). *On the Holy Spirit*. New York: St. Vladimir's Seminary Press.

Benedict (1975). *The Rule of St. Benedict*. New York: Image Books (Doubleday).

Bernard, of Clairvaux, Saint (1971). *On the Song of Songs I*. Spencer, Mass.: Cistercian Publications.

———. (1976). *On the Song of Songs II*. Kalamazoo, Mich.: Cistercian Publications.

———. (1980). *Treatises II: The Steps of Humility and Pride; On Loving God*. Kalamazoo, Mich.: Cistercian Publications.

Betz, Hans Dieter (1985). The Sermon on the Mount (Matt. 5:3–7:27): Its Literary Genre and Function. In *Essays on the Sermon on the Mount*, 1–16. Philadelphia: Fortress Press.

Bloom, Harold (1973). *The Anxiety of Influence: A Theory of Poetry*. New York: Oxford University Press.

Bobrinskoy, Boris (1984). "The Indwelling of the Spirit in Christ." *St. Vladimir's Theological Quarterly* **28**: 49–65.

———. (1986). "Revelation of the Spirit, Language Beyond Words." *Sobornost* **8**(1): 6–14.

Bochet, Isabelle (1982). *Saint Augustin et le Désir de Dieu*. Paris: Études Augustiniennes.

Bonner, Gerald (1986). "Augustine's Conception of Deification." *Journal of Theological Studies* **37**: 369–86.

Booth, Wayne C. (1988). *The Company We Keep: An Ethics of Fiction*. Berkeley: University of California Press.

Boswell, John (1980). *Christianity, Social Tolerance, and Homosexuality*. Chicago: University of Chicago Press.

Bourassa, Francois, S. I. (1966). "Sur la Traité de la Trinité." *Gregorianum* **47**: 254–85.

———. (1977). "Théologie trinitaire chez saint [sic] Augustin." *Gregorianum* **58**: 675–718.

———. (1978). "Théologie trinitaire de Saint Augustin—II." *Gregorianum* **59**: 375–412.

Bouwsma, William J. (1988). *John Calvin: A Sixteenth Century Portrait*. New York: Oxford University Press.

———. (1990). Calvinism as Renaissance Artifact. In *John Calvin & the Church: A Prism of Reform*, ed. T. George, 28–41. Louisville: Westminster/John Knox.

Breen, Quirinus (1973). St. Thomas and Calvin as Theologians: A Comparison. In *The Heritage of John Calvin*, ed. J. H. Bratt, 23–39. Grand Rapids: Eerdmans.

Brown, Peter (1969). *Augustine of Hippo: A Biography*. Berkeley: University of California Press.

Bynum, Caroline Walker (1987). Religious Women in the Later Middle Ages. In *Christian Spirituality: High Middle Ages and Reformation*, ed. J. Raitt. Vol. 17 of *World Spirituality: An Encyclopedic History of the Religious Quest*, 3: 121–39. New York: Crossroad.

Calvin, John (1960). *Institutes of the Christian Religion*. 2 vols. Philadelphia: Westminster Press.

———. (1964). *The Second Epistle of Paul to the Corinthians, and the Epistles to Timothy, Titus and Philemon*. Grand Rapids: Eerdmans.

———. (1975). First Sermon on Pentecost. In *John Calvin: Selections from His Writings*, ed. J. Dillenberger, 560–73. Missoula, Mont.: Scholars Press.

Cary, Phillip (1992). "On Behalf of Classical Trinitarianism: A Critique of Rahner on the Trinity." *The Thomist* 56(3): 365–405.

Cavadini, John (1992). "The Structure and Intention of Augustine's *De Trinitate*." *Augustinian Studies* 23: 103–23.

Charry, Ellen T. (1991). "Literature as Scripture: Privileged Reading in Current Religious Reflection." *Soundings* 74(1–2): 65–99.

———. (1993). "Academic Theology in Pastoral Perspective." *Theology Today* L(1): 90–104.

Christian, William A., Sr. (1987). *Doctrines of Religious Communities: A Philosophical Study*. New Haven: Yale University Press.

Cunningham, David S. (1991). *Faithful Persuasion: In Aid of a Rhetoric of Christian Theology*. Notre Dame: University of Notre Dame Press.

Cushman, Robert E. (1958). *Therapeia: Plato's Conception of Philosophy*. Chapel Hill, N.C.: University of North Carolina Press.

Davies, W. D. (1955). *Paul and Rabbinic Judaism*. London: S. P. C. K. Press.

Dawson, David (1995). *Literary Theory: Guides to Theological Inquiry*. Minneapolis: Fortress Press.

Delattre, Roland A. (1970). "Beauty and Politics: Toward a Theological Anthropology." *Union Seminary Quarterly Review* 25(4): 401–19.

Despland, Michel (1985). *The Education of Desire*. Toronto: University of Toronto Press.

Dowey, Edward A. (1952). *The Knowledge of God in Calvin's Theology*. New York: Columbia University Press.

Eadmer (1970). *Life and Conversation of St. Anselm: A Scholastic Miscellany*. New York: Macmillan.

Eldridge, Richard (1989). *On Moral Personhood: Philosophy, Literature, Criticism, and Self-Understanding*. Chicago: University of Chicago Press.

Farley, Edward (1983). *Theologia: The Fragmentation and Unity of Theological Education*. Philadelphia: Fortress Press.

Fox, Margaret Mary (1939). *The Life and Times of St. Basil the Great as Revealed in His Works*. Washington, D.C.: Catholic University of America Press.

Fredriksen, Paula (1988). "Beyond the Body/Soul Dichotomy." *Recherches Augustiniennes* XXIII: 87–114.

Gadamer, Hans-Georg (1988). *Truth and Method*. New York: Crossroad.

Gaskin, J. C. A. (1993). Hume on Religion. In *Cambridge Companion to Hume*, ed. D. F. Norton, 313–44. Cambridge: Cambridge University Press.

Gilligan, Carol (1982). *In a Different Voice*. Cambridge: Harvard University Press.

Greer, R. A. (1986). *Broken Lights and Mended Lives: Theology and Common Life in the Early Church*. University Park, PA: Pennsylvania State University Press.

Gregg, Robert C., and Dennis Groh (1981). *Early Arianism: A View of Salvation*. Philadelphia: Fortress Press.

Gregory, of Nyssa (1954). An Answer to Ablabius: That We Should Not Think of Saying There Are Three Gods. In *Christology of the Later Fathers,*. ed. E. R. Hardy, 256–67. Philadelphia: Westminster Press.

Guelich, Robert (1982). *The Sermon on the Mount*. Dallas: Word Publishing.

Gunton, Colin E. (1991). *The Promise of Trinitarian Theology*. Edinburgh: T. & T. Clark.

Gustafson, James M. (1986). Moral Discernment in the Christian Life. In *Norm and Context in Christian Ethics*, ed. G. Outka and P. Ramsey, 17–36. New York: Scribner's.

Hanson, R. P. C. (1988). *The Search of the Christian Doctrine of God: The Arian Controversy* 318–381. Edinburgh: T. & T. Clark.

Harries, Richard (1987). On the Brink of Universalism. In *Julian: Woman of Our Day*, ed. R. Llewelyn, 41–60. Mystic, Conn.: Twenty-Third Publications.

Hauerwas, Stanley (1975). *Character and the Christian Life*. San Antonio: Trinity University Press.

———. (1981). *A Community of Character*. Notre Dame: University of Notre Dame Press.

Haykin, Michael A. G. (1986). "'In the Cloud and in the Sea': Basil of Caesarea and the Exegesis of 1 Cor. 10:2." *Vigilae Christianae* **40**: 135–44.

———. (1988). "'A Sense of Awe in the Presence of the Ineffable': 1 Cor. 2.11–12 in the Pneumatomachian Controversy of the Fourth Century." *Scottish Journal of Theology* **41**: 341–57.

Helfgott, Benjamin W. (1954). *The Doctrine of Election in Tannaitic Literature*. New York: King's Crown Press.

Heyer, George S. (1965). St. Anselm on the Harmony Between God's Mercy and God's Justice. In *The Heritage of Christian Thought*, ed. R. E. Cushman and E. Grislis, 31–40. New York: Harper & Row.

Hill, Edmund, O.P. (1973). "St. Augustine's *De Trinitate*." *Revue des Etudes Augustiniennes* 19: 277–86.

Hume, David (1970). *Dialogues Concerning Natural Religion*. Indianapolis: Bobbs Merrill.

———. (1988). *An Enquiry Concerning Human Understanding*. LaSalle, Ill.: Open Court.

Hunsinger, Deborah van Deusen (1995). *Theology and Pastoral Counseling: A New Interdisciplinary Approach*. Grand Rapids: Eerdmans.

Jaeger, Werner (1944). *Paideia: The Ideals of Greek Culture*. 3 vols. Oxford: Basil Blackwell.

Jantzen, Grace M. (1987). Conspicuous Sanctity and Religious Belief. In *The Rationality of Religious Belief*, ed. W. J. Abraham and S. W. Holtzer, 121–40. Oxford: Clarendon Press.

———. (1988). *Julian of Norwich: Mystic and Theologian*. New York: Paulist Press.

Jaspers, Karl (1962). *Plato and Augustine*. New York: Harcourt, Brace, Jovanovich.

Jenson, Robert W. (1982). *The Triune Identity*. Philadelphia: Fortress Press.

Jones, L. Gregory (1990). *Transformed Judgment: Toward a Trinitarian Account of the Moral Life*. Notre Dame: University of Notre Dame Press.

Julian, of Norwich (1978). *Julian of Norwich: Showings*. New York: Paulist Press.

Kannengiesser, Charles (1983). *Athanase d'Alexandrie Eveque et Ecrivain*. Paris: Beauchesne.

———. (1988). "St. Athanasius of Alexandria Rediscovered: His Political and Pastoral Achievement." *Coptic Church Review: A Quarterly of Contemporary Patristic Studies* **9**: 68–74.

Kant, Immanuel (1965). *Critique of Pure Reason.* New York: St. Martin's Press.

Karam, Cyril (1979). "Saint Basil on the Holy Spirit—Some Aspects of His Theology." *Word and Spirit: A Monastic Review* 1: 137–64.

Kempe, Margery (1985). *The Book of Margery Kempe.* London: Penguin Books.

Kieckhefer, Richard (1984). *Unquiet Souls: Fourteenth-Century Saints and Their Religious Milieu.* Chicago: University of Chicago Press.

Kissinger, Warren S. (1975). *The Sermon on the Mount: A History of Interpretation and Bibliography.* Metuchen, N.J.: Scarecrow Press and American Theological Library Association.

Kopecek, Thomas A. (1979). *A History of Neo-Arianism.* Cambridge, Mass.: Philadelphia Patristic Foundation.

Kurz, William S., S. J. (1985). Kenotic Imitation of Paul and of Christ in Philippians 2 and 3. In *Discipleship in the New Testament,.* ed. F. F. Segovia, 103–26. Philadelphia: Fortress Press.

LaCugna, Catherine Mowry (1991a). *God for Us: The Trinity and Christian Life.* San Francisco: Harper.

———. (1991b). The Trinitarian Mystery of God. In *Systematic Theology: Roman Catholic Perspectives,* ed. Francis Schüssler Fiorenza and J. P. Galvin, I: 152–92. Minneapolis: Fortress Press.

———. (1992). "The Practical Trinity." *The Christian Century:* 678–82.

Ladner, Gerhard B. (1967). *The Idea of Reform: Its Impact on Christian Thought and Action in the Age of the Fathers.* New York: Harper.

Lapsley, James N. (1986). "The 'Self,' Its Vicissitudes and Possibilities: An Essay in Theological Anthropology." *Pastoral Psychology* 35(1): 23–45.

Leith, John H. (1982). *Creeds of the Churches.* Atlanta: John Knox.

———. (1989). *John Calvin's Doctrine of the Christian Life.* Louisville: Westminster/John Knox Press.

Lincoln, Andrew T. (1990). *Ephesians.* Dallas: Word Books.

Locke, John (1964). *An Essay Concerning Human Understanding.* New York: The New American Library.

———. (1983). *The Reasonableness of Christianity.* Stanford: Stanford University Press.

Louth, Andrew (1981). *The Origins of the Christian Mystical Tradition: From Plato to Denys.* Oxford: Clarendon.

———. (1983). *Discerning the Mystery: An Essay on the Nature of Theology.* Oxford: Clarendon.

Luz, Ulrich (1989). *Matthew 1–7: A Continental Commentary.* Minneapolis: Fortress Press.

Lynch, Joseph H. (1992). *The Medieval Church: A Brief History.* London and New York: Longman.

MacIntyre, Alasdair (1984). *After Virtue: A Study in Moral Theory.* Notre Dame, Ind.: University of Notre Dame Press.

Malherbe, Abraham J. (1986). *Moral Exhortation, A Greco-Roman Sourcebook.* Philadelphia: Westminster Press.

———. (1987). *Paul and the Thessalonians: The Philosophic Tradition of Pastoral Care.* Philadelphia: Fortress Press.

Markus, R. A. (1990). Augustine: A Defence of Christian Mediocrity. In *The End of Ancient Christianity,* 45–62. New York: Cambridge University Press.

McGuire, Brian Patrick (1974). "Love, Friendship, and Sex in the Eleventh Century: The Experience of Anselm." *Studia Theologica* 28: 111–52.

Meeks, Wayne A. (1990). The Circle of Reference in Pauline Morality. In *Greeks, Romans, and Christians: Essays in Honor of Abraham J. Malherbe*, ed. D. L. Balch, E. Ferguson, and W. A. Meeks, 305–17. Minneapolis: Fortress Press.

Meier, John P. (1976). *Law and History in Matthew's Gospel: A Redactional Study of Mt. 5:17–48*. Rome: Biblical Institute Press.

Mendieta, Emmanuel Amand de. (1965). "The 'Unwritten" and 'Secret' Apostolic Traditions in the Theological Thought of St. Basil of Caesarea." Vol. 13. Occasional Papers. *Scottish Journal of Theology*.

Mitchell, Basil (1973). *The Justification of Religious Belief*. New York: Oxford University Press.

Montefiore, C. G., and H. Loewe (1974). *A Rabbinic Anthology*. New York: Schocken Books.

Neusner, Jacob, ed. (1988). *The Mishnah: A New Translation*. New Haven: Yale University Press.

Newman, John Henry (1910). *Essays Critical and Historical*. London: Longmans, Green, & Co.

Nichols, Aidan, O.P. (1990). "St. Thomas Aquinas on the Passion of Christ: A Reading of Summa Theologiae IIIa, q.46." *Scottish Journal of Theology* 43(4): 447–459.

Nussbaum, Martha C. (1990). *Love's Knowledge: Essays on Philosophy and Literature*. New York: Oxford University Press.

Nyssa, Gregory (1954). An Answer to Ablabius: That We Should Not Think of Saying There Are Three Gods. In *Christology of the Later Fathers*, ed. E. R. Hardy, Philadelphia: Westminster Press: 256–67.

O'Callaghan, Paul (1986). "La Mediacion de Christo en su Pasion." *Scripta Theologica* 18(3): 771–98.

Origen, of Alexandria ([1885] 1989). De Principiis. In *Ante-Nicene Fathers*. Edinburgh: T. & T. Clark; Grand Rapids: Eerdmans. **IV**: 237–384.

Overman, J. Andrew (1990). *Matthew's Gospel and Formative Judaism: The Social World of the Matthean Community*. Minneapolis: Fortress Press.

Palliser, Margaret Ann, O.P. (1992). *Christ, Our Mother of Mercy*. Berlin and New York: Walter de Gruyter.

Pelagius (1981). Letter to Demetrias. In *Theological Anthropology*, ed. J. P. Burns, 39–55. Philadelphia: Fortress.

Pelikan, Jaroslav (1962). *The Light of the World: A Basic Image in Early Christian Thought*. New York: Harper.

Penelhum, Terence (1993). Hume's Moral Psychology. In *Cambridge Companion to Hume*, ed. D. F. Norton, 117–47. New York and Cambridge: Cambridge University Press.

Plaskow, Judith (1980). *Sex, Sin, and Grace: Women's Experience and the Theologies of Reinhold Niebuhr and Paul Tillich*. Lanham, Md.: University Press of America.

Prestige, G. L. (1952). *God in Patristic Thought*. London: S. P. C. K.

Rahner, Karl (1961). *God, Christ, Mary and Grace*. Vol. 1 of his *Theological Investigations*. Baltimore: Helicon Press.

———. (1966). *More Recent Writings*. Vol. IV of his *Theological Investigations*. Baltimore: Helicon Press.

Roques, René (1970). Structure et caractères de la prière Anselmienne. In *Sola Ratione: Anselm-Studien für Pater Dr. h. c. Franciscus Salesius Schmitt*, Helmut K. Kahlenberger, B. Geyer, and A. Hufragel, eds., 119–87. Stuttgart-Bad Cannstatt: Friedrich Fromman.

Sanders, E. P. (1977). *Paul and Palestinian Judaism: A Comparison of Patterns of Religion.* Philadelphia: Fortress Press.

———. (1990). *Jewish Law from Jesus to the Mishnah: Five Studies.* London: SCM Press; Philadelphia: Trinity Press International.

Schleiermacher, F. D. E. (1986). *The Christian Faith.* Edinburgh: T. & T. Clark.

Schweitzer, Albert (1931). *The Mysticism of Paul the Apostle.* New York: Henry Holt.

Sherry, Patrick (1984). *Spirit, Saints, and Immortality.* Albany: State University of New York Press.

Slusser, Michael (1985). "Review of Athanese d'Alexandrie by Charles Kannengiesser." *Theological Studies* **46**: 144–6.

Soskice, Janet Martin (1985). *Metaphor and Religious Language.* Oxford: Clarendon Press.

Southern, R. W. (1990). *Saint Anselm: A Portrait in a Landscape.* Cambridge: Cambridge University Press.

Stambaugh, John E., and David L. Balch (1986). *The New Testament in Its Social Environment.* Philadelphia: Westminster Press.

Stead, Christopher (1985). "Review of Athanase d'Alexandrie by Charles Kannengiesser." *Journal of Theological Studies* **36**: 220–9.

Stendahl, Krister (1976). Paul and the Introspective Conscience of the West. In his *Paul among Jews and Gentiles,* 78–96. Philadelphia: Fortress Press.

Tannehill, Robert C. (1970). "The 'Focal Instance' as a Form of New Testament Speech: A Study of Matthew 5:39b–42." *Journal of Religion* **50**(4): 372–85.

Taylor, Charles (1989). *Sources of the Self: The Making of the Modern Identity.* Cambridge: Harvard University Press.

Thomas, Aquinas, Saint (1964). *Christian Theology.* Vol. 1 of *Summa Theologiae.* London: Blackfriars.

———. (1965). *The Passion of Christ.* Vol. 54 of *Summa Theologiae.* London: Blackfriars.

———. (1974). *Faith.* Vol. 31 of *Summa Theologiae.* London: Blackfriars.

Tillich, Paul (1963). *Systematic Theology.* Vol. III. Chicago: University of Chicago Press.

Vaughn, Sally N. (1987). *Anselm of Bec and Robert of Meulan: The Innocence of the Dove and the Wisdom of the Serpent.* Berkeley: University of California Press.

Walker, C. R. (1952). "St. Anselm—A Reevaluation." *Scottish Journal of Theology* **5**: 362–73.

Wild, Robert A., S. J. (1985). "Be Imitators of God": Discipleship in the Letter to the Ephesians. In *Discipleship in the New Testament,* ed. F. F. Segovia, 128–33. Philadelphia: Fortress Press.

Wood, Allen W. (1992). Rational Theology, Moral Faith, and Religion. In *Cambridge Companion to Kant,* ed. P. Guyer, 394–416. New York: Cambridge University Press.

Wood, Charles M. (1994). The Aim of Christian Theology. In his *An Invitation to Theological Study,* 98–108. Valley Forge, Pa.: Trinity Press International.

Index